Ronny Boogaart, Timothy Colleman, Gijsbert Rutten (Eds.)
Extending the Scope of Construction Grammar

Cognitive Linguistics Research

Editors
Dirk Geeraerts
John R. Taylor

Honorary editors
René Dirven
Ronald W. Langacker

Volume 54

Extending the Scope of Construction Grammar

Edited by
Ronny Boogaart
Timothy Colleman
Gijsbert Rutten

DE GRUYTER
MOUTON

ISBN 978-3-11-055504-2
e-ISBN (PDF) 978-3-11-036627-3
e-ISBN (EPUB) 978-3-11-039326-2
ISSN 1861-4132

Library of Congress Cataloging-in-Publication Data
A CIP catalog record for this book has been applied for at the Library of Congress.

Bibliographic information published by the Deutsche Nationalbibliothek
The Deutsche Nationalbibliothek lists this publication in the Deutsche Nationalbibliografie;
detailed bibliographic data are available on the Internet at http://dnb.dnb.de.

© 2017 Walter de Gruyter GmbH, Berlin/Boston
This volume is text- and page-identical with the hardback published in 2014.
Printing and binding: CPI books GmbH, Leck
Typesetting: RoyalStandard, Hong Kong
♾ Printed on acid-free paper
Printed in Germany

www.degruyter.com

Table of contents

Ronny Boogaart, Timothy Colleman, and Gijsbert Rutten
1 Constructions all the way everywhere: Four new directions in constructionist research —— 1

I Methodological advances

Natalia Levshina and Kris Heylen
2 A radically data-driven Construction Grammar: Experiments with Dutch causative constructions —— 17

Barend Beekhuizen and Rens Bod
3 Automating construction work: Data-Oriented Parsing and constructivist accounts of language acquisition —— 47

II Construction morphology

Geert Booij and Matthias Hüning
4 Affixoids and constructional idioms —— 77

Alan Scott
5 The survival and use of case morphology in Modern Dutch —— 107

III Constructions in variation and change

Freek Van de Velde
6 Degeneracy: The maintenance of constructional networks —— 141

Gijsbert Rutten and Marijke van der Wal
7 Social and constructional diffusion: Relative clauses in seventeenth- and eighteenth-century Dutch —— 181

Muriel Norde, Bernard De Clerck, and Timothy Colleman
8 The emergence of non-canonical degree modifiers in non-standard varieties of Dutch: A constructionalization perspective —— 207

Bert Cappelle
9 **Conventional combinations in pockets of productivity: English resultatives and Dutch ditransitives expressing excess** —— 251

IV Constructions in interaction

Jörg Bücker
10 *Und mit der Party, wie wollen wir das organisieren?* **Tying constructions with the preposition *mit* in German talk-in-interaction** —— 285

Wolfgang Imo
11 **Appositions in monologue, increments in dialogue? On appositions and apposition-like patterns in spoken German and their status as constructions** —— 321

Camilla Wide
12 **Constructions as resources in interaction: Syntactically unintegrated *att* 'that'-clauses in spoken Swedish** —— 353

Index —— 381

Ronny Boogaart, Timothy Colleman, and Gijsbert Rutten
1 Constructions all the way everywhere: Four new directions in constructionist research

1 From Construction Grammar(s) to constructionally informed linguistics

Some ten years ago, Adele Goldberg summarized one of the basic tenets of constructionist approaches to language – viz. the view that the *whole* of grammar consists of a structured network of conventionalized form/meaning-pairings – in the often-quoted catchphrase "It's constructions all the way down!" (cf. Goldberg 2003: 223, 2006: 18). An important part of what presently goes on in the field of cognitive linguistics, broadly construed, could in the same vein be described informally as "It's constructions *all the way everywhere*". Indeed, linguistic research on a broad variety of language phenomena seems to be increasingly informed by constructionist ideas about the organization of grammar and the nature and acquisition of grammatical knowledge.

While construction grammar was intended as a theory that would account for the *entirety* of language right from the start, it can be observed that, until fairly recently, the majority of existing work in its various strands was concerned with the elucidation of the syntax and semantics of selected complex (in the sense of "multi-word") constructions from present-day standard English or the present-day standard variety of another language. The seminal publications of the 1980s and early 1990s on the formal and semantic idiosyncrasies of by-now notorious bits and pieces of the grammar of present-day standard (American) English strove for completeness in that they gave centre stage to grammatical patterns which were deemed too "peripheral" to merit linguistic attention in mainstream generative grammar (e.g. Fillmore, Kay, and O'Connor 1988 on the *let alone* construction, Lakoff 1987 on the presentational *there*-construction) and/or in that they did not solely focus on the formal properties of the investigated constructions but also, crucially, on their semantics (e.g. Goldberg 1992, 1995 on the semantics of the ditransitive construction and other argument structure constructions). In this way, the emerging family of constructionist approaches immediately cast its net wider than was customary in the then-dominant grammatical theories. However, while the groundbreaking work laid by the above-mentioned and other early studies is not to be underplayed or minimized, it can also be observed that there is more to accounting for the "entirety" of language than doing away with the core/periphery distinction and adopting a holistic approach to grammar and meaning. Sure enough, the investigation of "idiosyncratic" or otherwise noteworthy bits of contemporary grammar remains a worthwhile enterprise in its own right, which can potentially lead to new insights on the network structure of the grammar and as such is central to the constructionist agenda. Still, if construction grammar truly wants to develop into an overall theory of language, it should address a variety of other questions and issues as well, ranging from issues related to the cognitive representation of constructions, over issues of lectal variation in the properties of constructions and the structure of the constructicon, to topics as diverse as the emergence of constructions and constructional meaning (both ontogenetically and phylogenetically), the validity of constructions for cross-linguistic comparison, the role of constructions in interaction and dialogue, et cetera, et cetera. And, in fact, it has. In recent years, construction-based linguistics has been expanding to other domains and methodologies and important progress has been made in several of the above-mentioned domains – as is evident also from the breadth of coverage of the papers included in the recent handbook by Hoffmann and Trousdale (2013), to give just one example.

The present volume is comprised of 11 original research articles which represent and illustrate such emerging new research directions in construction-based linguistics, and which are organized into four complementary sections, viz. (i) methodological advances, (ii) construction morphology, (ii) variation and change and (iv) interaction. About half of these papers originated in a workshop on 'The construction grammar of Dutch' held in Leiden, the Netherlands on March 25–26, 2011 and co-organized by the Leiden University Centre of Linguistics (LUCL) and the Ghent University Linguistics Department. The other papers were solicited by the editors in order to further reinforce the thematic coherence of the volume as well as to broaden its language focus. In the next sections, we proceed to a detailed overview of the contents of the four sections, taking care to position each of the four selected sub-fields in the wider context of the extending scope of constructionist approaches.

Before we move on, however, it should be stressed that this increase of scope in construction grammar could just as well be described as a process in which various other branches of linguistics have started incorporating constructionist ideas and terminology. Construction grammar has never been a single unified framework. As is well-known, there rather is a family of constructionist approaches – several different construction grammars, so to speak – which share certain key ideas, most prominently including the symbolic view of syntax and the concept of stored form/meaning-pairings as constituting the basic units of grammatical organization, but which also display substantial mutual differences (see, e.g., Goldberg 2003, 2013; Croft and Cruse 2004; Östman and Fried 2005; Langacker 2005 for discussion). In addition, there are many scholars whose work is informed by these foundational constructionist views on grammar but who would not necessarily dub themselves construction grammarians, let alone commit themselves to any of the well-established strands of construction grammar, such as Berkeley Construction Grammar (Fillmore 1988; Fried and Östman 2004), Cognitive Construction Grammar (Goldberg 1995, 2006), Radical Construction Grammar (Croft 2001), Sign-Based Construction Grammar (Sag 2012), and so on. The papers in this volume are all *constructionally informed* in important respects, but they display different degrees of adherence to constructionist formalism and use a variety of notational styles.

2 Methodological advances

The fact that the volume starts off with a separate section on methodological advances should of course not be taken to imply that the chapters in the remaining three sections have no bearing whatsoever on methodological innovation in constructionist linguistics. What sets the two chapters in this section apart from the rest, however, is that their *primary* aim is to illustrate the great potential for constructional analysis of advanced new methodologies from computational linguistics.

Goldberg (2003: 219) states that the constructionist approaches emerging in the 1980s and 1990s had a number of assumptions in common with mainstream generative linguistics, such as the view "that it is essential to consider language as a cognitive (mental) system" and the acknowledgement "that there must be a way to combine structures to create novel utterances". It can be observed that, in addition to these shared theoretical assumptions, there was a striking methodological parallel, too: the above-mentioned near-exclusive focus on (decontextualized) standard language(s) in the early days of construction grammar was coupled with a near-exclusive reliance on *introspective* data. Since then, constructionist linguistics has come a long way, leading Gries (2013: 94) to observe that "empirically speaking, Construction Grammar as a family of closely related grammars is probably one of the methodologically most pluralistic fields, as it utilizes a large number of different data and methodologies." The chapter by **Natalia Levshina and Kris Heylen** presents a radically data-driven approach to constructional semantics based on Semantic Vector Space models. The paper starts out from the observation that corpus-based studies of constructional semantics often employ semantic classifications of the nouns, verbs, etc. filling the slots of the construction(s) under investigation – which are either defined *a priori*, for instance in order to include a "semantic verb class" label as a predictor variable in a regression study of an argument structure alternation, or *a posteriori*, as in the interpretation of the results from a collexeme analysis – but that these classifications themselves are more often than not ad hoc and largely based on introspection. The authors make a case for bottom-up semantic classifications based on Semantic Vector Spaces, a distributional method widely used in computational linguistics, which computes an overall collocational profile for all the target words attested in a given corpus on the basis of their co-occurrences with all other (content) words in the corpus. The method is shown at work on the basis of a set of 6,863 corpus instances of the near-synonymous Dutch causative constructions with *doen* 'do' and *laten* 'let': the results from this case study do not only corroborate earlier observations about the semantic determinants of the *doen/laten*-alternation but also provide empirical evidence about the optimal level of granularity of semantic classifications.

The chapter by **Barend Beekhuizen and Rens Bod** is concerned with the computational modeling of the *acquisition* of constructions. As is well-known, constructionist theories embrace a *usage-based* view on grammar and language acquisition: a crucial assumption is that constructions are learned from the input, through generalization over encountered examples (see, e.g., Tomasello 2003; Goldberg 2006). Over the last decade, a number of formalizations have been developed which are aimed at modeling this learning process, such as Fluid Construction Grammar (Steels 2011) and Embodied Construction Grammar (Chang 2008). Beekhuizen and Bod's chapter adds to this growing body of literature at the intersection of construction grammar and computational linguistics: the authors present the modeling procedure of Data-Oriented Parsing (DOP) as well as its unsupervised incarnation U-DOP and propose an extension of this formalism that is able to incorporate meaning (μ-DOP). The results from an initial experiment with artificial data show that this extended model can acquire both compositional and idiomatic structures from a noisy data set, using one and the same learning mechanism.

3 Construction morphology

In the second section of the volume, the constructional approach to grammar is extended to the field of morphology. While it is a crucial assumption of constructionist linguistics that there is no fundamental distinction between words and morphemes on the one hand and multi-word grammatical patterns on the other, grammar being a vast repository of conventionalized form/meaning-pairings of varying levels of formal complexity, it can also be observed that the attention of construction grammarians has always been primarily focused on the upper and middle parts of the lexicon-syntax cline, i.e. on phrasal and clause-level constructions. Until very recently, in-depth constructionist analyses of morphological phenomena were in fact scarce. The chapters in this section both take the landmark publication on construction morphology by Booij (2010) as their point of departure, while embarking upon new territory through a comparative outlook, as in the chapter by Booij and Hüning, or by the application of construction morphology to language history, as in the chapter by Scott.

In their chapter on 'Affixoids and constructional idioms', **Geert Booij and Matthias Hüning** discuss the category of affixoids, i.e. compound constituents with an affix-like behaviour as in the German case of *fähig* 'able'. This occurs in complex adjectives such as *veränderungsfähig* 'able to change', where the original meaning of the adjective is maintained. There are, however, also examples such as *kreditfähig* 'fit for getting credit', where a related though different meaning occurs, which is restricted to complex words. Booij and Hüning argue that it is not necessary to introduce a new category such as affixoid to account for such phenomena. Instead, they argue that research on affixoids has illustrated that there is no sharp distinction between derivation and compounding. Affixes and lexical words are at the two ends of a scale and the same is true for the two word formation processes, i.e. derivation and compounding. In between, there are formations with properties of both sides. While *affixoid* may be a useful descriptive term for the bound meanings of words when embedded in complex words, their behaviour can be insightfully accounted for within the framework of construction morphology, which does not make an absolute distinction between compounding and derivation. From a constructionist point of view, affixoids can be characterized as the lexically specified parts of so-called constructional idioms, that is, subschemas for compounding that are partially lexically fixed, with specific semantic properties. This analysis of affixoids fits into a conception of the lexicon as hierarchical, with different layers of abstraction at which the word formation possibilities of a language are specified.

Alan Scott, in his chapter on 'The survival and use of case morphology in Modern Dutch', discusses relics in present-day Dutch of the language's now defunct case system, in particular the use of what once were regular genitive forms in examples such as *een nieuw hoofdstuk in de geschiedenis der verkeerstechnologie* 'lit. a new chapter in the history of the:GEN traffic-technology'. Scott uses a usage-based diachronic approach in order to account for the survival of this piece of case morphology into Modern Dutch, incorporating corpus analyses from sixteenth- and seventeenth-century Dutch up to the present day. He analyzes how constructions with *der* became isolated from a dying case system and reinterpreted as an open frame construction within which, unexpectedly, agreement morphology was preserved. Building on Booij (2010), Scott suggests that the construction in question involves a non-canonical type of construction-dependent morphology. Having offered an account of the survival of *der* in the history of Dutch, Scott goes on to discuss the use of constructions with *der* in present-day language. It turns out that in present-day Dutch, constructions with *der* constitute a stylistic tool mainly used in specific registers and contexts, which Scott interprets as an example of the interplay of construction morphology and (morpho-)pragmatics.

4 Constructions in variation and change

The more or less exclusive focus on decontextualized "standard" language in the early days of construction grammar is a thing of the past: recent years have seen a marked increase in studies combining a construction-based view on grammar with an interest in issues of language variation and change. This shift in constructionist attention can be related to three more general trends in contemporary (cognitive) linguistics. First, since the mid-2000s, there has been an increasing rapprochement between constructional approaches to language change and research on *grammaticalization*. While constructions have to a certain extent always played an important role in theories of grammaticalization – see, e.g., Lehman's (1992: 402) often-quoted observation that "grammaticalization does not merely seize a word or morpheme [...] but the whole construction formed by the syntagmatic relations of the elements in question" – the arrival of constructionist theories of grammar has inspired grammaticalization scholars to refine the notions of "construction" and "constructional network" and to further reflect on the exact role of constructions as the input and/or outcome of processes of language change (see, e.g., Traugott 2008a, 2008b; Trousdale 2010, 2012; Traugott and Trousdale 2013; Noël 2007; Hilpert 2013). A second larger trend is the advent of Cognitive Sociolinguistics, a novel field of research that integrates methods and models from Cognitive Linguistics on the one hand and (variationist) sociolinguistics on the other, with a view to the uncovering of socio-cognitive dimensions of meaning (Kristiansen and Dirven 2008; Geeraerts, Kristiansen, and Peirsman 2010; Harder 2010; Pütz, Robinson, and Reif 2012). Needless to say, there is a social dimension to *constructional* meanings, too: several of the papers in, for instance, the edited volume by Geeraerts, Kristiansen and

Peirsman (2010) are explicitly constructionist in their approach to grammar. Thirdly, and related to the previous trend, there has been a kind of methodological turn in Cognitive Linguistics research at large, including various strands of construction grammar, in the form of an increasing reliance on *empirical methods of data investigation* – which can of course be related to the *usage-based* view on language and language acquisition embraced in Cognitive Linguistic theorizing. As pointed out by Geeraerts (2006: 30), doing corpus research implies coming to terms with variation in the data, as bringing in real language data automatically brings in sociolinguistic variation. In addition to the above-mentioned studies, we can also refer to Hoffmann and Trousdale (2010), Fried (2013), Östman and Trousdale (2013) and Hollmann (2013) for further discussion of the ways in which and reasons why construction grammar is particularly suited to deal with the inherent variability of language.

The first two chapters in this section focus on long-term constructional change. **Freek Van de Velde**'s chapter 'Degeneracy: The maintenance of constructional networks' applies the biological concept of *degeneracy* to language variation and change, arguing that language is a complex adaptive system not unlike, for instance, ant colonies. Degeneracy is a technical term from evolutionary biology for the phenomenon that structurally different elements can fulfil the same function. An example from biology is thermoregulation in the human body, which is degenerately controlled by perspiration, arteriolar vasodilation, shivering, countercurrent flow, wearing protective clothing, huddling, and so on. A simple example from the Germanic languages is the coexistence of the expression of the past tense by ablaut and by a dental suffix (English *spoke* vs. *talked*). Degeneracy is related to the notion of redundancy, but one of the differences is that degenerate features may play a role elsewhere in the system as well. Applying degeneracy to language, Van de Velde argues that horizontal or paradigmatic relations in construction networks – in which related constructions in a functional domain are mutually defined by differential values they take on a set of grammatical parameters – can be transmitted through time, even if the specific grammatical parameters on which they are defined are under threat. In other words, related functions are often degenerately expressed by different forms, which in the context of form-function change is important, according to Van de Velde, in that such changes should not be seen as renewal, i.e. compensating for the loss of a grammatical strategy by the development of something new. Rather, form-function changes involve the strengthening of degenerately already available resources, which can extend to new domains when a subsystem comes under pressure. To make this argument, Van de Velde discusses two case studies from the history of Dutch, viz. argument realization in experience processes and adverbial subordination.

The second chapter in this section, 'Social and constructional diffusion. Relative clauses in seventeenth- and eighteenth-century Dutch', written by **Gijsbert Rutten and Marijke van der Wal**, argues that a full account of language variation and change should combine constructional analyses and sociolinguistic research. Focusing on a case of morphosyntactic change in Dutch, viz. the rise of *w*-relativizers such as *waar* 'where' at the expense of *d*-relativizers such as *daar* 'lit. there, where', Rutten and Van der Wal claim that the trajectory of this change is subject to different types of diffusion. Using a corpus of private letters by writers with various social backgrounds, they show that the change displays social variation in the late seventeenth century as well as in the late eighteenth century, with the upper (middle) ranks of society behaving more progressively than the lower (middle) ranks. Zooming in on formulaic sequences, which are very characteristic of these historic private letters, they also argue that the change from *d-* to *w*-relativizers displays constructional diffusion, that is, the change proceeds through constructions. As sound changes may affect concrete words at different rates (lexical diffusion), similarly morphosyntactic changes may affect constructions at different paces (constructional diffusion).

The chapter by **Muriel Norde, Bernard De Clerck, and Timothy Colleman**, entitled 'The emergence of non-canonical degree modifiers in non-standard varieties of Dutch: A constructionalization perspective' shifts the focus to incipient language change. It is concerned with a set of high-quantity expressions that are all developing degree modifier uses in (substandard varieties of) present-day Dutch, thus adding to the large and diverse set of available degree modifiers in the language, a class that is particularly prone to language change due to rapid pragmatic wear and tear. The four cases singled out for the investigation are *massa's* ('masses'), *duizend* ('thousand'), *een partij* ('a batch') and *tig* ('umpteen'). On the basis of data from a variety of informal web sources, the authors lay bare similarities and differences between these cases as different instantiations of the quantifier-to-degree modifier pathway of change, and they discuss these cases of incipient constructional change in terms of Traugott and Trousdale's (2013) recent theory on (grammatical) constructionalization.

Hand in hand with the increasing attention for issues of intralingual variation and change discussed in the beginning of this section, construction grammarians have in recent years also taken a wider interest in issues of *cross-linguistic* comparison, see for instance the volume edited by Boas (2010a). In the introduction to that volume, Boas (2010b: 15) reflects on the potential of constructions for language comparison and concludes that "[s]ince constructions are linguistic signs that pair [phonological, morphological, syntactic, semantic, and pragmatic] aspects, they are extremely well suited to capture all of the different (and partially idiosyncratic) distributional properties of grammatical structure across languages simultaneously." In the present volume, this constructional approach to contrastive linguistics is represented by the chapter by **Bert Cappelle** on 'Conventional combinations in pockets of productivity: English resultatives and Dutch ditransitives expressing excess'. Cappelle starts off from a classic example from the early days of construction grammar, viz. *Pat sneezed the napkin off the table*, first discussed in Goldberg (1995). He argues against the view that such examples underscore the existence of a productive caused-motion argument structure construction by showing that the pattern is in fact idiosyncratically constrained in ways that are not predicted by the semantics of the general construction. Rather, Cappelle argues, following recent work by Kay (2013), such novel uses are better treated as analogical extensions from more conventional three-argument verbs, such as *blow*. Focusing on the so-called Body Part *Off* Construction (e.g. *work one's head off*) (BPOC), Cappelle shows that the action-intensifying semantics of this pattern cannot simply be explained on the basis of the overall meaning of the caused-motion construction, with general pragmatic reasoning ruling out the literal resultative reading. The fact that a direct translation of the BPOC does not occur in Dutch, which does have the caused-motion construction, shows that the BPOC has to be learnt independently. Dutch has a couple of related caused-motion patterns expressing excess, but the most commonly used Dutch construction in this domain has ditransitive rather than resultative syntax. For both the Dutch and the English constructions, corpus data reveal some highly conventional combinations that may prevent the use of other combinations that could have been possible.

5 Constructions in interaction

The final section of the volume is dedicated to research conducted at the crossroads of construction grammar and conversation analysis. As a matter of principle, and in line with the theoretical presuppositions of Cognitive Linguistics, (most) constructionist approaches to grammar do not distinguish between semantic and discourse-functional properties of constructions, since both of these may become conventionally associated with specific forms. Moreover, in Cognitive Linguistics at large a development can be observed from an almost exclusive focus on the individual, subjective construal of reality to incorporating the social, intersubjective dimension of speaker-hearer-interaction (Verhagen 2005; Croft 2009). Still, in the words of Linell (2009: 97), "it is undeniable that many variants of CxG suffer from an interactional deficit". The absence of interactional approaches from, for instance, Hoffmann and Trousdale's (2013) handbook, should, however, not lead one to conclude that there have not been attempts to fill this hiatus, see, e.g., the German-language volumes edited by Deppermann, Fiehler, and Spranz Fogasy (2006), Günthner and Imo (2006), and Günthner and Brücker (2009). The chapters in this section likewise deal with discourse functions of selected grammatical patterns – viz. prepositional phrases (Brücker), appositions (Imo), and complement clauses (Wide) – that can be attested only in detailed qualitative analyses of situated interaction. All three authors explore the possibilities and limitations of combining a methodological commitment to conversation analysis with the degree of generalization that is inherent to the notions of "construction" and "constructional network".

In his contribution on 'Tying constructions with the preposition *mit* in German talk-in-interaction', **Jörg Bücker** demonstrates that not only particles, adverbs and conjunctions, but also prepositional phrases may be used as discourse-structuring devices. Specifically, for German *mit* ('with') + Noun Phrase it is shown that in spoken talk-in-interaction it often functions as a "tying construction": in such cases, the speaker uses it to refer to a topical antecedent in the preceding discourse that is considered to be accessible, to different degrees. Bücker distinguishes between two patterns – attributive and non-attributive uses of "tying" *mit* + Noun Phrase – that differ slightly in both form and in function. These differences, however, can be explained fully compositionally as resulting from their different positions in the clause and different degrees of subordination. Bücker argues, therefore, that only one encompassing mit_{tying} + Noun Phrase-construction needs to be assumed, modeled along the lines of Goldberg (1995), that can be realized as two different "constructs" in conversation.

Wolfgang Imo, in the chapter entitled 'Appositions in monologue, increments in dialogue? On appositions and apposition-like patterns in spoken German and their status as constructions', deals with patterns in conversation that, more or less, resemble what have traditionally been called *appositions*. He shows that in his non-monological data, not a single instance can be found of the classic, "wide scope" NP + NP apposition (as in *I met John, my old friend, in London*). Instead, interactional data feature a kind of pattern that resembles an apposition but that exhibits quite different properties, both in syntax and in function. Whereas in typical appositions the two NPs are juxtaposed, the second NP in the interactional pattern occurs at quite a distance from the first one. It may in fact be used after the so-called *right verb brace*, which is a strong signal for syntactic closure in German. In this respect, the second NP behaves more like a *syntactic unit expansion* or *increment*. As for its function, the "interactional" type of apposition is added "on line" to respond to a real or potential problem of understanding and is thus used to re-focus, paraphrase or repair a previous utterance. The NPs in such "very wide scope" or "peripheral" appositions do not necessarily refer to persons; the latter is a typical feature of wide scope appositions in written and monologic discourse. In addition to a *formal* and a *functional entry* for characterizing constructions, at least a *sequential entry* is needed to capture this type of information. In order to determine the exact relation between these apposition-like patterns and other syntactic constructions in a constructional network, more empirical data are required about the actual use of related syntactic patterns in conversation.

In the final chapter, 'Constructions as resources in interaction: syntactically unintegrated *att* 'that'-clauses in spoken Swedish', **Camilla Wide** analyses instances of *insubordination* with the complementizer *att* 'that' in spoken Swedish (both Swedish Swedish and Finnish Swedish): these "subordinate" clauses are syntactically unintegrated since they are used without a main clause. Wide focuses on the phenomenon of *discourse insubordination*, that has also been observed for independent complement clauses in German and Dutch. Rather than being licensed by the syntactic context, the use of such clauses is licensed by the interactional and pragmatic context. Wide distinguishes between two types: one with a rephrasing function and one with a reasoning function. In the first type, the speaker adds more specific information or makes the intended speech act, such as a question or a suggestion, more explicit. The second type equally relates to something said in the preceding discussion, but here the speaker expands the line of reasoning by expressing a consequence of what another speaker has said. The two types clearly fulfill different functions in interaction and they may have developed from a different source. However, whether or not they instantiate two different constructions in the sense of construction grammar depends on the weight that is given to semantic/functional differences, as compared to formal differentiation. If the relationship to the prior context is itself regarded as a formal or form-related feature, it would be possible to treat the two types as different nodes in a constructional network since their "external syntax" (Linell 2009) is different.

References

Boas, Hans C. (ed.). 2010a. *Contrastive Studies in Construction Grammar*. Amsterdam/Philadelphia: John Benjamins.
Boas, Hans C. 2010b. Comparing constructions across languages. In: Hans C. Boas (ed.) *Contrastive Studies in Construction Grammar*, 1–20. Amsterdam/Philadelphia: John Benjamins.
Booij, Geert. 2010. *Construction Morphology*. Oxford: Oxford University Press.
Chang, Nancy. 2008. Constructing grammar: A computational model of the emergence of early constructions. Ph.D. dissertation, Computer science department, University of California at Berkeley.

Croft, William. 2001. *Radical Construction Grammar: Syntactic Theory in Typological Perspective*. Oxford: Oxford University Press.
Croft, William. 2009. Towards a social cognitive linguistics. In: Vyvyan Evans and Stephanie Pourcel (eds), *New Directions in Cognitive Linguistics*, 395–420. Amsterdam/Philadelphia: John Benjamins.
Croft, William and D. Alan Cruse. 2004. *Cognitive Linguistics*. Cambridge: Cambridge University Press.
Deppermann, Arnulf, Reinhard Fiehler and Thomas Spranz-Fogasy (eds.). 2009. *Grammatik und Interaktion*. Radolfzell: Verlag für Gesprächsforschung.
Fillmore, Charles J. 1988. The mechanisms of "Construction Grammar". *Proceedings from the annual meeting of the Berkeley Linguistics Society* 14: 35–55.
Fillmore, Charles J., Paul Kay and Mary Kay O'Connor. 1988. Regularity and idiomaticity in grammatical constructions: The case of *let alone*. *Language* 64: 501–538.
Fried, Mirjam. 2013. Principles of constructional change. In: Thomas Hoffmann and Graeme Trousdale (eds.), *The Oxford handbook of Construction Grammar*, 419–437. Oxford: Oxford University Press.
Fried, Mirjam and Jan-Ola Östman. 2004. Construction Grammar: A thumbnail sketch. In: Mirjam Fried and Jan-Ola Östman (eds.), *Construction Grammar in a Cross-Language Perspective*, 11–86. Amsterdam/Philadelphia: John Benjamins.
Geeraerts, Dirk. 2006. Methodology in Cognitive Linguistics. In: Gitte Kristiansen, Michel Achard, René Dirven and Francisco J. De Mendoza Ibáñez (eds.), *Cognitive Linguistics: Current Applications and Future Perspectives*, 21–49. Berlin/New York: Mouton de Gruyter.
Geeraerts, Dirk, Gitte Kristiansen and Yves Peirsman (eds.). 2010. *Advances in Cognitive Sociolinguistics*. Berlin/New York: Mouton de Gruyter.
Goldberg, Adele E. 1992. The inherent semantics of argument structure: The case of the English ditransitive construction. *Cognitive Linguistics* 3: 37–74.
Goldberg, Adele E. 1995. *Constructions: A Construction Grammar Approach to Argument Structure*. Chicago: University of Chicago Press.
Goldberg, Adele E. 2003. Constructions: A new theoretical approach to language. *Trends in Cognitive Science* 7: 219–224.
Goldberg, Adele E. 2006. *Constructions at Work: The Nature of Generalization in Language*. Oxford: Oxford University Press.
Goldberg, Adele E. 2013. Constructionist approaches. In: Thomas Hoffmann and Graeme Trousdale (eds.), *The Oxford Handbook of Construction Grammar*, 15–31. Oxford: Oxford University Press.
Gries, Stefan Th. 2013. Data in Construction Grammar. In: Thomas Hoffmann and Graeme Trousdale (eds.), *The Oxford Handbook of Construction Grammar*, 93–108. Oxford: Oxford University Press.
Günthner, Susanne and Jörg Bücker (eds.). 2009. *Grammatik im Gespräch: Konstruktionen der Selbst- und Fremdpositionierung*. Berlin/New York: Mouton de Gruyter.
Günthner, Susanne and Wolfgang Imo (eds.). 2006. *Konstruktionen in der Interaktion*. Berlin/New York: Mouton de Gruyter.
Harder, Peter. 2010. *Meaning in Mind and Society: A Functional Contribution to the Social Turn in Cognitive Linguistics*. Berlin/New York: Mouton de Gruyter.
Hilpert, Martin. 2013. *Constructional change in English. Developments in Allomorphy, Word Formation, and Syntax*. Cambridge: Cambridge University Press.

Hoffmann, Thomas and Graeme Trousdale. 2010. Variation, change and constructions in English. *Cognitive Linguistics* 22: 1–23.
Hoffmann, Thomas and Graeme Trousdale (eds.). 2013. *The Oxford Handbook of Construction Grammar.* Oxford: Oxford University Press.
Hollmann, Willem. 2013. Constructions in cognitive sociolinguistics. In: Thomas Hoffmann and Graeme Trousdale (eds.), *The Oxford Handbook of Construction Grammar*, 491–509. Oxford: Oxford University Press.
Kay, Paul. 2013. The limits of (Construction) Grammar. In: Thomas Hoffmann and Graeme Trousdale (eds.), *The Oxford Handbook of Construction Grammar*, 32–48. Oxford: Oxford University Press.
Kristiansen, Gitte and René Dirven (eds.). 2008. *Cognitive Sociolinguistics: Language Variation, Cultural Models, Social Systems.* Berlin/New York: Mouton de Gruyter.
Lakoff, George. 1987. *Women, Fire and Dangerous Things: What Categories Reveal about the Mind.* Chicago: University of Chicago Press.
Langacker, Ronald. 2005. Construction Grammars: Cognitive, radical, and less so. In: Francisco J. Ruiz de Mendoza and Sandra Pena Cervel (eds.), *Cognitive Linguistics: Internal dynamics and interdisciplinary interaction*, 101–159. Berlin/New York: Mouton de Gruyter.
Lehmann, Christian. 1992. Word order change by grammaticalization. In: Marinel Gerritsen and Dieter Stein (eds.), *Internal and External Factors in Syntactic Change*, 395–416. Berlin/New York: Mouton de Gruyter.
Linell, Per. 2009. Grammatical constructions in dialogue. In: Alexander Bergs and Gabriele Diewald (eds.), *Context and Constructions*, 97–110. Amsterdam/Philadelphia: John Benjamins.
Noël, Dirk. 2007. Diachronic construction grammar and grammaticalization theory. *Functions of Language* 14: 177–202.
Pütz, Martin, Justyna A. Robinson and Monika Reif. 2012. The emergence of cognitive sociolinguistics: an introduction. *Review of Cognitive Linguistics* 10: 241–263.
Östman, Jan-Ola and Graeme Trousdale. 2013. Dialects, discourse, and construction grammar. In: Thomas Hoffmann and Graeme Trousdale (eds.), *The Oxford handbook of Construction Grammar*, 476–490. Oxford: Oxford University Press.
Östman, Jan-Ola and Mirjam Fried. 2005. The cognitive grounding of Construction Grammar. In: Jan-Ola Östman and Mirjam Fried (eds.), *Construction Grammars: Cognitive Grounding and Theoretical Extensions*, 1–13. Amsterdam/Philadelphia: John Benjamins.
Sag, Ivan. 2012. Sign-based Construction Grammar: An informal synopsis. In: Hans C. Boas and Ivan A. Sag (eds.), *Sign-Based Construction Grammar*, 69–202. Stanford: CSLI.
Steels, Luc (ed.). 2011. *Design Patterns in Fluid Construction Grammar.* Amsterdam/Philadelphia: John Benjamins.
Tomasello, Michael. 2003. *Constructing a Language: A Usage-Based Theory of Language Acquisition.* Cambridge, MA: Harvard University Press.
Traugott, Elizabeth Closs. 2008a. The grammaticalization of *NP of NP* patterns. In: Alexander Bergs and Gabriele Diewald (eds.), *Constructions and Language Change*, 23–45. Berlin/New York: Mouton de Gruyter.
Traugott, Elizabeth Closs. 2008b. Grammaticalization, constructions and the incremental development of language: suggestions from the development of degree modifiers in English. In: Regine Eckhardt, Gerhard Jäger and Tonjes Veenstra (eds.), *Variation, Selection, Development: Probing the Evolutionary Model of Language Change*, 219–250. Berlin/New York: Mouton de Gruyter.

Traugott, Elizabeth Closs and Graeme Trousdale. 2013. *Constructionalization and Constructional Changes*. Oxford: Oxford University Press.

Trousdale, Graeme. 2010. Issues in constructional approaches to grammaticalization in English. In: Katerina Stathi, Elke Gehweiler and Ekkehard König (eds.), *Grammaticalization: Current Views and Issues*, 51–71. Amsterdam/Philadelphia: John Benjamins.

Trousdale, Graeme. 2012. Grammaticalization, constructions and the grammaticalization of constructions. In: Kristin Davidse, Tine Breban, Lieselotte Brems and Tanja Mortelmans (eds.), *Grammaticalization and Language Change: New Reflections*, 167–198. Amsterdam/Philadelphia: John Benjamins.

Verhagen, Arie. 2005. *Constructions of Intersubjectivity: Discourse, Syntax and Cognition*. Oxford: Oxford University Press.

I Methodological advances

Natalia Levshina and Kris Heylen
2 A radically data-driven Construction Grammar: Experiments with Dutch causative constructions

1 The need for objective data-driven semantic classes[1]

Constructions are commonly defined as pairings of form and function (Goldberg 1995, 2006). The meaning, understood here as the concept or conceptual structure associated with a construction, is a crucial aspect of the latter's function. Although the meaning of a construction cannot always be reduced to the meaning of its components (e.g. Goldberg 1995), the semantic properties of its slot fillers can be used as a convenient heuristic to access the conventional uses of the construction in question. For instance, the central sense of the caused-motion construction (X CAUSES Y to MOVE Z, e.g. *She threw a coin in the Trevi fountain*) commonly involves a verb of directed physical action (*threw*), a movable physical object (*a coin*) and another physical object that can serve as a location (*the Trevi fountain*). Semantic classes of the slot fillers can be helpful in two ways. First, they can indicate the differences between the senses of one construction; second, they may reflect the division of "semantic labour" between two or more near-synonymous constructions.

Quantitative corpus-based studies of constructional semantics (including lexical semantics) frequently employ semantic classes. Table 1 lists some of the existing quantitative methods and approaches. They differ with regard to the research perspective: the researcher can either focus on the internal semantic structure of a construction, most commonly on its polysemy, or compare the distinctive features of functionally related constructions, for instance, near-synonyms, or "alternations". This distinction corresponds to the semasiological and onomasiological perspective, in more traditional semantic terms (Geeraerts, Grondelaers, and Bakema 1994). The other distinction is whether the semantic classes are determined *a priori* and form the basis of the subsequent analyses,

---

[1] This research project was partly funded by a grant from the Research Foundation of Flanders (FWO) (G.0330.08) awarded to Dirk Geeraerts and Dirk Speelman, the Quantitative Lexicology and Variational Linguistics Research Unit at the University of Leuven.

or they are inferred *a posteriori* in order to interpret the results (e.g. lists of distinctive collexemes). Yet, all those methods involve semantic classes of the slot fillers – exclusively or alongside other semantic features.

Table 1: Quantitative corpus-based methods in usage-based approaches to constructions (a selection)

	a priori **semantic classes**	*a posteriori* **semantic classes**
semasiological perspective (polysemy)	– Behavioural Profiles of a word's senses (Gries 2006) – Multidimensional Scaling-based semantic maps of linguistic categories (Levshina 2011)	(standard) Collostructional Analysis (Stefanowitsch and Gries 2003)
onomasiological perspective (near-synonymy)	– regressing on functionally similar constructions (e.g. Heylen 2005; Bresnan et al. 2007) – Behavioural Profiles of lexemes (Gries and Divjak 2006) – Correspondence Analysis maps of constructional spaces (Levshina, Geeraerts, and Speelman 2013)	Distinctive Collexeme Analysis (Gries and Stefanowitsch 2004)

However, the use of classifications is often problematic. If a researcher applies an *ad hoc* intuitive classification, (s)he runs the risk of missing some important distinctions or imposing irrelevant ones. Trying to avoid this caveat, many linguists apply ready-made classifications, such as the ones available in Levin (1993) or WordNet (Fellbaum 1998), which are based on more or less definite criteria or conventions. Still, this practice involves several conceptual and practical difficulties. First of all, ready-made conventional classifications are not available for many languages besides English. Second, the existing classifications tend to be incomplete, so that the researcher has to decide what to do with a large chunk of data that fall outside the classifications. In addition, many classifications, such as WordNet, are tree-like and contain several levels. In this situation, choosing the level of classification granularity (i.e., how deep one should prune the classification tree) becomes an empirical problem. One of the goals of the present paper is to develop a strategy of finding the optimal level of granularity on the basis of objective quantitative criteria.

The greatest problem, however, is that even the conventional classifications are largely introspective. More recently, there have been attempts to classify constructional slot fillers on the basis of large-scale corpus evidence. For instance,

Gries and Stefanowitsch (2010) have attempted to classify constructional collexemes with the help of a set of contextual features found in the corpus. The classes were evaluated qualitatively, the main criterion being semantic interpretability of the classes. Yet, if one adheres to the principles of empirical semantics (e.g. Geeraerts 2010a), it is at least just as important to present objective quantitative evidence that the choice of classification is justified by the facts of usage.

In this paper, we propose a novel objective distributional approach based on large-scale corpus data and rich contextual information. The core of the approach is Semantic Vector Spaces (Lin 1998), a method widely used in computational models of language. We demonstrate how the method can be used to choose between hundreds of possible classifications, arriving at the optimal one in terms of parsimony and predictive power for every particular set of near-synonymous constructions. We illustrate how the method works on the "alternation" of Dutch causative constructions with the auxiliaries *doen* 'do' and *laten* 'let'.

The structure of the article is as follows. In the following section, we introduce the object of the case study, the causative constructions in Dutch. Section 3 presents the general principles of the distributional models of Semantic Vector Spaces, followed by a description of the data and specific models in section 4. Section 5 reports the results of our classification experiments. In section 6, we discuss these results from a constructionist perspective and suggest some steps for future research.

2 Dutch causative constructions

Dutch periphrastic causatives consist of an auxiliary predicate (*doen* or *laten*), an effected predicate and several nominal slots, as shown in the example below:[2]

(1) De   politie   deed/liet   de auto   stoppen.
    the   police   did/let   the car   stop
    Causer   Auxiliary   Causee   Effected
                     Predicate   Predicate
    'The police stopped the car (let the car stop).'

---

[2] Some examples also contain an Affectee, which is the object of the Effected Predicate and the end point of the causation chain, e.g. *the window* in *The strong wind caused the tree to break the window*. Since Affectees expressed by NPs are infrequent in the corpus, the Affectee slot will not be considered in our experiments. See also Stukker (2005), who shows that the semantic classes of Affectees are not relevant for the choice between *doen* and *laten*.

Most of the corpus-based studies of these constructions (Kemmer and Verhagen 1994; Verhagen and Kemmer 1997; Stukker 2005) suggest that *doen* is an auxiliary that expresses direct causation. It is used to categorise causative situations in which the Causer uses its own energy to produce the caused event encoded by the Effected Predicate. On the other hand, the auxiliary *laten* refers to indirect causation, when "some other force besides the initiator is the most immediate source of energy of the effected event" (Verhagen and Kemmer 1997: 67). The semantics of *laten* also covers situations of letting. In fact, it represents a continuum from coercion to enablement and permission (Verhagen and Kemmer 1997; Speelman and Geeraerts 2009) with some ambiguous cases in between. For example, the construction in (2) suggests two interpretations:

(2) *Hij liet iedereen zijn roman lezen.*
  he let everyone his novel read
  'He had/let everyone read his novel.'

The most typical uses of *doen* are described as physical and affective causation. The former usually involves an inanimate Causer and Causee and a non-mental observable caused event:

(3) *De aardbeving deed de muren trillen.*
  the earthquake did the walls shake
  'The earthquake made the walls shake.'

Affective causation typically involves an inanimate stimulus (Causer), a human cognizer (Causee) and a mental caused event:

(4) *Je kapsel doet me denken aan een vogelnest.*
  your hairstyle does me think to a bird-nest
  'Your hairstyle reminds me of a bird's nest.'

As far as *laten* is concerned, its prototype is considered to be inducive causation, with a human Causer affecting a human Causee, normally intentionally and by means of communication (Stukker 2005). An example of inducive causation is given below:

(5) *De trainer liet de spelers loopoefeningen doen.*
  the coach let the players run-exercises do
  'The coach had the players do running exercises.'

Therefore, one can expect human Causers to be typical of *laten*, and non-human ones to favour *doen*. This is also what was found in previous quantitative multivariate studies (Speelman and Geeraerts 2009; Levshina 2011). The inherent semantic classes of the Causee (human being, abstract entity, artifact, etc.) have never shown strong effects in these previous analyses (Levshina 2011). However, the thematic roles of the Causee (quasi-patient or agent) have shown significant effects: *laten* is favoured by relatively agentive Causees, whereas *doen* is associated with patient-like affected Causees. The low relevance of the inherent semantic class of the Causee can be explained by the diverse roles of human Causees, who can be both relatively passive experiencers, as in (4), and active agents, as in (5).

As far as the Effected Predicate is concerned, our previous research (Levshina 2011) revealed a few distinctive verb classes at different levels of semantic specificity, from specific verbs to medium-grained semantic classes *à la* Levin and to highly abstract distinctions. This is in line with the constructionist approach, which claims that both exemplars and generalisations are stored in the speaker's memory (Langacker 1987; Goldberg 2006: 45–65). On the most lexically-specific level, some verbs, such as *denken aan* 'think of' are used exclusively with *doen*, and some others, such as *weten* 'know' and *wachten* 'wait', occur predominantly in the combination with *laten*. These expressions form low-level constructional pairings with specific meaning. Some exemplars of this type form clusters. For instance, the verbs of perception (*zien* 'see' and *horen* 'hear') are normally used with *laten*, whereas most predicates that designate internal mental processes – for instance, belief (*geloven* 'believe', *vermoeden* 'suppose'), emotion (*vrezen* 'fear') and decision (*besluiten* 'decide') – tend to occur with *doen*. In addition, verbs of quantitative change along a scale (*stijgen* 'rise', *toenemen* 'increase') also prefer *doen*. These clusters form the middle level of generalisation. Finally, on the most abstract level, *laten* is in general preferred by semantically and syntactically transitive verbs (*maken* 'make', *doden* 'kill'), whereas *doen* usually occurs with intransitive verbs with a patient-like first argument (*verdwijnen* 'disappear', *smelten* 'melt').

To summarise, one can expect a high effect of the semantic classes of the Causer and the Effected Predicate slots, and a weak effect of the Causee slot in predicting the choice between the two constructions. As for the Effected Predicate, it will also be interesting to see which level of granularity will be the optimal one in distinguishing between the constructions.

3 Semantic vector spaces

3.1 Origin

Semantic Vector Spaces (SVSs) have become the mainstay of modeling lexical semantics in Computational Linguistics over the last 20 years. Based on the hypothesis that semantically similar words tend to be used in similar contexts, these corpus-based approaches model the meaning of a word in terms of the contexts in which it appears. They have been applied to a wide variety of computational tasks – from Question Answering and Information Retrieval to automated essay scoring (Landauer and Dumais 1997) or the modeling of human behavior in psycholinguistic experiments (Lowe and McDonald 2000). SVSs were first developed during the so-called statistical turn in Natural Language Processing (NLP) in the 1990s, when NLP moved away from the then prevalent rule-based approach. They addressed the need to model semantics in a bottom-up, automated fashion from large amounts of corpus data, rather than having to rely on the time-consuming manual construction of lexical resources. As such, this data-oriented development in Computational Linguistics was not unlike the empirical and statistical turn observable today in Theoretical Linguistics, and in Cognitive Linguistics and Construction Grammar in particular. We will argue that SVSs can also be useful in more theoretically-oriented linguistic research in Construction Grammar. Thanks to their fully automatic, bottom-up analysis of the distribution of a word, SVS models are not only able to deal with enormous quantities of data; they also bypass the need for subjective human judgments and may bring to light patterns that escape the human eye.

The origin of SVSs can be traced back to a fundamental linguistic insight already expressed in the 1950s. Back then, a number of linguists and philosophers stressed the dependency, or even the identity, between the meaning of a word and its use. This view inspired John Rupert Firth's quote that "you shall know a word by the company it keeps" (Firth 1957), Ludwig Wittgenstein's "the meaning of a word is its use in the language" (1953), and Zelig Harris' (1954) insight that semantically similar words are used in similar contexts – a view which is now often referred to as the *distributional hypothesis*. In the (mainly) British tradition of Corpus Linguistics this hypothesis was put into practice by investigating the collocational behavior of words and identifying their idiomatic usage. SVSs can be seen as an extension and generalisation of collocational analysis. Instead of identifying only a restricted number of significant collocations as input for further qualitative analysis, SVSs track a word's co-occurrences with all other words in the corpus, resulting in a sort of over-all collocational profile that is the input for further quantitative analysis. More specifically, the similarity of collocational profiles is measured mathematically. The hypothesis is that words with a similar collocational profile will be semantically related and can thus be grouped into semantic classes.

3.2 Practical implementation

In practice, SVSs record the co-occurrence frequencies of a set of target words with a large set of context words in a given window around the target words.[3] The choice of target words depends on the task and can range from all words in the corpus (e.g. to automatically identify taxonomic relations in the whole of the vocabulary), or it can be limited to a set of words, like in our case, where we want to group only the nouns and verbs occurring in the Dutch causative constructions into semantic classes. The choice of context words can be said to be dependent on how well they are able to represent the semantics of the target words. A stop-list of highly frequent (function) words is usually excluded because they occur with almost all words and cannot therefore discriminate one set of semantically related words from another. Context words with very low frequencies simply do not occur with enough target words to be a basis of comparison. Most SVSs therefore use a few thousand highly frequent context words minus a stop list of function words. The co-occurrence frequencies between target and context words are stored in vectors and collected in a large matrix. Table 2 illustrates such a co-occurrence matrix with a handful of context words. In reality, the matrix is high-dimensional with thousands of target and context words: The length of the vectors, i.e. the number of columns, is equal to the number of context words, and the number of vectors (the rows) to the number of target words. As shown, many co-occurrence counts are zero, making matrices usually quite sparse. This is because words tend to co-occur with a limited set of context words, which is exactly the property that allows the technique to capture word semantics through context. In the toy matrix in Table 2, it is clear that *kiss* and *hug* must be semantically related because they have high co-occurrence frequencies with the same context words (*lovingly, mother, lovers*). The same holds for *kill* and *murder* that share high co-occurrence frequencies for *gun, psychopath, knife* and *cruelly*. *Soap*, on the other hand, has high co-occurrence frequencies with very different context words and thus is not related.

---

[3] See Turney and Pantel (2010) for an overview of implementations and applications.

Table 2: A matrix with imaginary co-occurrence frequencies of target words (rows) and contextual features (columns)

	gun	psychopath	knife	cruelly	lovingly	mother	lovers	...	detergent
kiss	2	2	0	0	89	56	98	...	0
hug	3	1	2	5	77	49	88	...	0
kill	10	59	67	69	0	8	12	...	1
murder	97	65	58	81	0	9	9	...	0
...	...	...				...	...	...	...
soap	0	0	0	0	1	0	1	...	67

To capture these collocational properties even better, the raw co-occurrence frequencies are usually weighted to represent collocational strength (e.g. Pointwise Mutual Information or Log Likelihood Ratio). This has the effect of giving a higher weight to very informative context words, i.e. those that co-occur only with a limited set of semantically related target words. For the vector comparison, Semantic Vector Spaces use a geometrical approach (hence Vector *Space*): the weighted co-occurrence frequencies can be seen as co-ordinates defining a point in a high-dimensional context feature space. Points closer together in the space are then semantically more related. Figure 1 shows a 2D subspace of the high-dimensional space where *kiss* and *hug* are close together based on their shared relatively high co-occurrence frequency with *lovingly* and relatively low co-occurrence frequency with *cruelly*, and vice versa for *kill* and *murder*.

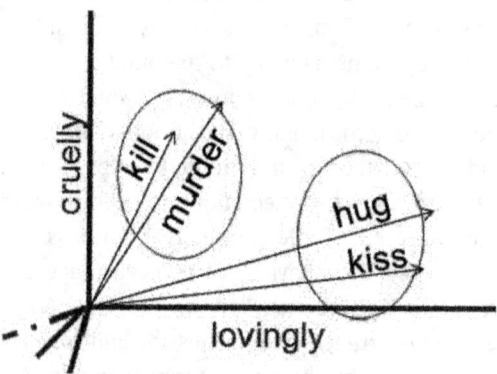

Figure 1: An imaginary 2D subspace of semantic vectors

As a proximity measure, most implementations use the cosine of the angle between the word vectors. If the angle is small, like between *kill* and *murder*, the cosine will be close to 1, indicating high similarity. If the angle is large, like between *kill* and *kiss*, the cosine is close to 0, indicating low similarity.[4] The computation of all pairwise cosine similarities between word vectors results in a word-by-word similarity matrix, shown in Table 3. Since the cosine is a symmetric similarity measure (the cosine of vector A with vector B is the same as the cosine of vector B with vector A), the matrix as a whole is also symmetric, with 1s on the diagonal (a target word is always completely similar with itself). Based on the similarity matrix, we can now derive for each target word a similarity ranking of all other target words. Depending on the application, the top most similar words can then be synonym candidates for inclusion in a thesaurus, or possible replacements in a search query to a Question Answering system. Important for this paper is that the similarity matrix can also be the input for a clustering algorithm that will try to identify groups of similar target words and hence semantic classes.

Table 3: Pairwise cosine similarities between word vectors (imaginary data)

	kiss	hug	kill	murder	...	soap
kiss	1	0.88	0.24	0.19	...	0.08
hug	0.88	1	0.18	0.26	...	0.11
kill	0.24	0.18	1	0.91	...	0.14
murder	0.19	0.26	0.91	1	...	0
...	...	...	...	...	1	...
soap	0.08	0.11	0.14	0	...	1

3.3 Different definitions of Context

Although all Semantic Vector Spaces share the basic ingredients described above, they come in many different flavors and implementations. To start with, there is a wide variety of possible settings for the more technical parameters like the frequency weighting function, the feature cut-off function or the similarity measure. However, the most important difference between the various implementations is how they define the notion of *context*. Recall that the basic principle behind SVSs is that a word's meaning can be modeled through the context it appears in. How context is defined, will necessarily influence the kind of semantics that is captured. In the description above, context was simply defined as the words co-occurring in a window around the target word, e.g. 5 words to the left and 5 words to the right. However, many other context definitions exist. A first

---

4 See Weeds, Weir and McCarthy (2004) for an overview and precise mathematical characterisation of different similarity measures, including the cosine.

obvious extension is varying the size of the context window. The extremes on this spectrum are, on the one hand, models that simply take the whole document as context, in which case words are similar if they tend to occur in the same documents. On the other hand, models can use simple bigrams, where only one word on the left or right is taken into account. Previous research (Peirsman, Heylen, and Geeraerts 2008) has shown that larger context windows lead to SVSs that capture looser, more associative semantic relations like *doctor-hospital* or *bird-sky*. Smaller context windows tend to find tighter, taxonomic relations like *doctor-nurse* (co-hyponym) or *bird-robin* (hyponym).

A second important aspect in the definition of context is the type of relation that holds between target and context words. In the models discussed so far, the relation is simply one of proximity without any further distinction between the context words within the chosen window. These models are therefore also called bag-of-words models. However, these models also record co-occurrences that are not very relevant or informative for the semantics of a given target word.

(6) *The teacher was startled by a barking dog on her way to work.*

In a sentence like (6), a bag-of-words model would include for the target word *dog* context words like *barking* – which is very informative – but also *teacher*, *startle*, *way* and *work* – which are much less informative. Therefore so-called dependency-based SVS models restrict the possible relation between target and context words by their syntactic or dependency relation. For example, an SVS can be construed to only include modifiers of the target noun, so that in sentence (6) only the highly informative *barking* is counted as context word. This results in fewer, but more semantically relevant context words. Of course, different dependency relations are relevant for different parts of speech: modifying adjectives are relevant for nouns but not for verbs. Therefore, these dependency-based SVSs are constructed for each part of speech separately. However, multiple dependency relations that are relevant for the same part of speech can be combined in a single SVS: A model for verbs can include adverbs, subject nouns, direct object nouns, prepositional complement nouns etc. In this case, most models define a context feature as the tuple [dependency relation, context word], so that [subject, dog] will be a different context feature from [object, dog]. In other words *dog* will be treated as a different context feature for *bite* in the sentences *A dog bites a man* and *A man bites a dog*. Additionally, the dependency relation between context and target word need not be binary: It can in principle consist of a dependency path of arbitrary length. In practice, only paths of three are commonly used to capture dependency relations involving prepositions, e.g. prepositional complements to verbs or modifying prepositional phrases to nouns.

(7) We listen to the radio.

In a sentence like (7), the target verb *listen* then has the context feature [object, to, object, radio], indicating that *listen* has a prepositional complement *radio* introduced by the preposition *to*.[5] Previous research (Heylen et al. 2008; Heylen, Peirsman, and Geeraerts 2009) has shown that dependency-based models tend to find even tighter semantic relations than the small-window bag of words models. They are especially good at identifying near-synonyms like *hospital* and *clinic* or *monkey* and *ape*.

Finally, a third way of defining context is specifically relevant for verbs and relies purely on a verb's syntactic behavior. Whereas the previous approaches all looked at the lexical context of a target word (be it syntactically restricted or not), these models only use the schematic syntactic slots or *subcategorisation frames* that a verb occurs with.

(8) Ellen bought her girlfriend a book for her birthday.

In (8), the context feature extracted for *buy* would be the tuple [subject, indirect object, direct object, prepositional adjunct], indicating only the attested syntactic arguments without any lexical information. Subcategorisation frame SVSs have been developed in a separate research tradition (see Schulte im Walde 2009 for an overview) based on the insights of (neo)structuralists like Lucien Tesnière, Juri Apresjan and Beth Levin that a verb's meaning is closely connected to its syntactic behavior and the arguments it governs. More specifically, semantically similar verbs are said to show the same alternation patterns in the syntactic arguments they take, which allows to derive semantic verb classes similar to Levin's (1993) classification. The implementations vary further in two respects. Firstly, they differ in the number of possible argument types taken into consideration. Some only look at the bare NP arguments (subject, direct object, indirect object), others include all arguments (prepositional complements, obligatory adverbs etc.), and the most inclusive models also take into account adjuncts (e.g. temporal, locational or benefactive adverbial expressions). Secondly, subcategorisation-frame models also differ with respect to the amount of lexico-semantic information they take into account. As discussed

---

5 See Padó and Lapata (2007) for an overview of possible applications.

above, the basic approach is to include only schematic syntactic valency information, but some models add some high-level semantic information: this might be semantic classes of the NP arguments, e.g. distinguishing between animate and non-animate arguments, or information about the specific preposition introducing a prepositional complement. The extracted context feature for *buy* in (8) then becomes [animate subject, animate indirect object, inanimate direct object, inanimate prepositional adjunct introduced by *for*]. Previous research indicates that subcategorisation frame models are indeed able to capture verb classes based on event-type, like manner-of-motion verbs, position verbs or perception verbs (Schulte im Walde 2006).

On a more theoretical note, it is necessary to make a qualification regarding the status of the dependencies. SVSs and most other computational distributional models originate from the structuralist reductionist tradition of relational semantics (see Geeraerts 2010b: 165–170), which assumes the existence of the categories like "subject" and "direct object" and the corresponding dependency relations. However, these categories have a controversial status in the contemporary usage-based constructionist approaches. Whereas Langacker's Cognitive Grammar interprets such categories in an essentialist way, as primary and secondary focal points (e.g. Langacker 2005), the non-essentialist Radical and Cognitive Construction Grammars question this assumption (e.g. Croft 2001; Goldberg 2006: 205–226). However, they do not claim that there can be no generalisations over similar arguments, which share the same form, in different constructions. It is necessary to emphasise, though, that the cognitive reality of such categories and the criteria for their demarcation need empirical support (Goldberg 2006: 223). Our use of the pre-determined categories and corresponding dependencies in this study is explained solely by historical and practical reasons: most computational models, including syntactic parsers, use this kind of neostructuralist approach. Still, we hope that these categories and dependencies provide an acceptable approximation of the possible generalisations over the similar constituents and relationships across different constructions.

Different definitions of context will result in Semantic Vector Spaces that capture different types of semantic relations. A clustering based on these SVSs will therefore also lead to different groupings of nouns and verbs into semantic classes. It is not clear *a priori* which semantic classification is the most relevant for modeling the choice between the causative constructions in Dutch. Additionally, it is also unclear how many semantic classes we need to distinguish to model the constructional variation. In this paper, we will therefore construct a range of SVSs with different context definitions, both for the nouns that fill the Causer and Causee slot and for the verbs that fill the Effected Predicate slot. Based on these SVSs, we will cluster these nouns and verbs at different levels of granularity and test which classification predicts the use of *laten* and *doen* best. The following section describes the procedure in detail.

4 Data and design

4.1 Data

For this case study, we took 6,863 occurrences of the constructions with *doen* and *laten* from two large corpora of Dutch: the Twente News Corpus (Ordelman et al. 2007) and Leuven News Corpus.[6] The newspaper data consisted of equal samples of articles about politics, economy, music and football. Because the corpora were syntactically parsed, the information about the lexical fillers of the three main slots – the Causer, the Causee and the Effected Predicate – was extracted automatically and later checked manually. Some of the nominal slots were empty, especially the Causee in transitive constructions, as in (9):

(9) Ik liet het huis bouwen.
     I   let the house build
     'I had the house built.'

The objects of the classifications were all explicit non-pronominal slot fillers treated as types, or lemmata. In total, we obtained 2700 common and proper nouns in the function of the Causer, 1810 nouns filling the Causee slot, and 1155 verbs in the function of the Effected Predicates.

4.2 Distributional classes

The Semantic Vector Spaces were all constructed from the Twente Nieuws Corpus (380 million words, see Ordelman et al. 2007).[7] For the SVSs using syntactic dependency information, we used the version parsed with the Alpino dependency parser (van Noord 2006) whose dependency triples have been shown to be 90% accurate in the Twente Nieuws Corpus (Plank and Van Noord 2010). Following our discussion in section 3.3, we built SVS models with 3 different

---

[6] Leuven News Corpus is a large corpus of contemporary newspaper Dutch in Flanders. The corpus was compiled by the Quantitative Lexicology and Variational Linguistics Research Unit at the University of Leuven.
[7] No separate SVSs were constructed for Belgian Dutch (Leuven News Corpus). As a consequence, some typically Belgian Dutch verbs or verb meanings might have been disregarded.

types of context definition and with the slot fillers of the Dutch causative construction as target words:
1) bag-of-words models for nouns and verbs;
2) dependency-based models for nouns and verbs;
3) subcategorisation frame models for verbs only.

For the nouns filling the Causer and Causee slots in the *doen* en *laten* constructions, we only constructed one bag-of-words SVS and one dependency-based SVS (subcategorisation frame models are not relevant for nouns). This choice was based on previous research (Heylen et al. 2008; Peirsman, Heylen, and Geeraerts 2008) where these two models gave the best performance in finding tight semantic relations. The bag-of-words SVS had a relatively small context window of 5 words left and right of the target noun. The dependency-based SVS used 8 dependency relations distinguished by the Alpino parser that a noun can be involved in. These relations are listed in Table 4 with examples (the target noun is in italics and the context feature resulting from the dependency relation is underlined).[8] In the first four relations (su, obj1, pc, advPP), the target noun is regarded as the dependent element and the governing verb is counted as a context feature. In the next three relations (pmPP, adj, app) the noun is the head and the dependent adjective and/or noun is counted as a context feature. Finally, the co-ordination relation is a symmetric one and always generates two target noun/context noun pairs.

Table 4: Syntactic dependency relations of nouns. The target noun is in italics and the context feature resulting from the dependency relation is underlined

Abbr.	Dependency relation	example
su	subject	De *baby* slaapt. 'The baby sleeps.'
obj1	direct object	Hij eet een *appel*. 'He eats an apple.'
pc	prepositional complement	Ze luistert naar de *radio*. 'She listens to the radio.'
advPP	adverbial prepositional phrase	Hij woont in een *dorp*. 'He lives in a village.'
pmPP	post-modifying prepositional phrase	het *meisje* met de jurk 'the girl in the dress'
adj	adjective	de gelaarsde *kat* 'the booted cat'
app	apposition	de *koningin*, een wijze vrouw 'the queen, a wise woman'
cnj	co-ordination	de *krekel* en de mier 'the cricket and the ant' de krekel en de *mier*

---

[8] For a full description of the Alpino parsing scheme, see van Noord (2006).

Since previous research has shown several possible classification criteria of the Effected Predicates (see section 2), we focused on exploring different Semantic Vector Spaces for verbs. Within each of the 3 context definition types, we therefore varied the specific number and type of context features. Within the bag-of-word models, we varied the size of the window around the target verb and constructed a first model with a relatively small window size of 4 context words to the left and right, and a second model with a relatively large window of 15 words on either side. Within the dependency-based models we varied the number of different dependency relations. Based on the Alpino dependency parser, we can distinguish 23 different dependency relations that a verb can engage in. They are listed in Table 5. A first model only takes context features into account that are based on the 3 bare NP arguments (su, obj1, obj2). A second model uses all 7 arguments to extract context features (su, obj1, obj2, pc, ld, ldprep, predc) and, finally, the third model took all 13 dependency relations with a lexically full element into account (su, obj1, obj2, pc, ld, me, ldPP, adv, advPP, predm, predc, invomte, invte).[9]

Table 5: An overview of syntactic dependency relations of verbs. The target verb is in italics and the context feature resulting from the dependency relation is underlined

Abbr.	Relation	Example
su	subject	Het meisje *slaapt*. 'The girl sleeps.'
sup	cataphoric subject	Het *blijkt* dat... 'It appears that...'
obj1	direct object	Hij *eet* een appel. 'He eats an apple.'
pobj1	cataphoric object	...of ik het *betreur* dat... 'whether I regret it that...'
obj2	indirect object	Ze *geeft* papa een kus. 'She gives daddy a kiss.'
se	reflexive	Hij *schaamt* zich. Lit. 'He shames himself (i.e., He is ashamed).'
svp	separable affix	Je *lacht* me uit. Lit. 'You laugh me out (i.e., You're mocking me).'
pc	prepositional complement	Ze *luistert* naar de radio. 'She listens to the radio.'
me	measure complement	Het *kost* 20 euro. 'It costs 20 euro's.'
ld	locative complement	Ze *werkt* thuis. 'She works at home.'

---

[9] Since dependency-based models, like bag-of-words models only select lexically full words as context words (excluding function words), we only took those dependency relations into account where there is a lexically full dependant of the verb (a noun, adjective or other verb). This excludes relations like cataphoric object (pobj1) or reflexive (se), but also the clausal arguments where the dependent is not a single lexically full word.

ldPP	locative prepositional phrase	Ze *rijdt* naar huis. 'She is driving home.'
adv	adverbial complement	Je *zingt* goed. 'You sing well.'
advPP	adverbial prepositional phrase	Hij *komt* over 2 weken. 'He's coming in two weeks' time.'
predm	predicative modifier	Hij *kwam* dronken thuis. 'He came home drunk.'
predc	predicative complement	Dat *smaakt* lekker. 'That tastes nice.'
ccl	complement clause	Hij *zegt* dat hij komt. 'He says that he is coming.'
cclof	complement clause (choice)	Ze *vraagt* of je komt. 'She asks whether you're coming.'
cvte	complement verb	Ze *staat* te praten. Lit. 'She stands talking (i.e., She is talking).'
cvom	complement verb (goal)	We *reizen* om te leren. 'We travel to learn.'
invaux	auxiliary verb	Ik *kan* lezen. 'I can read.'
invte	semi-auxiliary verb	Hij *ligt* te slapen. Lit. 'He lies sleeping (i.e., He is sleeping).'
invomte	semi-auxiliary (goal)	Ik probeer om te slapen. 'I try to sleep.'
invaanhet	progressive marker	Ik ben aan het lezen. Lit. 'I am at reading (i.e., I am reading).'

Within the subcategorisation frame models, we varied both the syntactic positions that could be included in a subcategorisation frame and the amount of lexico-semantic information about the elements filling the syntactic positions. The syntactic positions are based on the same 23 dependency relations in Table 5. Again, we made 3 subdivisions for the types of relations: the 5 bare NP arguments (su, sup, se, obj1, obj2); all 9 arguments (su, sup, se, obj1, obj2, pc, ld, ldprep, predc); all 23 dependency relations. The lexico-semantic information on the syntactic position fillers could be of 4 types: (i) no lexico-semantic information; (ii) the specific preposition introducing the dependent in pc, ldPP and advPP; (iii) the semantic class of a dependent noun; (iv) both the specific preposition and the semantic noun class. For the semantic noun classes, we used the second highest ancestor of the noun in the Dutch WordNet (Vossen 1998). This resulted in 11 semantic noun classes: animate being, object, situation, action, utterance, property, thought, part, group, place, time. If the noun was not present in the Dutch WordNet, we reverted to a syntax-only subcategorisation frame feature. If the noun belonged to more than one semantic class (because of polysemy), the most frequent overall class was used.

An overview of the models can be found in Table 6, together with the abbreviations used in the rest of the article. For all models, the maximum number of context features was restricted to the 4000 most frequent context features (excluding 122 function words). Both target and context words were processed on the lemma level (i.e., generalising over word-forms). In all models, the co-occurrence frequencies were weighted with the Pointwise Mutual Information index. For all the SVS models, the similarity between target word vectors was measured with the cosine. This resulted in 16 similarity matrices for verbs, and 2 similarity matrices for nouns.

Table 6: An overview of the models and classifications

Context definition	Causer and Causee (nouns)		Effected Predicate (verbs)	
	feature selection	no. clusters	feature selection	no. clusters
Bag of words	5 words left and right: BOW5	2–100	4 words left and right: BOW4	5–100
			15 words left and right: BOW15	5–100
Dependency-based	8 dependencies: DEPREL8	2–100	3 dependencies: Vbarel	5–100
			7 dependencies: Varel	5–100
			13 dependencies: rVrel	5–100
Subcat. frame	–	–	Syntax only	
			5 dependencies: 5syn	5–100
			9 dependencies:: 9syn	5–100
			23 dependencies: 23syn	5–100
			Preposition information	
			9 dependencies: 9relprep	5–100
			23 dependencies: 23relprep	5–100
			Sem.Class information	
			5 dependencies: 5sclass	5–100
			9 dependencies: 9sclass	5–100
			23 dependencies: 23sclass	5–100
			Prep. + Sem.Class information	
			5 dependencies: 5richsubcat	5–100
			9 dependencies: 9richsubcat	5–100
			23 dependencies: 23richsubcat	5–100

The similarity matrices were the input for a hierarchical cluster analysis (e.g. Everitt et al. 2001) that groups the noun and verb lemmata into semantic classes. We experimented with different numbers of classes, ranging from 2 to 100 for the Causers and Causees (all numbers from 2 to 10 and then intervals of 5, totalling 27 different clusterings), and ranging from 5 to 100 for the Effected Predicates (intervals of 5, totalling 20 different clusterings). Together with the different context definitions and feature selection criteria, this gives 54 possible semantic classifications of the Causer and Causee nouns and 240 possible semantic classifications of the Effected Predicate verbs.

4.3 The objective criterion for the evaluation of classifications

The next question is, how to choose the optimal classification from this richness? In previous research, the classifications were evaluated against an *a priori* manually created 'gold standard' (Schulte im Walde 2006) or *a posteriori* intuitively (Stefanowitsch and Gries 2010). In this study, we propose an entirely objective and data-driven criterion. The evaluation of the models is carried out according to the power of the classes in predicting the use of *doen* or *laten* in the above-mentioned sample of 6,863 observations. Obviously, the predictive power of a classification will be greater if the lexemes that belong to one and the same class will also tend to be used in contexts with only one of the two auxiliaries. In other words, the predictive power is actually an operationalisation of the success of discrimination between the lexemes that tend to be used with *doen* and the ones that are attracted to *laten* (cf. distinctive collexemes in the Distinctive Collexeme Analysis developed by Gries and Stefanowitsch 2004).

In this case study, we used several well-known statistical measurements of the predictive power: C, Somer's D_{xy}, Nagelkerke's R^2, Gamma and AIC (Hosmer & Lemeshow 2000; Baayen 2008). All statistical analyses were performed in R (R Development Core Team 2010). Since most of the parameters displayed very similar behaviour, in the discussion of the results we will limit ourselves to the concordance index C, which is believed to be one of the most objective estimators (Hosmer and Lemeshow 2000: 160–164). This statistic usually falls in the range between 0.5 (random prediction) and 1 (perfect prediction). If $C < 0.7$, this suggests no discrimination; if $0.7 \leq C < 0.8$, the prediction is acceptable; if $0.8 \leq C < 0.9$, the model has excellent discrimination; and if $C \geq 0.9$, the prediction is outstanding. A good model combines a low number of classes with high predictive power. The results of our experiments are presented in the next section.

5 Results of the classification experiments

In this section, we discuss the results of the classification experiments for every slot individually. In the last subsection, we also present the results for all three slots taken together.

5.1 Classification of the Causers

As mentioned in the previous section, we had two SVS models of the Causer nouns: the one with the lexical information only (*BOW*), and the one where the lexical information was enriched with the syntactic information about the eight dependency relations (*DepRel8*). For both models, we also tested different clustering solutions with the number of classes from 2 to 100. Figure 2 shows how the C index rapidly goes up from the very beginning, which indicates that the relevant semantic distinctions are captured by a relatively small number of classes. The syntactically enriched model performs much better than the simple bag-of-words model. This finding corroborates the results in Gries & Stefanowitsch 2010 (section 2.2), which also compared a bag-of-words model with a syntactically more precise one. The starting value for the syntactically enriched model with

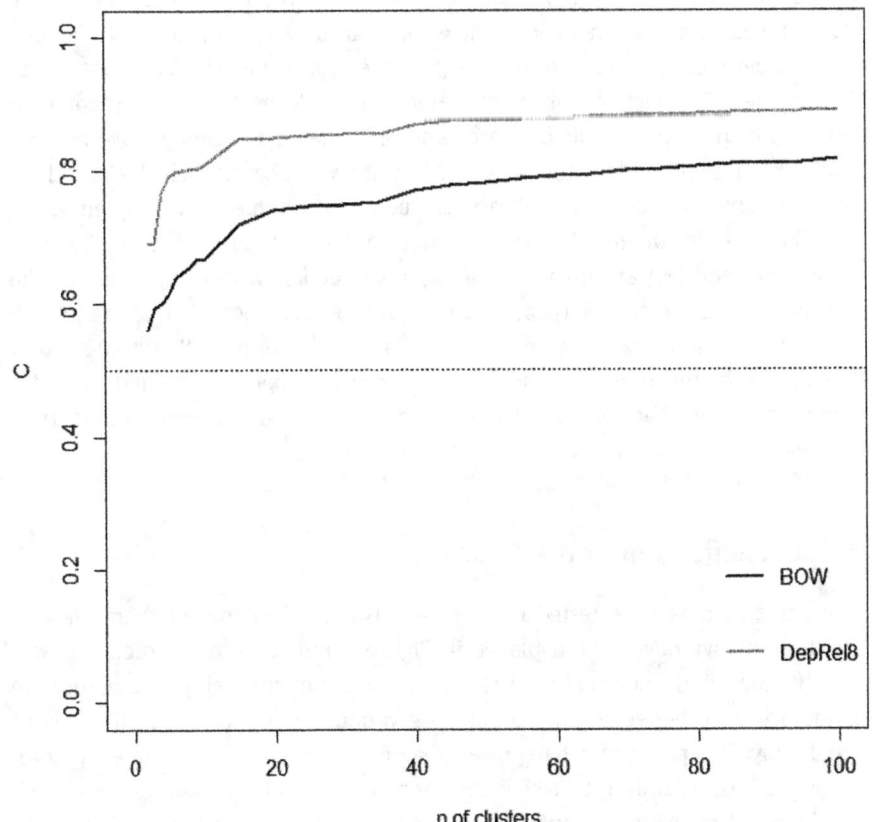

Figure 2: The Causer: predictive power of two models, for different number of classes

two classes only is already 0.69, and for six classes it is 0.80, which is considered to be good. The 100-cluster syntactically enriched solution has the highest value ($C = 0.89$), but its predictive power is not dramatically different from the more parsimonious classifications with a smaller number of classes.

Let us consider the classification with 6 clusters, which is quite successful in discriminating between the *doen* and *laten* observations. The classification includes a cluster with predominantly inanimate concrete and abstract nouns: *cd* 'cd', *cijfer* 'digit', *herstel* 'recovery', *stem* 'voice', *aanslag* 'attack', *afwezigheid* 'absence', *resultaat* 'result', etc. Cluster 2 (the numbering is arbitrary) contained mostly football- and music-related nouns denoting people and organisations: *Feyenoord* (a football club in the Netherlands), *dirigent* 'conductor', *speler* 'player', *orkest* 'orchestra' etc., although there were a few exceptions, such as *beurs* 'stock exchange', which comes from economy-related articles. Cluster 3 included some proper names of conductors and common and proper nouns denoting political and other agents: *Gergiev* (a Russian conductor), *Van Hecke* (a Belgian politician), *secretaris-generaal* 'General Secretary', *Harnoncourt* (an Austrian conductor) etc. Cluster 4 contained many geographical names, which are frequently used in newspaper articles to refer to the government metonymically: *Verenigde Staten* 'the US', *Amerika*, *Washington*, etc. Cluster 5 included mostly common nouns, which denote people in charge and organisations: *regering* 'government', *minister* 'minister', *bedrijf* 'company', *trainer* 'trainer'. The sixth cluster contained only 7 nouns with very low collocability due to an extremely low frequency.

The majority of the observations that contain the Causers from Cluster 1 (inanimate entities) are instances of the construction with *doen*, whereas the nouns from Clusters 2–5 (people and organisations) occur more frequently with *laten*. Cluster 6 was too small for evaluation. The findings therefore support the results of the previous studies. The distinction between animate and inanimate Causers had very high predictive power in all previous multivariate analyses.

5.2 Classification of the Causees

The same models were tested on the Causee nouns. Neither of them showed much predictive power, as displayed in Figure 3, although the predictive power slowly grows with the number of clusters. This is not surprising: the higher the granularity, the better the individual observations are fitted, but at the cost of parsimony. This poor predictive power (maximum $C = 0.74$) corroborates the previous studies, according to which the inherent semantic classes of the Causee are largely irrelevant, in contrast with the thematic role of the participant in bringing about the effected event.

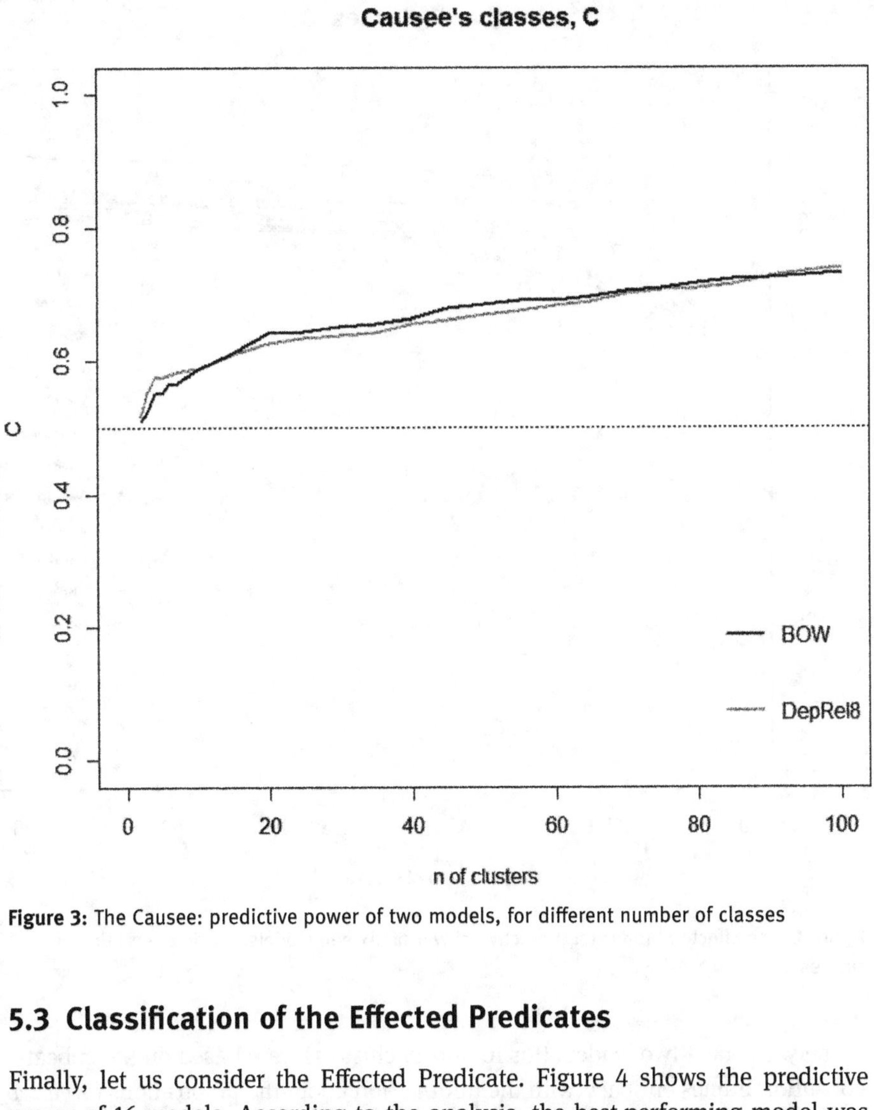

Figure 3: The Causee: predictive power of two models, for different number of classes

5.3 Classification of the Effected Predicates

Finally, let us consider the Effected Predicate. Figure 4 shows the predictive power of 16 models. According to the analysis, the best-performing model was *23syn* (the upper line), the model with information about the subcategorisation frames based on 23 syntactic relations without any additional information, although some other models were more successful for a very small number of classes, as one can see from Figure 4. It is interesting that the model *9richsubcat*, which was the leader when the number of clusters was very small (C = 0.68 with 5 classes), contained information about the subcategorisation frames enriched with the information about the prepositions and semantic noun classes. As the number of clusters grew, the leadership was taken over by other models.

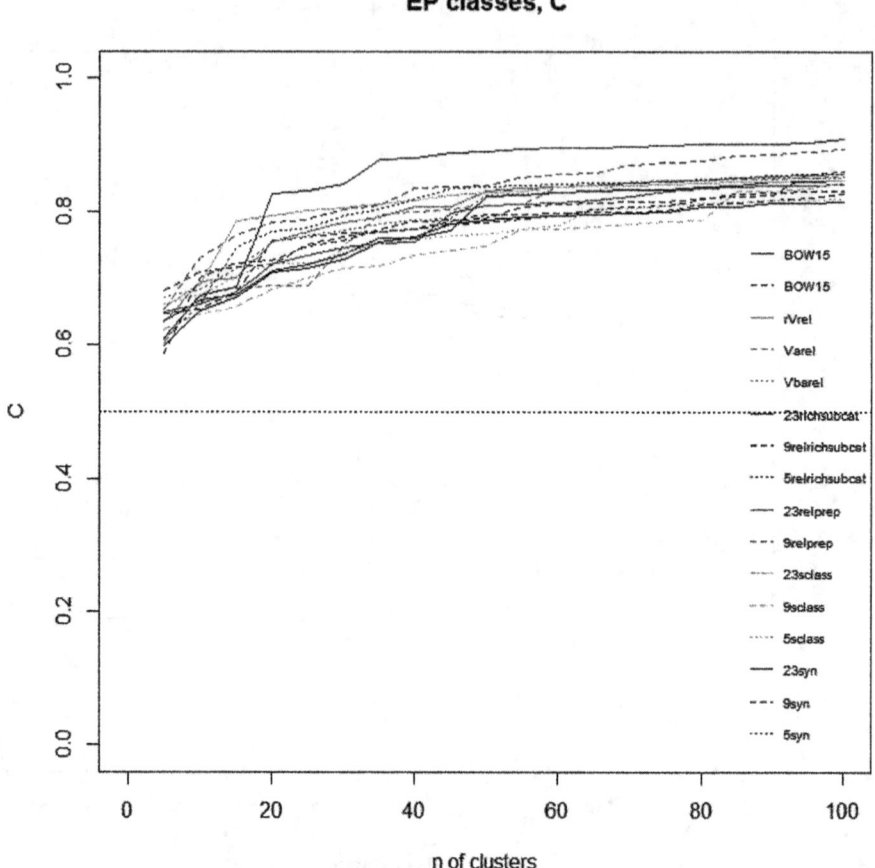

Figure 4: The Effected Predicate: predictive power of sixteen models, for different number of classes

Namely, the next two leaders (for 10 and 15 clusters) were based on the subcategorisation frames enriched with the information about the prepositions (*9relprep* with 10 clusters, $C = 0.73$) and semantic noun classes (*23sclass* with 15 clusters, $C = 0.79$). From 20 verb classes on, the simple subcategorisation frames based on 23 dependencies without additional information yielded the best results (*23syn* with 20 clusters, $C = 0.83$), although the model was closely followed by *9relprep*, which involved subcategorisation frames based on 9 syntactic relationships and prepositions, especially for large numbers of clusters. The bag-of-words models performed on average worse than most other models, although the large window model (*BOW15*) was slightly more successful than the small window one (*BOW4*). Another poorly performing model was *9sclass* (subcategorisation frames based on only 9 syntactic relations, enriched with the information about noun classes). All this suggests that the abstract constructional information is vital for a successful verb classification, and that this information should be very detailed and go beyond the main arguments. We can also conclude that the semantic and prepositional information does not add much, and even makes the classification less successful, when we have 20 and more classes.

The increase in the predictive power was gradual, so that the optimal classification into 35 clusters ($C = 0.88$) – the number after which the predictive power does not increase substantially – was medium-grained. Only three of these clusters contain verbs that predominantly co-occurred with *doen* in the test sample. These classes are interpretable as verbs of qualitative and configurational change of state (e.g. *herleven* 'come to life again', *kantelen* 'tip over', *smelten* 'melt', *verslappen* 'weaken', *vervagen* 'fade'), verbs of quantitative change along a scale (e.g. *stijgen* 'go up', *dalen* 'go down', *groeien* 'grow', *zakken* 'fall') and verbs of various mental processes, emotions and beliefs (e.g. *denken* 'think', *vermoeden* 'suppose', *geloven* 'believe', *besluiten* 'decide, conclude', *vrezen* 'fear', *hopen* 'hope').

Most of the clusters showed a higher proportion of *laten*, as was the case with the Causer (see section 5.1). One of them was the cluster containing predominantly verbs of communication: *schrijven* 'write', *uitleggen* 'explain', *adviseren* 'advise', *vertellen* 'tell'. Another cluster contained many verbs of change of possession and possessional deprivation: *geven* 'give', *ontnemen* 'take, rob', *leveren* 'deliver', *verkopen* 'sell'. Yet another one mainly consisted of verbs of searching, active perception and testing, e.g. *onderzoeken* 'explore', *bekijken* 'have a look (at)', *toetsen* 'test'. Most of these imply a volitional human Causee and a human Causer, who represents an authority and gives orders (10). The presence of such semantic frames and scenarios of causation implies that the combinations of the three slot fillers are not arbitrary. From this follows that the combined effect of the semantic classes of the Causer, Causee and Effected Predicate on the choice of the auxiliary is probably not additive. We will come back to this observation later.

(10)   *Obama   laat   alle   kerncentrales   VS   onderzoeken.*
      Obama   lets   all   nuclear-stations   US   check
      'Obama orders to check all nuclear power stations in the US.'

Another cluster contains verbs related to putting and bringing (*leggen* 'lay', *zetten* 'set', *stellen* 'put', *brengen* 'bring'), which imply an active Causee that brings about a change in the location or position of another entity. Yet another one had verbs of motion, such as *draaien* 'turn round', *glijden* 'slide', *rijden* 'ride', *vliegen* 'fly', which also involve a certain degree of autonomy on the part of the Causee.

However, many other classes were more difficult to interpret. For instance, one of the clusters with a very high proportion of *laten* contained verbs of perception (*zien* 'see', *voelen* 'feel'), the verbs *weten* 'know', *kennen* 'know, be acquainted', *maken* 'make', *doen* 'do', *blijken* 'appear', *schijnen* 'shine, appear', *zijn* 'be', *worden* 'become' and *hebben* 'have'. It is difficult to say why these verbs go together. Probably this is an effect of the overall high frequency and broad constructional repertoire of these verbs. In this respect, this cluster was similar to another one, which contained the semi-auxiliary or light verbs prototypically related to motion or position: *gaan* 'go', *zitten* 'sit', *staan* 'stand', *vallen* 'fall', *komen* 'come'. Note that many of these verbs in the vague clusters are strongly associated with *laten* (see section 2).

In general, many of these classes strikingly resemble Levin's (1993) classification. This similarity can be explained by the fact that both Levin's "alternations" and subcategorisation frames reflect the distribution of verbs in constructions. However, our approach is finer-grained (more possible constructions are examined), probabilistic and treats every construction on its own, not as a part of an alternation pair.

5.4 Combined classes of three slots

In addition, we compared the models with the three slots taken together. The 5 to 100 classes of the Effected Predicates were combined with 2, 5, 10, 15, 20 and 30 classes of the Causer and the Causee. The best-performing models only were tested: *depRel8* for the Causer and *23syn* for the Effected Predicate. For the Causee, also *depRel8* was chosen, although it did not perform better than the bag-of-words model. The C index for these different classifications is displayed in Figure 5.

The results of the combined classifications show that adding the semantic information about the Causer and Causee to the information about the Effected Predicate does increase the predictive power, but the effect is non-additive. The effect is significant for the small number of the Effected Predicates, but as the verb classes become finer-grained and more successful in the prediction, the impact of the nominal classes becomes smaller. Also the difference in the granularity of the nominal slot classifications becomes less evident as the number of the verb classes and the predictive power grow.[10]

---

[10] Unfortunately, we were unable to test the statistical interactions of the slot fillers due to data sparseness.

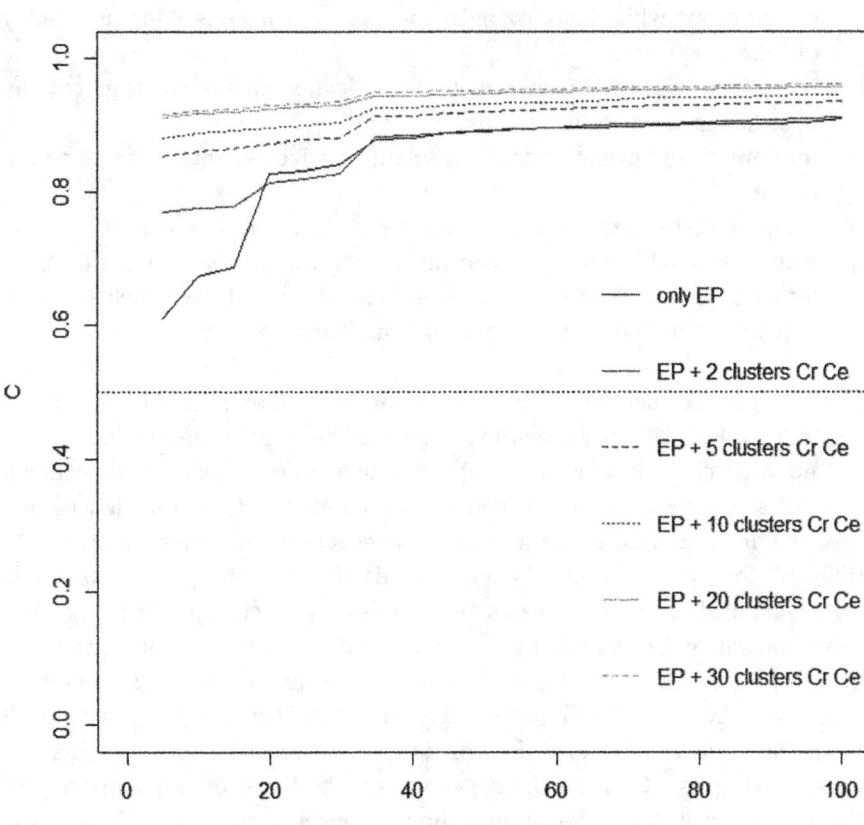

Figure 5: Thee slots together: predictive power of the best-performing individual classifications

6 General discussion and conclusions

In this paper, we have demonstrated how Semantic Vector Spaces, an approach in computational linguistics, can be transferred to Construction Grammar and used to model constructional semantics. Our approach offers the following epistemological advantages in comparison with introspective manual semantic analysis (in the extreme case, mere eye-balling of the contexts):

– It allows one to find the optimal semantic classification of constructional slot fillers, based on their usage;

- It takes into account the frequencies of semantic classes in near-synonymous constructions, which has a cognitive interpretation in terms of the cue validity of collexeme classes;
- It provides objective evidence about the optimal level of semantic granularity of semantic descriptions;
- It allows one to detect semantic regularities, which might otherwise go unnoticed;
- It allows one to explore larger amounts of data than it would be possible manually, and, in principle, can provide distribution-based classifications for all collexemes that occur in the corpus. As a result, the conclusions are robust from both the quantitative and qualitative perspectives.

In addition, the co-occurrence matrices that were used for this case study can be easily "recycled" for other construction-oriented case studies in Dutch.

Apart from the demonstration of a new method for studying constructional semantics, the results of the experiments have theoretical consequences. For instance, in section 5.4 we found that the effects of the semantic classes of the different slots are non-additive. In other words, the predictive power of the three slots combined together is smaller than the sum predictive power of the slots taken separately. Why should this be the case? A possible explanation might be as follows. If a word is compatible with the meaning of the construction, as assumed in Construction Grammar, then there should be coherence among all slots. This statement is called the Principle of Semantic Coherence by Stefanowitsch and Gries (2005: 11). The coherence can be based on different types of knowledge, for instance, frame-semantic relationships, as in example (10). The information stored in one slot therefore interacts with the information from the other slots. This non-additivity can serve as evidence that the semantics of constructions is not reducible to the semantics of the constructional components.

Another interesting finding is that the most parsimonious classification of the Causers has fewer classes than that of the Effected Predicates. In general, noun classifications tend to be organised taxonomically as trees with long branches, for instance, 'entity' – 'concrete object' – 'living being' – 'animal' – 'mammal' – 'carnivore' – 'canine' – 'dog' – 'bulldog', whereas verbs constitute far less hierarchically structured 'bushes' (the hyper- and hyponymy chains in the WordNet provide a nice illustration). This difference can be explained by the complex semantic structure of verbs, which normally involves a configuration of participants, spatiotemporal characteristics of the event, image schemata, social frames and scenarios, and other information. To organise these heterogeneous abstract semantic structures in a consistent tree-like hierarchy with a high level of generalisation is problematic. It seems plausible that verbs are organised in a large number of small local clusters. We need very detailed contextual information (in our approach, many possible subcategorisation frames) to capture these small classes.

Perhaps the most intriguing finding concerns the type of distributional context. Both in the case of the Causers and the Effected Predicates, the maximally syntactic (constructional) models perform the best (cf. Gries and Stefanowitsch 2010). One may wonder why this should be the case. We would like to propose the following explanation. The abstract syntactic context features highlight the syntactically (constructionally) relevant semantic properties of lexemes (e.g. animacy or inanimacy). These features may also be relevant for the prediction of other constructions beside the causatives with *doen* and *laten*. According to this hypothesis, one can expect the more syntactically enriched models to perform better than more lexically specific models in all sets of near-synonymous syntactic constructions. Future research will show if this hypothesis is correct.

The approach also has to face a few challenges in the future. First of all, a more realistic approach would require word sense disambiguation. For instance, it would be necessary to treat *denken* in the sense 'think (of)' separately from *denken* as 'think (that)' and even 'think (about)'. Another important problem is pronominal reference resolution, which would allow us to use all occurrences of the constructions in the testing set and get a more complete picture.

The results also suggest that a medium level of granularity is optimal for classification of the Effected Predicates. However, as we pointed out in section 2, the speaker's knowledge about the constructions may have several interacting levels of generalisation. So far, we have pruned the clustering tree only at one level. In future experiments, we are planning to test different levels of granularity simultaneously, which may allow us to integrate both higher-level generalisations and specific exemplars of the constructions.

From a broader interdisciplinary perspective, this study has demonstrated that the neostructuralist distributional models perform quite well in finding relevant semantic similarities between constructional slot fillers. We expect that fully construction-based bottom-up models, free from any aprioristic assumptions about the syntactic categories and relations, will further improve the performance and make the approach even more radically data-driven. One of the possibilities, for instance, would be to use unsupervised stochastic grammar induction from raw data on the basis of existing Data Oriented Processing models (e.g. Beekhuizen and Bod, this volume). A practical implementation of this approach will bridge the gap between the computational models of semantics and usage-based Construction Grammar.

References

Baayen, R. Harald. 2008. *Analyzing Linguistic Data: A Practical Introduction to Statistics Using R*. Cambridge: Cambridge University Press.

Bresnan, Joan, Anna Cueni, Tatiana Nikitina and R. Harald Baayen. 2007. Predicting the dative alternation. In Gerlof Bouma, Irene Kramer and Joost Zwarts (eds.), *Cognitive Foundations of Interpretation*, 69–94. Amsterdam: Royal Netherlands Academy of Science.

Croft, William. 2001. *Radical Construction Grammar: Syntactic Theory in Typological Perspective*. Oxford: Oxford University Press.

Everitt, Brian S., Sabine Landau and Morven Leese. 2001. *Cluster Analysis*. London: Arnold.

Fellbaum, Christiane (ed.). 1998. *WordNet: An Electronic Lexical Database*. Cambridge, MA: MIT Press.

Firth, John R. 1957. A synopsis of linguistic theory 1930–1955. In: John R. Firth (ed.), *Studies in Linguistic Analysis*, 1–32. Oxford: Blackwell.

Geeraerts, Dirk. 2010a. The doctor and the semantician. In: Dylan Glynn and Kerstin Fischer (eds.), *Quantitative Methods in Cognitive Semantics: Corpus-driven Approaches*, 63–78. Berlin/New York: Mouton de Gruyter.

Geeraerts, Dirk. 2010b. *Theories of Lexical Semantics*. Oxford: Oxford University Press.

Geeraerts, Dirk, Stefan Grondelaers and Peter Bakema. 1994. *The Structure of Lexical Variation: Meaning, Naming, and Context*. Berlin/New York: Mouton de Gruyter.

Goldberg, Adele E. 1995. *Constructions. A Construction Grammar Approach to Argument Structure*. Chicago: University of Chicago Press.

Goldberg, Adele E. 2006. *Constructions at Work: The Nature of Generalization in Language*. Oxford: Oxford University Press.

Gries, Stefan Th. 2006. Corpus-based methods and Cognitive Semantics: The many senses of *to run*. In: Stefan Th. Gries & Anatol Stefanowitsch (eds.), *Corpora in Cognitive Linguistics: Corpus-based Approaches to Syntax and Lexis*, 57–99. Berlin/New York: Mouton de Gruyter.

Gries, Stefan Th. and Dagmar Divjak. 2006. Ways of trying in Russian: Clustering behavioral profiles. *Corpus Linguistics and Linguistic Theory* 2: 23–60.

Gries, Stefan Th. and Anatol Stefanowitsch. 2004. Extending collostructional analysis: A corpus-based perspective on "alternations". *International Journal of Corpus Linguistics* 9: 97–129.

Gries, Stefan Th. and Anatol Stefanowitsch. 2010. Cluster analysis and the identification of collexeme classes. In: John Newman & Sally Rice (eds.), *Empirical and Experimental Methods in Cognitive/Functional Research*, 73–90. Stanford: CSLI.

Harris, Zellig. 1954. Distributional structure. *Word* 10: 146–162.

Heylen, Kris. 2005. A quantitative corpus study of German word order variation. In Stephan Kepser & Magda Reis (eds.), *Linguistic evidence: Empirical, Theoretical and Computational Perspectives*, 241–264. Berlin/New York: Mouton de Gruyter.

Heylen, Kris, Yves Peirsman, Dirk Geeraerts and Dirk Speelman. 2008. Modelling word similarity: An evaluation of automatic synonymy extraction algorithms. In: *Proceedings of the 6th International Conference on Language Resources and Evaluation (LREC 2008), Marrakesh, Morocco, 23–30 May 2008*, 3243–3249. Marrakesh: European Language Resources Association.

Heylen, Kris, Yves Peirsman and Dirk Geeraerts. 2009. Automatic synonymy extraction: A comparison of syntactic context models. In: S. Verberne, Hans van Halteren and Peter-Arno Coppen (eds.), *Computational Linguistics in the Netherlands 2007: Selected Papers from the Eighteenth CLIN Meeting*, 101–116. Utrecht: LOT publications.
Hosmer, David W. and Stanley Lemeshow. 2000. *Applied Logistic Regression*. New Yprk: Wiley.
Kemmer, Suzanne and Arie Verhagen. 1994. The grammar of causatives and the conceptual structure of events. *Cognitive Linguistics* 5: 115–156.
Landauer, Thomas K. and Susan T. Dumais. 1997. A solution to Plato's problem: The latent semantic analysis theory of acquisition, induction and representation of knowledge. *Psychological Review* 104: 211–240.
Langacker, Ronald W. 1987. *The Foundations of Cognitive Grammar. Volume I: Theoretical prerequisites*. Stanford: Stanford University Press.
Langacker, Ronald W. 2005. Construction Grammars: Cognitive, radical, and less so. In: F. J. Ruiz de Mendoza Ibáñez and M. Sandra Peña Cervel (eds.), *Cognitive Linguistics: Internal Dynamics and Interdisciplinary Interaction*, 101–159. Berlin/New York: Mouton de Gruyter.
Levin, Beth. 1993. *English Verb Classes and Alternations: A Preliminary Investigation*. Chicago: University of Chicago Press.
Levshina, Natalia. 2011. Doe wat je niet laten kan. A usage-based analysis of Dutch causative constructions. Ph.D. dissertation, Department of Linguistics, University of Leuven.
Levshina, Natalia, Dirk Geeraerts and Dirk Speelman. 2013. Mapping constructional spaces: A contrastive study of English and Dutch analytic causatives. *Linguistics* 51: 825–854.
Lin, Dekang. 1998. Automatic retrieval and clustering of similar words. In: Christian Boitet and Pete Whitelock (eds.), *Proceedings of the 36th Annual Meeting of the Association for Computational Linguistics and 17th International Conference on Computational Linguistics, COLING-ACL '98, August 10–14, 1998, Université de Montréal, Montréal, Quebec, Canada*, 768–774. San Francisco: Morgan Kaufmann.
Lowe, Will and Scott McDonald. 2000. The direct route: Mediated priming in semantic space. In: Lila R. Gleitman and Aravind K. Joshi (eds.), *Proceedings of the 22nd Annual Conference of the Cognitive Science Society*, 675–680. Wheat Ridge, CO: Cognitive Science Society.
Noord, Gertjan van. 2006. At last parsing is now operational. In: Piet Mertens, Cédrick Fairon, Anne Dister and Patrick Watrin (eds.), *Actes de la 13e Conference sur le Traitement Automatique des Langues Naturelles*, 20–42. Leuven: Leuven University Press.
Ordelman, Roeland, Franciska de Jong, Arjan van Hessen and Henri Hondorp. 2007. TwNC: A multifaceted Dutch news corpus. *ELRA Newsletter* 12 (3–4). Available at: http://doc.utwente.nl/68090/ (last accessed 20 October 2011).
Padó, Sebastian and Mirella Lapata. 2007. Dependency-based construction of semantic space models. *Computational Linguistics* 33: 161–199.
Peirsman, Yves, Kris Heylen and Dirk Geeraerts. 2008. Size matters: Tight and loose context definitions in English word space models. In: Marco Baroni, Stefan Evert and Alessandro Lenci (eds.), *Proceedings of the ESSLLI Workshop on Distributional Lexical Semantics: Bridging the Gap between Semantic Theory and Computational Simulations*, 34–41. Hamburg: ESSLLI.
Plank, Barbara and Gertjan van Noord. 2010. Dutch dependency parser performance across domains. In: Eline Westerhout, Thomas Markus and Paola Monachesi (eds.), *Computational Linguistics in the Netherlands 2010: Selected Papers from the Twentieth CLIN Meeting*, 123–138. Utrecht: LOT publications.

R Development Core Team. 2010. R: A language and environment for statistical computing. R Foundation for Statistical Computing, Vienna. URL http://www.R-project.org/.

Turney, Peter D. and Patrick Pantel. 2010. From frequency to meaning: Vector space models of semantics. *Journal of Artificial Intelligence Research* 37: 141–188.

Schulte im Walde, Sabine. 2006. Experiments on the automatic induction of German semantic verb classes. *Computational Linguistics* 32: 159–194.

Schulte im Walde, Sabine. 2009. The induction of verb frames and verb classes from corpora. In: Anke Lüdeling and Merja Kytö (eds.), *Corpus Linguistics: An International Handbook*, 952–972. Berlin/New Tork: Mouton de Gruyter.

Speelman, Dirk and Dirk Geeraerts. 2009. Causes for causatives: The case of Dutch *doen* and *laten*. In: Ted Sanders & Eve Sweetser (eds.), *Linguistics of Causality*, 173–204. Berlin/New York: Mouton de Gruyter.

Stefanowitsch, Anatol and Stefan Th. Gries. 2003. Collostructions: Investigating the interaction between words and constructions. *International Journal of Corpus Linguistics* 8: 209–243.

Stefanowitsch, Anatol and Stefan Th. Gries. 2005. Covarying collexemes. *Corpus Linguistics and Linguistic Theory* 1: 1–43.

Stukker, Ninke. 2005. Causality marking across levels of language structure. Ph.D. dissertation, Department of Linguistics, University of Utrecht.

Verhagen, Arie and Suzanne Kemmer. 1997. Interaction and causation: Causative constructions in Modern Standard Dutch. *Journal of Pragmatics* 27: 61–82.

Vossen, Piek (ed.). 1998. *EuroWordNet: A Multilingual Database with Lexical Semantic Networks for European Languages*. Dordrecht: Kluwer.

Weeds, Julie, David Weir and Diana McCarthy. 2004. Characterising measures of lexical distributional similarity. In: *COLING 2004: Proceedings of the 20th international conference on Computational Linguistics*, 1015–1021. Geneva: University of Geneva.

Wittgenstein, Ludwig. 1953. *Philosophical Investigations*. Oxford: Blackwell.

Barend Beekhuizen and Rens Bod
3 Automating construction work: Data-Oriented Parsing and constructivist accounts of language acquisition

1 Introduction

Our world is filled with a vast array of objects and their relations and properties. Human infants face the magnificent task of processing experiences with the outside world in such a way that they can later on respond in an adequate manner when similar, but non-identical experiences present themselves. We can call this processing "learning" and an important question studied throughout the cognitive sciences is how humans do it. One domain for which this question is especially important, is that of linguistic systems of communication, as the complexity and open-endedness found therein has led many to believe that some architectural aspects of the cognitive representations of the phenomenon are not learnable from positive linguistic input alone. This assumption has led to the conclusion that these representations are innately present in the language learner and that there are cognitive mechanisms innately tuned or geared towards acquiring a language (such as a "principles and parameters" approach, cf. Wunderlich 2007). With the linguistic nativist conviction comes the assumption that the representations used are of a fairly abstract nature – after all, the learner would have to be able to acquire any of the thousands of languages being used around the world. Nativists, especially within the Minimalist framework (Chomsky 1993), further support this assumption by pointing to the economy of representation as a driving factor for having a system that is as compact as possible. Importantly, the innate knowledge is part of a mental module pertaining only to language. That is, the representations the learner starts with are domain-specific.

Another school of thought, the empiricist one, states the child does not come equipped with inborn, domain-specific knowledge concerning the architecture or properties of a communication system to be acquired. The acquisition of the complexities of linguistic structure are explained (as far as they are not theory-internal concerns that depend on one's preconception of the cognitive representation, cf. Tomasello 2003: 7) from experience, through domain-general structure-finding mechanisms such as categorization, schematization and social understanding. Importantly, these mechanisms and representational biases have to exist in the learner's mind prior to the acquisition of a language system.

Hence, usage-based theorists cannot be argued to believe in a blank-slate learner. The crucial difference from a linguistic nativist position is that the mechanisms and biases are not specific to language, but are shared with other cognitive domains because they either are functions of how the brain in general works (e.g., working memory, entrenchment processes, abstraction) or are part of known evolved cognitive modules (e.g., the figure-ground distinction from the visual system, notions of object permanence). With the nativist position being the dominant one for the last decades, researchers of the empiricist bent face the task of showing that there are flaws in the empirical observations or subsequent inferential processes leading to linguistic nativist conclusions. At the same time, it is crucial that empiricist theorists develop a substitutive, positive, account of language acquisition through experience and domain-general skills. Important work showing flaws in nativist reasoning and providing a novel account has been done. Construction Grammar, in many of its flavors (Langacker 1989; Goldberg 1995; Croft and Cruse 2004), as well as non-constructivist work in language acquisition (Peters 1983) shows how the nativists' assumed divisions between the core and periphery of the grammar, meaning and the grammar, and linguistic competence and performance cannot be maintained, and at the same time presents an empiricist account of how the architecture and content of linguistic representation emerges as an interaction between a multitude of factors. The work of Tomasello and colleagues (Tomasello 2003) has shown how understanding other people's (communicative) intentions is crucial for and supportive of acquiring a language, demonstrating how a thitherto overlooked aspect of human cognition solves some of the nativist arguments against acquiring a grammar from experience, as well as presenting a coherent explanation of linguistic development.

In this paper, we would like to add something to the developing usage-based constructivist narrative. This contribution is in part a methodological enrichment and in part an account of the possible domain-general cognitive mechanisms behind the acquisition of the grammatical structures. We believe that computational modeling is an important means for providing us with important insights in the theoretical perspective. First of all, it forces us to translate our fuzzy and imprecise natural-language definitions into extremely precise computational ones. Although this often means a loss in accuracy of description (we will have to give up on the description of some aspects of natural language for our model to be understandable), it provides a gain in the testability of certain claims. Using a well-defined model, then, we can assess claims pertaining to the architecture and content of the representations, the processing mechanisms and the timescales on which these operate.

The computational model we present in this paper is Data-Oriented Parsing or DOP (Scha 1990; Bod 1998, Bod, Scha & Sima'an 2003), and its instantiations

Unsupervised Data-Oriented Parsing (U-DOP) and Meaningful Unsupervised Data-Oriented Parsing (μDOP). The Data-Oriented family of models addresses the question how processing complex, structured exemplars, such as linguistic experiences, may lead to a cognitive system by means of which a language user can assign structure to novel exemplars. As such, it is not a theory about the content of representations, but rather a discovery procedure (for learners and linguists alike) for cognitively useful structured representations. In the following sections, we explain the basic ideas behind the models in greater detail, link it to constructivist assumptions and show how the diverse models can be applied to questions about the acquisition of grammar.

2 Data-Oriented Parsing

A core question in the usage-based approach to language acquisition is that of grammatical productivity. How does a learner, be it an artificial one or one of flesh and blood, know, after having seen a number of exemplars, what patterns it should use to produce and interpret novel utterances? Although many informal discussions of the process have been given (Tomasello 2003; Goldberg 2006), often with reference to Gentner's more formalized work on analogy (Gentner 1983), few models of discovering the productive grammatical units of a language have been developed so far. Similarly, no existing description of construction grammar's parsing principles offers us an account of recombining these productive fragments into analyses of novel utterances. Such an account is desirable, as it can help validate learnability claims and adds to the possibilities for evaluating the theory against the data. It should be noted that construction grammar and usage-based theories are not alone in their lack of precise definitions; it seems that any current linguistic theory has given up on the construction of a precise, testable model of language use and language acquisition.

Formalizations of learning mechanisms for acquiring a grammar such as Embodied Construction Grammar (Chang 2008) and Fluid Construction Grammar (van Trijp et al. 2009) have been developed over the last decade. Other systems that have claimed relevance to usage-based theorizing are Memory-Based Learning (Daelemans and Van den Bosch 2005) and the memory-access and parsing framework developed by Jurafsky (1996). All of these add to our understanding, and insights from these different approaches complement DOP's contribution, namely a precise account of how Gestalt-like linguistic units can be discovered in the data. The proposed mechanisms of Data-Oriented Parsing obviously cannot capture the wealth of linguistic phenomena described in full detail, but aim to give us insight in how complex representations can be acquired from the input data, and as such can help understand the domain-general learning processes in want of further specification.

2.1 Data-Oriented Parsing as a constructional learner

Suppose a learner has processed several exemplars, or structured representations of utterances. When processing novel utterances, the learner can draw on this inventory by recombining its parts in order to come up with an analysis of the novel utterance.

Now, a novel utterance, say the one in example (1), can be analyzed using parts of the processed utterances in Figure 1. Let us define a legal part, or subtree of a tree representation to be a connected subgraph in which all sisterhood relations of the original tree hold (see Bod and Kaplan 1998 for a more precise definition). Maintaining the sisterhood means that given the first tree in Figure 1, we can have a fragment of S going to NP and VP, but not S going just to NP (without its VP sister). But most importantly, it is not just the small parts that can be re-used, larger fragments can be used in analyzing novel utterances as well. The main claim of Data-Oriented Parsing is that all fragments, irrespective of size, can be used in analyzing novel utterances. Given this starting point, we have many ways of analyzing sentence (1). Some of these are given in Figure 2. We analyze novel utterances by using a legal part of an utterance the learner has seen and "substituting" its leftmost non-terminal symbol (that is: grammatical symbols, such as 'S', 'Det' and 'PP') with another part the learner has already seen. This procedure is repeated until there are no non-terminal symbols left, that is: all words of the utterance are present in the analysis.[1] The symbol of this substitution operation is '∘'.

(1) *She saw the dress with the telescope*

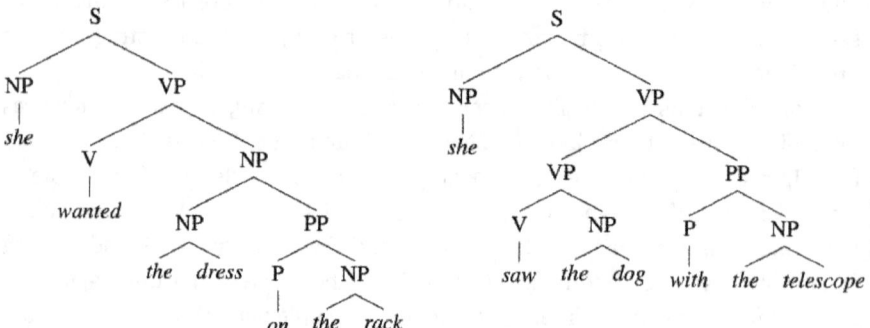

Figure 1: A corpus of two processed utterances

---

[1] This procedure may strike some readers as very top-down. Although it is presented as such, the same principles can be applied in a bottom-up parsing algorithm equally well.

What we see in Figure 2 is that there are multiple analyses possible for the novel utterance, and there are multiple ways to arrive at a single analysis. We call each of these ways of arriving at an analysis a derivation and a resulting analysis (which can emerge through different derivations) a parse. The first and third derivation thus give us the same parse tree, but get there in different ways. The first tree uses only the smallest fragments possible, while the third tree re-uses larger fragments of the earlier processed experiences.

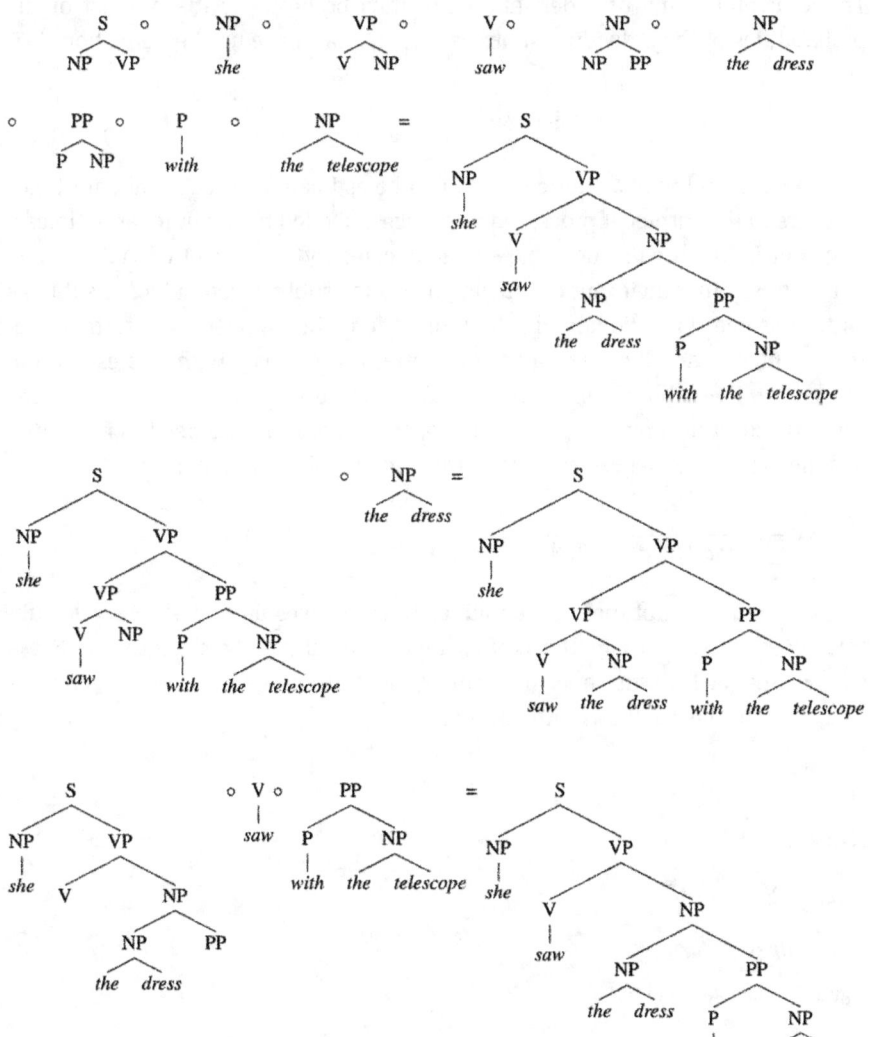

Figure 2: Three derivations of *she saw the dress with the telescope*

Now, given this structural ambiguity (traditionally: the PP-attachment problem), the learner has to choose which of the possible analyses to consider as the right one. This is where the frequencies of the fragments come in. First, consider a derivation to be a complex event consisting of a number of smaller events, viz. the subtrees. Suppose that each of these subtrees has a certain probability. This would mean that the probability of the event of them occurring together would be the joint probability of all of the individual events of selecting that subtree. The joint probability of a derivation can thus be given by the product of the probabilities of the individual subtrees $t_1 \ldots t_n$ that make up the derivation d:

$$P(d) = P(t_1 \circ t_2 \circ \ldots \circ t_n) = \prod_{i=1}^{n} P(t_i)$$

The probability of a subtree, then, can be estimated by the number of times it occurs in the corpus of processed utterances, divided by the number of times a fragment is found with the same syntactic category at the root of that subtree. This is to say that the event of drawing a specific subtree from a bag of subtrees with the same syntactic label in the root node is the number of times that subtree occurs divided by the number of subtrees in the bag. With this estimation procedure, the subtree competes with all other subtrees that can occur at the same place in a derivation, viz. at an open position in another fragment that has the syntactic category of that subtree. Stated more formally:

$$P(t) = \frac{|t|}{\sum_{t': root(t') = root(t)} |t'|}$$

The estimation of these probabilities thus involves finding all possible subtree types in all trees in the corpus and establishing their frequency. For a simple tree such as the one in Figure 3, we can extract all possible subtrees and arrive at the set shown in Figure 4.

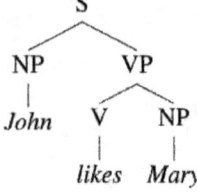

Figure 3: A simple parse tree

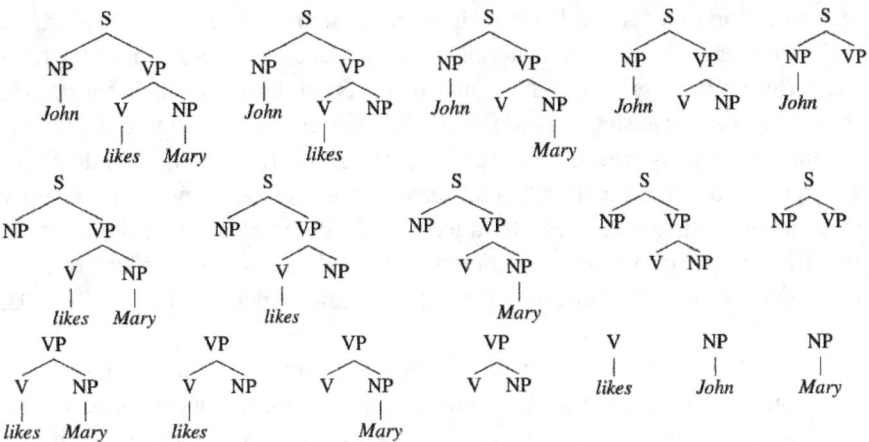

Figure 4: All subtrees of the tree in Figure 3

Now, we have multiple derivations leading to the same parse of an utterance, as we have seen in Figure 2. We determine the probability of a parse to be the sum of the probabilities of all derivations yielding that parse tree. Again, this is grounded in relatively simple probability theory: the probability of a parse is the probability of either derivation one leading to that parse, or derivation two, or derivation three, and so forth, and so it is the sum of the probabilities of the individual events. For any parse tree t we can thus calculate the probability as follows:

$$P(t) = \sum_{d \text{ is a derivation of } t} P(d)$$

We then select the parse with the highest probability mass to be the most likely analysis of the novel utterance (cf. Zuidema 2006 for a discussion of this and other estimation and evaluation methods).

It is important to note that, using the same mechanisms, DOP can also generate utterances from the grammar. This process boils down to probabilistically selecting a subtree fragment rooted in the starting label, and expanding its open substitution sited by other subtrees. When coupled with meaning, this approach can give us a Data-Oriented generator as well.

2.2 DOP as a usage-based, constructionist model

DOP shares most of its core principles with the usage-based constructionist approach. In this section, we discuss on what theoretical positions DOP and the usage-based constructionist approach converge.[2]

---

[2] For a more thorough discussion of the principles of experience, heterogeneity and redundancy, see Beekhuizen, Bod, and Zuidema (2013).

An important effect of this modeling procedure is that the most likely parses will be the ones that have derivations consisting of a few larger subtrees. Why is this? The probability of a derivation will generally be higher if it consists of fewer subtrees because there are fewer subtree probabilities to multiply. Hence, the model has a bias towards interpreting utterances by using as few and hence as large fragments as possible. In that sense, the model tries to maximize analogy with the previously processed utterances and by doing so, the model adheres to the usage-based principles that grammatical productivity comes about through experience and a domain-general ability to make schemas (Tomasello 2003; Gentner 1983).

The reliance on experience is another aspect on which usage-based constructionist approaches and DOP converge. First of all, the hypothesis space of possible grammatical constructions emerges through the experience with language, as well as the conception that we have to understand language, at least to some extent, hierarchically (see Frank, Bod, and Christiansen 2012 for arguments why hierarchical processing is not a procedure applied all the time). Hierarchicality, then, does not have to be the a priori template for a learner to understand language. The learner may start with a number of possible data structures, some of which are hierarchical and some are not, and find out, in response to processing the data that a hierarchical template to store, process and produce language may be an optimal cognitive strategy (Perfors, Tenenbaum, and Wonnacott 2010). For this paper, we assume that this property of language has been discovered.

Secondly, experience means that routinization and Gestalt-like effects take place (Bybee 2006). It is well known that frequency affects language use, at the very least by governing choice among acceptable alternatives (Schuchardt 1885; Mehler and Carey 1968; Jurafsky 2003). DOP incorporates this insight by allowing for larger fragments to be stored and used as Gestalts in linguistic processing. Moreover, the trade-off between computation (composing two fragments by the substitution operator) and storage (using one larger fragments) is driven by frequency as well: the more likely the parts are relative to the whole, the more likely a computed analysis (as opposed to a retrieved one) is. But most importantly: it does not have to be either/or. Because all derivations, whether they are directly retrieved as one chunk, or composed of minimal bits, are used in calculating the probability of the analysis, DOP avoids the rule-list fallacy (Langacker 1989: chapter 1): language users maintain both, sometimes perhaps redundantly.

Furthermore, DOP starts from the same maximalist conception of language as constructionist approaches do. This conception entails a couple of things. First, the basic building blocks are heterogeneous in size. This means that they can be small, like words or depth-one rules, or larger. And it means that they can be abstract, having no lexical material, or highly concrete. An important insight following from this principle and the previous one is that rules and exemplars are not ontologically different entities, but are created out of the same matter, viz. processed experience. Every subtree in DOP then, is a schema from the processed experience that can be recombined with parts of other experiences to understand something novel. These ideas resonate core properties of a constructivist, usage-based understanding of grammatical knowledge (Croft and Cruse 2004: chapters 10 and 11).

Finally, the inventory of the basic building blocks may be redundant, as hinted at earlier. DOP gives the artificial learner fragments which it can, in principle, build up out of other subtrees it has. The idiom *What time is it?* can of course be built up out of its components, but there is reason to believe that language users keep a representation of the whole in mind as well (Bybee 2006).[3]

Although this is not a position shared by all constructionist linguists (Construction Grammar (Fillmore and Kay 1996) tries to minimize redundancy for instance), the usage-based theorists seem to embrace this idea. Accepting redundancy as a core property of the linguistic system follows rather naturally from the rejection that linguistic structure has to be either stored as a rule or as a list (i.e., the rule-list fallacy, cf. Langacker 1989).

In fact, the DOP framework has been used to address issues in language acquisition that relate to the issues of heterogeneity and redundancy. Given a hypothesis space of all possible subtrees, we can find out what set of subtrees was most likely used in deriving an utterance. Without going into the details, Borensztajn, Zuidema, and Bod (2008) did so for a syntactically annotated corpus of young children's utterances. What they showed was that, in line with the usage-based perspective, the most likely subtrees behind the children's utterances become more abstract with age. More examples of applying the DOP principle to language acquisition can be seen in the next sections.

2.3 Analogy, acquisition and the unlearnable

If we think about DOP as a model of language acquisition, the model effectively says that children acquire grammar by constructing analogies with previous utterances, guided by statistical generalization. This starting point, of using analogy to construct a grammar, has not gone unchallenged in linguistic theorizing. Examples of linearly similar but structurally different sentences, as discussed by Pinker (1979) and Chomsky (1986), show how proportional analogy,

---

[3] That is, regardless of whether this whole is opaque to the user or whether its constituency is transparent.

the simplest format of analogical reasoning, might lead a learner to wrong conclusions (this particular example being Pinker's):

(2) *John likes fish* : *John likes chicken* :: *John might fish* : *John might chicken*

(3) *Swimming in the sea is dangerous* : *The sea is dangerous* ::
Swimming in the rivers is dangerous : *The rivers is dangerous*

As Pinker and Chomsky correctly point out, analogies like these do not hold because there is no notion of structural dependency, nor a concept of syntactic category that would be required to make them work. However, this is not a problem of analogical reasoning per se, but rather of the structure and content of the input analogical reasoning applies to. Analogical reasoning can be described as trying to solve a problem (categorizing an object, parsing an utterance) by comparing our knowledge about the object to a knowledge base of similar objects. If we grant people the ability to infer grammatical categories and hierarchical representations for sentences, analogical reasoning over such a knowledge base would not come up with the erroneous predictions of the grammaticality of *John might chicken*. If we let the the learner make the analysis without anything like grammatical categories or a notion of hierarchical structure, we do arrive at this prediction. Hence, it is not the mechanism that yields ungrammatical results, it is the nature of the content.

An extension of the original DOP model presented in the previous sections, Unsupervised Data-Oriented Parsing, or U-DOP, has been developed as an attempt to address this issue. Unsupervised techniques, developed in machine learning, allow a learner to build up some representation (of structure or categories, for instance), without having 'correct' representations for a set of training items (which would be supervised learning). Instantiated in U-DOP, these techniques grant the learner the domain-general starting point of understanding data as hierarchically structured, that is, as containing different levels of analysis, in which a concept on one level is *triggered by* (communicatively, cf. Verhagen 2009) or *consists of* (cognitively) small, less inclusive parts, but do not give the learner the correct analyses of the structure to train on. These assumptions are not language-specific, as we can apply the template of meronymy (the *consists-of* relation) to our understanding of body parts, artefacts, grouping relations of identical individuals, only in language we combine it with symbolic understanding (the *triggered-by* relation).

Using the idea that language is hierarchical and a stricter notion of analogical reasoning, U-DOP can be shown to predict the ungrammaticality of *The rivers is dangerous* (Bod 2009). It also predicts that a child can learn that, if it wants to form a polar interrogative of a sentence like (4), it is not the first (as in example 5) but the second *is* (as in example 6) that is produced at the front of the utterance.

(4) *The man who is sick is singing.*

(5) **Is the man who sick is singing?*

(6) *Is the man who is sick singing?*

How does the model acquire these dependencies correctly? Unlike DOP, U-DOP assumes that the learner does not know how to interpret its initial input. Instead, the learner will store all possible analyses of the input, and uses that as a basis for extracting subtrees and estimating their probabilities. Furthermore, we leave the problem of syntactic categories out of scope for now, focussing solely on the hierarchical structure. Effectively, all nodes in the tree representation, except for the lexical leafs, are of the same category, say 'X', and can thus be substituted for one another with the combination operation. So, suppose the U-DOP learner has heard the two utterances the dog walks and watch the dog. Each of these has two possible analyses:

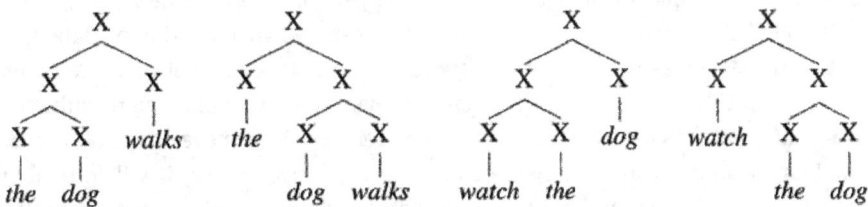

Figure 5: The analysis of the two utterances *the dog walks* and *watch the dog*

From this collection of all possible analyses, we can extract all possible subtrees, just like we did with DOP. What will become immediately clear, is that a subtree like [[*the*]$_X$ [*dog*]$_X$]$_X$ forms a reliable constituent, being found in two out of four parse trees. A less reliable subtree is [[*dog*]$_X$ [*walks*]$_X$]$_X$, which is only found in one parse tree. Using these subtrees, then, we can infer the hierarchical structure of an unseen utterance.

In order to do this, we use a stricter notion of analogy than in DOP. U-DOP starts from the insight that the more similar a novel analysis is to earlier analyses, the better an analysis it is. The model will therefore choose in the first place that parse tree that has the shortest derivation. We consider the length of the derivation to be the number of subtrees used in that derivation. Often, there are multiple parse trees that have an equally long derivation. In that case, the learner selects the most probable parse among the ones that have the shortest derivations. The probability of the parse is calculated as in DOP. This idea of selecting the most probable parse from among the shortest-derivations (MPSD) is in essence a probability driven model of analogy.

When we train this model on child-directed speech, we can simulate the acquisition of hierarchical structure and grammatical dependency. If we train U-DOP on the Adam corpus (Brown 1973), which consists of two hours of child directed speech per fortnight over the course of approximately two years, which constitutes only a fraction of a child's input, the model correctly assigns more probability to a sentence like 6 than to one with the wrong auxiliary at the sentence-initial position 5 (Bod and Smets 2012)

Why is this of interest? The issue of auxiliary-fronting with subjects that have relative clauses has been a parade case for nativist approaches to grammar. Crain (1991) and others have tried to argue that the fact that children make no errors like the one in (5) when learning these patterns shows that they directly home in on the correct hypothesis, i.e. that there is a main clause and a subordinate clause, and that the auxiliary in main clause ought to be fronted. U-DOP uses no concepts of 'clause' to explain the phenomenon, but grounds it in the experience of a learner and its attempt to stick as close as possible to that experience. A typical nativist argument against the use of experience is that this specific construction is rarely, if ever, observed in the primary data, yet children seem be sensitive to the difference in grammaticality between examples (6) and (5). U-DOP tackles this problem by saying that we can combine subtrees from different processed utterances. A learner may have never seen a case of auxiliary fronting with a subject containing a relative clause, it will probably have processed some auxiliary fronting without subjects with a relative clause as well as some relative clauses in other grammatical constellations.

Subtrees from these parses make the learner able to produce a more probable short derivation for sentences like example (6), but not for cases like (5). A pattern like *the X who is X* might be used, along with *is X singing*. However, the model will have never or very scarcely seen patterns like *who sick* or *is X is singing*. Because of this, the model will find more probable short derivations for the good pattern, and longer, or less likely derivations for the erroneous one. The observed behavior of the model is in line with the pattern of errors observed in Ambridge, Rowland, and Pine (2008)

Moreover, this manner of analyzing the learnability of complex grammatical phenomena can be extended to other cases. Whereas most empiricist computational linguists use a specific model to address a specific phenomenon in order to refute nativist explanations (e.g., auxiliary fronting (Clark and Eyraud 2006) or anaphoric *one* (Foraker, Regier, Khetarpal, Perfors, and Tenenbaum 2009)),[4] Bod and Smets (2012) show that a single, unified model, viz. U-DOP, can learn (virtually) all existing cases of hierarchical dependencies that are thought of as unlearnable. Work like this complements the analysis done by Pullum and Scholz (2002) and shows how general learning and structuring principles may lead to the behavior or judgements we can observe. As such, they provide us with a cognitively leaner, simpler and hence a priori more likely model of the acquisition of grammatical structure.

3 Meaning

One crucial aspect of constructional approaches has been ostensibly lacking from the discussion so far: meaning. Constructional theories hold that the grammatical building blocks are pairings of some signifying form with a signified meaning. Although much work in DOP has been done on grammatical form per se, the model is not incompatible with this approach to grammar. In fact, the model has no restriction on the representations it processes, as long as they are well-formed according to some formal criterion. This follows from the claim that DOP is a domain-general learner; as such it has to be able to detect structure regardless of the topology or content of the structure.

DOP has a long history in trying to accommodate meaningful representations. (Bonnema, Bod, and Scha 1997) can be seen as a first attempt. In this model, the syntactic representations on the tree's nodes were enriched with lambda-calculus logical formulae. Later developments were the integration of DOP and Lexical-Functional Grammar (LFG-DOP, Bod and Kaplan 1998) and Head-Driven Phrase Structure Grammar (HPSG-DOP, Arnold and Linardaki 2007). Building on the insights of these models, we propose an unsupervised variant of Data-Oriented Parsing that incorporates meaning. Because this is the first exploration of an unsupervised learning mechanism to meaning-enriched structures, we chose not to use the rich representations of LFG or HPSG, but rather take a very simple and limited formalism to illustrate the priniciple. We will show how it functions, how a learner may derive productive patterns with it, and what its limitations are.

---

4 See Clark and Lappin (2011) for an overview of different refutations using different models.

3.1 A U-DOP approach to learning meaningful grammars

What would acquiring a grammar involve, if we use the constructionist starting point of form-meaning pairings as the basic building blocks of a language? First of all, the problem of learning the mapping has become bigger, as not only word-meaning mappings have to be learned, but also mappings between all other kinds of constructions and meanings. Secondly, the learner would have to have some mechanism for arriving at a set of schemas, productive and less so, that allow it to talk about novel events and understand novel utterances. Thirdly, the model would have to be incremental: we cannot expect a real language learner to wait until it has seen some number of utterances. As we will see, incrementality in fact does not make the problem bigger, but can function as a bootstrap for the learner.

The basic idea behind meaningful U-DOP, or μ-DOP, is that a learner analyzes a sentence using meaningful, heterogeneously sized and possibly redundant hierarchical representations. It starts analyzing utterances with the fragments it knows already, and then maps the unanalyzed parts of the utterance with parts of the semantic situation that are unexpressed in the analysis, thereby filling the gaps in its knowledge. Next, it decomposes these analyses and adds them to its knowledge base.

In this experiment, we describe a learner that can deal with very simple meaning representations. For understanding more complex semantic operations, obviously more complex representations are needed. The goal, however, is not to develop an account of meaning, but rather to show how DOP can acquire symbolic structures (i.e., form-meaning pairings) of different size, complexity and abstractness. By doing so, we show how the concept of building up meaningful constructions works with an unsupervised Data-Oriented model and how the acquired representations are in line with the constructivist understanding of language. As such, we argue that DOP is a substrate-neutral learner (as long as the substrate can be structured in some graphical way), that can be thought of as domain-general.

How can we envisage the representation of an analysis in μ-DOP to which the dataoriented learning algorithm applies? It has to contain hierarchical structures, meaning representations and representations of words. As a simple formalism for representing meaning, we use predicate logic, restricted to representations of predicates and entities. The semantic representations take the place of the syntactic categories of DOP as the contents of the nodes in the analyses. A node may contain a value of a variable (predicate or entity), denoted as P:WATCH for the predicate WATCH or E:JOHN for the entity JOHN, or denote an operation on its constituent parts. WATCH(E_1, MARY), for instance, means that there is some entity that fills the slot position e1 that can be found somewhere else in the subtree. Fragments like these can be combined by logical composition. Suppose we have the fragments in Figure 6. We can compose these and the interpretation will be HIT(JOHN, BILL), as the slots with which the two small, word-like subtrees are combined, dictate which entity is the first argument (E_1) and which the second (E_2). Not all (legal) fragments can be composed: the subtrees in Figure 8 cannot be composed, as there is no slot in the subtree to the left to fit P:HIT to: both open positions are of the category E.

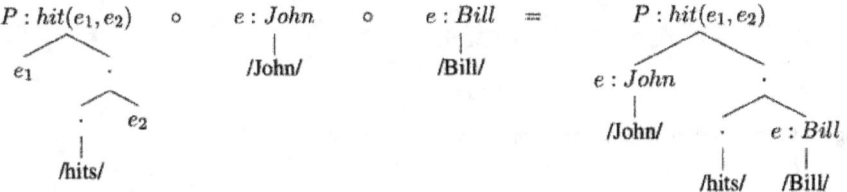

Figure 6: Legal composition of three subtrees. The empty nodes (visualized with • as the node label) are necessary to preserve binarity, but do not have any analytical significance. The character before the colon in the top-node of a subtree represents the semantic category of the subtree

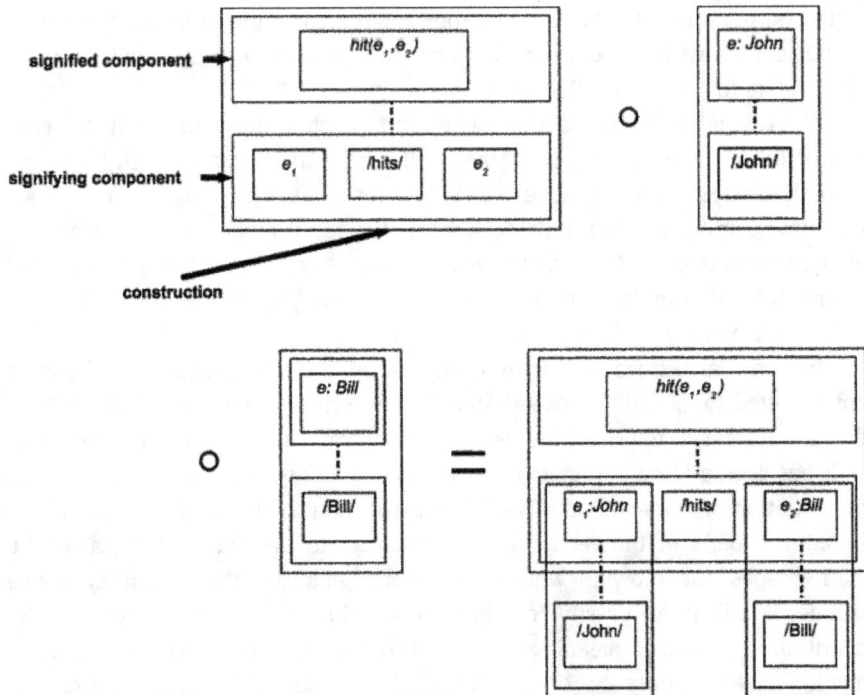

Figure 7: The composition of Figure 6, represented in box diagrammes. Note that the two poles of the construction correspond to Verhagen's (2009) conception of the construction as a symbolic assembly

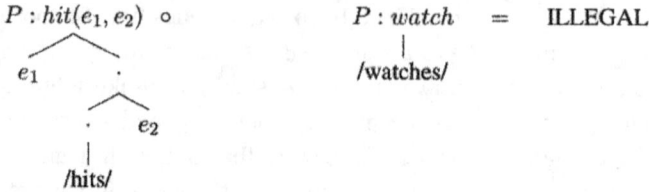

Figure 8: Illegal composition of two subtrees

Figure 9: The starting knowledge of the model in the example

Let us look at the learning procedure taking us to an inventory of such subtrees step by step. First, the learner analyzes a sentence using its inventory of grammatical patterns. Initially, this inventory is empty, but as the learner processes more utterances, it will become bigger. Suppose for the sake of the argument that the learner knows that the word *John* means that there is an entity called John, or E:JOHN. This can be represented as a simple subtree, connecting a node E:JOHN with a node *John*. Suppose the learner also knows that the word *Mary* refers to an entity called Mary.

The learner hears an utterance like *John watches Mary*, uttered in the context of John watching Mary and Mary walking. What the learner will try to do, then, is analyze this utterance using its known constructions, i.c. the word-meaning pairing for *John* and for *Mary*. If the learner does not know how to analyze the utterance, it can use a meaningless binary subtree (with a very small probability) to combine any two fragments. Analyzing *John watches Mary* we arrive at two analyses, as follows.

In both parse trees, we arrive at an interpretation that involves at least an entity called John and one called Mary. When trying to understand what situation the utterance refers to, the learner can now exclude that of Mary walking, as it has seen a known fragment that refers to John, who is not a participant in the situation of Mary walking. The learner will then try to complete the analysis by adding parts of the semantic representation to the analyses. Because the learner does not know to what nodes of the analyses these representations belong, it will try all possible combinations and store them in its memory. The distribution of unseen meanings is guided by the constraint that the same fragment of meaning does not occur twice in the utterance. This constraint can be seen as a form of a mutual exclusivity constraint or as more simple Gricean pragmatic reasoning (i.c. balancing the maxims of quality and quantity).

To what observed situations can the partial analyses in Figure 10 apply? Recall that two situations take place, viz. John watching Mary and Mary walking. The second can be excluded, as John, who was found to be referred to in both analyses, is no part of it. This leaves us the first one, and the model will try to complete its analyses using parts of that meaning. If there were more situations compatible with the inferred meaning in an analysis, all of them would be used in the add-unseen-meaning step to complete that analysis.

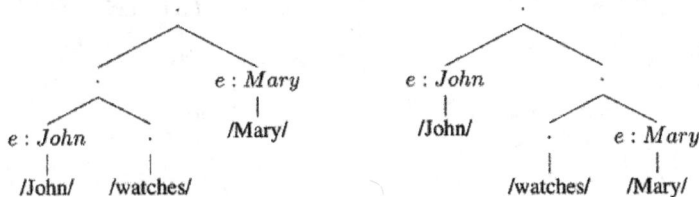

Figure 10: Two analyses of *John watches Mary*

In our example, we have two analyses, both of which can be mapped to the situation WATCH(JOHN, MARY). In both cases, the learner has found the meaning E: JOHN and E:MARY and hence it is missing the part WATCH(E1, E2). This partial semantic representation can be further decomposed into P(E1, E2) and P:WATCH (in general: the models tries all decompositions of the unobserved parts of the meaning) and these partial representations can be distributed over the nodes in the tree that were unanalyzed according to the constraint discussed before. This is effectively a U-DOP approach to semantic representations: we take all parts of all missing semantic representations, all nodes in the tree analyses of an utterance and map them to each other, letting the statistics decide which ones would be relevant for analyzing novel utterances. For the first analysis of *John watches Mary* and the representations we found missing, we can add them to the partial analysis in the ways given in Figure 11.

Using these completed representations, we can update our inventory of subtrees that can be reused in analyzing new utterances. We define DOP's decomposition operation here to take all connected subgraphs of the parse tree that have both a root node with a semantic representation, and only leaf nodes with either semantic or phonological representations in them. That is, the two subtrees in Figure 13 are excluded on these grounds (not a meaningful root, not all leaf nodes are meaningful), whereas all legal subtrees of the third completed analysis in Figure 11 are given in Figure 12. When decomposing a tree, leaf nodes retain only the type and its index, so that an indexed slot comes into existence. The non-trivial part of the decomposition operation is that a tree can be decomposed only at nodes where a meaning representation is found; nodes lacking these are taken to be 'internal' (signified with a dot '·') and are not used in the interpretation process in any way, but are retained only to maintain (the positive computational properties of) binarity.

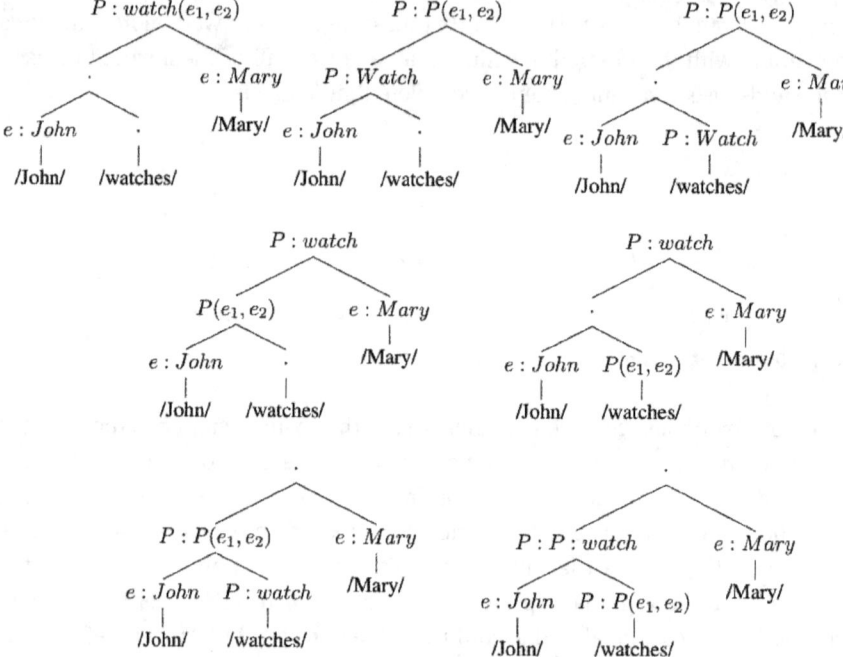

Figure 11: All additions of unseen meaning to the first analysis in Figure 10

Among these decompositions, we can find various structures that remind us of constructions as we know them. There are words, fully open patterns, ones with only lexical items as leaf nodes and everything in between. All of these have the same ingredients: a graph structuring the part-whole relations with phonological or semantic structure as the content of the nodes. Our procedure, of trying to parse an utterance, adding the unseen parts of the meaning to unanalyzed parts of the utterance and decomposing that thus provides a learner with a way of discovering the patterns that are useful for understanding novel language material.

However, in a more realistic setting, there may be many analyses that are incorrect and thus harm the model if their parts are added to the inventory of fragments. Do we add all of these to the knowledge base for interpreting the next utterance too? In fact, we don't have to, as DOP provides us with a good mechanism to separate the wheat from the chaff, namely the probabilities of the analyses.

As in DOP, the most likely analysis of an utterance is the analysis that has the highest probability mass summed over all of its derivations. The probability mass of a derivation, then, is given by the joint probability of all the subtrees used. Since the model has to add unseen rules, we have to reserve some small probability for these. We do so by smoothing the probability of the seen rules, so that some probability mass becomes available for the unseen components.[5]

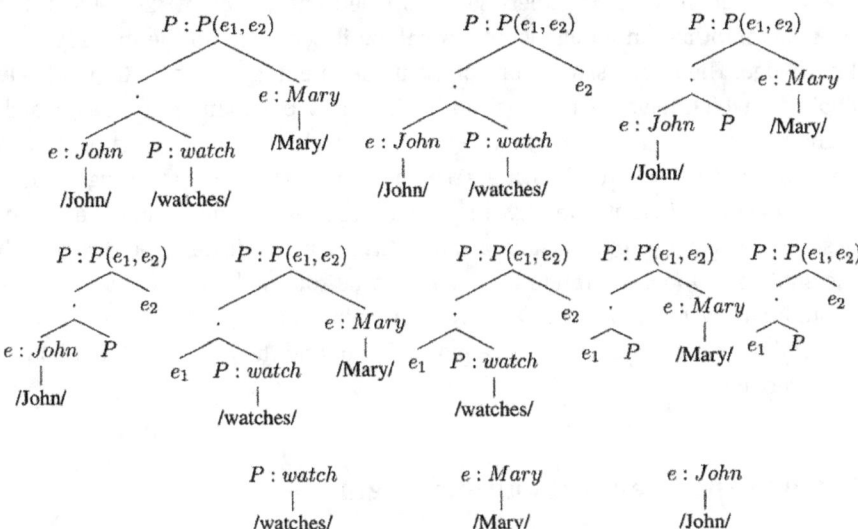

Figure 12: Legal subtrees of the third analysis in Figure 11

Figure 13: Illegal subtrees of the third analysis in Figure 11

We weight all parse trees by their probability before decomposing them, so that the subtrees from the more likely analyses will be more likely to be reused in subsequent analyses. The subtrees in Figure 12 thus are not added to the inventory of patterns with a frequency of one, but with a frequency of one times the probability of the derivation. After all subtrees are added, we can recalculate the probability of every subtree in the same way as we did with DOP, viz. by dividing its (weighted) frequency by the summed (weighted) frequencies of all subtrees sharing the exact content of the root node, i.e. the semantic representation of it.

---

5 More precisely, we used Simple Good-Turing smoothing (Gale and Sampson 1995).

Expanding the DOP-idea to another representation, we can see what Data-Oriented Parsing can and cannot do, as well as what the assumptions of the model are. The model is not a category learner: semantic structures and their combinatoriality, and sound structures are assumed as given information to the model. The power of DOP is then to recognize productive, complex patterns in the structured data given these assumptions. To this end, the model tries all possible structures (the unsupervised component) as guided by the context, but uses this information judiciously by weighing it according to the model's prior knowledge. The main assumptions of the model are in the construction of likely analyses, which have been argued to be driven by pragmatic processes (match with the situation and a mutual exclusivity bias), and the deconstruction of complex wholes, where slots are assumed to be necessary meaningful. This latter constraint is motivated by a learner's desire to communicate: if a slot of a subtree specifies some meaning (an entity or a predicate) co-indexed with the subtree's global interpretation pattern in its root node, the learner can use it productively for generating and understanding novel utterances. If no such constraint is present, the pattern cannot be used, and the learner will not bother to extract it.

3.2 An experiment with artificial data

Can the model described above induce a grammar from utterances and situations these utterances are found in? As an initial test, we used artificial data loosely based on natural language to see if the model was able to discover patterns that allowed it to find the situation that the utterance was intended to refer to. The model saw each sentence paired with seven situations (which are represented as predicate-argument structures), of which one was the intended one. There were eight entities, (ABE, BEN, CARL, DIDI, ED, FAY, GEROLD, HANNAH), four single-place predicates (LAUGH, CRY, TURN.FIFTY, DIE, and four two place predicates (SEE, SHAVE, HIT, PUSH). In total, there were $8 \times 4 + 8 \times 8 \times 4$ possible predicate-argument structures. Obviously, this is a gross oversimplification of the issues a child faces (it ignores the packaging problem (Gentner 1982; Gleitman 1990), does not use extralinguistic understanding of speaker intentions (Tomasello 2001) and overly restricts the space of possible situations), but as a toy example demonstrating the dynamics of the model, it will do.

The intended predicate was expressed by a simple subject-verb-object sentence if it was transitive (e.g. *Carl hits Ben* for HIT(CARL, BEN), and a subject-verb sentence if it was intransitive (e.g. *Carl cries* for CRY(CARL)). If the subject and object were coreferential, the pronoun *himself* was used at the object position (e.g. *Carl hits himself* for HITS(CARL, CARL)), except in the case of the predicate SHAVE, where the object is simply not expressed if it is coreferential with the subject (e.g. *Gerold shaves* for SHAVES(GEROLD, GEROLD)). Two other exceptions are the predicate TURN.FIFTY, which is expressed with the verb-object idiom *see Abe*, so TURN.FIFTY(DIDI) is expressed with *Didi sees Abe*,[6] and the predicate DIE, which is expressed with the verb-object idiom *kick bucket*, so DIE(CARL) is expressed with *Carl kicks bucket*.

Using this system, we can generate artificial data. From our 288 possible predicateargument structures, we select seven at random for every entry. One of these seven is expressed according to the rules mentioned above. With this procedure, we generated twenty data sets of 1200 entries each. Because we are sampling, we have to repeat the experiment so that we know the results are not due to chance. Moreover, this gives us an insight in what it might mean for the cognitive representation of different learners acquiring a grammar from (slightly) different input. Furthermore, note that unlike in the example we gave earlier, here the model starts with an empty inventory. It will thus have to learn words, grammatical patterns and their meanings.

We measure the success of the model by evaluating if it can find the correct situation given the utterance. Because µ-DOP is a discovery mechanism rather than a declarative model of how the grammar should look like, we cannot evaluate if the parses are good or not, only whether they lead to interpretations that were intended. We will have a closer, more qualitative look at the parse trees that the model produces.

How well can the model find the intended predicate-argument structure from among the seven ongoing situations at that moment? Figure 14 shows the performance at each trial for all of the twenty simulations, with every dot standing for the average of the model's performance over the twenty samples. So, after having seen zero utterances, the model will be inconclusive about what situation utterance one refers to, and will therefore predict none of them correctly. With only a few subtrees in its inventory, it will be making mistakes, but we can see that after about 250 situations the model reached its asymptotic peak in performance at understanding around 90% of cases correctly.[7]

---

[6] For the puzzled reader, this idiom is loosely based on the Dutch idiom *Abraham zien*, lit: 'to see Abraham'; 'to turn fifty'.

[7] It should be noted here that the line in the figure oversmooths the data; it should be interpreted as merely indicating that the model displays a learning curve leading up to an asymptote. The actual curve seems to rise in a much steeper way.

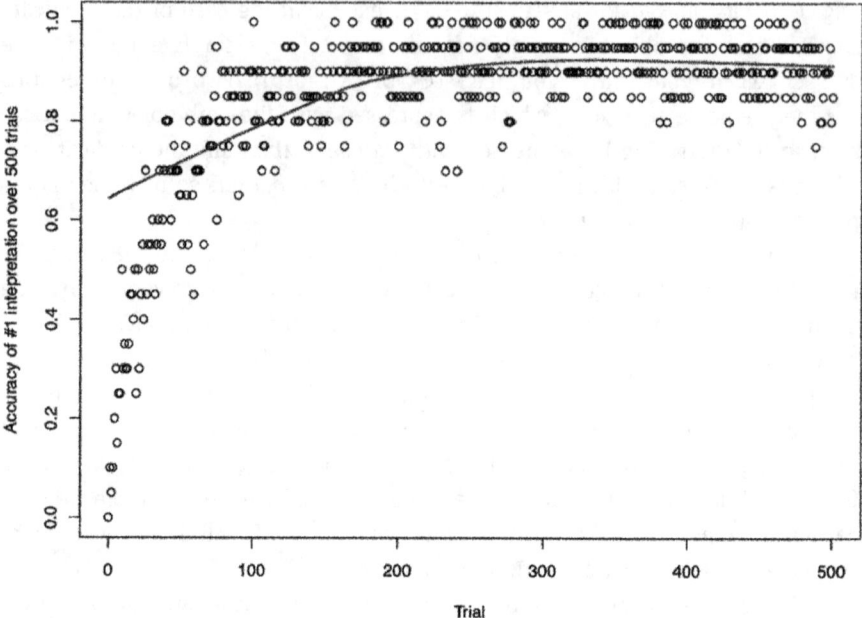

Figure 14: The average accuracy of μ-DOP in the first 500 trials

So exactly what patterns does the learner use to understand the utterances? Let us take a closer look at three cases.

First, the intransitive pattern was after a few instances being used as a fully abstract pattern. So the most likely derivation of a sentence like *Abe walks* is the one in Figure 15. The model probably directly inferred this abstraction, because the semantic representations are very simple. Given these simple representations, the generalization quickly pays off: breaking down the analysis into its smallest component parts allows the learner to use the words and the more abstract pattern. Note that this means that there are no restrictions on the nature of P : there is nothing witholding the parser from substituting P with a transitive predicate like P : see

$$P(e_1) \atop e_1 \ \ P \quad \circ \quad {e : Abe \atop /Abe/} \quad \circ \quad {P : walk \atop /walks/} \quad = \quad {P(e_1) \atop e : Abe \ \ P : walk \atop /Abe/ \ \ /walks/}$$

Figure 15: Most likely derivation for *Abe walks*

A second case is that of the *sees Abe*-construction (meaning that the subject turns fifty). This case is interesting, because it shows the effect of slightly different inputs on the learners. Recall that we generated twenty different corpora of utterance-situation pairs. Because all of these are different, learners might extract different patterns. It may be that later they converge on the same representation, after having seen more evidence, but they may also retain different representations. As long as this does not hamper communication, that is not a problem. For the *sees Abe*-construction, we see such a development. Basically, there are two paths the learners take. In the first, they almost directly infer that *sees + Abe* is a chunk that should be treated as a whole and that combines with the intransitive pattern and a subject to form a parse (see Analysis 1 in Figure 16). However, six out of fourteen learners started with another, communicatively correct analysis, viz. Analysis 2 in 16. These analyses lead to the same interpretation, and hence are fine for these six learners to use. However, after having seen more utterance-situation pairs, all learners abandon Analysis 2 in favor of Analysis 1. Arguably, they do so because the patterns decomposed from Analysis 1 will be reinforced more over other analyses (the pattern where *Ed + sees* means E:ED and the one where *Abe* means P:TURN.FIFTY can only be used rarely, and hence will obtain lower frequency scores over time, whereas *Ed* meaning E:ED are often reused in analyzing all sorts of sentences.

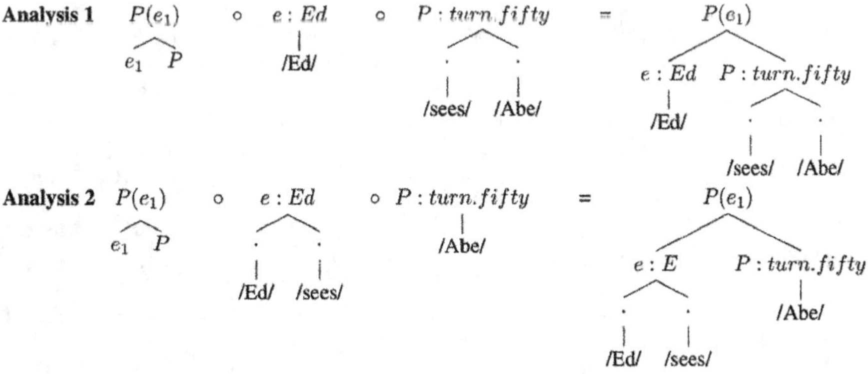

Figure 16: Two analyses of *Ed sees Abe* in the situation where TURN.FIFTY(ED) is present

Another interesting aspect of the sees A construction is that it is ambiguous, in principle, between a literal reading (SEE(E_1, ABE)) and an idiomatic one (TURN.FIFTY(E_1)). Thus, when facing a sentence *Ed sees Abe* and both the situations SEE(ED, ABE) and TURN.FIFTY(ED) are present in its context, the model cannot make a well-founded choice. In our experiment, the learner selected the former situation as the intended one, presumably because of the higher frequency of SEE(E_1, E_2) situations (with eight subject and eight objects: 64 instances) than TURN.FIFTY(E_1) situations (with only eight subjects: 8 instances). A final case is that of the no-reflexive construction. With the predicate shave and a coreferential subject and object, the reflexive is left out, so SHAVE(BEN, BEN) is expressed as *Ben shaves*. How does the learner respond to these sentences? In nineteen out of twenty cases, it will arrive at an analysis such as the one in Analysis 1 (Figure 17), where it has a pattern stating that there is a two-place predicate of which the coreferential argument is the first element (e1) and the predicate the second. This means that the model constructs a generalization that is too broad: this pattern could now in principle also be used to parse and produce (ungrammatical) utterances like *Ed sees* for the situation SEE(ED, ED). However, the model has no grounds of restricting this overgeneralization: there is an incentive to extract the third subtree (the 'word' *shaves*) from a more verb-island like pattern, viz. its use in the transitive argument-structure construction, where it fits the P-slot. We see here the effect of the whole system being interconnected by sharing members or parts of constructions. If it were not for the transitive pattern combining with the word *shaves* (or [P:SHAVE [*shaves*]]), the no-reflexive sentences would have probably been analyzed using a more restrictive pattern like '[[E$_1$] [P:SHAVE [*shaves*]]] meaning SHAVE(E$_1$, E$_1$)'.

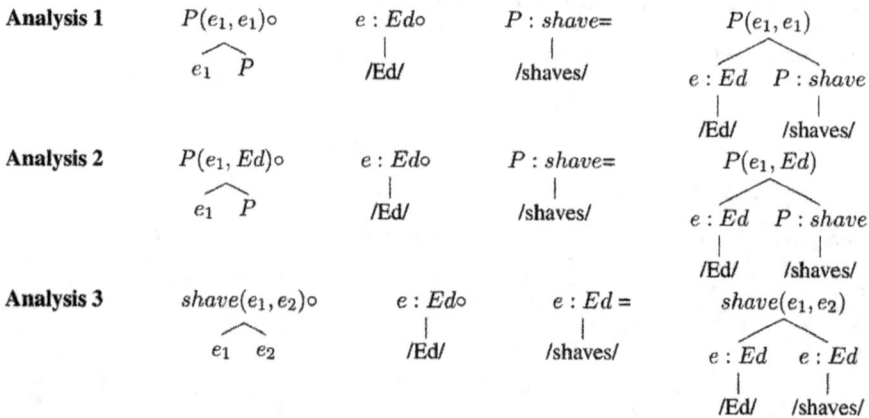

Figure 17: Three analyses of the no-reflexive sentence type

But apart from Analysis 1, the model also comes up with other analyses. In six simulations, the learner started with a pattern like in Analysis 3, that is, one in which the word form *shaves* is paired with a range of entities and there is a pattern that states that if you juxtapose two entities, the interpretation is that the first entity shaves the second. After having seen more utterances, five out of six learners give up on this pattern in favor of Analysis 1, whereas one keeps using Analysis 2 and Analysis 3 for this sentence type. In one case, the learner starts with Analysis 2 and shifts to Analysis 1 after a while.

What these cases show, is that the model can acquire both compositional and idiomatic structures from the data, using one and the same mechanism. It makes overgeneralizations, which is realistic, and the learners arrive at different representations on the basis of slightly different inputs, but converge mostly after having seen more evidence.

3.3 Approaching the learner: whither μ-DOP?

Any formalization will leave certain questions unanswered: indeed, the formalization of a language learner from a constructivist perspective is an AI-complete problem, as not only linguistic structure, but also conceptual structure and the memory system will have to be modeled. Model criticism on these levels is nevertheless very welcome and helps modelers develop more realistic models. Extending the representational formalism would be required to be able to understand alternations of the argument structure patterns (e.g., passivization and clefting), for instance, but this point does not bear on the essential learning strategy proposed by DOP, but rather on the nature of the structure in the input. We will discuss one further criticism in this paragraph that does relate to DOP's structure discovering mechanism, acknowledging the essential limitations present to the current line of reasoning.

One central problem with the μ-DOP approach is the fact that it allows for all possible fragments from the beginning onwards. This means that after having processed its first experience, the learner already has a (weak) generalization of, say, the subject preceding the verb. We have seen how the intransitive pattern is directly generalized to its most abstract form. This direct generalization is obviously unrealistic in the light of early language being rather holophrase-based. We can expect a learner to go about in a more conservative manner, only making a schema after it has seen multiple instances of an utterance. Much effort has been spent within the framework of Bayesian learning to understand how a conservative learner can create patterns that are both restrictive and openended enough to avoid both undergeneralization and overgeneralization (Stolcke 1994, O'Donnell, Snedeker, Tenenbaum, and Goodman 2011), and it is in similar mechanisms that our understanding of generalization has to be looked at (see also Beekhuizen, Bod, and Zuidema 2013).

4 Conclusion

In this paper, we have tried to show the potential of formal models for the constructivist approach to grammatical structure. We presented a domain-general, meronymy-based learning mechanism, viz. Data-Oriented Parsing, and show how it can be used as an unsupervised learning mechanism (U-DOP) to address learnability issues using constructivist principles such as heterogeneity of representation size and redundancy. We further gave an example of how we can incorporate meaning in U-DOP and showed how such a model can in principle learn from noisy data, although it remains to be seen how such a model behaves given naturalistic data. Although the specifics of the presented models may not be viable (perhaps there are problems with the learning mechanism, perhaps there are cognitively unrealistic assumptions), they show at least how we can formalize our understanding of linguistic learners in such a way that we can shed light on known phenomena and perhaps discover new ones.

References

Ambridge, Ben, Caroline Rowland, and Julian Pine. 2008. Is structure dependence an innate constraint? New experimental evidence from children's complex-question production. *Cognitive Science* 32: 222–255.

Arnold, Doug and Evita Linardaki. 2007. HPSG-DOP: Towards exemplar-based HPSG. In: *Proceedings of the European Summer School of Language, Logic and Information*.

Beekhuizen, Barend F., Rens Bod, and Willem Zuidema. 2013. Refining the all-fragments assumption: The search for parsimony in redundancy. *Language and Speech* 56: 257–264.

Bod, Rens. 1998. *Beyond Grammar: An Experience-Based Theory of Language*. CSLI, Stanford, CA.

Bod, Rens. 2009. From exemplar to grammar: A probabilistic analogy-based model of language learning. *Cognitive Science* 33: 752–793.

Bod, Rens and Ronald Kaplan. 1998. A probabilistic corpus-driven model for lexical-functional analysis. In: *Proceedings of ACL/COLING*, 145–151.

Bod, Rens, Remko Scha, and Khalil Sima'an (eds.). 2003. *Data-Oriented Parsing*. Chicago, IL: University of Chicago Press.

Bod, Rens and Margaux Smets. 2012. Empiricist solutions to nativist puzzles by means of unsupervised TSG. In: *Proceedings EACL*.

Bonnema, Remko, Rens Bod, and Remko Scha. 1997. A DOP Model for semantic interpretation. In: *Proceedings ACL-EACL*.

Borensztajn, Gideon, Willem Zuidema, and Rens Bod. 2008. Childrens grammars grow more abstract with age. Evidence from an automatic procedure for identifying the productive units of language. In: *Proceedings of the Annual Conference of the Cognitive Science Society*, 175–188.

Brown, Roger. 1973. *A First Language*. Harvard University Press, Cambridge, MA.

Bybee, Joan. 2006. From usage to grammar: The mind's response to repetition. *Language* 82: 711–733.

Chang, Nancy C.-L. 2008. Constructing grammar: A computational model of the emergence of early constructions. Dissertation, University of California, Berkeley.

Chomsky, Noam. 1986. *Knowledge of Language: Its Nature, Origin, and Use*. Westport, CT: Praeger.

Chomsky, Noam. 1993. A minimalist program for linguistic theory. In: K. L. Hale and S. J. Keyser (eds.), *The view from Building 20: Essays in linguistics in honor of Sylvain Bromberger*, 1–52. Cambridge, MA: MIT Press.

Clark, Alexander and Rémi Eyraud. 2006. Learning auxiliary fronting with grammatical inference. In: *Proceedings CoNLL*, 125–132.

Clark, Alexander and Shalom Lappin. 2011. *Linguistic Nativism and the Poverty of the Stimulus*. London: WileyBlackwell.

Crain, Stephan. 1991. Language acquisition in the absence of experience. *Behavioral and Brain Sciences* 14: 597–612.

Croft, William and D. Alan Cruse. 2004. *Cognitive Linguistics*. Cambridge: Cambridge University Press.

Daelemans, Walter and Antal van den Bosch. 2005. *Memory-Based Language Processing*. Cambridge: Cambridge University Press.

Fillmore, Charles J. and Paul Kay. 1996. *Construction Grammar*. Manuscript, University of California at Berkeley Department of linguistics.

Foraker, Stephani, Terry Regier, Naveen Khetarpal, Amy Perfors, and Joshua Tenenbaum. 2009. Indirect evidence and the poverty of the stimulus: The case of anaphoric one. *Cognitive Science* 33: 287–300.

Frank, Stefan L., Rens Bod, and Morten Christiansen. 2012. How hierarchical is language use? *Proceedings Biological sciences / The Royal Society* 279: 4522–4531.

Gale, William A. and Geoffrey Sampson. 1995. Good-Turing frequency estimation without tears. *Journal of Quantitative Linguistics* 2: 217–237.

Gentner, Dedre. 1982. Why nouns are learned before verbs: Linguistic relativity versus natural partitioning. In Stan A. Kuczaj II (ed.). *Language Development. Volume 2: Language, Thought, and Culture*, 301–334. Hillsdale, New Jersey: Lawrence Erlbaum Associates.

Gentner, Dedre. 1983. Structure-mapping: A theoretical framework for analogy. *Cognitive Science* 7: 155–170.

Gleitman, Lila. 1990. Sources of verb meanings. *Language Acquisition* 1: 3–55.

Goldberg, Adele E. 1995. *Constructions. A Construction Grammar Approach to Argument Structure*. Chicago, IL: Chicago University Press.

Goldberg, Adele E. 2006. *Constructions at Work. The Nature of Generalization in Language*. Oxford: Oxford University Press.

Jurafsky, Daniel. 1996. A probabilistic model of lexical and syntactic access and disambiguation. *Cognitive Science* 20: 137–194.

Jurafsky, Daniel. 2003. Probabilistic modeling in psycholinguistics: Linguistic comprehension and production. In: R. Bod, J. Hay and S. Jannedy (eds.), *Probabilistic Linguistics*, 39–94. Cambridge, MA: MIT Press.

Langacker, Ronald W. 1989. *Foundations of Cognitive Grammar, Volume I*. Stanford, CA: Stanford University Press.

Mehler, Jacques and Peter Carey. 1968. The interaction of veracity and syntax in the processing of sentences. *Perception and Psychophysics* 3: 109–111.

O'Donnell, Timothy J., Jesse Snedeker, Joshua B. Tenenbaum, and Noah D. Goodman. 2011. Productivity and reuse in language. In: *Proceedings CogSci*.

Perfors, Amy, Joshua B. Tenenbaum, and Elizabeth Wonnacott. 2010. Variability, negative evidence, and the acquisition of verb argument constructions. *Journal of Child Language* 37: 607–642.

Peters, Ann M. 1983. *The Units of Language Acquisition*. Cambridge: Cambridge University Press.

Pinker, Steven. 1979. Formal models of language learning. *Cognition* 7: 217–83.

Pullum, Geoffrey K. and Barbara C. Scholz. 2002. Empirical assessment of stimulus poverty arguments. *The Linguistic Review* 19: 9–50.

Scha, Remko. 1990. Taaltheorie en taaltechnologie; competence en performance [Linguistic theory and linguistic technology]. In: R. de Kort and G. Leerdam (eds.), *Computertoepassingen in de Neerlandistiek*, 7–22. Almere: LVVN.

Schuchardt, Hugo. 1885. *Ueber die Lautgesetze: Gegen die Junggrammatiker*. Berlin: Robert Oppenheim.

Stolcke, Andreas. 1994. Bayesian learning of probabilistic language models. Dissertation, University of California, Berkeley.

Tomasello, Michael. 2001. Perceiving intentions and learning words in the second year of life. In: M. Bowerman and S. C. Levinson (eds.), *Language Acquisition and Conceptual Development*, 132–158. Cambridge: Cambridge University Press.

Tomasello, Michael. 2003. *Constructing a Language: A Usage-Based Theory of Language Acquisition*. Cambridge, MA: Harvard University Press.

Trijp, Remi van, Luc Steels, Katrien Beuls, and Pieter Wellens. 2009. Fluid Construction Grammar: The new kid on the block. In: *Proceedings ACL*.

Verhagen, Arie. 2009. The conception of constructions as complex signs. Emergence of structure and reduction to usage. *Constructions and Frames* 1: 119–152.

Wunderlich, Dieter. 2007. Why assume UG? In: M. Penke and A. Rosenbach (eds.), *What counts as evidence in linguistics?*, 147–174. Amsterdam/Philadelphia: John Benjamins.

Zuidema, Willem. 2006. Theoretical evaluation of estimation methods for data-oriented parsing. In: *Proceedings EACL*.

II Construction morphology

Geert Booij and Matthias Hüning
4 Affixoids and constructional idioms

1 Introduction

Affixoids are compound constituents with an affix-like behaviour. An example from German is the adjective *fähig* 'able' that occurs in a huge number of German complex adjectives as their rightmost constituent. Wills collected about 1000 adjective types with *fähig* (Wills 1986). This is illustrated in (1):

(1) a. *veränderungs-fähig* 'able to change'
wandlungs-fähig 'able to change'

b. *umlaut-fähig* 'fit for undergoing Umlaut'
kredit-fähig 'fit for getting credit'

In the complex words (1a) we observe the original meaning of the adjective *fähig* 'able' which can be predicated of animate entities that can perform intentional actions. It is with this meaning that the adjective *fähig* can be used as free form, without forming part of a compound, as in *Er ist fähig sich zu entscheiden* 'He is able to make a decision'. In (1b) we find a different though related meaning of *fähig*, 'fit for'. This bound meaning of the adjective *fähig*, in combination with the observation that this use of *fähig* is very productive in complex words, is why some linguists of German have qualified this word as an affixoid. Its use looks similar to that of derivational affixes, the only difference being that derivational affixes are bound morphemes, whereas morphemes like *fähig* are lexical morphemes that have unbound meanings as well, and thus can be used as words.

Another example of an affixoid is the German adjective *frei* 'free' that, like its English and Dutch equivalents *free* and *vrij* respectively has developed the more general meaning 'without what is denoted by the base word' when used as the right constituent of compounds, as in *alcohol-frei* 'without alcohol'.[1] The use of this affixoid presupposes that the presence of what the base word denotes is a slightly negative evaluation. For instance, by using the adjective *sugar-free* instead of *sugar-less*, we imply that the presence of sugar is evaluated negatively, for instance, since it is not good for your health.

---

[1] This morpheme is also used with verbal base nouns, as in *bügel-frei* 'lit. iron-free, no iron', where *-frei* has the related meaning 'without the necessity of'.

The reason for giving a special status to German words like *fähig* and *frei* is that the use of these words with their bound meaning is not restricted to one or a few compounds, but can be used productively with this bound meaning for the formation of new adjectives. Hence, this phenomenon is not just a matter of lexicalization of individual words, it concerns a series of words that share their second constituent.

Both first and second constituents of Dutch and German compounds may exhibit this type of behaviour, and therefore, we find lists of both prefixoids and suffixoids of these languages in the relevant literature (Ascoop and Leuschner 2006; Decroos and Leuschner 2008; Leuschner 2010). A survey of such affixoids in Dutch can be found in Meesters (2004). In this paper, we will focus on affixoid phenomena in Dutch and German as well (cf. the comparison of compounding in both languages in Hüning and Schlücker 2010).

Examples of noun prefixoids are German *Riesen* 'giant' with the meaning 'enormous', as in *Riesen-erfolg* 'enormous success', and Dutch *hoofd* 'head' with the meaning 'main', as in *hoofd-probleem* 'lit. head problem, main problem' (Booij 2010a). An example of an adjective that is used as prefixoid is Dutch *oud* 'old' with the meaning 'former', as in *oud-leerling* 'ex-pupil' (Van Goethem 2008):

(2) a. *Riesen-durst* 'enormous thirst'
Riesen-enttäuschung 'enormous disappointment'
Riesen-erfolg 'enormous success'
Riesen-überraschung 'enormous surprise'

b. *hoofd-bezwaar* 'main objection'
hoofd-gedachte 'main thought'
hoofd-oorzaak 'main cause'
hoofd-probleem 'main problem'

c. *oud-Ajacied* 'former Ajax-player'
oud-burgemeester 'former mayor'
oud-collega 'former colleague'
oud-leerling 'former pupil'

The Dutch adjective *oud* when used in this way imposes the semantic restriction that the base word has to denote a human being with a particular social role. Hence, a noun like *oud-huis* 'former house' is ill-formed. In German, the use of its equivalent *Alt* is even more restricted, as it is only used to denote former political functions, as in *Alt-Kanzler* 'former chancellor'.

The theoretical question at issue here is whether we should introduce a new category of morphemes, that of affixoids, to account for the phenomena discussed above. This issue is raised by Schmidt, who argued against this category used in a number of descriptive studies of German morphology (Schmidt 1987). Schmidt's main point is that there is no good reason to introduce a third category besides the categories *affix* and *compound constituent*. According to Schmidt, the fact that a word has a special meaning when embedded in a compound is nothing special, as the choice of one of the meanings of a polysemous word often correlates with the context in which that word occurs. On the other hand, Stevens wants to maintain the notion *affixoid*, as it is relevant for describing and understanding morphological change, in particular the rise of derivational affixes from compound constituents (Stevens 2000, 2005). Stevens mentions among others the following tests for determining whether a morpheme is an affixoid:

(3) "a. Affixoids in spoken languages are not just serial but usually very productive. They are the basis for new formations.

b. Affixoids exist alongside a formally identical, and usually free "parent" morph. This means that there are two linguistic items identical in form and one is derived from the other.

c. The meaning of the affixoid is more generalized and abstract than the formally identical parent. In contrast to some affixes, the affixoid does not express grammatical relations (like person, case, tense, etc.)." (Stevens 2005: 73).

These tests reflect the idea that affixoid morphemes have acquired a more abstract meaning than their lexemic counterpart, and that they can be used productively with this meaning.

Because of such criteria, Elsen (2009), too, comes to the conclusion that there is a need for a third category of morphemes besides the categories of lexical morphemes and affixes. She wants to introduce the category *affixoid* and a corresponding word formation process, the *affixoid formation*, in order to account for the peculiarities of the complex words involved. While we do appreciate her careful and accurate overview of the discussion about the notion of affixoid, we are not convinced that it should be necessary to introduce new categories. What the discussion illustrates is mainly that there is no sharp distinction between derivation and compounding. Affixes and lexical words are at the two ends of a scale and the same is true for the two word formation processes, i.e. derivation and compounding. In between, there are formations with aspects of the both sides. The term affixoid is a useful descriptive term to denote the phenomenon of bound meanings for words when embedded in complex words. Their behaviour can be insightfully accounted for in the model of the hierarchical lexicon proposed within the framework of Construction Morphology (Booij 2010b). This model provides a formalism that does not force us to make an absolute distinction between compounding and derivation. Affixoids can be characterized as the lexically specified parts of constructional idioms (section 2). Constructional idioms for compounds are schemas for subsets of compounds in which one of the slots is lexically fixed. In section 3, we adduce additional arguments for the necessity of such subschemas, and discuss the problem of how to account for the differences in productivity of affixoids. In section 4, we argue that the use of the notion *constructional idiom* can be fruitfully extended to other subsets of compounds in which one of the constituents has special properties. Section 5 summarizes our findings and conclusions, and relates them briefly to how the rise of derivational affixes from compound constituents can be understood.

2 Affixoids and constructional idioms

What is it supposed to mean that a morpheme is called an affixoid? One option is to assume that such a morpheme has two entries in the lexicon, one as a lexical morpheme, and one as an affix, in the list of affixes of the language, each with their specific meaning or range of meanings. However, this is not very enlightening. For instance, if we were to list German *fähig* as a suffix, we have to specify that it creates adjectives, whereas this follows from the right-hand headedness of German compounds if we consider *fähig* as an adjective, even in words like *kredit-fähig*, where *fähig* carries the specific meaning restricted to the context of compounds.

We can keep the insights behind the notion of affixoid without introducing an additional category of morphemes besides lexical morphemes and bound morphemes by assuming a hierarchical lexicon, i.e. a lexicon with different layers of abstraction (Booij 2005; 2010a, b) Complex words with affixoids are compounds in which one of the constituents has a special, sometimes more abstract, meaning that can be used productively for the formation of new compounds. Hence, the phenomenon of affixoids is one of the arguments for a hierarchical lexicon in which schemas and subschemas are used. In the case of German *frei*, for instance, the general compound patterns $[NA]_A$ and $[VA]_A$ dominate the following subschemas:

(4) <[N$_i$ [frei]$_{Aj}$]$_{Ak}$ ↔ [without$_j$ SEM$_i$]$_k$>   Pragmatics: the presence of SEM$_i$
is evaluated negatively

A schema, marked by angled brackets is a correlation (indicated by the double arrow), of the form (left part) and meaning (right part) of a set of linguistic expressions. Correlations between subparts of the formal structure and the semantic structure are indicated by means of co-indexation.

The hierarchical lexicon of German contains schemas for compounds at various levels of abstraction. All German compounds are right-headed, which is expressed at the highest level of abstraction since the variable for syntactic category of the right constituent (Y) is identical to that of the compound as a whole. The semantic specification expresses that a compound of the type Y is a kind of Y with some relation to the modifier constituent X. At a lower level we specify constructional idioms such as (4), which in their turn dominate individual compounds of the relevant type:

(5) <[X$_i$ Y$_j$]$_{Yk}$ ↔ [SEM$_j$ with relation R to SEM$_i$]$_k$>
|
<[N$_i$ [frei]$_{Aj}$]$_{Ak}$ ↔ [without$_j$ SEM$_i$]$_k$>
|
<[[alkohol]$_{Ni}$ [frei]$_{Aj}$]$_{Ak}$ ↔ [without$_j$ SEM$_i$]$_k$>

Each level motivates properties of the next lower level, and serves to reduce the degree of arbitrariness between meaning and form in certain sets of compounds. That is, both the schemas and the fully specified individual complex words that instantiate these patterns are stored in the lexicon. Thus, expression is given to the fact that abstract morphological schemas depend for their existence on fully specified words.

The word-constructional schema in (4) can be qualified as a constructional idiom (that is, a schema with both variable slots and lexically specified slots), since one of the positions is lexically specified, whereas the other position is open (Jackendoff 2002). Such constructional idioms for compounds serve to express that the specified compound constituents have meanings that are different from those of the corresponding words used as free forms. In addition, this format expresses that the specific bound meaning is potentially productive, because the other position in the constructional idiom is a variable.[2]

---

[2] The relevance of the notion *constructional idiom at the word level* for the proper characterization of the affixoid behaviour of words has also been argued to be relevant for languages such as Greek (Ralli et al. 2008), French (Van Goethem 2008, 2010), Mandarin Chinese (Arcodia 2011) and Japanese (Namiki 2010). A constructional idiom analysis of some German affixoids (*-stück*, *-fall* and *-werk*) is defended in Zifonun (2012).

The criterion of 'bound meaning' is important. There are many sets of compounds that share either their first or their second constituent. As long as this shared constituent has the same meaning as when used as a separate word, there is no reason to assume a constructional idiom for such a set of compounds. For instance, Dutch has a lot of compounds with the word *molen* 'mill' as their right constituent. Since the meaning of *molen* in such compounds does not deviate from the meaning of *molen* as an independent word, there is no reason to assume a constructional idiom with *molen*.

It is, however, not always easy to decide whether a certain meaning is to be characterized as 'bound' or belongs to the polysemous semantic spectrum of the free form, the word. This can be illustrated by *frei* as well. Like its Dutch counterpart *vrij*, German *frei* has developed the 'without X' meaning also for the adjective (*frei von Sorgen* 'without a care, not hindered by a care'). This means, that it is difficult to delimit the bound meaning from one of the semantic possibilities of the original word, especially since it is not clear whether this meaning developed independently with that word or on the basis of the bound meaning through a process that has been called 'debonding' by Norde (2009) who sees this as a possible case of degrammaticalization (cf. also section 3.2 on the reinterpretation of affixoids).

The use of constructional idioms for sets of compounds serves to account for the polysemy of the specified words: in addition to one or more meanings that these words have when used by themselves, they have another (but related) meaning when used as part of a compound.

The existence of constructional idioms for words with affixoid behaviour may manifest itself in specific semantic and/or formal properties. Recall that the Dutch adjective *oud* when used as an affixoid with the meaning 'former' can only be added to nouns denoting social roles of human beings, whereas the adjective *oud* with its literal sense of 'old' in phrases combines with all sorts of nouns. An additional observation on the affixoid use of *oud* is that in words beginning with *oud-*, main stress is on the second constituent, whereas normally, AN compounds carry their main stress on their first constituent, as in *brúinbrood* 'brown bread', *gróot-vader* 'grandfather'. In this respect, *oud-* behaves similarly to prefixes like *ex-* 'ex-'. That is, we have to specify the specific stress pattern of *oud*-compounds with this meaning as part of the relevant constructional schema. In sum, the following subschema for Dutch AN compounds has to be assumed:

(6) $<[[oud]_{Ai} [N_j]]_{Nk} \leftrightarrow [former_i \ SEM_j]_k>$
    Conditions: N_j carries main stress; N_j = social role

After this brief sketch of the way in which affixoids can be represented within a hierarchical lexicon model, we now turn to a number of properties of affixoids that show that they need to be singled out as forming special subclasses of compounds.

3 The need for constructional idioms

Why do we need constructional idioms as characterizations of the various patterns if we list the members of the various word families anyway? Apart from their redundancy rule function (the statement of systematic patterns of interpretation for subsets of compounds), there are some other observations that suggest that such schemas can be abstracted and used by native speakers.

First of all, many of these affixoids are productive. Therefore, we need to account for this productive use of affixoids with a schema with a variable (section 3.1). In addition, affixoids may undergo a process of reinterpretation which suggests that their productive affixoid meaning is recognized by language users (section 3.2). This is also clear from grammatical replication and borrowing (section 3.3). Affixoids are also the historical source of affixes (section 3.4). Finally, in section 3.5. it is shown that we need a more abstract compounding schema for all compounds that begin with a word with intensifier meaning, because such compound constituents can all be repeated in emphatic coordination.

3.1 Degrees of productivity

Given the characterization of affixoids as lexical morphemes with a bound meaning, we may wonder to what extent productivity should be seen as a necessary property of affixoids. Consider the use of *steen* 'brick, stone' in the following Dutch N+A compounds taken from the latest electronic edition of *Van Dale Groot Woordenboek der Nederlandse Taal*:

(7) *steen-dood* 'very dead'
    steen-goed 'very good'
    steen-hard 'very hard'
    steen-koud 'very cold'
    steen-rijk 'very rich'

These are the only AN compounds beginning with *steen* listed in this dictionary, apart from *steen-rood* 'red as a stone'.[3] The part *steen* expresses the meaning 'very'. *Van Dale* also has an entry *steen-*, with a hyphen right after the morpheme, thus suggesting that this morpheme is used as a prefixoid. It is glossed as *in hoge mate* 'to a high degree', and the example provided in the prefixoid entry is the compound adjective *steen-dood* 'very dead', an adjective that is being used indeed, as a Google search reveals. Thus, we see class expansion in the sense that *steen* 'stone' is used as a modifier for a larger class of adjectives than the literal meaning of *steen* would make us to expect. (This literal meaning may still be linked to the meanings of *steenhard* and *steenkoud*.) However, this use of *steen* as an intensifier is not productive. For instance, we do not find *steen-slecht* 'very bad' besides *steen-goed* 'very good' in actual language use, and it does not feel as a correct adjective for speakers of Dutch. Hence, what we have to do with here is a closed set of compounds that begin with the same word, hence a word family, where some of the lexicalized compounds share the lexicalized meaning of this first word.

Another example of a word family of compounds with a lexicalized meaning for the first constituent is the set of compounds beginning with *dood* 'death'. The following words, among others, where *dood* means 'very', are listed in the *Van Dale* dictionary:

(10) *dood-gemoedereerd* 'without any hesitation'
      dood-gewoon 'very normal'
      dood-leuk 'very nice'
      dood-moe 'very tired'
      dood-ongelukkig 'very unhappy'
      dood-op 'very tired'
      dood-simpel 'very simple'
      dood-stil 'very quiet'
      dood-ziek 'very ill'

Again, *Van Dale* lists this morpheme as a prefix(oid) *dood-*, with the meaning 'very'. The word is also listed as one of the affixoids of Dutch in Leuschner (2010). However, this word cannot be used productively as an intensifier prefixoid. For instance, *dood-* does not combine straightforwardly with other adjectives that denote an unpleasant state, such as ?*dood-lelijk* 'very ugly', or ?*dood-gemeen* 'very nasty'.

---

[3] The adjective *steen-rood* 'red as stone' is an instantiation of the class of NA compounds with a comparative meaning, also exemplified by compounds like *sneeuw-wit* 'snow-white, white as snow'.

In contrast to these unproductive prefixoids, the prefixoid *reuze-* 'enormous, very' appears to be attached to a wide range of adjectives, as illustrated in (11) (Google search, 09.03.2012), and can easily be attached to new adjectives:

(11) *reuze-arm* 'very poor'
reuze-bekakt 'very posh'
reuze-beleefd 'very polite'
reuze-bijzonder 'very special'
reuze-eigenwijs 'very conceited'
reuze-gemeen 'very nasty'
reuze-gewoon 'very common'
reuze-gezellig 'very cosy'
reuze-lief 'very sweet'
reuze-stout 'very naughty'
reuze-verwend 'very spoiled'

Its productivity can also be illustrated by the combination of *reuze-* with recent loan words, as in *reuze-cool* 'very cool' or *reuze-soft* 'very soft'.

Complex words that share one or more morphemes form word families, and there is a wealth of evidence that word families form an important ingredient in the structure of the mental lexicon (Schlücker and Plag 2011; Schreuder and Baayen 1997). Constructional idioms can be seen as characterizations of specific types of word families consisting of compounds that either have the same modifier constituent or the same head, and with a special bound meaning for the common constituent. Hence, it is very well possible that language users discover the common bound meaning of a lexical morpheme in a number of related conventionalized complex words. Should this common meaning always be expressed by an abstract schema, that is, a constructional idiom? Does the assumption of an abstract schema imply that the pattern is productive?

There are two possible approaches to the problem of productivity. One option is to make an absolute distinction between incidental extension of a pattern by means of analogy, where a specific existing complex word forms the model, versus extension of a pattern by means of an abstract schema, in which case there is no specific word that serves as the model. For instance, the word *pis-link* 'lit. piss-angry, very angry' may have been coined in analogy to the compound *pis-nijdig* 'very angry', the only other existing compound in which *pis* 'piss' has the intensifier meaning, combined with an adjective with the same meaning. On the other hand, we cannot identify a specific compound as the model for the use of *reuze-* as an intensifier, and thus the affixoid use of *reuze-* can be specified in a schema.

The Van Dale Dutch dictionary seems to follow this model, since words such as *dood-*, *steen-*, *reuze-* have a separate entry for their use as intensifier, whereas there is no entry *pis-*, only an entry *pis*. Similarly, there is no prefix entry for *straat-* with the meaning 'very', as there is only one adjective of this type, *straat-arm* 'lit. street-poor, poverty-stricken'.[4]

However, some compound families such as those for *steen-* and *dood-* discussed above do have a number of members, and yet, it is hard to extend the relevant compound family. That is, we may assume a schema to characterize such a compound family, but the existence of such a schema should not necessarily imply that the pattern expressed is productive.

Recall that the use of schemas does not imply that the individual instantiations are not listed themselves. Schemas therefore have a secondary status, and depend for their existence on sets of complex words with a shared property.

What determines productivity in the sense of *extensibility* of a pattern? Extensibility is determined by at least two factors: type frequency, and the occurrence of new forms. Type frequency will boost productivity, as stressed by Barðdal (2008). For instance, since there are many Dutch words with *reuze-* it will be easier to make a new compound beginning with this morpheme. Yet, type frequency in itself is not enough, as shown by *dood-*: Dutch has a reasonable number of words of this type, yet it is hard to make a new word of this type because we do not come across new words with *dood-* as first constituent. This supports the view that the extension of classes of words with affixoids is in principle always based on analogical relationships (Karsdorp and Hüning 2012). These analogical relationships between similar words will be (re)activated every time a new word of the relevant type is coined (Abbot-Smith and Tomasello 2006). Hence, the abstract schema characterizing the set of words with a particular affixoid will be more readily available, the more it is used for new words, and this will boost its productivity. This issue is also treated in a number of articles by Hüning (Hüning 2009; 2010a, b) and in van Santen (2010).

In sum, constructional idioms that characterize sets of compounds may vary in their degree of productivity. This degree of productivity is determined by type frequency and the frequency of new coinings.

The problem broached here is the same that holds for word formation in general. How can we account for differences in degree of productivity between different derivational affixes and different types of compounding? Such gradual differences cannot be expressed in a formal, structural fashion. Therefore, we

---

4 *Van Dale's* Dutch French dictionary explicitly mentions a prefix *straat-*, but this pertains to the literal meaning of *straat* in compounds. This shows that the use of the notion 'prefix' in this dictionary is rather erratic.

have to distinguish between the common structural properties of a set of complex words as expressed by constructional schemas, and the actual extensibility of the relevant class of complex words. Productivity is not a purely structural matter, but a multi-factorial phenomenon. The actual productivity of a morphological pattern is partially determined by type frequency, but also by functional factors such as the naming function, stylistic variation, register, style, fashion, the need for distinguishing oneself, etc. But we do not only need sociolinguistics and pragmatics; in order "to come to a full understanding of the challenging phenomenon of morphological productivity, a truly interdisciplinary data-driven research effort is required" (Baayen 2009: 917).

An example of regional variation is the productive use of the noun *kei-* as a prefixoid intensifier as used in *kei-hard* 'lit. rock-hard, hard as a rock'. The use of *kei-* can also be found in words like *kei-gaaf* 'very cool', *kei-jammer* 'very deplorable', *kei-gezellig* 'very cosy, *kei-komisch* 'very comical', and *kei-makkelijk* 'very easy'; the use of these words is characteristic for the southeast region of the Netherlands and is used in particular by youngsters.

3.2 Reinterpretation of affixoids

In some compounds with an affixoid constituent this affixoid is reanalyzed as an adjective, as illustrated here for German and Dutch. This is a case of back formation: the first word is given the status of adjective by reinterpreting NN compounds as AN compounds. This type of reanalysis is also referred to as *debonding* (Norde 2009). This reinterpretation is possible because the initial nouns function semantically as intensifiers. The relevant constructional idioms are illustrated in (12), with the Dutch nouns *kut* 'cunt', *reuze* 'giant', and *top* 'top', and the German nouns *Hammer* 'hammer' (in informal and substandard German), *Klasse* 'class', and *Spitze* 'top'; the reinterpretation as adjectives is given in (13):

(12) Dutch
    a. *kut-ding* 'bad thing'
       kut-gevoel 'bad feeling'
       kut-smoes 'bad excuse'

    b. *reuze-dorst* 'enormous thirst'
       reuze-vader 'great father'
       reuze-vriendelijk 'very kind'

c. *top-conditie* 'top-condition'
   top-prestatie 'top-achievement'
   top-productie 'top-production'

German
d. *das Hammer-gefühl* 'the great feeling'
   das Hammer-teil 'the great thing'
   die Hammer-vorstellung 'the great performance'

e. *das Klasse-fahrrad* 'the marvelous bike'
   die Klasse-vorstellung 'the marvelous performance'
   das Klasse-weib 'the marvelous woman'

f. *das Spitzen-erzeugnis* 'the top product'
   die Spitzen-leistung 'the top performance'
   die Spitzen-vorstellung 'the top performance'

(13) Dutch:
reuze 'great'
kut 'bad'
top 'excellent'
German:
hammer 'great'
klasse 'excellent, marvelous'
spitze 'excellent, top'

In the case of Dutch, the linking element *-e* in *reuze* (the lexical morpheme is *reus* 'giant'), is preserved in the adjectival use of these words, which confirms the source of these adjectives, reinterpretation of a noun compound constituent with a bound meaning. However, this does not apply to German where the form *spitze*, the form of the word in isolation, rather than *spitzen* is used. Note that the adjectival reinterpretation is reflected by the spelling of the German examples, as only nouns are spelled with initial capital letters.

The resulting adjectives are mainly used in predicate position (or as adverbs); this may have to with the origin of these adjectives from nouns:

(14) Dutch
a. Dat   vind ik erg   reuze van jullie
   That find I   very   giant of   you
   'I appreciate your doing very much'

b. *Die videokaart is niet erg top*
   That videocard is not very top
   'That is not a very good videocard'

c. *Dit vind ik erg kut*
   That find I very cunt
   'I find that very bad'

German
d. *Ich finde den Film total klasse.*
   I find the film totally class.
   'I find that film very good.'

e. *Das Konzert war ja hammer.*
   The concert was yes hammer.
   'The concert was fantastic.'

f. *Sein Auftritt war total spitze.*
   His performance was totally top.
   'His performance was fantastic.'

Use as attributive adjectives is possible in informal varieties of Dutch. For instance, the word *kut*, originally a noun, may occur in attributive position when used as an adjective of depreciation, with the inflection typical for pronominal adjectives, and also with a superlative form (Google search, 06.03.2012). However, in German, words like *klasse* and *spitze* cannot be inflected as regular adjectives, which results in minimal pairs like (15h–i):

(15) Dutch
   a. *een kutt-e werk-houding*
      a cunt-INFL work-attitude
      'a bad attitude towards work'

   b. *kutt-e tekenfilms*
      cunt-INFL cartoons
      'worthless cartoons'

   c. *Frans is een kut-vak, maar wiskunde blijft het kut-st*
      French is a cunt-subject but math stays the cunt-est
      'French is a nasty subject but math stays the nastiest'

   d. *een heel topp-e dame*
      a very top-INFL lady
      'an excellent lady'

e. *erg   topp-e   film*
   very   top-INFL movie
   'very good movie'

German
f. *eine   klasse   Frau* (compare *eine bös-e Frau* 'an angry woman')
   a   class   woman
   'an excellent woman'

g. *ein   klasse   Hund* (compare *ein bös-er Hund* 'an angry dog')
   a   class   dog
   'an excellent dog'

h. *ein   spitz-er   Bleistift*
   a   sharp-INFL pencil
   'a sharp pencil'

i. *ein spitze Bleistift*
   'an excellent pencil'

Reinterpretation of noun affixoids as adjectives is thus an indication that language users master the relevant productive constructional idioms.

Other examples of this type of reinterpretation are the Dutch nouns *doorsnee* 'lit. sectional plane, average', *luxe* 'lit. luxury, luxurious' and *standaard* 'lit. standard, common'. These three nouns all function as adjectives as well, as can be concluded from the fact that they can be modified by an adverb such as *erg* 'very', and are used as a predicate:

(16) *Dat klinkt erg doorsnee* 'That sounds very average'
     Een erg luxe oplossing 'A very luxurious solution'
     Ik vind hem erg standaard 'I find him very common'

These three nouns are also used productively as the first part of NN compounds, with the meanings indicated above, and it is this productive use of a bound meaning that gave rise to their being used as adjectives. Note that the same meaning development took place in English for *standard*, and it may well be that the intensive contact between English and Dutch plays a role in boosting this parallel use of English *standard* and Dutch *standaard*.

Thus, this reinterpretation shows that language users grasp the compound subpatterns with these productive meanings that started as bound meanings for compound constituents.

3.3 Affixoids may lead to affixes

The change of an affixoid into an affix can be observed by comparing the Dutch noun *hoofd* 'head' and its German prefix counterpart *Haupt-* 'main'. In German, the word *Haupt* that is the historical equivalent of Dutch *hoofd* has been superseded by the word *Kopf* to denote the upper body part. In the text of Bach's *Matthew Passion* (composed in 1727) we can still observe the use of *Haupt* as a free form in the choral *Oh Haupt voll Blut und Wunden* 'O head full of blood and wounds', but the productive use of *Haupt* as a free word is no longer possible in modern German, and has gradually disappeared. This is why in present-day grammars of German the morpheme *Haupt-* in words like *Haupt-bahnhof* 'central station' and *Haupt-sache* 'main issue' is qualified as a prefix. In other words, a prefixoid becomes a real prefix if the relevant word is no longer a free lexical item. The additional condition is that the prefixoid has a meaning that can be used productively. The loss of a word that is also listed as part of a complex word will not lead to an affix, but only lead to a cranberry morpheme (that is, a morpheme that only occurs as compound constituent) if that morpheme is not used for coining new words. This is the case for words like Dutch *bruide-gom*, German *Bräuti-gam* and English *bride-groom* (all with the same meaning), where *gom*, *gam* and *groom* are cranberry morphemes. Hence, we do not consider the bound morphemes *gom*, *gam* or *groom* suffixes.

The rise of affixes from affixoids requires that language users conclude to abstract patterns that characterizes sets of compounds with the same bound meaning for one of their constituents, and thus supports the use of constructional idioms for the proper characterization of affixoids.

3.4 Replication and borrowing

Replication is the phenomenon that a grammatical pattern is borrowed from one language into another. The recognition of affixoid patterns is confirmed by the observation that such patterns may be replicated by other languages. An example of this type of grammatical replication is the use of the word for 'top' in various European languages with the meaning 'of high quality'; it may well originate in the affixoid use of this word in English (Heine and Kuteva 2006):

(17) English *top-*
Dutch *top-*
German *Spitzen-*
Swedish *topp-*
Finnish *huippu-*

Heine and Kuteva (2006: 62) mention another example from Finnish, the use of the Finnish equivalent of English *key* with the meaning 'central, most important': *avain-asema* 'key position', and *avain-hahmo* 'key figure'. This pattern is also found in Dutch, as in *sleutelpositie* 'key position' and *sleutelbijdrage* 'key contribution'.

Affixoids may be borrowed and attached to base words of the borrowing language. An example is German *über*. This word is used as a preposition, an adverb, and an adjective. In addition, it is used as part of particle verbs, complex verbs, nouns, and adjectives:

(18) a. *über den Rücken* 'across the back'
 b. *über 80 Gäste* 'more than 80 guests'
 c. *Es ist noch Kaffee über* 'There is still coffee left'
 d. *über-nehmen* 'to take over'
 e. *über-setzen* 'to translate'
 f. *Über-kontrolle* 'too much checking'
 g. *über-deutlich* 'excessively clear'

Similar though not identical patterns of polysemy can be found for English *over* and Dutch *over*. This polysemy implies that there is a number of subentries for *über* in the German lexicon. Some of these meanings are tied to their occurrence in specific classes of complex words. For instance, the use of *über* with the meaning 'beyond the standard level, to an excessive measure' is tied to its occurrence in nouns and adjectives (18f–g). With nouns it may be used with the meaning 'extreme', with adjectives with the meaning 'excessively':

(19) a. *Über-mensch* 'super human being, super-man'
 Über-doktor 'super-doctor'

 b. *über-deutlich* 'excessively clear'
 über-glücklich 'excessively happy'
 über-füllt 'over-crowded'

These uses of *über* are productive, and can be easily extended to new nouns or adjectives of German. Hence, these uses of *über* should be specified by means of constructional idioms of the form [*über*-A]$_A$ and [*über*-N]$_N$, with the specific meanings of *über* specified. This use of *über* is probably based on Nietzsche's word *Über-mensch* that became well known in European philosophy and literature, translated as *super-man* in English (as in Shaw's play *Men and supermen*). The relevant meaning of *über* has subsequently been extended to many new compounds. It has also been borrowed in English. The English examples below are from the NY Times Archives on the internet:[5]

(20) a. with N: *über-burger, über-guru, über-diva, über-style, über-station wagon, über-close up, über-shopper, über-producer, über-caterer*

b. with A: *über-hip, über-talented, über-traditional, über-catchy*

Examples from British English are given in Renouf (2007):

(21) a. with N: *über-pundit, über-talkshow, über-mogul*

b. with A: *über-hyped, über-media-saturated, über-waif*

In Dutch one also finds lots of new words with *über* on the internet, as in *über-gewelddadig* 'extremely violent', *über-lekker* 'very nice', *über-lijp* 'very smart' (adjectives) and *über-professor* 'super-professor' and *uber-nicht* 'extremely gay person' (nouns). This use of *über* is taken over from English rather then directly from German (Forche 2011).

The borrowing of affixes through an intermediate language is a common phenomenon. The prefix *non-* is used in Dutch before adjectives and nouns, as in *non-figuratief* 'non-figurative' and *non-fictie* 'non-fiction'. This prefix *non-* is originally a Latinate negative word, but is probably borrowed as a prefix from English where it has become very productive, as in *non-food* and *non-issue*. Similarly, as suggested by van der Sijs (1996: 113), the productive use of the Latin morpheme *super-* as a prefix in Dutch may have been influenced by the very productive use of this prefix in English.

The borrowing of German *über* in Dutch through English discussed above thus confirms the similar status of affixes and affixoids with respect to grammatical replication in the sense of Heine and Kuteva (2006). In sum, grammatical replication requires that some users of the replicating language have discovered a pattern in the source language, which makes it possible to transfer that pattern to the target language.

3.5 Emphatic coordination

For a proper characterization of Dutch we need to be able to refer to the class of initial morphemes of complex words that express an intensifier meaning (discussed as elative compounds in Hoeksema (2012), since it is exactly this class

---

[5] This English prefixoid *über* has various other spelling forms such as *uber*, *ueber* and *Uber* (Forche 2011).

of morphemes that can be repeated in order to express emphatic meaning (Booij 2010b: 59):

(22) a. noun prefixoids

bere- en bere-goed
bear- and bear-good
'very, very good'

bloed- en bloed-mooi
blood- and blood-beautiful
'very, very beautiful'

dood- en dood-ziek
death- and death-ill
'very, very ill'

kei- en kei-leuk
boulder- and boulder-cool
'very, very cool'

pis- en pis-nijdig
piss- and piss-angry
'very, very angry'

poep- en poep-arm
shit- and shit-poor
'very, very poor'

reuze- en reuze-tevreden
giant- and giant-pleased
'very, very pleased'

steen- en steen-rijk
stone- and stone-rich
'very, very rich'

stok- en stok-kreupel
stick- and stick-crippled
'very, very crippled'

stront- en stront-lazerus
shit- and shit-drunk
'very, very drunk'

b. adjective prefixoids
dol- en dol-komisch
mad- and mad-comical
'very, very comical'

stom- en stom-dronken
dumb- and dumb-drunk
'very, very drunk'

c. verb prefixoids
kots- en kots-beu
puke- and puke-sick
'very, very sick of'

loei- en loei-heet
thump- and thump-hot
'very, very hot'

piep- en piep-klein
peep- and peep-small
'very, very small'

The same kind of repetitive coordination with emphatic effect is possible with Dutch intensifiers that correspond to prepositions such as *door* 'through' and *in* 'in':

(23) a. *door- en door-nat*
through- and through-wet
'wet through and through'

b. *in- en in-triest*
in- and in-sad
'very, very sad'

If we want to make a generalization as to which elements can occur in such repetitive coordination, we need to be able to refer to the class of compound-initial morphemes with intensifier meaning. The crucial condition for this form of repetition is a semantic one: whatever the lexical category or the degree of productivity, the first word must carry the meaning of intensification:

(24) $<[x \text{ } en \text{ } x \text{ } A_i]_{Aj} \leftrightarrow [\text{very high degree of SEM}_i]_j> \approx$
$<[x \text{ } A_i]_{Aj} \leftrightarrow [\text{high degree of SEM}_i]_j>$

The symbol ≈ indicates that the two schemas are paradigmatically related. The second of these schemas is a general schema that dominates the various constructional idioms for complex words with a first constituent that carries an intensifier meaning. Generalization (24) presupposes the following constructional idiom, which is then instantiated by a large set of compound adjectives with various kinds of intensifying modifiers such as *door* in *doornat*:

(25) <[x A_i]$_{Aj}$ ↔   [high degree of SEM_i]$_j$>
       |
       <[door [nat]$_{Ai}$]$_{Aj}$ ↔   [high degree of SEM_i]$_j$>

Emphatic repetition of this type is also possible in Frisian that has a number of intensifier affixoids (Hoekstra 1998), such as:

(26) *dea* 'death'   *dea-bang* 'very afraid'
                         dea-gewoon 'very common'
      poer 'pure'   *poer-lilk* 'very ugly'
                         poer-verlegen 'very shy'
      troch 'through' *troch-kâld* 'very cold'
                         troch-waarm 'very warm'

Like in Dutch, the intensifier affixoid can be repeated in Frisian by means of coordination with the conjunction *en* 'and', or the older form of this conjunction, *ende*:

(27) *poer-ende-poer-swart* 'pure-and-pure-black, very, very black'
      troch-ende-troch-kâld 'very, very cold'

The possibility of using the old form of the conjunction, *ende*, shows that this is not a regular form of coordination, but a special form of repetition for which a separate coordinative subschema has to be assumed, with *ende* as conjunction.

This pattern of emphatic repetition applies to all initial compound constituents with an intensifier meaning, including those instantiated by one of a few compounds only, such as those in (28), Dutch compounds in which the first constituent has the intensifier meaning in one compound only:

(28) *boter- en boter-zacht* 'butter- and butter-soft, very soft'
      pis- en pis-nijdig 'piss- and piss-angry, very angry'
      spin- en spin-nijdig 'spider- and spider-angry, very angry'
      ziels- en ziels-gelukkig 'soul- and soul-happy, very happy'

We cannot assume a constructional idiom for the intensifier nouns *boter-*, *pis-*, *spin-*, and *ziels-*, as they occur in these compounds only. Yet, they pattern with the other, more productive intensifier prefixoids. This means that these compounds are instantiations of the general very schema in (25), although they do not instantiate a constructional idiom of their own.

4 Constructional idioms for bound lexemes

The concept *constructional idiom at the word level* that was argued for in the preceding sections to be a useful concept for the characterization of affixoids, appears to be applicable to a number of related phenomena, cases in which words and phrases when used as compound constituents have specific properties: (i) complex words that only appear as parts of compounds, (ii) allomorphs of words as compound constituents, and (iii) phrasal constituents. These are discussed in the following subsections.

4.1 Complex words as bound elements

Complex words may exhibit the same behaviour as affixoids in the sense that their occurrence is bound to their being embedded in compounds. Consider the German deverbal noun *Mach-er* 'mak-er', discussed in detail in Joeres (1995). Joeres' observation is that the complex word *-macher* with the regular meaning 'maker' is very productive as part of compounds, whereas it has a lexicalized meaning when used as an autonomous lexeme, namely 'strong personality who achieves a lot'. Joeres (1995: 151) concludes that *-macher* can be qualified as a 'Halbsuffix', that is, an affixoid. Note, however, that that *macher* is not one morpheme, as was the case for the affixoids discussed above, but consists of two morphemes, the verbal stem *mach-* 'make' and the agentive suffix *-er*. Examples of this type of compounding in German are:

(29) with A as first constituent
Fit-macher 'fit-maker'
Krank-macher 'ill-maker'
Wach-macher 'awake-maker'

with N as first constituent
Baby-macher 'baby-maker'
Eis-macher 'ice-maker'
Programm-macher 'program-maker'

Different from what is at stake with the affixoids discussed in section 3, the meaning of *macher* in these words is completely regular: it has the meaning 'entity that causes or creates something'. This meaning, however, is only available within compounds, and not for the word *Macher* in isolation, which only has the lexicalized meaning mentioned above. In order to account for its bound use, we may assume the following constructional idioms for this class of compounds:

(30) $< [A_i \ [[mach]_V \ er]_{Nj} \ ]_{Nk} \ \leftrightarrow \ [\text{who causes to be SEM}_i]_k >$
$< [N_i \ [[mach]_V \ er]_{Nj} \ ]_{Nk} \ \leftrightarrow \ [\text{who creates SEM}_i]_k >$

These are unifications of two independently motivated word formation schemas, $[NN]_N$ or $[AN]_N$ on the one hand, and $[V\text{-}er]_N$ on the other, with the V-slot lexically specified as *mach*. Note that the interpretation of *mach* 'make' depends on the lexical category of the first constituent: CAUSE with As, CREATE with Ns. These subschemas express the dependence of the use of *macher* with these meanings on its being embedded in a compound.

There are more cases in Dutch where complex words do not function as words in isolation, or only with a specific meaning (as was the case for German *Macher*). Examples are compounds headed by the deverbal noun *kun-de* 'skill, knowledge' which has acquired the meaning of 'science' when used as compound head:

(31) *bodem-kunde* 'soil-science, geology?'
bouw-kunde 'build-science, architectural science'
dier-kunde 'animal-science, zoology'
taal-kunde 'language-science, linguistics'

These and other nouns ending in -*kunde* denote various sciences. Thus, a specific constructional idiom has developed in Dutch of the form

(32) $<[N/V]_i \ [kunde]_{Nj}]_{Nk} \leftrightarrow [\text{science}_j \text{ of SEM}_i]_k$

Other examples of derived words that function in similar ways as building blocks of compounds are -*aard-ig, -vorm-ig, -zinn-ig*. These are denominal adjectives ending in the suffix -*ig* derived from the following nouns:

(33) *aard* 'nature'
vorm 'form'
zin 'sense'

The adjectives *aardig* 'nice' and *zinnig* 'sensible' do occur as separate words, but not with the meanings that they have in compounds; the word *vormig* only occurs as the head of adjectival compounds:

(34) a. *boos-aard-ig* 'angry-nature-ed, malignant'
eigen-aard-ig 'own-nature-ed, peculiar'

b. *blad-vorm-ig* 'leaf-shap-ed'
cirkel-vorm-ig 'circle-shap-ed'

c. *diep-zinn-ig* 'deep-sense-ed, profound'
eigen-zinn-ig 'self-willed'

The bound use of these complex adjectives can be characterized by constructional idioms of the following type:

(35) <[A$_i$ [[aard]$_{Nj}$ ig]$_A$]$_{Ak}$ ↔ [having property$_j$ SEM$_i$]$_k$>
<[N$_i$ [[vorm]$_{Nj}$ ig]$_A$]$_{Ak}$ ↔ [having form$_j$ SEM$_i$]$_k$>
<[A$_i$ [[zinn]$_{Nj}$ ig]$_A$]$_{Ak}$ ↔ [having mental disposition with property SEM$_i$]$_k$>

The formal structures of these complex adjectives are unifications of independently motivated morphological structures, AA compounds and complex adjectives of the form [N-*ig*]$_A$. Yet, we should specify them as part of the hierarchical lexicon, as the denominal adjectives by themselves either do not exist at all, or have a different meaning when used as independent words.

The constituent *-aardig* may have lost its internal structure for language users, because *aardig* in isolation means 'nice'. This lack of transparency can also be observed in the use of the denominal adjective *-matig* derived from the noun *maat* 'measure'. The word *matig* in isolation means 'moderate'. As the following examples illustrate, it functions to turn a noun into its corresponding adjective, in which the meaning of *maat* plays no role:

(36) *beroep* 'profession'   *beroeps-matig* 'professional'
dwang 'compulsion'   *dwang-matig* 'compulsory'
gevoel 'instinct'   *gevoels-matig* 'instinctive'
kunst 'art'   *kunst-matig* 'artificial'
recht 'law'   *recht-matig* 'legal'
wet 'law'   *wet-matig* 'regular, legal'

The same observation applies to the German equivalent of *-aardig*, the bound constituent *-artig*, where the constituent *Art* 'character' is probably no longer recognized, and -*mäßig*, the equivalent of -*matig*, where the meaning of *Maß* 'measure' is not relevant anymore:

(37) *bös-artig* 'bad-natured'
gut-artig 'good-natured'
groß-artig 'great'
gefühls-mäßig 'instinctive'
recht-mäßig 'legal'
gesetz-mäßig 'regular, legal'

The complex Dutch noun *gang-er* 'goer' is a bound word, only to be used as constituent of compounds, such as:

(38) *bedevaart-gang-er* 'pilgrimage-go-er'
kerk-gang-er 'church-go-er'
Mekka-gang-er 'Mekka-go-er'

The word *ganger* cannot be used in isolation. According to the *Woordenboek der Nederlandsche Taal*, it used to be a word of Dutch that could be used as a free word with the meaning 'goer', but this is no longer possible. The class of compounds with -*ganger* can easily be extended, as the following examples illustrate. In the modifier slot geographical names can be inserted, but also other nouns that denote a destination:

(39) *Amsterdam-gang-er* 'Amsterdam-go-er'
Berlijn-gang-er 'Berlin-go-er'
Heiloo-gang-er 'Heiloo-go-er'
Parijs-gang-er 'Paris-go-er'
congres-gang-er 'conference-go-er'
museum-gang-er 'museum-go-er'
zee-gang-er 'sea-go-er'

Hence, the following constructional idiom must be assumed for Dutch:

(40) <[N_i [gang-er]$_{Nj}$]$_{Nk}$ ↔ [goer$_j$ to SEM$_i$]$_k$>

Note that unlike English *goer*, the constituent *ganger* is not derived from the present-day verbal stem *ga* 'go'. The noun *gang* 'going' does exist, but *gang* in *ganger* is an old infinitive. So even though the suffix -*er* may be recognized as these words are agent nouns, there is no motivation for a category label for *gang*. Hence, *ganger* is only formally complex, still formally being recognizable as an agent noun.

4.2 Allomorphy

Constructional idioms for subsets of compounds enable us to express specific properties of words when embedded in compounds which are not restricted to one lexicalized compound, and can be used to coin new compounds. This special property can also be a phonological property: compounds may require a particular allomorph of a word used as compound constituent.

As observed in Booij (2010b: Chapter 3), the Dutch noun *eer* 'honour' has an allomorph *ere*. The short form is the effect of a historical process of schwa apocope. The long form is still used in fixed expressions such as *Ere wie ere toekomt* 'Honour to whom deserves honour', and in old religious songs. Both the short and the long form occur in the modifier slot of NN compounds:

(41) a. *eer-betoon* 'honour-show, mark of honour'
eer-bewijs 'honour-proof, mark of honour'
eer gevoel 'honour-sense, sense of honour'

b. *ere-divisie* 'honour-division, premier league'
ere-dienst 'honour-service, religious service'
ere-boog 'honour-arch, triumphal arch'

However, it is only the long form that is used if it carries the meaning 'honorary', and that can be used for coining new compounds with the meaning 'honorary x'. In that sense, the noun *ere* has become a prefixoid, and this meaning of the allomorph *ere* has to be specified in a constructional idiom:

(42) *ere-lid* / *eer-lid 'honour-member, honorary member'
ere-voorzitter / *eer-voorzitter 'honour-president, honorary president'

The rise of this constructional idiom is another example of how the word formation possibilities of Dutch are extended, through the availability of a special bound morpheme for the expression of the notion 'honorary'.

4.3 Phrases as bound constituents of compounds

The use of linguistic constructs with an idiosyncratic meaning when embedded in compounds is not restricted to the mono-morphemic constituents discussed in section 4.1. Phrases can be used in the same way. An example of the compound-bound use of a phrase is *huis-tuin-en-keuken* 'house-garden-and-kitchen' with the meaning 'run of the mill, ordinary', as in:

(43) *huis-tuin-en-keuken-adverteerders* 'ordinary advertisers'
huis-tuin-en-keuken-onderwerpen 'ordinary topics'
huis-tuin-en-keuken-chirurgie 'ordinary surgery'
huis-tuin-en-keuken-tandarts 'ordinary dentist'
huis-tuin-en-keuken-ongevallen 'ordinary accidents'
huis-tuin-en-keuken-klussen 'ordinary chores'

The use of this phrase as the modifier constituent of compounds is extremely productive. In fact, the English gloss, the phrase *run of the mill*, exhibits the same behaviour. Originally it meant to refer to products that come directly from the mill in an ungraded state, and may contain imperfections. Its use has been extended, and this NP functions as a modifier with the meaning 'ordinary'. In German, the phrasal word constituent *(Feld,)Wald-und-Wiesen* is used for this purpose.

This way of using phrases can be accounted for by making use of constructional idioms. The phrase *huis-tuin-en-keuken* defines an extensive word family of compounds, and this pattern can be extended easily. In this case, the term *affixoid* would not be adequate for the simple reason that this constituent is complex, and even phrasal in nature.

5 Conclusions

The expressive power of the word formation system of Dutch, in particular its compounding system, is enhanced continuously through the emergence of new constructional idioms. These are subschemas for compounding that are partially lexically fixed, with specific semantic properties. These constructional idioms enable the language user to encode a larger variety of meanings by means of compounds. In addition, they are the source of new affixes, as illustrated by the German prefix *Haupt-*.

These phenomena lend support to a conception of the lexicon as defended in Construction Morphology: a hierarchical lexicon with different layers of abstraction at which the word formation possibilities of a language are specified. This model of the lexicon provides an adequate framework for representing affixoids and other cases of bound meanings for words and phrases, and bound allomorphy for words, embedded in compounds. In sum, subschemas in a hierarchical lexicon provide a structural interpretation of affixoids that makes a special theoretical status of affixoids unnecessary.

References

Abbot-Smith, Kisten and Michael Tomasello. 2006. Exemplar-learning and schematization in a usage-based account of syntactic acquisition. *The Linguistic Review* 23: 275–290.

Arcodia, Giorgio F. 2011. A *Construction Morphology* account of derivation in Mandarin Chinese. *Morphology* 21: 89–130.

Ascoop, Kristin and Torsten Leuschner. 2006. Affixoidhungrig? Skitbra! Comparing affixoids in Swedish and German. *Sprachtypologie und Universalienforschung* 59: 241–252.

Baayen, R. Harald. 2009. Corpus linguistics in morphology: Morphological productivity. In: Anke Lüdeling and Merja Kytö (eds.), *Corpus Linguistics. An International Handbook*, 900–17. Berlin/New York: Mouton de Gruyter.

Barðdal, Jóhanna. 2008. *Productivity. Evidence from Case and Argument Structure in Icelandic.* Amsterdam/Philadelphia: John Benjamins.

Booij, Geert. 2005. Compounding and derivation: Evidence for Construction Morphology. In: Wolfgang U. Dressler, Dieter Kastovsky, Oskar E. Pfeiffer, and Franz Rainer (eds.), *Morphology and its Demarcations*, 109–32. Amsterdam Philadelphia: John Benjamins.

Booij, Geert. 2010a. Compound construction: Schemas or analogy? A Construction Morphology perspective. In: Sergio Scalise and Irene Vogel (eds.), *Cross-disciplinary Issues in Compounding*, 93–108. Amsterdam/Philadelphia: John Benjamins.

Booij, Geert. 2010b. *Construction Morphology.* Oxford: Oxford University Press.

Decroos, Nancy and Torsten Leuschner. 2008. Wortbildung zwischen System und Norm: Affixoiden im Deutschen und im Niederländischen. *Sprachwissenschaft* 33: 1–34.

Elsen, Hilke. 2009. Affixoide: Nur was benannt wird, kann auch verstanden werden. *Deutsche Sprache* 4: 316–33.

Forche, Christian R. 2011. The über-phenomenon. Überlegungen zur Entlehnung von über- ins Englische. M.A. Paper. Program Sprachen Europas, Freie Universität Berlin.

Goethem, Kristel van. 2008. *Oud-leerling* versus *ancien élève*. A comparative study of adjectives grammaticalizing into prefixes in Dutch and French. *Morphology* 18: 27–49.

Goethem, Kristel van. 2010. The French construction *nouveau* + past participle revisited: Arguments in favour of a prefixoid analysis of *nouveau*. *Folia Linguistica* 44: 163–78.

Heine, Bernd and Tania Kuteva. 2006. *The Changing Languages of Europe.* Oxford: Oxford University Press.

Hoeksema, Jack. 2012. Elative compounds in Dutch: Properties and developments. In: Guido Oebel (ed.), *Intensivierungskonzepte bei Adjektiven und Adverbien im Sprachvergleich / Cross-linguistic Comparison of Intensified Adjectives and Adverbs*, 97–142. Hamburg: Verlag dr. Kovač.

Hoekstra, Jarich. 1998. *Fryske Wurdfoarming* [Frisian wordformation]. Louwert: Fryske Akademy.

Hüning, Matthias. 2009. Semantic niches and analogy in word formation. *Languages in Contrast* 9: 183–201.

Hüning, Matthias. 2010a. Productiviteit in taal en taalgebruik. Overwegingen vanuit een diachroon perspectief [Productivity in language and language use. Considerations from a diachronic perspective]. *Voortgang. Jaarboek voor de Neerlandistiek* 28: 51–69.
Hüning, Matthias. 2010b. Wortbildung im niederländisch-deutschen Sprachvergleich. In: L. Gunkel and G. Zifonun (eds.), *Deutsch im Sprachvergleich. Grammatische Kontraste und Konvergenzen*, 161–186. Berlin/New York: de Gruyter.
Hüning, Matthias and Barbara Schlücker. 2010. Konvergenz und Divergenz in der Wortbildung – Komposition im Niederländischen und im Deutschen. In: Antje Dammel, Sebastian Kürschner, and Damaris Nübling (eds.), *Kontrastive Germanistische Linguistik*, 783–825. Hildesheim etc.: Georg Olms Verlag.
Jackendoff, Ray. 2002. *Foundations of Language*. Oxford: Oxford University Press.
Joeres, Rolf. 1995. *Wortbildungen mit -macher im Althochdeutschen, Mittelhochdeutschen und Neuhochdeutschen*. Heidelberg: Universitätsverlag C. Winter.
Karsdorp, Folgert and Matthias Hüning. 2012. De relatie tussen schema's en analogische verbindingen [The relation between schemas and analogical combinations]. *Nederlandse Taalkunde* 17: 261–67.
Leuschner, Torsten. 2010. Ausnahmepianist fettgeschreckt – inbleich! Deutsche, niederländische und schwedische präfixoide im Spanningsfeld von Genealogie, Kreativität und Norm. In: Antje Dammel, Sebastian Kürschner, and Damaris Nübling (eds.), *Kontrastive Germanische Linguistik*, 863–892. Hildesheim etc: Georg Olms Verlag.
Meesters, Gert. 2004. *Marginale Morfologie in het Nederlands. Paradigmatische Samenstellingen, Neo-klassieke Composita en Splintercomposita* [Marginal morphology in Dutch. Pradigmatic compounds, neo-classical compounds and splinter compounds]. Gent: Koninklijke Academie voor Nederlandse Taal- en Letterkunde.
Namiki, Takayasu. 2010. Morphological variation in Japanese compounds: The case of *hoodai* and the notion of "compound-specific meaning". *Lingua* 120: 2367–2387.
Norde, Muriel. 2009. *Degrammaticalization*. Oxford: Oxford University Press.
Ralli, Angela, Geert Booij, Sergio Scalise, and Athanasios Karasimos (eds.). 2008 *Morphology and Dialectology. On-line Proceedings of the Sixth Mediterranean Morphology Meeting (MMM 6), Ithaca, 27–30 September 2007*. Patras: University of Patras.
Renouf, Antoinette. 2007. Tracing lexical productivity and creativity in the British media. In: J. Munat (ed.), *Lexical Creativity, Texts and Contexts*, 61–88. Amsterdam/Philadelphia: John Benjamins.
Santen, Ariane van. 2010. Betekenis: de sturende kracht van woordvorming [Meaning: the steering power of word formation]. *Voortgang. Jaarboek voor de Neerlandistiek* 28.7–27.
Schlücker, Barbara and Ingo Plag. 2011. Compound or phrase? Analogy in naming. *Lingua* 121: 1539–1551.
Schmidt, Günter Dietrich. 1987. Das Affixoid. Zur Notwendigkeit und Brauchbarkeit eines beliebten Zwischenbegriffs der Wortbildung. In: Rainer Wimmer and Gisela Zifonun (eds.), *Deutsche Lehnwortbildung: Beiträge zur Erforschung der Wortbildung mit entlehnten WB-Einheiten im Deutschen*, 53–101. Tübingen: Narr.
Schreuder, Rob and R. Harald Baayen. 1997. How complex simplex words can be. *Journal of Memory and Language* 37: 118–139.
Sijs, Nicoline van der. 1996. *Leenwoordenboek. De Invloed van Andere Talen op het Nederlands* [Book of loans. The influence of other languages on Dutch]. The Hague: SDU Uitgeverij.
Stevens, Christopher. M. 2000. The derivational suffixes and suffixoids of Old Saxon: A panchronic approach to a linguistic category. *American Journal of Germanic Linguistics and Literatures* 12: 53–79.

Stevens, Christopher M. 2005. Revisiting the affixoid debate. On the grammaticalization of the word. In: Torsten Leuschner, Tanja Mortelmans, and Sarah de Groodt (eds.), *Grammatikalisierung im Deutschen*, 71–83. Berlin/New York: de Gruyter.
Wills, Wolfram. 1986. *Wortbildungstendenzen in der deutschen Gegenwartssprache*. Tübingen: Gunter Narr.
Zifonun, Gisela. 2012. Komposition (oder Halbaffigierung) zum Ausdruck von Nominalaspect: *Schmuckstück, Glücksfall* und *Zuckerwerk*. In: Livio Gaeta and Barbara Schlücker (eds.), *Das Deutsche als kompositionsfreudige Sprache. Strukturelle Eigenschaften und systembezogene Aspekte*, 101–34. Berlin/New York: de Gruyter.

Alan K. Scott
5 The survival and use of case morphology in Modern Dutch

1 Introduction[1]

1.1 The purpose of this research

The aim of this chapter is to explore the usefulness of a Construction Grammar approach in accounting for morphosyntactic phenomena which are not the unmarked, default variant in any given situation. Such phenomena, despite their marginality, may nonetheless be *regular* in the sense defined by Barðdal (2008: 30) as "[t]he application of a morphological pattern to create new word forms of already existing words" (with reference to morphology) and "[t]he application of a syntactic process to create new instances of already existing syntactic patterns" (with reference to syntax). The chapter focuses on one regular but marginal construction in modern standard Dutch; it is exemplified in (1), in which the relevant parts are in boldface.

(1) a. *een nieuw hoofdstuk* in **de geschiedenis der** **verkeerstechnologie**
    a   new   chapter   in the history   the.GEN traffic-technology
    'a new chapter in the history of traffic technology'
    (*INL 27 Mil.*, March 1994)

  b. *Neem de maat* van **de breedte der** **plastic zakken**.
    take the measurement of the width   the.GEN plastic bags
    'Measure the width of the plastic bags.' (*INL 27 Mil.*, October 1994)

This construction, in which the genitive definite article *der* connects two noun phrases, is one of several in modern Dutch which developed from the now defunct genitive case. Some constructions, such as possessive -*s* (2a) and the partitive construction (2b), preserve the former genitive ending -*s* which is now used as an invariant marker (see Booij 2010: 211–231).

---

[1] I thank audience members at the *Construction Grammar of Dutch* workshop in Leiden and the *Interfaces in Language III* conference in Canterbury for their useful feedback and suggestions. The work here builds both on the paper presented in Leiden and on Scott (2014: Chapter 5). The data and examples presented here overlap to a degree with those in Scott (2014); however, the analysis presented here has a different focus. This research was carried out as part of a Leverhulme Early Career Research Fellowship.

(2) a. *Albertiens   hart*
        Albertien.POSS   heart
        'Albertien's heart' (*Eindhoven*, novels and short stories, 21549)

        uw   vaders   handen
        your   father.POSS   hands
        'your father's hands' (*Eindhoven*, news magazines, 7846)

   b.   *iets   heel   lastigs*
        something   very   difficult.PART
        'something very difficult' (from Booij 2010: 226)

In contrast, the genitive fragment studied here – referred to here both as the *adnominal genitive construction* and, on account of its structure, as *x der y* – maintains an agreement relationship between the determiner *der* and the noun in *y*; this agreement seems to resemble the relationship that would have held when the case system was intact (for more justification on this, see Scott 2011, 2012a).

Within a Construction Grammar framework, and on the basis of general usage-based principles, this chapter addresses the manner of the preservation of the adnominal genitive construction, and the structural and pragmatic aspects of its present-day use. Having sketched out the diachronic development of case morphology in Dutch, this chapter addresses the synchronic structural characteristics of the adnominal genitive construction in modern Dutch. Then, on the basis of 16th–19th century corpus data, a usage-based explanation is proposed for how the *x der y* construction was able to survive while morphological case marking was otherwise lost from Dutch. The focus then shifts to the present-day language: first, a structural explanation within Construction Grammar is posited to account for the productivity of the *x der y* construction, then the pragmatic meaning of the construction, and the consequences of using it in various registers, are considered.

1.2 A usage-based approach

The research presented here takes a usage-based approach to the study of grammar, assuming that knowledge of language is informed and shaped by experience of language, and that language users' relationship with their language follows general cognitive principles; through exposure to repetition, language users identify abstract structures which they use as the basis for their own language use (see, e.g., Langacker 2000; Bybee 2006a, 2006b, 2010). These recurring abstract structures, or *constructions* (or *schemata*), become entrenched through familiarity (Langacker 2000: 3): they combine information on form (i.e. structure) and meaning (including pragmatic information) (Rumelhart 1980: 34; Goldberg 2009: 94; Bybee 2010: 76). Construction Grammar, the view that grammar consists of constructions and is informed by an individual's experience of his or her language, is one usage-based approach. In Construction Grammar, syntax and morphology are accounted for by the same principles, differing only in relative complexity (Goldberg 2009: 95). The aspects of a usage-based, constructional approach most relevant to the phenomenon under discussion are returned to throughout section 3.

1.3 Data

The analysis presented in this paper is based on usage data from historical and modern corpora (summarised in Table 1) and from attestations from broadcast media and the web.

Table 1: The corpora used in this investigation (arranged chronologically by start date)

Corpus	Written or spoken	Contents	Total tokens	Period
Early Modern Dutch Corpus (EMDC)	written	diaries, drama, prose (fiction, academic, non-academic)	c. 300,000	16th–19th century
Eindhoven	written (83.3%), spoken (16.7%)	journalism, popular science, fiction, speech	c. 720,000	1960–1973
Corpus Gesproken Nederlands (CGN)	spoken	conversations, broadcasts, lectures, speeches; read-aloud texts	c. 9 million	1991–2003
INL 27 Miljoen Woorden Krantencorpus (INL 27 Mil.)	written	journalism (*NRC Handelsblad*)	c. 27 million	1994–1995

The *Early Modern Dutch Corpus* (*EMDC*) was compiled especially for the project of which the research reported here forms a part. The aim was to produce a balanced corpus of written language use covering a variety of text types, from relatively informal egodocuments to formal academic prose. To this end, a corpus was compiled from texts held by the online *Digitale Bibliotheek voor de Nederlandse Letteren* (*DBNL*); the corpus contains three sub-corpora of 100,000 tokens each: the *Gouden Eeuw* 'golden age' (16th and 17th centuries combined, following the distinction made in the *DBNL*), the 18th century and the 19th century. Each of these sub-corpora consists of five genre-defined sub-corpora of 20,000 tokens each: diaries, drama, fictional prose, academic prose and non-academic prose. The genres and registers covered were chosen so as to exploit the various text types covered within the *DBNL* as far as possible.

The orthography of the corpus examples, both historical and modern, is reproduced unaltered throughout this chapter.

2 Case morphology in Dutch

At the start of its existence as a language in its own right, Dutch had a morphological case-marking system comprising nominative, genitive, dative and accusative cases (although this system was in decline and syncretic to some degree, as noted by van der Horst 2008: 145),[2] and a three-way gender distinction (masculine, feminine and neuter). Case and gender agreement within the noun phrase was marked on the determiner, any adjectives, and on some nouns (particularly masculine and neuter singulars in the genitive). This is exemplified in (3).

(3) *de aller bloeyenste Eeuwe des*
the all blossoming.SUPER century the.GEN.NEUT.SG
Roomschen Rijckx
Roman.GEN.NEUT.SG empire.GEN.NEUT.SG
'the most blossoming century of the Roman Empire' (*EMDC*, 16th–17th century, Academic)

Deflection caused the loss of morphological case marking from spoken Dutch during the Middle Dutch period, and the weakening and eventual loss of the masculine-feminine nominal gender distinction in northern Dutch, which is attested from the 16th century onwards (van der Horst 2008: 803), by the early modern period. Both morphological case marking and the masculine-feminine distinction remained in the written language until the early 20th century as part of the norm of the standardised written code. The manifestations of deflection most relevant to the adnominal use of the genitive case were the competition from the *van*-construction (4), whose suppression of the adnominal genitive gained strength throughout the Middle Dutch period (Weerman and de Wit 1999:

---

[2] Van der Horst's exact description is of "vier min of meer te onderscheiden naamvallen" ["four more or less distinguishable cases"] (2008: 145).

1158), and the exaptation of the possessive -s construction (5) from the originally masculine and neuter singular genitive suffix -s which, in its new role, could also be attached to feminine nouns and was only marked once in the noun phrase, meaning that a determiner in the noun phrase would remain uninflected (see, e.g., Booij 2010: 216–222). The construction exemplified in (4) is now the default means of connecting two noun phrases in a possessive or partitive relationship, rather than two adjacent noun phrases (one of which is morphologically marked as genitive), which is possible in a language with morphological case marking (see, e.g., Weerman 1997: 437).

(4) eene   vande   nieuwe   predicanten
    one   of-the   new   ministers
    'one of the new ministers' (*EMDC*, 16th–17th century, Diaries)

(5) voor-by de   Bruydts   huys   quam   ryden
    past   the.Ø   bride.POSS   house   came   ride
    'came riding past the bride's house' (*EMDC*, 16th–17th century, Fictional Prose)[3]

From the 16th century onwards, starting with the first true grammar of Dutch, *Twe-spraack* (1584), grammarians customarily included a morphological case system – sometimes with six cases after the Latin model (e.g. *Twe-spraack* 1584; van Heule [1625/1626] 1953), or with four cases (e.g. Bilderdijk 1826; Weiland 1805) – and the three-way gender distinction in their norm; indeed, knowledge of the latter was a necessity for accurate use of the former (van der Wal and van Bree 2008: 241–244, 294–296). Over time, a number of the grammarians started to take usage into account; for instance, by noting – and, often, prescribing – the register-based division of labour between synthetic case marking in formal language and analytic alternatives in less formal language (e.g. ten Kate 1723: 334–340; Weiland 1805: 76). By the 19th century there was a discrepancy between spoken language and the old fashioned written language (Willemyns 2003: 110). Morphological case marking was long gone from speech (e.g. Muller 1891: 201–202); as a written phenomenon, it had become an orthographical matter (van der Horst and van der Horst 1999: 311) and was finally lost from the written language as a result of spelling reforms in the first half of the 20th century.

---

3 Notice that, since the gender of *huis* 'house' is neuter, this example does not involve a compound whose constituents are written apart; for this to be the case, the example would have to read *het Bruydts huis* 'the bride-house, i.e. ?bridal house'. The determiner *de* in (3) clearly refers to *Bruydt* and not to *huis*.

3 The adnominal genitive

This section deals with structural aspects of the adnominal genitive fragment, which is introduced in 3.1. An explanation for the preservation of the fragment is proposed in 3.2, and a theoretical account of the construction in modern Dutch is suggested in 3.3.

3.1 The *x der y* fragment

In modern Dutch the default construction for connecting two noun phrases in a broadly possessive or partitive relationship is a periphrastic construction involving a prepositional phrase, namely the *van*-construction (6).

(6) de pioniersdagen van de nederlandse televisie
 the pioneer-days of the Dutch television
 'the early days of Dutch television' (*Eindhoven*, daily newspapers, 109)

As was noted in section 2, given the lack of morphological case marking, only the structure NP PP is possible;[4] the structure NP NP, in which one of the noun phrases is genitive-marked, is no longer possible (Weerman 1997: 437). Nevertheless, as exemplified in (1) and (8), modern Dutch retains an NP NP construction in which the second noun phrase is genitive-marked, which performs the same role as the default *van*-construction, namely connecting the two noun phrases in a possessive or partitive relationship. The present-day use of the adnominal genitive construction, along with that of other surviving genitive remnants, is portrayed in detail in Scott (2011). The most important points are reprised in this section as a basis to the analysis that follows in the rest of the chapter.

In the *x der y* construction, the noun phrase *y* is the complement of – and, often, denotes the possessor of – the noun phrase *x*. The matter of whether *der* should be considered a fixed element which simply binds *x* and *y*, or whether it is more closely linked to *y*, is considered later in this section. The element *der* was originally the genitive case definite article for singular feminine nouns and

---

[4] An exception to this, pointed out by one of the reviewers, is the partitive construction, e.g. *een glas wijn* 'a glass wine, i.e. a glass of wine', which does have the structure NP NP, i.e. [een glas] [wijn]. In earlier periods of Dutch, the right-hand noun phrase was genitive-marked, e.g. *een glas wyns* 'a glass wine.GEN, i.e. a glass of wine' and *den laesten droppel bloets* 'the last drop blood.GEN, i.e. the last drop of blood' (both examples: *EMDC*, 16th–17th century).

plural nouns of all genders. Following the complete loss of morphological case marking from Dutch – that is, from speech and, centuries later, writing – the element *der* is now exclusive to the adnominal genitive construction and to fixed phrases and names formed when the genitive was still part of an active case system (even if only in the written language). Two examples of the latter are given in (7). In short, as far as the production of novel phrases is concerned, *der* is not used outside the *x der y* construction.

(7) a. phrase:
    in   de   loop   der   jaren
    in   the course the.GEN years
    'over the years'

   b. name:
    Nationale Maatschappij der   Belgische Spoorwegen
    national   company   the.GEN Belgian   railways
    'Belgian National Railway Company'

It is contended here (as in Scott 2011, 2012a) that, despite its limited use compared to the *van*-construction, the adnominal genitive construction is productive. It fits the definitions of regularity or *regular performance* in the sense given by Barðdal (2008: 30) and noted in 1.1 above. The use of *x der y* to produce novel phrases is the focus of this paper; lexicalised phrases such as those in (7) are not considered further (and are not included in the calculations made on the basis of the corpus data), although their likely role in maintaining the preservation of the familiarity of the *x der y* structure is acknowledged.

A study of the use of the *x der y* fragment in modern Dutch using data from the modern corpora listed in Table 1 identified two trends in the nature of the nouns that occur in position *y*: most nouns occurring in *y* are plural (Table 2) and, among the singular nouns, most are derivatives (Table 3) (Scott 2011); an example of the former is given in (8a) and an example of the latter is given in (8b). Each singular derived noun that occurs in *y* ends in a suffix that was formerly associated with feminine gender.

(8) a. de   leider   der   Democraten
     the   leader the.GEN democrats
     'the leader of the democrats' (*INL 27 Mil.*, April 1994)

   b. de   bronnen der   weldadigheid
     the sources the.GEN charity
     'the sources of charity' (*Eindhoven*, popular science, 36149)

Table 2: The relative occurrence of singular and plural nouns in all attestations of *x der y* in the corpora (in tokens and as a proportion of the total) (adapted from Scott 2011: 113)

Singular noun	Plural noun
617	1441
30.0%	70.0%

Table 3: The relative occurrence of simplex and derived nouns among the *x der y* examples in which *y* is singular (in tokens and as a proportion of the total) (adapted from Scott 2011: 114)

Simplex noun	Derived noun
170	447
27.6%	72.4%

The dominance of plural nouns in *y* is not an epiphenomenon of a dominance of plural nouns in the language as a whole: the *Eindhoven* corpus, in which nouns are tagged as singular or plural, contains 93,620 singular nouns (74.1%) and 32,688 plural nouns (25.9%) (Scott 2012a: 90). Morphologically simplex nouns – i.e. those lacking a (synchronically) transparent morphological structure, whether inflectional or derivational – are rare in the data studied, accounting for just 170 (8.3%) of the 2058 tokens of *x der y*. It is assumed that this does not reflect a general rarity of simplex nouns in the language as a whole.

The noun heading *y* appears most frequently unmodified, as in (1), (7a) and (8). The noun may, however, be modified by one or more adjectives (7b, 9a), or an even more complex phrase (9b,c). The option to increase the complexity of *y* is accounted for in the formalisation in 3.3.3.

(9) a. *de arm der wrekende gerechtigheid*
 the arm the.GEN avenging justice
 'the arm of avenging justice' (*INL 27 Mil.*, April 1995)

 b. *die der inmiddels sterk geromaniseerde kelten*
 those the.GEN meanwhile strongly romanised Celts
 'those of the meanwhile strongly Romanised Celts' (*Eindhoven*, popular science, 35100)

c. *de huidige omstandigheden der tijdens de Tweede*
   the current circumstances the.GEN during the second
   Wereldoorlog door de Japanse (militaire) autoriteiten
   world-war through the Japanese (military) authorities
   tot prostitutie gedwongen vrouwen
   to prostitution forced women
   'the current circumstances of the women who were forced to prostitution by the Japanese (military) authorities during the Second World War' (*INL 27 Mil.*, Sept. 1994)

3.2 The preservation of *x der y*

The question of how the adnominal genitive fragment *x der y* was able to survive while genitive morphology (and case morphology in general) was lost from Dutch is addressed here. I argue that it was not only prescription, but also usage and repetition that preserved *x der y*.

In previous work (Scott 2011: 130, 2012a: 97) it was hypothesised – in the absence of quantified historical data – that speakers' familiarity with *x der y* led to its reanalysis as a means of connecting two noun phrases even as their familiarity with case morphology declined. In this section, on the basis of usage data from a balanced corpus of written 16th–19th century Dutch from various genres, it is posited that *x der y* survived due to the *conserving effect* (see Bybee 2006a: 10) resulting from its high token frequency. In particular, I argue that the general cognitive process of *chunking* – in which one memorised unit, a *chunk*, is combined with other chunks to form greater or more complex chunks (e.g. Bybee 2010: 34–37) – led to the identification of *x der y* as a pairing of function and form (i.e. as a construction) and, within this construction, to the forming of associations between the construction and nouns ending in particular suffixes. This type of chunking denotes a chunk whose constituents are not adjacent; it is therefore referred to here as *discontinuous chunking*. Bybee (2010: 36), discussing interruption by whole words or phrases (as in the English *drives X mad* construction) notes that "chunks do not have to be continuous – they can be interrupted by open classes of items"; the discontinuous chunks described here, in contrast, are interrupted by the base of a derived singular noun.

Originally, two constituent orders were possible with the adnominal genitive, prenominal (10a) and postnominal (10b):

(10) a. prenominal:
   *En pas **der** woorden klank verstaen.*
   and just the.GEN words sound understand.
   'And just understand the sound of the words.'
   (*EMDC*, 18th century, drama)

b. postnominal:
   ende   vande   ongheoorsaemheijt   der   onderzaten   tot
   and   of-the   disobendience   the.GEN   subjects   to

Andtweerpen   ende   te   *Doornicke*
Antwerp   and   to   Doornik
'and of the disobedience of the subjects in Antwerp and in Doornik [Tournai]' (*EMDC*, 16th–17th century, diaries)

Overall, postnominal order had a much higher token frequency than prenominal order in 16th–19th century Dutch (Table 4); thus, the structure *x DET y* was more familiar than *DET y x*. In the data, the 21 16th–17th century tokens of prenominal genitives with a feminine noun exclusively involved a masculine/neuter singular determiner (usually *des* or *'s*) (11a), which is also true of one of the two 18th century prenominal feminine singulars; the four 19th century examples all involved the noun *majesteit* 'majesty', which is feminine but refers in context to a male monarch (11b). This, combined with the paucity of prenominal examples with a plural noun, underlines the rarity of the determiner *der* in prenominal genitives and its attendant association with postnominal order.

(11) a.   aen   **des**   ***Compagnies***   *sijde*
           on   the.GEN   company.GEN   side
           'at the company's side' (*EMDC*, 16th–17th century, non-academic prose)

     b.   met   **uwer**   ***Majesteits***   *verlof*
           with   you.GEN   majesty.GEN   permission
           'with your majesty's permission' (*EMDC*, 19th century, drama)

Table 4: Pre- and postnominal genitives in the three equal-sized sub-corpora of the Early Modern Dutch Corpus (in tokens and, in italics, as a proportion of the total pre- and postnominal genitive tokens for each gender and number in each period)[5]

Period	Masculine		Feminine		Neuter		Plural	
	pre-	post-	pre-	post-	pre-	post-	pre-	post-
16th–17th century	77	75	21	116	9	76	16	190
	50.7%	*49.3%*	*15.3%*	*84.7%*	*10.6%*	*89.4%*	*7.8%*	*92.2%*
18th century	13	38	2	149	15	50	3	213
	25.5%	*74.5%*	*1.3%*	*98.7%*	*23.1%*	*76.9%*	*1.4%*	*98.6%*
19th century	21	33	4	239	8	29	6	296
	38.9%	*61.1%*	*1.6%*	*98.4%*	*21.6%*	*78.4%*	*2.0%*	*98.0%*

---

[5] Table 4 excludes examples in which the gender of the noun was unclear, or in which the noun had more than one gender.

Additionally, within postnominal order, in the *EMDC*, it was found that the genitive determiner *der* is by far the most frequent genitive marker in all three sub-corpora. This is shown in Table 5, which also shows that the markers used with feminine singular nouns and plural nouns of all genders generally have a higher token frequency than those which occur with singular masculine and neuter nouns. From the 16th to the 19th century, the masculine/neuter singular markers tend to decrease in use while the feminine singular/all genders plural markers tend to increase in use. The genitive structure with the consistently highest token frequency, and which therefore would have been the most familiar genitive structure, was *x der y*.

Table 5: The occurrence of genitive markers in postnominal order in the *Early Modern Dutch Corpus* (in tokens) (listed in alphabetical order by marker; excluding markers with 0 tokens in all sub-corpora)

			16th–17th century	18th century	19th century
Feminine singular & all genders plural	der	the.GEN	251	304	447
	dezer	these.GEN	15	7	10
	dier	they.GEN	2	1	12
	ener	a/one.GEN	0	6	19
	harer	her.GEN	1	3	6
	hunner	their.GEN	0	6	6
	mijner	my.GEN	1	16	18
	onzer	our.GEN	3	5	10
	uwer	your.GEN	2	0	2
	zijner	his/its.GEN	7	11	27
Masculine/neuter singular	des	the.GEN	117	70	33
	dezes	these.GEN	2	4	1
	eens	a/one.GEN	1	1	1
	haars	her.GEN	0	3	1
	huns	their.GEN	0	0	1
	mijns	my.GEN	2	0	7
	onzes	our.GEN	5	3	1
	uws	your.GEN	0	1	3
	zijns	his/its.GEN	5	0	4

In addition to having the highest token frequency of any genitive determiner, *der*, which could be used with any plural noun as well as with feminine singular nouns, also had a particularly high type frequency.

The unit-like nature of *x der y*, in addition to its high token and type frequencies, must also have been conducive to its preservation. (Note that while *x des y-s* and *des y-s x* were also unit-like, they lacked the frequency and flexibility of *x der y*.) Whereas, as deflection took hold, case endings on individual lexemes within the noun phrase became increasingly unfamiliar to language users and constituent order became the principal means of marking syntactic roles, the adnominal genitive structure (whose prime exponent was *x der y*) remained a coherent unit into which two noun phrases could be placed at either side of the element binding them together. Familiarity through high token frequency led to the chunking of *x der y*, whose entrenchment was straightforward as it was both self-contained and highly familiar. Having become entrenched as a means of connecting two noun phrases, it remained in use and outlived the case system of which it had once been a part. Thus, the conserving effect of its high token frequency (and high type frequency), along with its unit-like nature, led to the survival of *x der y*.

One matter that is harder to explain on the basis of the diachronic usage data is the predominance in position *y* in modern Dutch of plural nouns and singular nouns ending in a suffix that was previously associated with feminine gender. It would be expected that, over time, these nouns became ever more frequent in position *y* at the expense of other types of noun. The relative proportion of plural nouns in position *y* actually fell in 16th–19th century Dutch (Table 6), while, amongst the singular nouns, the relative proportion of derived feminine nouns in position *y* also decreased over time (Table 7).

Table 6: The occurrence of singular and plural nouns in the *x der y* structure in 16th–19th century Dutch

	Singular	Plural
16th–17th century	90 35.9%	161 64.1%
18th century	122 40.1%	182 59.9%
19th century	213 47.5%	235 52.5%

Table 7: The occurrence of simplex and derived feminine singular nouns in the *x der y* structure in 16th–19th century Dutch (excluding ungrammatical examples)

	Simplex	Derived feminine
16th–17th century	45 50.0%	45 50.0%
18th century	58 47.5%	64 52.5%
19th century	129 60.6%	84 39.4%

These developments seem to disprove the hypothesis that token frequency caused plural and derived feminine singular nouns to become associated with the *x der y* structure. However, the figures presented in Tables 6 and 7 are more likely to indicate language users' increasing familiarity with case morphology and the lexical gender of nouns. This can be observed particularly in the 18th and 19th centuries as a result of increasing awareness of the prescribed norm for written language (Scott 2012b; for instance, the accuracy of use of case morphology actually increased over time, even as the system weakened in the spoken language). Certainly, the increased occurrence of simplex nouns from the 18th century to the 19th corresponds to other evidence of an increasing awareness of certain aspects of case and gender morphology from the 18th to the 19th century (Scott 2012b). Language users would accordingly have known which nouns to treat as feminine (and therefore use with the determiner *der*); this applied not only to derived nouns, which were recognisable as feminine on account of their suffix, but also simplex nouns whose feminine gender had been learnt. Following the loss of the masculine/feminine distinction as part of the early 20th century spelling reforms, the knowledge of which simplex nouns were feminine and could therefore be combined with *der* was also lost (perhaps with the exception of certain feminine simplex nouns that had frequently occurred in *x der y*).

Language users' knowledge of which complex nouns could appear in the *x der y* construction was preserved through familiarity and, as far as singular nouns are concerned, through discontinuous chunking. The *y* slot became associated with plural nouns and this connection remained beyond the end of the case system; thus, *[der [plural noun]]* became a chunk within *x der y*. As language users became increasingly unfamiliar with which nouns were lexically feminine, they could no longer use simplex nouns in position *y*. Formerly feminine derived nouns, on the other hand, were still used in position *y*. The reason for this appears to be their suffix. Nouns ending in (ex-)feminine derivational suffixes would have been familiar in position *y*. This would have led, via abstraction, to discontinuous chunks consisting of the determiner *der* and a suffix, separated by the base to which the suffix was attached (12). Once language users had encountered sufficient tokens of *der* with a noun ending in a certain suffix, the construction illustrated in (12), containing the determiner and the suffix (but not the base of the noun) as fixed elements, became part of their linguistic knowledge and they were able to produce their own, novel formations on this basis. Later in this paper (section 3.3.2) it is proposed that this process remains the basis of the productivity of *x der y* in present-day Dutch.

(12) [[x] [der ___suffix]]
 [[x] [der ___heid]]

 het   licht der   waarheid
 the   light the.GEN.FEM.SG/PLU   truth
 'the light of the truth' (EMDC, 18th century, academic)

When the case system was still active, nouns were inserted into *y* by analogy – "the process by which a speaker comes to use a novel item in a construction" (Bybee 2010: 57) – with already encountered formations, based on the suffix of the noun in *y*. These "*der* ___ suffix" chunks would have become self-perpetuating; originally based on examples formed as part of the original case system (or at least the codified written language case system), new formations are now possible based on other recent formations which postdate the loss of the case system; such self-perpetuation of constructions is described by Kemmer and Barlow (2000: ix) as a "feedback loop" in which "[l]anguage productions are not only products of the speaker's linguistic system, but they also provide input for other speakers' systems". More specifically, it is an instance of *abstraction*, defined by Langacker (2000: 4) as "the emergence of a structure through reinforcement of the commonality inherent in multiple experiences". Once-feminine suffixes, as well as plurality, still identified nouns as being able to be used with *der*. Following its preservation through the conserving effect, and then, after the spelling reforms which eradicated the last remnants of case morphology, it continued although its type frequency had been reduced to certain nouns identifiable through their morphological structure. (An alternative analysis that the occurrence of nouns in *y* is determined by their semantic characteristics is tested in 3.3.1.)

It is necessary to address the fact that only the *x der y* structure was preserved and not its masculine and neuter singular equivalent (and, as shown in Table 5, the second most frequently occurring genitive structure) *x des y-s*, which the above account does not explain. (Although a handful of novel formations in the data have the *x des y-s* structure, all strongly resemble fixed phrases with the structure.) Again, the answer appears to be frequency-based. Although *x des y-s* had a relatively high token frequency during the 16th–17th century (albeit lower than *x der y*), its token frequency, along with that of most masculine/neuter singular genitive markers, fell steadily from the 16th to the 19th century, while that of *x der y*, along with most feminine singular and all genders plural genitive markers, rose (see Table 5). A number of factors hindered the use of *x des y-s*. Structurally, the attachment of the suffix *-s* to the noun, while emphasising the genitive marking, increases complexity by adding inflection to a singular noun (an anomaly in modern Dutch morphosyntax); furthermore, given its present-day familiarity from lexicalised phrases (Scott 2011: 104, 116), such as *een steen* *des aanstoots* 'a stone the.GEN offence.GEN, i.e. a bone of contention' and *de dag des oordeels* 'the day the.GEN judgement.GEN, i.e. judgement day', it might also introduce an archaic character (at least for some language users) (van Haeringen 1956: 33; Scott 2011: 116). In contrast, *x der y* leaves the noun in *y* unaltered. The token frequency of *x des y-s* was less than half of that of *x der y* in the 16th/17th century; it was therefore less familiar to language users. Furthermore, compared to *x der y*, its type frequency was relatively low: although *x des y-s* could potentially have become associated – through discontinuous chunking – with derived nouns ending in masculine agent suffixes, or with the neuter conversions of verb infinitives, this appears not to have happened. While *x der y* could involve any plural noun and any noun ending in certain suffixes, as well as any other feminine noun, *x des y-s* was restricted to a far smaller group of nouns. Although a number of entrenched *x des y-s* phrases survived into modern Dutch and possibly serve as models for the handful of novel *x des y-s* formations that still appear (Scott 2011: 105), they tend to be high frequency items and may therefore not be parsed by language users (see Bybee 2006a: 95). Although the grammarians were broadly successful in preserving genitive morphology in the written language until the early 20th century, the *x des y-s* construction – and, indeed, masculine/neuter singular genitive constructions in general – stands as one example in which their efforts were less successful.

Alongside the structural, usage-based reasons for the preservation of the *x der y* fragment, it is likely that pragmatic factors also played a part. In section 4 the construction's strong association with formal written language is shown. Its preservation may well therefore be linked to the conservative nature of prestige varieties and their tendency to preserve archaising features as status markers (as argued for phonological features by, for instance, Kroch 1978).

3.3 A formal account of *x der y*

The strong association of particular types of nouns – to wit, plural nouns and singular nouns ending a derivational suffix formerly associated with feminine gender – with position *y* in the adnominal genitive construction suggests that an agreement relationship holds between *der* and the noun heading the noun phrase *y*. Thus, when formalising the construction (in 3.3.3), a binary structure of *x* and *der y* is posited. Given the relative rarity of morphologically simplex nouns in *y*, the morphological structure of the nouns that head *y* appears to be the key to their ability to appear in the construction. In this section, two hypotheses are tested to explain the agreement that takes place in the *x der y* structure: on one view, the construction involves morphological agreement, i.e. the nouns that appear in *y* are licensed to do so by their structure (3.3.2). However, given that this kind of morphological agreement died out in Dutch in the early 20th century (section 2), a synchronically more probable hypothesis is considered first (in 3.3.1), in which nouns appear in *y* on account of their semantic properties.

3.3.1 Semantic agreement in *x der y*

In the original Dutch case system, the relationship between *der* and *y* was one of gender and number agreement: the genitive determiner *der* was selected to agree with feminine singular nouns and plural nouns of any gender. However, as was noted in section 2, present-day standard Dutch no longer has a distinct feminine lexical gender, masculine and feminine having fallen together to form the "common" gender. Thus, the notion that the (ex-)feminine marker *der* is still involved in gender-based agreement today appears far-fetched.

In modern standard (Netherlandic) Dutch, pronoun assignment is often determined by the semantic characteristics of the noun to which the pronoun refers rather than the lexical gender of the noun (e.g. Audring 2006; Kraaikamp 2012). Of particular relevance to the present investigation, which deals with the continued use of a former feminine determiner (i.e. *der*), nouns denoting collective human referents, and some nouns denoting an abstract concept, may be referred to with a feminine pronoun (Audring 2006: 92). The nouns denoting these referents are often derived nouns ending in a formerly feminine suffix (13),[6] i.e. the singular nouns which occur in position *y* of the *x der y* construction.

(13) a. *Wat vreemd dat de* **overheid** *haar eigen regels niet kent*
what strange that the government her own rules not knows
'How strange that the government doesn't know its (literally: her) own rules.'
(http://www.nrc.nl/rechtenbestuur/2011/10/08/strafrecht-is-voor-de-ander-niet-voor-de-overheid-zelf/ [accessed 17.7.13])

b. *en toen de Fransen in 1672 binnenvielen sloot de*
and when the French in 1672 invaded closed the
universiteit haar *poorten*
university her gates
'and when the French invaded in 1672, the university closed its (literally: her) gates'
(http://www2.nijmegen.nl/content/84633/1923_de_katholieke_universiteit_nijmegen_wordt_opgericht [accessed 17.7.13])

---

[6] This is confirmed, for instance, by a wildcard-based search for nouns ending in particular suffixes, in the electronic dictionary van Dale (2005–2008).

Many of the singular nouns which occurred in *x der y* when the case system was intact would have denoted abstract concepts and collective human referents. The association between *der* and such nouns would have been preserved within the *x der y* construction as it became entrenched. A hypothesis to be tested is, therefore, that the placement of a noun in *y* is based on the noun's semantics; any connection to morphological structure would be, on this view, coincidental. In order to test this hypothesis, it is necessary to concentrate on the simplex nouns that occur in *y*, and the complex nouns in *y* that do not end in a "feminine" suffix. If the simplex nouns in *y* also denote abstract concepts and collective human referents, the assignment of nouns to position *y* is likely to be semantics-based. If the complex nouns that occur in *y* may also end in a "masculine" or neuter suffix, this too would suggest semantically based agreement between *der* and *y*.

In Table 8, the 170 simplex nouns occurring in position *y* in novel examples are categorised according to the semantic nature of their referent. When the semantic nature of the simplex nouns – regardless of their gender – in position *y* is considered, the hypothesis that nouns appear in *y* on the basis of their semantics is supported. The simplex nouns tend to denote abstract entities or collective human referents.

Table 8: The semantic nature of the referents of the simplex singular nouns occurring in *y*. (Examples from the *Eindhoven* corpus.)

Semantic nature	Example	Tokens
abstract inanimate	*de grondleggers der moraal* 'the founders the.GEN morality'	85
place	*het middelpunt der provinciale hoofdstad* 'the middle-point the.GEN provincial capital'	37
collective human	*de opkomst der arbeidersklasse* 'the rise the.GEN working class'	32
concrete inanimate	*de wanden der lichtbeuk* 'the walls the.GEN clerestory'	9
human (individual)	*de heiligheid der moeder* 'the holiness the.GEN mother'	5
animal	*de droeve klachten der reine duif* 'the sorrowful laments the.GEN pure dove'	2

The referents of the simplex nouns in *x der y* are only rarely concrete inanimate referents, individual humans, or animals. Thus, position *y* is associated with abstract and collective human nouns, regardless of whether or not those nouns are morphologically transparent. If derived nouns ending in non-"feminine" suffixes, but denoting abstract or collective human referents, appeared in position *y*, the semantic agreement hypothesis would be further supported. Nouns ending in *-dom*, which occurs on neuter and ex-masculine nouns, and *-schap*, which occurs on neuter and ex-feminine nouns, generally denote abstract and collective human referents and therefore could be used in position *y*. In the data, however, only one *-dom*-noun occurs in the adnominal genitive (14); otherwise, the *van*-construction is used.

(14) de   vaagheid   der   ouderdom
     the   vagueness   the.GEN.FEM.SG   parenthood
     'the vagueness of parenthood' (*INL 27 Mil.*, January 1994)

The *-schap*-nouns are particularly useful when testing whether the nouns that appear in *y* do so on the basis of morphologically based or semantically based principles. They all denote collective human or abstract referents so, under the "semantic" hypothesis, any *-schap*-noun should be able to occur in *y*. However, in the data, only the formerly feminine *-schap*-nouns occur in *y*. To test whether this is a general trend or whether it is specific to the data studied, all the neuter *-schap*-nouns which occurred in the *van*-construction in the data were searched for on the web in combination with the determiner *der*. Only isolated occurrences were found; examples are given in (15). One of the reviewers considers the examples in (15) to be errors made by a writer using a high-register construction that he/she does not master; another reviewer notes that a formation with the common/"feminine" *zwangerschap*, i.e. *x der zwangerschap*, is more acceptable than one with the neuter *moederschap*, i.e. *x der moederschap*; see also the example in (15c). The evidence here suggests that language users are aware of which *-schap*-nouns may occur in *x der y*.

(15) a. ?ter   bevordering   der   gezelschap
        to-the   encouragement   the.GEN   party
        'for the encouragement of the party'
        (http://www.waarmaarraar.nl/forum/6/ID/1819044/GO/6175/
        Rijmelarij_2_-.html [accessed 17.7.13])

   b. ?het   stokje   der   leiderschap
      the   stick.DIM   the.GEN   leadership
      'the baton of leadership'
      (http://essay.utwente.nl/57910/1/scriptie_Mars.pdf [accessed 17.7.13];
      occurs in a quotation from a book written in 1983)

c. ?*in   naam   der   moederschap*
      in   name   the.GEN   motherhood
      'in the name of motherhood'
      (http://baby-op-komst.nl/forum/topic/2535/zwangeren-maart-2009-
      deel-3.html?page=12 [accessed 17.7.13])

Accordingly, even though it would fit with modern Dutch pronoun gender assignment, the hypothesis that there is a semantically determined relationship between *der* and the noun in *y* is not wholly supported by the data. Despite the semantic patterns observed in Table 8, the dubiousness of formations such as those in (15) suggest that semantics alone cannot be the basis of the agreement between *der* and *y*; semantics can at most only be part of the explanation.[7] Therefore, a morphologically based hypothesis is tested in the following section.

3.3.2 Morphological agreement in *x der y*

In this section it is hypothesised that the nouns which occur in *y* must agree morphologically with *der*. It is suggested that this is the result of discontinuous chunking (see section 3.2), through which the genitive marker *der* became associated with particular derivational suffixes. The accessibility of the internal morphological structure of the nouns involved to the *x der y* construction, and the absence of this relationship elsewhere in modern Dutch, suggests that the agreement between *der* and the noun in *y* is an example of what Booij (2010: 211) terms *construction-dependent morphology*, in which a morphological marker, otherwise lost from a language, plays a new role within a particular construction (see also Scott 2012a: 99–101).

Originally the relation between *der* and *y* was number-based for plural nouns, and gender-based for singular nouns. Thus, a noun could appear in *y* if it was plural or if it was singular and lexically feminine. The occurrence of plural nouns in *y* appears to be a straightforward continuation of the original adnominal genitive construction; the occurrence of singular nouns in *y* in present-day Dutch is trickier to explain. The conclusion of section 3.3.1 was that a noun is placed in *y* on the basis of that noun's morphological structure, not its semantics. Furthermore, the data show the occurrence of morphologically simplex words to be relatively rare in *x der y*. It is therefore assumed here is that a noun's morphological structure is the key to its occurrence in *x der y*.

---

[7] I am grateful to the editors for encouraging me to clarify my thoughts on this matter.

As a continuation of the discontinuous chunking that led to its survival (as proposed in 3.2), the use of the adnominal genitive construction is still based on discontinuous chunks (sub-schemata), each one specifying nouns ending in a particular suffix. Accordingly, a present-day Dutch speaker, having encountered sufficient tokens of *x der y* involving nouns ending in the relevant suffixes (the input) will, on the basis of the usage-based principles summarised in 1.2, generalise those tokens to identify the various *x der y* sub-schemata; the possibility of including an adjective (termed *z* in the formalisations that follow) to modify the noun in *y* will also be noted. This is illustrated in (16) using the example of the *-heid*-sub-schema. These sub-schemata can then be used to produce novel formations; at the same time, the speaker notices that there are certain register-based restrictions which characterise the adnominal genitive construction: these are the topic of section 4.

(16) Input:

de spiraal	**der** eenzaam**heid**	'the spiral the.GEN loneliness'
de engel	**der** gerechtig**heid**	'the angel the.GEN justice'
het imago	**der** onnozel**heid**	'the image the.GEN silliness'
de grenzen	**der** redelijk**heid**	'the borders the.GEN rationality'
de wet	**der** waarschijnlijk**heid**	'the law the.GEN probability'
de zaak	**der elektrische** veilig**heid**	'the matter the.GEN electric securit
het sobere deel	**der kenbare** waar**heid**	'the sober part the.GEN known trut

(Sources, respectively: *INL 27 Mil.*, April 1995; *INL 27 Mil.*, January 1994; *INL 27 Mil.*, May 1994; *Eindhoven*, spoken, 40722; *INL 27 Mil.*, March 1994; *INL 27 Mil.*, February 1994; *INL 27 Mil.*, March 1994)

Generalisation:

[[x_{NP}] [*der* [z]$_{ADJ}$ ___*heid*$_{NP}$]] (i.e. any noun ending in *-heid* may follow *der*)

Notes: *x* is a string, i.e. a whole NP, of any complexity
an adjective *z* may be inserted between *der* and the noun[8]

The identification of structures through experience and repetition is also the basis of the sub-schema for plural nouns: once sufficient plural nouns have been encountered following *der*, the pattern is generalised to apply to any plural noun and used as the basis of further novel formations.

---

8 For now, the adjective *z* has simply been placed between *der* and the noun to indicate the possibility of its occurrence; its hierarchical position in the binary structure of the noun phrase is accounted for more precisely in (19).

The identification and entrenchment of the various sub-schemata of *x der y* through discontinuous chunking does not necessarily preclude non-discontinuous (i.e. prototypical) chunking of *der* along with certain derived nouns which occur frequently in position *y*. Although these nouns could be identified as suitable for *x der y* on account of their ending, the frequency of nouns such as *bevolking* 'population', *democratie* 'democracy', *natie* 'nation', *techniek* 'technology' and *waarheid* 'truth' in the adnominal genitive construction suggests that *der bevolking*, *der democratie*, etc., become chunked in their own right to form sub-schemata such as those in (17), in which only position *x* is free for the insertion of a noun phrase.

(17) [[x_{NP}] [der bevolking]]   '*x* the.GEN population'
      [[x_{NP}] [der waarheid]]   '*x* the.GEN truth'

This notion also explains the occurrence of simplex nouns in position *y* since, clearly, discontinuous chunking is impossible with simplex nouns. A number of (formerly feminine) simplex nouns recur in *x der y*, such as *aarde* 'earth', *eeuw* 'century', *kerk* 'church', *wereld* 'world' and *zee* 'sea'. Accordingly, chunks such as *der aarde, der kerk*, and so on, can become entrenched to form sub-schemata such as those listed in (18), in which only position *x* is open. Some sub-schemata have specific properties: the sub-schema for *eeuw* allows the placement of an ordinal number before *eeuw* to specify the century, while those for *kerk* and *zee* allow for the placement of a lexeme before the noun to specify the church or sea, respectively.

(18) [[x_{NP}] [der aarde]]   '*x* the.GEN earth'
      [[x_{NP}] [der ORD.NUM eeuw]]   '*x* the.GEN __st/nd/rd/th century'
      [[x_{NP}] [der ADJ kerk]]   '*x* the.GEN ___ church'

General usage-based principles can account for the productive use of *x der y*; the structure of morphologically complex nouns serves as the basis for their occurrence in the construction. Given the rarity of simplex nouns in position *y*, the continued use of the adnominal genitive must be primarily morphologically governed. This is the basis of the formal account of the *x der y* construction which is put forward now in section 3.3.3.

3.3.3 A formalisation of *x der y*

In the preceding sections it was contended that the adnominal genitive construction in modern Dutch is a partially filled construction with, in its canonical form, two free positions: one, *x*, can be filled by any noun phrase (based on the intention of the language user); the other free position, *y*, can contain a noun phrase headed by a noun which has certain characteristics (either it is plural, or it is singular with a particular ending, or, less frequently, it is one of a – more or less – closed group of simplex nouns which, through usage, have become associated with the *x der y* pattern).

Accordingly, the modern Dutch adnominal genitive construction can be formalised as in (19). This develops further the formalisation proposed in Scott (2012a: 100); in (19), however, the formalisations are presented in such a way as to emphasise the emergence through discontinuous chunking of the various sub-schemata. The information on the noun phrase *y* relates to the head noun; the head noun may be modified by one or more adjectives or, rarely, a more complex phrase (n = 375 in the data; i.e. 18.2% of the total *x der y* tokens).

(19) **adnominal genitive construction (*x der y*)**
'*x* is the possession of *y* (in a broad sense); *x* is part of *y*; *x* is *y*'

basic schema: $[[x]_{NP} [der [[z]_{ADJ} [y]_{NP}]_{NP}]_{NP}]_{NP}$
y is either [+plural] or is [+singular, +common gender]

sub-schemata: $[[x]_{NP} [der [[z]_{ADJ} [N_{[+PLURAL]}]_{NP}]_{NP}]_{NP}]_{NP}$
de   leden   der   volgende   verenigingen
the   members   the.GEN   following   societies
'the members of the following societies' (CGN: fv800831.4)

$[[x]_{NP} [der [[z]_{ADJ} [\_\_\_DE]_{NP}]_{NP}]_{NP}]_{NP}$
het   pad   der   liefde
the   path   the.GEN   love
'the path of love' (*INL 27 Mil.*, June 1994)

$[[x]_{NP} [der [[z]_{ADJ} [\_\_\_HEID]_{NP}]_{NP}]_{NP}]_{NP}$
de   grenzen   der   hoorbaarheid
the   borders   the.GEN   audibility
'the borders (i.e. limits) of audibility' (*Eindhoven, popular science*, 31987)

$[[x]_{NP} [der [[z]_{ADJ} [\_\_\_IE]_{NP}]_{NP}]_{NP}]_{NP}$
het   grote   genie   der   corruptie
the   great   genius   the.GEN   corruption
'the great genius of corruption' (*INL 27 Mil.*, March 1995)

$[[x]_{NP} [der [[z]_{ADJ} [\_\_\_IEK]_{NP}]_{NP}]_{NP}]_{NP}$
het   terrein   der   orthopedagogiek
the   domain   the.GEN   ortho-pedagogy

'the domain of otho-pedagogy' (*Eindhoven*, popular science, 36654)

[[x]_NP [der [[z]_ADJ [___IJ]_NP]_NP]_NP]_NP
de   verplichtingen der   rederij
the   obligations   the.GEN   shipping-company
'the obligations of the shipping company' (*Eindhoven*, popular science, 32770)

[[x]_NP [der [[z]_ADJ [___ING]_NP]_NP]_NP]_NP
47   procent   der   bevolking
47   percent   the.GEN   population
'47% of the population' (*INL 27 Mil.*, June 1994)

[[x]_NP [der [[z]_ADJ [___ITEIT]_NP]_NP]_NP]_NP
het   bloed   der   experimentele   realiteit
the   blood   the.GEN   experimental   reality
'the blood of experimental reality' (*Eindhoven*, popular science, 33305)

[[x]_NP [der [[z]_ADJ [___NIS]_NP]_NP]_NP]_NP
de   volle   lading   der   geschiedenis
the   full   load   the.GEN   history
'the full load of history' (*INL 27 Mil.*, February 1994)

[[x]_NP [der [[z]_ADJ [___SCHAP]_NP]_NP]_NP]_NP
de   ijzeren   wet   der   dronkenschap
the   iron   law   the.GEN   drunkenness
'the iron law of drunkenness' (*INL 27 Mil.*, July 1994)

[[x]_NP [der [[z]_ADJ [___ST]_NP]_NP]_NP]_NP
de   zwanezang   der   schilderkunst
the   swansong   the.GEN   painting
'the swansong of the art of painting' (*INL 27 Mil.*, October 1994)

[[x]_NP [der [[z]_ADJ [___TE]_NP]_NP]_NP]_NP
de   modern   behandeling   der   bloederziekte
the   modern   treatment   the.GEN   haemophilia
'the modern treatment of haemophilia' (*Eindhoven*, family magazines, 16093)

[[x]$_{NP}$ [der [[z]$_{ADJ}$ [___UUR]$_{NP}$]$_{NP}$]$_{NP}$]$_{NP}$
het luilekkerland   der   pulp-literatuur
the land-of-plenty the.GEN pulp-literature
'the land of plenty of pulp literature' (*INL 27 Mil.*, May 1994)

[[x]$_{NP}$ [der [[z]$_{ADJ}$ [EX-FEMININE SIMPLEX]$_{NP}$]$_{NP}$]$_{NP}$]$_{NP}$
de   afgronden   der   menselijke   ziel
the   abysses   the.GEN   human   soul
'the abysses of the human soul' (*INL 27 Mil.*, April 1995)

The frequency in the data of each of these sub-schemata – as well as the number of tokens that fell outside the sub-schemata – is shown in Table 9. As already shown in Table 2, plural nouns are by far the most frequent type of noun in position *y*. Surprisingly, roughly a quarter of the singular nouns in *y* are simplex; however, this figure is actually made up of many tokens of a limited number of types. In contrast, many of the morphologically complex nouns only occur once in the data. The dominant complex noun types are those ending in *-ie*, *-ing* and *-heid*.

Table 9: The occurrence of the various types of noun in *y*

Nature of head noun of *y*		Total tokens	Proportion of total *x der y* tokens (%)	Proportion of singular *x der y* tokens (%)
plural		1441	70.0	
singular	simplex; ex-feminine	134	6.5	21.7
	ends in *-ie*	125	6.1	20.3
	ends in *-ing*	98	4.8	15.9
	ends in *-heid*	78	3.8	12.6
	simplex; other	36	1.7	5.8
	ends in *-iek*	28	1.4	4.5
	ends in *-uur*	26	1.3	4.2
	ends in *-nis*	22	1.1	3.6
	ends in *-de*	21	1	3.4
	ends in *-ij*	12	0.6	1.9
	ends in *-te*	11	0.5	1.8
	ends in *-schap*	10	0.5	1.6
	ends in *-st*	9	0.4	1.5
	ends in *-iteit*	7	0.3	1.1
Total:		2058 (singulars only: 617)		

This section has focused on the structural regularity of the adnominal genitive construction. The following section addresses the pragmatic constraints on the use of the construction.

4 (Morpho-)pragmatic aspects of the use of *x der y*: obsolete case morphology as a stylistic tool in Dutch and elsewhere

The use of the adnominal genitive is governed by a number of pragmatic factors: on the one hand, it appears to be a relatively unmarked (register-specific) alternative to the *van*-construction in formal written language; on the other hand, its use in informal speech and writing carries pragmatic consequences. This underlines the form-function characteristic of constructions and the importance of context to the use of particular constructions (Bybee 2006a: 291). The use of the adnominal genitive construction contains the information that the construction may be felicitously used in formal writing but that its use in informal language (written and spoken) while possible and acceptable, will stand out. Finally in this section, the use of obsolete case morphology as a stylistic tool in Dutch and elsewhere is briefly considered.

In the *Eindhoven* corpus of mid-20th century Dutch, which is divided into six genre-defined sub-corpora (daily newspapers, spoken language, family magazines, news magazines, popular science books, and novels and short stories), clear trends are visible in the use of the adnominal genitive both regarding the occurrence of novel formations produced using the construction, and regarding the number of genitive tokens relative to the number of tokens of the *van*-construction: the popular science sub-corpus contains by far the most novel genitive tokens (226 tokens; the novel genitives in the other written sub-corpora number between 26 and 49 tokens), and is also the sub-corpus in which the genitive is strongest against the *van*-construction: in interchangeable syntactic contexts, about 90% of the examples were formed with *van* and 10% with the genitive (in the other written sub-corpora, the ratio is circa 97% to 3%) (Scott 2011: 109, 123). Thus, the adnominal genitive construction has a clear association with the popular science genre, which appears to be particularly fertile ground for the production of novel genitive formations.

In derivational morphology, one of the characteristics of a productive construction is that, in addition to their intelligibility to language users, the products of the construction must not draw attention to themselves (see, e.g., Bauer 2001:

58–59, 62–71 on naturalness and creativity; also Bochner 1993: 4). Furthermore, the societal productivity of a particular construction is "suspect" if the products occur, for instance, only in "poetry or poetic and/or highly literary prose", or are "playful formations" (Bauer 2001: 57–58); it is also noted by Bauer (2001: 58) that, on some views, the very fact that a construction is used "consciously", i.e. deliberately, suggests that the construction is not productive. These criteria are valid when assessing the productivity of a marginal (or, indeed, any) morphosyntactic construction: if the products of a particular construction are intelligible to language users who encounter them, but are felt to be unusual or inappropriate (at least in certain pragmatic contexts), this would suggest that the productivity of that construction is either dubious, or is restricted to certain pragmatic contexts (e.g. a particular register or genre). Away from derivational morphology, this is the situation with the adnominal genitive fragment which, on the view noted above, would be unproductive even in the formal writing in which its use is unmarked.

The adnominal genitive is even rarer in spoken language than in writing: in the 9 million token *CGN*, only 17 novel *x der y* tokens (i.e. not as part of fixed expressions such as those exemplified in (7) above; on this, see also Scott 2011: 110) were found in the spontaneously produced speech (i.e. excluding read-aloud texts); two examples are given in (20).

(20) a. *streven naar een ratio van* **drieëndertig procent der** **studenten**
striving after a ratio of thirty-three percent the.GEN students
'striving for a ratio of thirty-three percent of the students'
(CGN: fv400010.70; ceremonial speech: opening of the academic year)

b. *'k zal nooit tot 't* **gilde der** **beste schrijvers** *uh toetreden.*
I shall never to the guild the.GEN best writers uh enter
'I'll never, uh, enter into the guild of the best writers.'
(CGN: fn007328.271; radio programme: *Forum*)

The use of *x der y* away from formal writing is strongly pragmatically restricted: while its use in formal speech, such as that of solemn speeches or journalistic radio broadcasts (indeed, most of the 17 *CGN* examples came from such sources), may not draw attention to itself, its use in informal speech and writing is both deliberate and, often, playful and ironic (cf. Merlini Barbaresi 2006: 334, who notes the presence of such pragmatic features in morphological constructions). That is to say, the pragmatic consequence of the use of *x der y* in informal language is the humour derived from the incongruence of using, in informal language, an archaising construction that is so strongly associated with formal, solemn style. Some informal examples are given in (21). Important to its use in informal registers is the fact that its continued entrenchment in formal language (and in numerous fixed expressions and names encountered in all registers) means that its products are always understood.

(21) En daarmee zijn we aan 't end der verbale
and with-that are we on the end the.GEN verbal
knuffeling gekomen, genaamd de podcast.
hugging come namely the podcast
'And, with that, we have come to the end of the verbal hugging, i.e. the podcast.' (Sofie Lemaire, *De Podcast van Sofie*, Studio Brussel, 4.2.11)

The Bootleg Beatles worden dan ook alom beschouwd
the Bootleg Beatles become then also generally regarded
als **de moeder der Beatles-coverbands**.
as the mother the.GEN Beatles-coverbands
'The Bootleg Beatles are, then, generally regarded as the mother of Beatles cover bands.'
(http://www.013.nl/event/2754_the_bootleg_beatles [accessed 17.7.13])

Aangezien de Vodafone's en KPN's van deze wereld maar
since the Vodafones and KPNs of this world just
bezig blijven met **het naaien der consumentjes**
busy remain with the screwing the.GEN consumer.DIM.PLU
moeten we iets anders verzinnen.
must we something else come-up-with
'Since the Vodafones and KPNs of this world just keep on screwing the little consumers we have to come up with something else.'
(http://www.geenstijl.nl/mt/archieven/2637161_pda.html [accessed 17.7.13])

Overall, although its marginality would class it as unproductive on some views, the adnominal genitive fragment is productively (if relatively infrequently) used in formal written Dutch. In informal Dutch, in contrast, the markedness of novel *x der y* formations suggests, on the one hand, that the construction is unproductive; on the other hand, given that novel formations are usually (at least in the data studied) well-formed and are deliberately deployed to achieve a particular effect, and that this effect is clear to readers or listeners, it can be concluded that the adnominal genitive enjoys a rather specialised (and restricted) productivity in informal Dutch.

Additionally, it is worth considering that some sub-schemata of *x der y* may be used in any register without necessarily drawing attention to themselves; this is, for example, the situation with the elective genitive construction (22) and the partitive use of *x der y* exemplified above in (20a).

(22) ik   heb   uit   betrouwbare   bron   dat   over   2   jaar   **de**
     I   have   from   reliable   source that   over   2   years   the
     iPod   der   iPods   uitkomt
     iPod   the.GEN   iPods   comes-out
     'I have it from a reliable source that the iPod of iPods will be coming out in two years.'
     (http://forum.fok.nl/topic/765906/1/999 [accessed 17.7.13])

   Klopt   naast   de   Oude   ICR   was   de   koploper
   that's-right beside   the   old   ICR   was   the   koploper
   de   trein   der   treinen.
   the   train   the.GEN   trains
   'That's right, beside the old *ICR* [*Intercityrijtuig* 'intercity carriage'] the *koploper* ['front runner'] was the train of trains.'
   (http://forum.opeenshadikhet.nl/viewtopic.php?f=3&t=4262&start=864 [accessed 17.7.13])

The use of obsolete case morphology as a stylistic tool is found beyond Dutch. Such use tends to occur when the morphology in question is still partly familiar to language users, e.g. because the case morphology had not been absent from the language for too long, or because the case morphology remains in use in other roles.

In German, as noted by Nishiwaki (2010: 1), one of the characters in Kurt Tucholsky's 1931 *Schloß Gripsholm* ['Gripsholm castle'], uses the archaic partitive genitive and the quirkiness – that is to say, the pragmatic markedness – of this usage is commented on by the narrator (23).

(23) "Hast du **schwedischen Geldes**?" fragte die Prinzessin träumerisch. Sie
     führte gern einen gebildeten Genitiv spazieren und war demzufolge sehr
     stolz darauf, immer "**Rats**" zu wissen. (Tucholsky [1931] 2000: 27)
     '"Do you have Swedish.GEN money.GEN?" asked the Princess dreamily. She
     liked to take an educated genitive for a walk und was accordingly very
     proud of always knowing "what to do.GEN [literally "advice.GEN"]".'

Examples of the use of case morphology as a stylistic tool in older Swedish are addressed by Norde (2007): in the 14th century, when case- and non-case-forms co-existed, poets would make use of a particular variant in order to maintain rhyme or metre, rather than to achieve morphosyntactic agreement; by the 17th century (and through to the 19th century), by which time case morphology was long lost from Swedish, case endings were used – often inaccurately – in order to achieve a solemn or formal effect; Norde (2007) also notes that this style was parodied at the time. The latter Swedish usage is parallel to the use of *x der y* in modern informal Dutch.

5 Conclusions

The findings of the paper suggest, following the principles set out in Booij (2010), that Construction Grammar can successfully be applied to morphology, both synchronically and diachronically. Building on a provisional proposal (Scott 2011: 130), it was contended that a usage-based, constructional framework can effectively account for the continued use in modern Dutch of a small fragment of the genitive case which was "left behind" as morphological case marking was lost. This fragment of the adnominal genitive case was able to be preserved as it remained useful to language users as a means of connecting two noun phrases in a possessive or partitive relationship. Thus, it continued to be used; this exercised a repetition effect which led to its entrenchment as a construction independent of the case system. One curiosity of its preservation was that the construction's association with nouns with a particular morphological structure was also retained through a process of discontinuous chunking, whereby the genitive marker and the derivational suffix of the head noun of the genitive noun phrase became entrenched, but not the base of the noun. As such, the word-internal morphological structure of the nouns concerned remained accessible for syntax. In present-day standard Dutch, the adnominal genitive is perpetuated through its use. Constructions contain not only information on form, but also on function, and the adnominal genitive construction contains the pragmatic restriction that it may be used fairly neutrally in formal language but that, in informal language, its use carries a mocking or ironic connotation, and attracts attention.

References

Audring, Jenny. 2006. Pronominal gender in spoken Dutch. *Journal of Germanic Linguistics* 18: 85–116.
Barðdal, Jóhanna. 2008. *Productivity: Evidence from Case and Argument Structure in Icelandic*. Amsterdam/Philadelphia: John Benjamins.

Barlow, Michael and Suzanne Kemmer (eds.). 2000. *Usage-based Models of Language.* Stanford, CA: CSLI Publications.
Bauer, Laurie. 2001. *Morphological Productivity.* Cambridge: Cambridge University Press.
Bilderdijk, Willem. 1826. *Nederlandsche Spraakleer* [Dutch grammar]. 's Gravenhage: J. Immerzeel, junior.
Bochner, Harry. 1993. *Simplicity in Generative Grammar.* Berlin/New York: Mouton de Gruyter.
Booij, Geert. 2010. *Construction Morphology.* Oxford: Oxford University Press.
Bybee, Joan. 2006a. *Frequency of Use and the Organization of Language.* Oxford: Oxford University Press.
Bybee, Joan. 2006b. From usage to grammar: The mind's response to repetition. *Language* 82: 711–733.
Bybee, Joan. 2010. *Language, Usage and Cognition.* Cambridge: Cambridge University Press.
van Dale. 2005–2008. *Elektronisch Groot Woordenboek van de Nederlandse Taal. Bijgewerkt tot 2008* [Electronic large dictionary of the Dutch language. Updated to 2008] (14th edition). Utrecht/Antwerpen: Van Dale Lexicografie.
Goldberg, Adele E. 2009. The nature of generalization in language. *Cognitive Linguistics* 20: 93–127.
Haeringen, C. B. van. 1956. *Nederlands tussen Duits en Engels* [Dutch between German and English]. The Hague: Servire.
Heule, Christiaan van. [1625/1626] 1953. *De Nederduytsche Grammatica ofte Spraec-konst* [Dutch grammar or grammar (literally "language-skill")]. Edited by W. J. H. Caron. Groningen/Djakarta: Wolters.
Horst, Joop van der and Kees van der Horst. 1999. *Geschiedenis van het Nederlands in de Twintigste Eeuw* [History of Dutch in the twentieth century]. Den Haag/Antwerpen: Sdu Uitgevers/Standaard Uitgeverij.
Horst, J. M. van der. 2008. *Geschiedenis van de Nederlandse Syntaxis* [History of Dutch syntax]. Leuven: Universitaire Pers Leuven.
Kate, Lambert ten. 1723. *Aenleiding tot de Kennisse van het Verhevene deel der Nederduitsche Sprake* [Introduction to knowledge of the elevated part of the Dutch language]. Amsterdam: Rudolph en Gerard Wetstein.
Kemmer, Suzanne and Michael Barlow. 2000. Introduction: A usage-based conception of language. In: Michael Barlow and Suzanne Kemmer (eds.), *Usage-based Models of Language*, vii–xxviii. Stanford, CA: CSLI Publications.
Kraaikamp, Margot. 2012. The semantics of the Dutch gender system. *Journal of Germanic Linguistics* 24: 193–232.
Kroch, Anthony. 1978. Toward a theory of social dialect variation. *Language in Society* 7: 17–36.
Langacker, Ronald W. 2000. A dynamic usage-based model. In: Michael Barlow and Suzanne Kemmer (eds.), *Usage-based Models of Language*, 1–63. Stanford, CA: CSLI Publications.
Merlini Barberesi, Letitia. 2006. Morphopragmatics. In: Keith Brown (ed.). *Encyclopedia of Language and Linguistics (2nd edition)*, 332–335. Amsterdam: Elsevier.
Muller, J. W. 1891. Spreektaal en schrijftaal in het Nederlandsch [Spoken language and written language in Dutch]. *Taal en Letteren* 1: 196–232.
Nishiwaki, Maiko. 2010. *Zur Semantik des deutschen Genitivs. Ein Modell der Funktionsableitung anhand des Althochdeutschen.* Hamburg: Buske.
Norde, Muriel. 2007. *Skåder glasenom på bordenom i Krogenom*: Naamvallen als stijlmiddel [*Skåder glasenom på bordenom i Krogenom*: Case as stylistic tool]. *Huginn ok Muninn* 5: 8–23.

Rumelhart, David E. 1980. Schemata: the building blocks of cognition. In: Randy J. Spiro, Bertram C. Bruce and William F. Brewer (eds.). *Theoretical Issues in Reading Comprehension: Perspectives from Cognitive Psychology, Linguistics, Artificial Intelligence, and Education*, 33–58. Hillsdale, NJ: Lawrence Erlbaum Associates.
Scott, Alan K. 2011. The position of the genitive in present-day Dutch. *Word Structure* 4: 104–135.
Scott, Alan K. 2012a. A constructionist account of the Modern Dutch adnominal genitive. In: Ferenc Kiefer, Mária Ladányi, and Péter Siptár (eds.). *Current Issues in Morphological Theory: (Ir)Regularity, Analogy and Frequency. Selected Papers from the 14th International Morphology Meeting, Budapest, 13–16 May 2010*, 83–103. Amsterdam/Philadelphia: John Benjamins.
Scott, Alan K. 2012b. Competition in possession marking in early modern Dutch. Paper presented at *Synchrony and diachrony: Variation and change in language history*, Worcester College, University of Oxford, 16 March 2012.
Scott, Alan K. 2014. *The Genitive Case in Dutch and German: A Study of Morphosyntactic Change in Codified Languages*. Leiden: Brill.
Tucholsky, Kurt. [1931] 2000. *Schloß Gripsholm. Eine Sommergeschichte*. Reinbek bei Hamburg: Rowohlt.
Twe-spraack. 1584. *Twe-spraack vande Nederduitsche Letterkunst ofte vant Spellen ende Eyghenschap des Nederduitschen Taals* [Dialogue on Dutch grammar, or on the spelling and nature of the Dutch language]. Leiden: Christoffel Plantyn.
Wal, Marijke van der and Cor van Bree. 2008. *Geschiedenis van het Nederlands* [History of Dutch]. Utrecht: Spectrum.
Weerman, Fred. 1997. On the relation between morphological and syntactic case. In: Ans van Kemenade and Nigel Vincent (eds.). *Parameters of Morphosyntactic Change*, 427–459. Cambridge: Cambridge University Press.
Weerman, Fred and Petra de Wit. 1999. The decline of the genitive in Dutch. *Linguistics* 37: 1155–1192.
Weiland, P. 1805. *Nederduitsche Spraakkunst* [Dutch grammar]. Amsterdam: Johannes Allart.
Willemyns, Roland. 2003. Dutch. In: Ana Deumert and Wim Vandenbussche (eds.). *Germanic Standardizations: Past to Present*, 93–125. Amsterdam/Philadelphia: John Benjamins.

III **Constructions in variation and change**

Freek Van de Velde
6 Degeneracy: The maintenance of constructional networks

1 Introduction

In this article it is argued that long-term drifts that destroy grammatical strategies a language disposes of in its functional domains are not as detrimental as one might think, thanks to a property that goes under the name of "degeneracy", a technical term from evolutionary biology for the phenomenon that structurally different elements can fulfil the same function. To bring out the diachronic effects of degeneracy, a construction grammar perspective will be taken, with special emphasis to the horizontal relations in constructional networks, which so far have been somewhat neglected in comparison with the vertical relations.

The article is structured as follows: in the remainder of this introduction, I will first introduce the concept of degeneracy, as this is not a familiar notion in linguistics. Second, I will detail what I understand by constructional networks in Construction Grammar. In section 2, I will introduce two cases of constructional networks: Dutch experience predicates and Dutch subordinate clauses. In section 3, I trace the diachrony of these constructional networks, showing how they are degenerately transformed. Section 4 rounds off with the conclusions.

1.1 Degeneracy

Like the stock market or ant colonies, language is a complex adaptive system (Holland 1992; Steels 2000; Beckner et al. 2009; Bybee 2010). Such systems display emergent properties that cannot be understood by looking at its individual components alone. One of these properties is what in biology is called "degeneracy". In this context, degeneracy has nothing to do with its common sense meaning of deterioration, but is a technical term for the phenomenon that structurally different elements can fulfil the same function (see Edelman and Gally 2001).

A simple example is thermoregulation in the human body, which is degenerately controlled by (a) perspiration, (b) arteriolar vasodilation, (c) shivering, (d) countercurrent flow, (e) wearing protective clothing, (f) huddling, etc. Degeneracy is related to the notion of redundancy, but one of the differences is that degenerate features may play a role elsewhere in the system as well. To stick to the example of thermoregulation in humans, consider the role of walking upright. This plays a role in thermoregulation, as the body catches less solar radiation and catches more wind, thus helping to keep the body cool in warm climates, but one would be hard pressed to maintain that thermoregulation is the sole function of our species' upright posture: it also adds to the expansion of the visual perimeter, and has energetic advantages in locomotion, for instance.

Degeneracy has been applied to biological complex adaptive systems, but hitherto its relevance for language has only been pointed out cursorily (Edelman and Gally 2001: 13764) and has never been studied in depth, despite the growing idea that language change can be modeled by appealing to general evolutionary processes (Croft 2000; Ritt 2004; Mufwene 2008; Rosenbach 2008; Steels 2011a).[1] In fact, the notion of degeneracy can be readily applied to various phenomena in language. Examples include:

(a) The marking of the plural by both umlaut and a plural suffix in German (e.g. *Mann – Männer*)
(b) the expression of past tense by ablaut and by a dental suffix (e.g. English *spoke* vs. *talked*)
(c) the expression of past time reference both by a prefixed "augment" *e-* and a suffixed sigmatic marker *-s-* in Ancient Greek and Old Indic aorists (e.g. Ancient Greek *é-lu-s-a* 'I unbound')
(d) Syntactic agreement markers (e.g. Gumawana *Komu ku-mwela* 'you 2SG-climb', see Siewierska 2004: 120–127)

Note that just as in biological degeneracy, there is no pure "redundancy" in these linguistic examples either: with regard to (a), it can be pointed out that both i-umlaut and *-er*-suffixation play a role elsewhere in the system as well (for deriving causatives and nomina actionis, respectively), with regard to (b) it can be pointed out that there is lexical differentiation between both strategies, and arguably also differences in meaning (see Bolinger 1980; Levin 2009), with regard to (c) it can be pointed out that the *e*-augment is also used in imperfects and the sigmatic infix is also used in the future, and with regard to (d) it can be pointed out that syntactic agreement is not redundant with non-pronominal subjects.

In language as well as in other communication codes, redundancy is beneficial as it offers protection against information loss in cases of signal perturbation. This is well-understood by computer programmers, who are familiar with in-built redundancy in their codes. Degeneracy offers the same "robustness"

---

[1] See also blog posts by Givón (Funknet, 14 Aug. 2011) and Winters (2011, http://replicatedtypo.com/robustness-evolvability-degeneracy-and-stuff-like-that/4026.html).

advantage, but has an additional advantage of "evolvability" (Whitacre and Bender 2010). Degeneracy increases the possibility of complex adaptive systems to move over the fitness landscape. It is precisely this second advantage that will be focused on in this paper. In form-function change in language, speakers renew their grammar. Degeneracy explains how this comes about without overhauling the semiotic code. A comparison with the example of thermoregulation of the human body can make this clear: many mammals use "horripilation" (or "piloerection"), the process of making one's fur stand on end, as a thermoregulatory process. Humans have lost this ability as a consequence of a long-term general process ("drift") of losing body hair, although a vestigial trait is still present in the form of *cutis anserine*, or goose bumps. The fact that thermoregulation is degenerate, means that it is robust to the loss of body hair. But there is more: degeneracy in thermoregulation not only increases robustness, but also evolvability, firstly because the hair loss has evolutionary advantages (e.g. in shedding lice, see Pagel 2007), and second because goose bumps are now available for refunctionalisation.

1.2 Networks in Construction Grammar

In the last 15 years or so, Construction Grammar has established itself firmly in linguistics. It meshes particularly well with usage-based approaches (see Bybee and Beckner 2010: 842–845), especially in the fields of variational linguistics, diachronic linguistics and language acquisition. Inevitably, the scope of what is understood by Construction Grammar has widened, so that it is nowadays more accurate to speak of Construction Grammars – plural – than of Construction Grammar (see Croft and Cruse 2004).

Some versions of Construction Grammar have added epithets to the name, as for instance Radical Construction Grammar (Croft 2001), Fluid Construction Grammar (Steels 2011b), Embodied Construction Grammar (Bergen and Chang 2013) or Sign-Based Construction Grammar (Michaelis 2009). Not all of these Construction Grammar variants share the same views on the ins and outs of the model, and they disagree on the technical representation. Still, there is a core creed to which most of them subscribe. Language is basically a fund of "constructions", pairings of form and meaning, of varying degrees of complexity, and these constructions form taxonomic networks. The vertical dimension of these networks revolves around the idea of schematicity: the higher positions in the network are occupied by schematic constructions, which hierarchically subsume the lower positions with (partially) specific instantiations of the abstract constructions. Whereas more traditional linguistic approaches have a division between syntax and the lexicon, constructional approaches to language generally reject such a division (see e.g. Croft and Cruse 2004: 255–256). In the words of Goldberg (2006: 18): "It's constructions all the way down".[2] Indeed, if schematic – that is lexically underspecified – constructions like the ditransitive for instance have their own idiosyncratic meaning that cannot be reduced to its parts (see Goldberg 1995), they do not differ really from individual words, as they realise an irreducible form-function correspondence. The same applies to the level below the word: in Construction Grammar bound morphemes convey meaning in a way not unlike free morphemes (see Booij 2010 in defence of Constructional Morphology; also see Booij and Hüning, this volume).[3] The various types of constructions can be classified according to the dimension atomic-complex and the dimension schematic-specific, which are orthogonal to each other. As becomes clear in Table 1, the latter dimension is gradual in nature: partially schematic atomic constructions are bound morphemes and partially schematic complex constructions are multi-word constructions with a mixture of lexically fixed parts and lexically underspecified slots.

Table 1: Different types of constructions

	Schematic	Partially schematic	Specific
Atomic	N	-s	cat
Complex	[$_{Transitive}$ NP V NP]	[V [Poss *way*] PP]	*let alone*

Constructions of different sizes, from fully lexically instantiated multi-word expressions (e.g. *kick the bucket*) over partially lexically instantiated constructions like the *way*-construction (see Goldberg 1996; Israel 1996), over bound morphemes (e.g. the third person verbal ending -s) to fully lexically underspecified constructions (e.g. the ditransitive construction), form a giant network, and each

---

[2] There is disagreement about whether fully instantiated constructions (also called "constructs") also count as constructions (see Taylor 2004 for a critique; see also Norde, De Clerck, and Colleman, this volume).
[3] This is not a new idea, but goes back to at least Bloomfield, and it is one of the foundational principles of the Columbia School of Linguistics, as set out by Diver (Huffman 2001). Van der Horst (1995: 239) interestingly points out that there seems to be an iconic relation between form and meaning such that concrete, lexical meaning is encoded by concrete lexemes, whereas bound morphemes and even less "material", non-segmental *signifiants* (e.g. word order regularities such as V2 (verb-second) or dependent-before-head) have a more organising *signifié*. In other words: it would be strange to have a language that expresses a meaning like 'cat' or 'table' with a bound morpheme, let alone with a non-segmental form, and it would be equally strange to mark illocution with a lexical verb or an auxiliary (see Hengeveld 2004: 1198–1199). See Van de Velde (2009: 144) for the incorporation of this idea in grammaticalisation theory.

node in this network has its own features that specify the meaning import of that particular construction. The whole network of constructions in a particular language is called the Constructicon (Evans 2007: 42), and is in essence an extended version of what other theories would regard as the Lexicon, enriched with non-lexical constructions.[4]

Along the vertical schematic-specific dimension in the Constructicon the lower concrete constructions "are sanctioned by" and "inherit features from" the higher schematic construction, and features from lower nodes in the network "percolate" upward to the higher nodes. An example of a – partial and simplified – hierarchical network is shown in Figure 1. The top node is the maximally underspecified "transitive" construction. At the next level there are nodes for the ditransitive, the transitive resultative and the reflexive construction. These three constructions are all sanctioned by the transitive construction, but in different ways: the ditransitive is an "extension" of the transitive construction with an extra participant, the transitive resultative is a blend of the transitive and a resultative predicate, and the reflexive is a lexically more specific instantiation of the transitive, in which the direct object Noun Phrase is filled with the reflexive pronoun. Fully instantiated versions of the ditransitive and the transitive resultative constructions are examples like *Hij heeft haar een brief gestuurd* ('He sent her a letter') and *Hij kuste haar bewusteloos* ('He kissed her unconscious'), respectively. At the same time, there are other nodes in the hierarchy that represent constructions that draw on different parent constructions. One of these is a construction that may be called "fake object resultative construction", an instantiation of which is *Hij loopt zijn schoenen stuk* (lit. 'He walks his shoes broken'). In actual fact, it is not really a separate construction next to the transitive resultative construction, but an extension of it by inserting a normally intransitive verb (*lopen* 'walk') in a resultative construction frame, by a process called "coercion". This process shows the power of Construction Grammar, which has fewer difficulties with such constructions than traditional grammar. The intermarriage between the reflexive and the fake object resultative yields a construction which for convenience sake has been termed "fake reflexive resultative" in the network in Figure 1. Constructs instantiating it are of the type *Hij schreeuwt zich schor* (lit. 'He shouts himself hoarse'). The offshoot of the ditransitive construction and the reflexive is the ditransitive reflexive (*Ronny gunt zich een verzetje*, lit. 'Ronny grants himself a distraction'), and the combination of this ditransitive reflexive with the caused motion construction gives us the Dutch *weg*-construction, which is similar to the English *way*-construction, but has a somewhat different form (see Verhagen 2002, 2003).

---

4 The term *constructicon* is said to be originally coined by Jurafsky (1992).

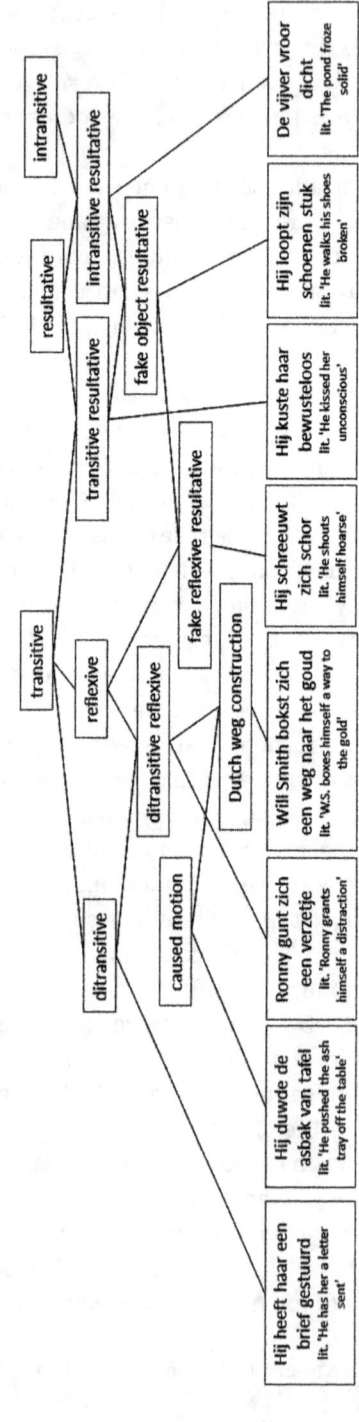

Figure 1: A hierarchical network of constructions in Dutch

The kind of hierarchical network of constructions with inheritance relations illustrated in Figure 1 is well-known, and features in various scholarly articles on Construction Grammar. There is, however, another respect in which constructions form a network: rather than just forming a hierarchical structure, constructions can also be related to each other on what could be called the horizontal axis.[5] What I have in mind here is a network where the form-function relation of a particular construction may be partly motivated in relation to its neighbours. This view on networks is familiar from phonology and morphology, but is less often applied to syntax. Before discussing syntactic examples in section 2, I will first elucidate the horizontal relations in a network in phonology and morphology.

In phonology, segmental elements can be related to abstract nodes higher up in the hierarchy thus forming a network not unlike the type illustrated in Figure 1. In Dutch, /ɛ/ or /ɔ/ are instantiations at the lowest level of the higher abstract node "short front vowel" and "short back vowel", respectively. The latter nodes straightforwardly instantiate nodes of an even higher level. This is all illustrated in Figure 2.

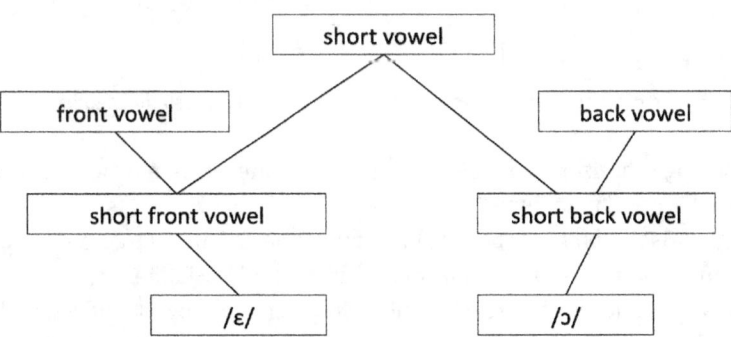

Figure 2: Partial hierarchical network in Dutch phonology

The hierarchical network can be enriched by adding lines for horizontal relations. There is a relationship between the two vowels at the lowest level:

---

[5] Taylor (2004) also embraces the idea of constructions forming networks: "(...) each unit stands at the hub of a network of relations to other units" (2004: 49) and speaks about horizontal relations in constructions, but he refers to something else, viz. the relationship between a structure and a larger structure of which it is a part, e.g. the relation between a Noun Phrase and the clause in which the Noun Phrase functions as, say, a direct object. By contrast, horizontal networks in this paper refer to structures of differential relationships between NPs functioning as subjects, direct objects, indirect objects etc. (see section 2.2).

they share the features [+vowel] and [+short] and are differentiated by the feature [±front] (and also [±rounded], but this is ignored here in order not to complicate the issue unnecessarily). It is not just the vowels themselves that entertain this horizontal relation, but the abstract nodes as well. The boxes for front vowels and back vowels are not just arbitrary notions, but are in a contrastive set ([+front] and [−front]), and the different values impact on the meaning. By contrast, the nodes [reflexive], [ditransitive] and [resultative] in Figure 1 do not stand in such a contrastive relation: there is no sensible interpretation of [+reflexive] as [−ditransitive]. In Figure 3, double-headed arrows are added to bring out the horizontal relationships in the phonological network.

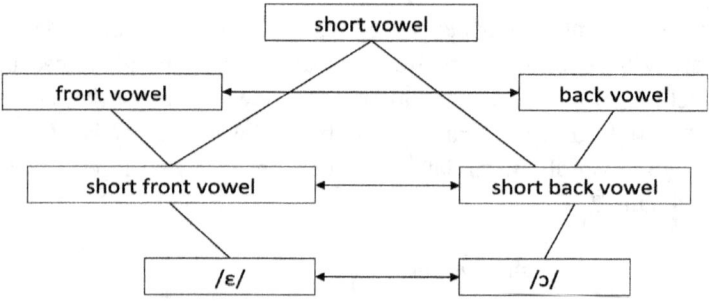

Figure 3: Partial hierarchical network in Dutch phonology with horizontal relations added

In morphology, horizontal relations in networks are well-known, and are mostly referred to as "paradigms". The Dutch verb forms *spreek* (speak.1SG), *spreekt* (speak.2/3SG), *spreken* (speak.PL) are all connected in a large network, but their mutual relation is, again, not one of instantiation. Rather they are at the same hierarchical level and are horizontally differentiated by the inflectional endings.[6] The horizontal relations in the constructional network in Figure 4 are again visualised by double-headed arrows. The existence of similar "paradigms" outside conjugation or declination has received less attention. Nonetheless, horizontal relations in constructional networks can be discerned at the level of syntax as well, as will be shown in the next section.

---

[6] The situation is complicated by the existence of homonymous forms: *spreek* is also the imperative form of the verb *spreken* and *spreken* can be an infinitive as well as a plural form. Moreover, with post-verbal subjects, the form for 2SG is not *spreekt* but *spreek*. These complications will be ignored in the present paper, where the morphological example merely has an expository function.

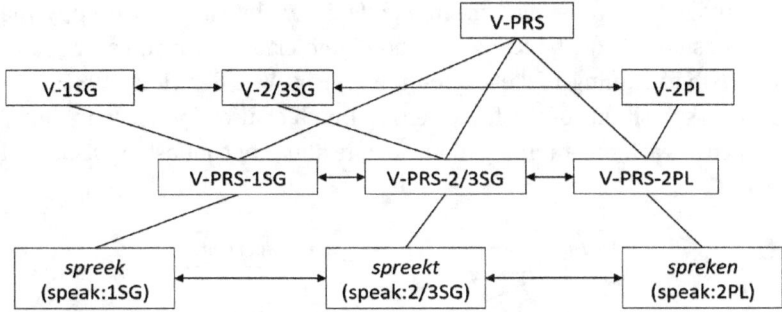

Figure 4: A hierarchical network with horizontal relations added

2 Horizontal constructional relations in syntax

In the previous section, we have added horizontal lines to the phonological and morphological networks that take the same form as the typical networks in Construction Grammar of the type illustrated in Figure 1. In itself, adding such horizontal lines does not yield new insights to what we know, of course. Contrastive relations have always been recognised in phonology and morphology, and they feature prominently in all handbooks of classical languages. The question that arises is to what extent such horizontal relationships also play a role in syntax, where the existence of paradigms is less obvious, or at least less often explicitly acknowledged. What would constitute a syntactic paradigm – a set of alternating forms with related meaning differences?

In sections 2.1–2.3, three examples are introduced of horizontally defined syntactic constructions in a network: (i) the position of the finite verb in Dutch clauses, (ii) the case frames of Dutch experience predicates and (iii) the integration of subordinate clauses in Dutch. The latter two examples will be of special interest, as they will be at the focus of the diachronic investigation in section 3.

2.1 The position of finite verbs in Dutch clauses

One example of a syntactic paradigm defined by horizontal relations in a network is the position of the finite verb in Dutch clauses (or German clauses, for that matter). In declarative main clauses, the verb is in second position (often abbreviated as "V2" position). The finite verb can occur in other positions as well, however, and these positions have a syntactic meaning: initial verbs (V1) occur in polarity questions, conditionals and imperatives. These contexts can be unified under "non-assertive" meaning.[7] Finite verbs can also occupy the clause-final position (Vn)[8], typically in subordinate clauses, which can be seen as conveying the meaning of "backgrounding" (see Van der Horst 1984: 172–175). The various positions of the finite verb in Dutch clauses form a "paradigm" and are related to each other through horizontal relations of contrast, as visualised in Figure 5.[9]

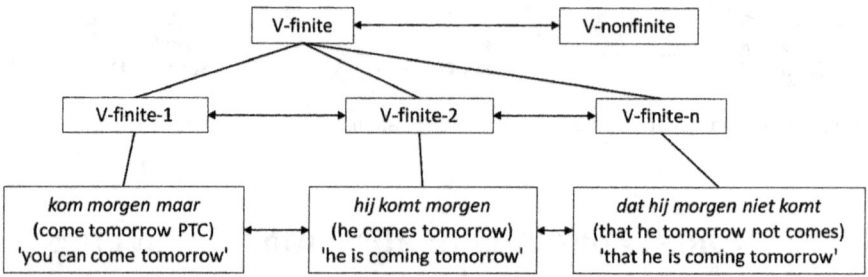

Figure 5: The position of the finite verb in Dutch clauses as a constructional network with horizontal relations

2.2 Case frames in Dutch experience predicates

Another example of a set of constructions entertaining horizontal relations of contrast is the argument realisation network in Middle Dutch. Middle Dutch relies on case frames for indicating the agentivity of the participants (Van de Velde 2004). Agentivity can be broken down into features like volition, responsibility, control, animacy, instigation, movement etc. (Lakoff 1977; Dowty 1991; Næss 2007; Grimm 2011, among others). Glossing over the details, which are much discussed but are not our immediate concern here, the whole system is then fairly straightforward, and is well-known from other Indo-European languages: the nominative is used for animate participants, exerting volitional control and instigating the action. Accusatives, on the other hand, are used for non-agentive undergoers, who have no control over the action expressed by the

---

7 See Goldberg and Del Giudice (2005) for a similar proposal concerning the historically related English subject-auxiliary inversion.
8 Vn does not necessarily mean the very last position in the clause. Hence, it is more accurate to speak about V-late than about V-final.
9 Interestingly, the syntacticisation of V1 and V-late is probably a diachronic corollary of the emergence of V2 (see Hopper 1975; Van der Horst 2008): V1 and V-late only acquired grammatical significance *in contrast to* V2. This shows that the horizontal lines do capture something substantive in language.

predicate. The dative case is used for sentient, volitional, but non-instigating participants (see Næss 2007: 198 for a similar proposal), and genitives are used for mainly inanimate patients that are not fully affected by the action expressed by the predicate. This yields a cline of cases, as represented in (1), in which dative and genitive occupy the space in the middle, between the highly agentive nominative and the highly patientive accusative.

(1) AGENTIVE   nominative – dative – genitive – accusative   NON-AGENTIVE
                                                              (PATIENTIVE)

These are the prototypical functions of the different cases, from which language users can deviate on semantic grounds.[10] It is, for instance, not uncommon to encounter animate accusatives, and to the extent that animacy is correlated with (or part of) agentivity, this poses a conflict. The accusative then highlights the fact that the undergoer is non-instigating, fully affected etc., glossing over the animacy aspect. In languages where the animacy is given higher priority, this can lead to so-called differential object marking, as in Spanish or Afrikaans, where animate objects can be preceded by a preposition, *a* and *vir*, respectively.

An insightful way to account for the assignment of case in Middle Dutch is by taking a constructional approach, in which, unlike in a projectionist approach (see Levin and Rappaport Hovav 2005 for this term), verbs do not assign case automatically according to the valency with which they are registered in the lexicon, but rather select a case frame that contributes its own constructional meaning. The whole system can best be seen at work in verbs that do not straightforwardly map onto the prototypical process in which an actor exerts physical force to affect an undergoer (*hit, destroy, break* ...). This is, for instance, the case with so-called experience processes, expressing mental and sometimes also physical experiences such as *amaze, wonder, annoy, forget* etc. It is not clear who is the instigator in the case of *annoy*, and whether the participants involved – the experiencer or the stimulus – are volitionally implicated. Nor is it clear to what extent the annoyee is really affected. A similar case can be made for *amaze* and *forget*, for instance. What we see in Middle Dutch then, is that such verbs occur with a wide range of case frames. For the verb *wonderen*

---

10 In fact, the use of case-marking in argument realisation is derivative from their earlier function in spatial marking (see also the localist hypothesis). With the exception of the nominative, which probably is merely the absence of case (Van der Horst 2008: 145, referring to Schuchardt), the cases also have or had a role in the expression of essive relations. Accusative could be used to express adessive (cf. Latin *Romam ire*) and the genitive, as its name suggests, expresses the abessive, or "source", whether the source of possession, the source of an experience etc.

('amaze', 'astonish', 'surprise'), the examples in (2) to (5) give an idea of the attested variation.[11]

(2) NOMINATIVE-STIMULUS, DATIVE-EXPERIENCER
Sere   wonderde   Pharaone   sine   vulmaectheit   so   scone
much   amazed   Pharao:DAT   his:NOM perfection:NOM so   beautiful
'Pharao was amazed by his very beautiful perfection.' (MNW, s.v. wonderen)

(3) GENITIVE-STIMULUS, DATIVE-EXPERIENCER
Des   wondert   mi   utermaten
this:GEN   amazes   me:DAT   highly
'I was highly astonished by this.' (MNW s.v. wonderen)

(4) NOMINATIVE-EXPERIENCER, ACCUSATIVE-STIMULUS
Die   goede   man,   die   in   clenen   dingen   die
the   good   man   who:NOM in   little   things   the:ACC

grootheit   van   onsen   here   plach   te   wonderne   wel   zere
greatness:ACC of   our:DAT   lord:DAT   used   to   amaze   well   very
'The good man, who used to be highly amazed about the greatness of our lord by little things.' (MNW, s.v. wonderen)

(5) NOMINATIVE-EXPERIENCER, GENITIVE-STIMULUS
Si   wondrens   sere   algader
they:NOM   wonder=this:GEN   much   altogether
'They were all highly astonished about this.' (MNW, s.v. wonderen)

The language user can opt for the strategy of pressing the experience verb *wonderen* in the canonical transitive mould, as for example in (4). But since the experiencer is a non-prototypical agent, it may be encoded as a dative as well, and since the stimulus as well is a non-prototypical agent or patient, it can get genitive encoding. As is shown in (3), there is no need to have a nominative-marked subject. The so-called impersonal construction has a third person singular verb with obliquely marked participants. This shows that the classical two-way typological distinction between experiencer-subject and experiencer-object verbs

---

[11] The examples under (2)–(5) do not exhaust all the possibilities. Apart from case-based argument realisation, there were also voice-based strategies (see Van de Velde 2004 and below). For a resolution of the difficulties posed by case syncretism etc., see Van de Velde (2004: 73–76).

is a gross oversimplification for Middle Dutch (unless the notion of subject is stretched considerably).¹²

In Van de Velde (2004) it is shown that the distribution of the different constructions over the experiencer verbs is semantically motivated: verbs with an inherently more agentive experiencer (e.g. *denken* 'think') are statistically more likely to go with case frames that acknowledge the agentivity of the experiencer, whereas verbs with an inherently less agentive experiencer (e.g. *ontbreken* 'lack') are more likely to encode the experiencer as an undergoer. Verbs like *wonderen* take a middle position, and excel in the use of the impersonal construction exemplified in (3). Focusing on the cases where the verbs come with two arguments, thus ignoring cases like (6) and (7) without an explicit stimulus and without an experiencer respectively, the different case frames can be ordered on a cline from agentive to non-agentive experiencers, see Table 2. Experiencers are seen as maximally agentive when they are the subject of a regular transitive nominative-accusative construction, as this is the construction that is used for straightforwardly transitive verbs like *break, destroy* etc. Marking the stimulus with genitive case decreases the agentivity of the experiencer as the stimulus is now represented as not fully affected, and thus somehow escapes the control of the experiencer. The next level is the so-called "impersonal construction" with a dative and a genitive argument, representing a twofold deviance from the transitive frame. The experiencer can be represented as even less agentive, when the stimulus is in the nominative, marking the latter as the starting point of the causal chain.

(6) NOMINATIVE-EXPERIENCER, NO STIMULUS
Alle diet sagen an, wonderden wijf ende man
all who=it saw to amazed woman and man
'All who saw it, both women and men were amazed.' (MNW, s.v. wonderen)

(7) GENITIVE-STIMULUS, NO EXPERIENCER
Waer dat zake dat zijns ontbrake
were it case that he:GEN lack
'If it is the case that he is lacking (= he is dead).' (MNW, s.v. ontbreken)

---

12 I will not dwell on the applicability of the notion subject in non-canonically case-marked predicates in Middle Dutch. On this topic, see Weerman (1988), Eythórsson and Barðdal (2005) and Barðdal and Eythórsson (2012).

Table 2: Case frames ordered on a cline of experiencer agentivity

AGENTIVE EXPERIENCER
Experiencer-nominative; Stimulus-accusative
Experiencer-nominative; Stimulus-genitive
Experiencer-dative; Stimulus-genitive
Experiencer-dative; Stimulus-nominative
NON-AGENTIVE EXPERIENCER

The graph in Figure 6 (based on Van de Velde 2004, with data from the citation corpus of MNW) shows that the case frames are non-randomly distributed over different types of verbs: inherently more "agentive-experiencer" verbs select constructions higher on the cline in Table 2, and vice versa. The correlation is statistically significant.[13]

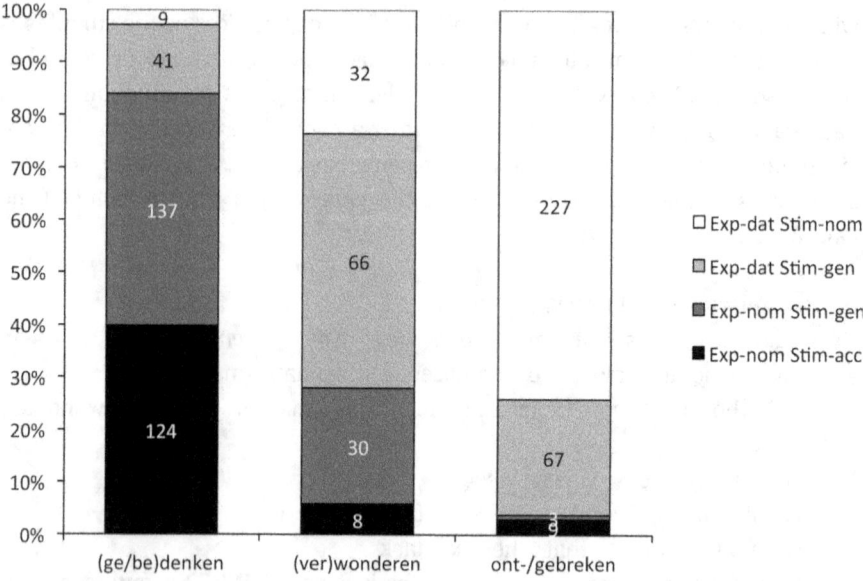

Figure 6: Distribution of constructions over various types of experiencer verbs

The different case frames combining with the experience predicates are horizontally related in the constructional network: differences in meaning are correlated with differences in form, in such a way that we get a cline of closely-

---

[13] Kendall's Tau-b, a test for association, indicates a correlation of 0.69 (Asymptotic Standard Error = 0.02). Chi-Square: p < 0.0001.

related constructions, which are distinguished from one another in the values they have for a set of features. For constructions with experience predicates, the cline goes from "agentive experiencer" to "non-agentive experiencer", and the constructions that form aggregate points on a cline do not entertain a hierarchical relation to each other, but are related in a horizontal way. The case frames can be seen as a cluster of constructions at a certain horizontal level in a constructional network (see also Trousdale 2008: 308, Figure 3 for a visualisation).

2.3 Subordination

In the domain of clause combining, the degree of syntactic integration may iconically correspond to the degree of semantic integration (see Cristofaro 2003). Starting from the layered structure of the clause in which arguments and satellites are attached at various levels from the predicate up to the clause (Foley and Van Valin 1984; Hengeveld 1989; Cinque 1999), it can be shown that lower-level satellites such as time adverbial clauses tend to be better integrated than higher-level relations such as concessives (see Lehmann 1988; Hengeveld 1998; Croft 2001; and, specifically for Dutch, Smessaert et al. 2005). The question is of course how to measure "integration". For Dutch, we are in the fortunate position that its verb-second main clauses offer a clue to integration: if the subordinate clause triggers inversion in the main clause, it is integrated, as it occupies the first position, "pushing" the subject to post-verbal position. If, on the other hand, the subordinate clause is followed by subject-verb word order (no inversion), then it is in left-detached position.[14] By way of illustration, let us take a look at two different types of syntactic constructions:

(8) Toen   hij   thuis   kwam,   begon   het   te   regenen.
    when   he   home   came   began   it   to   rain
    'When he arrived home, it started to rain.'

(9) *Toen hij   thuis   kwam,   het   begon   te   regenen.
    when   he   home   came   it   began   to   rain

(10) Al   is   hij   ziek,   hij   komt   toch.
     even_if   is   he   ill   he   comes   anyway
     'Even if he is ill, he is still coming.'

---

[14] I assume the reader has a basic idea of the word order principles in Dutch clauses. If not, the reader can be referred to Haeseryn et al. (1997: 1221–1400), Verstraete (2003) or Zwart (2011).

(11) *Al   is   hij   ziek, komt   hij   toch.
     even_if   is   he   ill   comes he   anyway

The temporal subordinate clause in (8) obligatorily triggers inversion in the main clause, whereas the concessive clause in (10) is obligatorily followed by subject-verb word order.[15] This is not a coincidence, but iconically reflects the higher level of attachment of concessive clauses. If the only indication of the level of attachment would be the presence or absence of inversion in the main clause, this would of course be a circular argument, but fortunately, there are other semantic and formal considerations: temporal adverbial clauses trigger tense agreement ("consecutio temporum"), but concessive clauses can under certain circumstances bail out, see (12) vs. (13).

(12) Toen   hij   thuis   kwam/*komt,   begon   het te   regenen.
     when   he   home   came/comes   began   it   to   rain
     'When he arrived/*arrives home, it started to rain.'

(13) Al   staat/stond   hij   niet   als   erg   betrouwbaar   bekend,
     even_if   stands/stood   he   not   as   very   reliable   known
     hij   sprak   toen   de   waarheid.
     he   spoke   then   the   truth
     'Even if he is/was not known to be very reliable, he nevertheless spoke the truth back then.'

This can be seen as an indication that the (ook) al-concessive clauses are less integrated in the main clause, the reason being that they are separately asserted. This also explains why they behave differently with regard to clefting: concessives cannot (easily) be clefted (see Smessaert et al. 2005), and why concessives more easily allow speech act adverbs, such as *eerlijk gezegd* ('honestly said').[16]

What examples (8)–(11) show is that integration vs. non-integration as signaled by the presence or absence of inversion of the main clause verb is a

---

[15] Note that *(ook) al* concessives are different in another respect as well: they do not feature verb-final syntax of typical subordinate clauses, but rather have verb-initial (in fact V2) syntax in the subordinate clause. I will come back to this issue below.

[16] Space limitations prevent an in-depth illustration of all possible types of subordinate adverbial clauses in Dutch. I will ignore the fact that there is a third pattern: semi-integration, in which the subordinate clause is in left-detached position, but is resumed by a correlative element in sentence-initial position in the main clause, so that the subordinate clause is at the

cue for the language user to partly assess the semantics of the subordinate clause. In principle, one could argue that the integration of the subordinate clause is lexically projected from the conjunction, but this is not the case. Just as with argument realisation, a constructional approach is superior over a projectionist approach, as the template (integration/non-integration) carries meaning of its own, although some degree of convention always limits the possible variation. In the case of integration/non-integration, the semantic contribution of the constructional template can be seen at work in the use of several conjunctions which allow both construals. As shown by Smessaert et al. (2005), many a Dutch conjunction occurs both in integrated and non-integrated patterns (e.g. *aangezien* 'since', *vooraleer* 'before', *als* 'if', *terwijl* 'while', *tenzij* 'unless'), but the two construals yield different readings. Take for instance the conditional conjunction *als*. If the conditional clause modifies the state-of-affairs, the conditional is integrated and triggers inversion in the main clause. If the conditional clause modifies the speech act, it is attached at a higher level. There is a vast literature on the topic (Davison 1981; van der Auwera 1986; Sweetser 1990, among others), but the difference can easily be illustrated with the set of examples under (14)–(15).

(14) Als   het   regent,   word   je   nat.
     if   it   rains   get   you   wet
     'If it rains, you'll get wet.'

(15) Als   je   het   nog   niet   gezien   hebt,   het   regent   buiten.
     if   you   it   yet   not   seen   have   it   rains   outside
     'In case you haven't noticed, it's raining outside.'

There are other conditionals introduced by *als* that fail to trigger inversion in the main clause, but the non-integrated nature is motivated here as well: either they border on concessive meaning, as in (16) (from König and van der Auwera 1988: 112), or they are subjunctive (or counterfactual), as in (17) (from

---

same time integrated and non-integrated. The picture is rather complicated for Dutch (see König and Van der Auwera 1988 and Van der Horst 2008 for details). The reason this pattern is ignored is that it only rarely occurs as the only possible pattern in Present-day Dutch (see Smessaert et al. 2005, appendix A). Furthermore, I will concentrate on sentence-initial subordinate clauses only here. Also, the presence of the subordinator *dat* is not taken into consideration here. In some subordinate adverbial clauses, it is obligatory (e.g. *omdat*), in other subordinate adverbial clauses, it is optional (be it substandard) (e.g. *toen dat, hoewel dat*) and in still other contexts it is excluded (e.g. *als *dat*).

König and van der Auwera 1988: 114). Note that in the latter case, integrative construal with inversion is also possible, unlike conditionals like (16).

(16) Als   ik   als schilder slecht was, als metselaar was
     if   I   as   painter   bad   was   as   mason   was
     ik   echter   een   katastrofe/succes.
     I   however   a   catastrophe/success
     'If I was bad as a painter, as a mason however I was a catastrophe/success.'

(17) Als ik in jouw plaats was, ik zou   hem aanklagen.
     if   I   in your place   was   I   would him sue
     'If I were in your position, I would sue him.'

To summarise, integrated vs. non-integrated patterns of subordinate clauses are horizontally related in their constructional network. It is only in contrast to integration that non-integration is semiotically meaningful. There is cross-linguistic variation in the absolute degree of syntactic integration of time adverbial clauses, and it is only by comparing the different subordinate constructions that the motivation becomes clear, so that whatever degree of integration a temporal subordinate clause has in a language, it will not be less integrated than a concessive clause. The precise formal features that define the network are language-specific: obviously, the criterion of inversion only works in a V2 language (see also Verstraete 2003).

3 The diachrony of horizontal constructional relations

3.1 Language change as a "threat" to horizontal constructional relations

In the previous sections, a number of horizontally organised constructional networks have been discussed, to wit, vowel features, verbal inflection, position of the finite verb, case frames in experience predicates, and integration of subordinate clauses. Evidently, each of these networks can get tousled when one of the differential values increases its scope. Suppose all vowels become [+ front], then the difference between [+ front] and [− front] is no longer able to discriminate words. Or suppose that analogical leveling in verbal inflection paradigms blots out the person desinences. In that case, the inflectional paradigm ceases to exist.

This is not so far-fetched: the history of the verbal inflection in Proto-Germanic, Dutch, English and Afrikaans is largely one of far-reaching analogical leveling.

In the syntactic case studies, introduced in section 2, language change similarly can bring down the network of horizontal relations. In principle, Dutch could extend its V2 to subordinate clauses, thereby obliterating the semiotically relevant distinction between V2 and Vn. Again, this is not far-fetched, as such a change occurred in English. In the following sections 3.1 and 3.2, a closer look is taken at the history of the other two syntactic examples, as these have in fact come under pressure by diachronic drifts elsewhere in the language system. The case frames in Dutch experience predicates came under pressure in Middle Dutch, and the integration level of subordinate clauses has recently come under pressure.

In both cases, however, it can be shown that the semantic differences that are formally expressed by the horizontally related nodes, survive. The reason is that these semantic differences are degenerately expressed. Crucially, the degenerate strategies are *not* instances of what is traditionally called "renewal" (Hopper and Traugott 2003: 122–124): it is not the case that language users come up with new ways to express semantic distinctions which they used to express differently. Rather, grammatical strategies that already existed in the language and already played a role in the functional domain at issue are seized upon to "rescue" the system.

3.2 Case study 1: Case frames in Dutch experience predicates

The delicate case-frame network laid out in Table 2 came under pressure when the case system of Middle Dutch broke down in a process that is commonly called "deflection". When dative- and genitive-marked objects die out, the constructions that deviate from the canonical transitive construction become indistinguishable.

As is well-known, the loss of case in Dutch was compensated for by the increased use of prepositions. It is easy, however, to be misled by this metaphor of "compensation". In its naive form, it could be taken to suggest that prepositions arose when the case system broke down. This does not conform to the actual facts, however. Prepositions already existed in Middle Dutch, and were used in combination with case. A more accurate way of describing the actual development is that an already existing strategy was exploited by language users. This is a clear case of degeneracy: prepositions were not specifically designed as a trade-off means of expressing case in argument realisation, and the two strategies are not always completely interchangeable, but there is a certain amount of functional overlap so that the language system can sustain loss of one of the strategies. By way of illustration, take example (18), where the impersonal construction is realised by encoding the stimulus as a prepositional object introduced by *van* which is equivalent to the genitive in other contexts, such as possession, as well.

(18) *Hen   allen   wonderde* **van** *dien*
     they:DAT all:DAT amazed   **of**   this:DAT
     'They were all amazed by this.' (MNW s.v. wonderen)

Still, this strategy was not exploited in full, as the substitution of a dative by a prepositional object introduced by *aan* or *voor* does not appear to occur. (If the preposition *aan* occurs, it is one of the alternatives to the *van* preposition for encoding the stimulus, see 19 and below).[17, 18]

(19) *Alle konsten daer   men sich   **aen** verwondert*
     all   arts   where one himself to   amazes
     'All arts by which one is amazed.' (WNT s.v. verwonderen (I))

There is one construction in present-day Dutch that closely resembles the Middle Dutch impersonal construction, as neither of its arguments is encoded as subject, see (20) and (21). The subject role is taken by a dummy *het* ('it'), the stimulus argument is marked by the preposition *aan* ('to') and the experiencer is encoded as an object, with oblique forms in case of pronominal realisation, as in (20). The construction is odd as it does not occur with those verbs that were most strongly associated with the impersonal construction in Middle Dutch, such as *(be/ver)wonderen*, but rather with a few verbs that belong to the stimulus-subject category: *ontbreken, mangelen, schorten*, all of which can be glossed 'lack'.

(20) *Het ontbreekt hem aan geld.*
     it   lacks   him to   money
     'He lacks money.'

(21) *Het ontbreekt die   mensen aan geld.*
     it   lacks   those people to   money
     'Those people lack money.'

---

[17] The analysis of (19) is complicated because the complement of the preposition is *daer*, constituting what is called in Dutch grammar a (separable) pronominal adverb.
[18] Other prepositions occur as well: *af, in, om, in, over* (see WNT s.v. verwonderen I).

To summarise, while degenerate marking by preposition existed and was exploited to partially make up for the gradual loss of case inflection, there was no full hand-off between both strategies: prepositional marking did not reach its full potential. Instead, language users relied on other degenerate strategies.

One of these degenerate strategies was the increased use of the plain transitive construction with experiencer subjects: over the centuries, Dutch experiencer predicates undergo a drift towards more experiencer-subjects. The drift from dative-experiencers to nominative-experiencers is by no means restricted to Dutch. It is a cross-linguistically rather common tendency and has been analysed from the perspective of grammaticalisation (see Haspelmath 1998: 338–340). From the perspective of Construction Grammar, the process has been ascribed to the extension/schematisation of the transitive construction (Trousdale 2008). For Dutch, this extension of the transitive construction is corroborated by a corpus study on *(be/ver)wonderen* 'amaze', the prime example of an experience verb that tended to occur in the impersonal construction in Middle Dutch (see Figure 6).[19] Using data from two corpora, KLASLIT and LITEROM, the bar chart in Figure 7 shows a diachronic increase in the use of the transitive construction after Middle Dutch.[20] Transitive constructions are those with a subject

---

[19] The prefixes *be-* and *ver-* have an impact on the meaning of the verb, of course. *Bewonderen*, with the applicative *be-* prefix involves higher agentivity on the part of the experiencer. The question is whether to include *bewonderen* in the corpus study. Its applicative nature implies a strong tendency to occur in the transitive construction, and it could be argued that it would be better to leave the instances of *bewonderen* out of the corpus study, as it risks to overestimate the transitivity drift. Still, there are good reasons to retain *bewonderen* in the counts. First, it semantically overlaps with *(ver)wonderen*: on the one hand Middle Dutch *(ver)wonderen* could carry the meaning of present-day Dutch *bewonderen* ('admire'), as in the following example: *Nochtan so verwondert die natuer die suverlijcheit* ('Still, nature admires pureness') (MNW s.v. suverlijcheit). On the other hand, Early Modern Dutch *bewonderen* does not consistently mean 'admire', but can be used in the sense of 'amaze' as well (see WNT s.v. bewonderen). Moreover, it does not consistently occur in the plain transitive experiencer-subject construction, but occurs in the inverted source-subject construction (*Het bewonderde mij* 'it APPL=amazed me' (WNT s.v. bewonderen)) and in the reflexive as well, as in: *Zoo men (...) binnens-Lands nog sommige Kaakenbeenderen van Walvisschen, 't zy in Klai, Veen of Zand, verkalkt of versteend mogte ontdekken, behoeft men zig ... deswegens niet te bewonderen* ('If one would discover some calcified or petrified whale cheek bones inland, be it in clay, peat or sand, one should not be amazed by it') (WNT s.v. bewonderen). In short, there is no hard and fast distinction, neither in meaning nor in argument realisation, between *bewonderen* on the one hand and *(ver)wonderen* on the other hand. This is the reason why we treat *bewonderen* and *verwonderen* together in the corpus study. I will return to the role of the prefixes below.

[20] The correlation is statistically significant: Kendall's Tau-b 0.28, ASE 0.07. Chi-Square: $p < 0.0001$.

and a non-prepositional object. Examples are given in (22)–(23). Dutch has not decidedly converged on experiencer-subjects for its transitive construal, but allows stimulus-subjects as well, but Figure 8 shows that within the group of transitive constructions, the experiencer is nevertheless increasingly likely to be encoded as subject – a process which has been observed in English too (see Allen 1995).[21]

(22) Ik   bewonder hun   schaamteloosheid.
     I   admire   their shamelessness
     'I admire their shamelessness.' (21st century, LITEROM)

(23) Neen, maar het verwondert me   niet.
     no   but   it   astonishes me   not
     'No, but it does not surprise me.' (21st century, LITEROM)

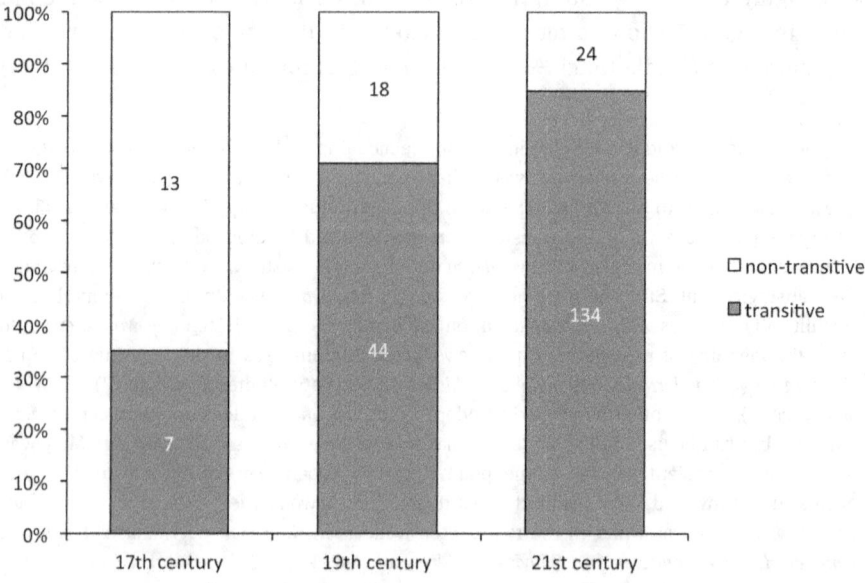

Figure 7: The diachrony of the transitive construction with *(be/ver)wonderen* in Modern Dutch

---

[21] The correlation is statistically significant: Kendall's Tau-b 0.56, ASE 0.04. Chi-Square: $p < 0.0001$.

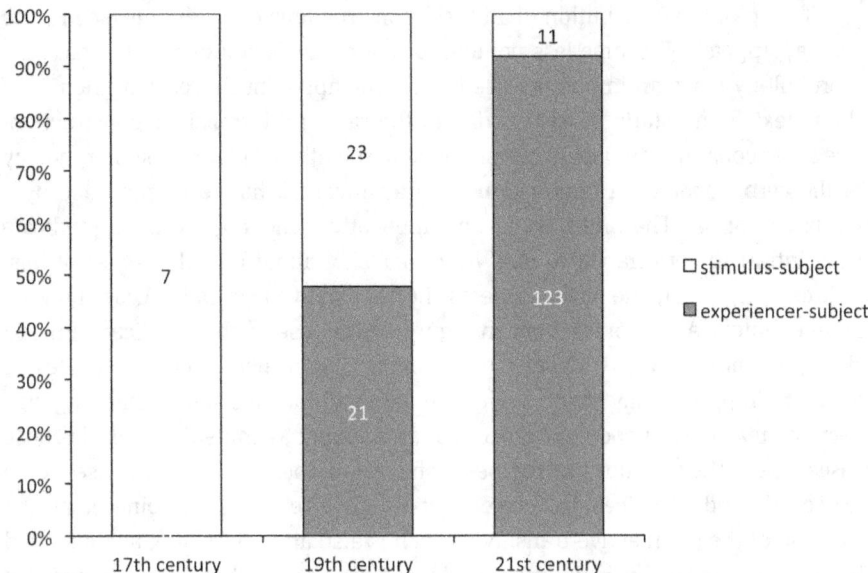

Figure 8: Experiencer-subject vs. stimulus-subject in *(be/ver)wonderen*

A closer look at the diachrony of the argument realisation of *(be/ver)wonderen* shows, however, that the transitivity drift is not the only thing that is going on. Dutch turns out to deploy other degenerate ways to maintain the meaning differences primarily carried by case frames in Middle Dutch. Rather than yielding completely to an undifferentiated transitive construction, Dutch exploited existing voice distinctions to re-establish the middle ground that was formerly covered by (double-)oblique case frames. More specifically, there are two constructions that take over this function, namely the reflexive, exemplified in (24), and the static passive, exemplified in (25). Again, we are dealing with degeneracy here, rather than pure renewal, as the reflexive and the (static) passive already existed in Middle Dutch, and just extended their use (frequency and context) in Dutch.

(24) Ik   verwonder   mij   daarover.
     I   amaze   myself   there_about
     'That amazes me.' (21st century, LITEROM)

(25) ... dat   je   over   alles   even   verwonderd   was.
         that you   about   everything   equally   amazed   were
     '... that you were equally amazed by everything.' (21st century, LITEROM)

If we plot the distribution of all these constructions through time (see Figure 9), they appear to become less popular, but our view is clouded by the fact that morphology plays an important role here.[22] The apparent decrease in the use of the reflexive and static passive is due to the rise in the transitive construction. The latter construction, however, cannot be used without altering the morphology of the verb *wonderen*. In order to use it transitively, it has to be preceded by a prefix *ver-* or *be-*. The prefix *be-* has an applicative function, turning a predicate from intransitive to transitive (e.g. *be-zingen* 'sing about'). In this sense, it has, to a certain extent, the same value as the nominative-accusative case frame in Middle Dutch. As becomes clear in Figure 10, the use of this applicative prefix rises precipitously over the centuries – indeed, plain *wonderen* is not attested anymore in present-day Dutch.[23] The rise of the applicative shows that language users increasingly encode the process of amazement as transitive. Still, in those cases where they do not use the *be-* prefix, there does seem to be a rise in the use of the other voices (reflexive + static passive voice combined), at the expense of the plain active-transitive, which is also an option here, as illustrated in (23). This is shown in Figure 11, which gives the diachronic distribution of the constructions ignoring the observations with a *be-* prefix.[24] This shows that although language users increasingly rely on the transitive construction, and on the experiencer-subject version of it, they also increasingly use voice-based constructions when they want to deviate from the plain transitive construction.

---

[22] Making the "construction" variable binary by amalgamating the reflexive and the static passive in one category, as opposed to the active transitive, yields the following results: Kendall Tau-b: 0.56, ASE 0.10. Chi-Square: $p < 0.0001$.

[23] The reason why Figure 10 plots more observations is that the non-finite contexts (and imperatives) could be included as well, which were obviously ignored in the figures on argument realisation above. The figures have been analysed with a Cochran-Mantel-Haenszel statistic, which tests a matrix with an ordinal variable in the columns and a nominal variable in the rows for the alternative hypothesis that the row mean scores differ. In the case at hand, it tests whether the use for either of the three forms (Ø-*wonderen*, *ver-wonderen*, *be-wonderen*) shifts through time. The test value corresponds to a p-value < 0.0001.

[24] The results show that the correlation observed in Figure 9 disappears: Kendall's Tau-b 0.06 (ASE 0.10). Chi-Square $p = 0.12$. (But note that absence of evidence of an association is not the same as evidence of absence of an association.)

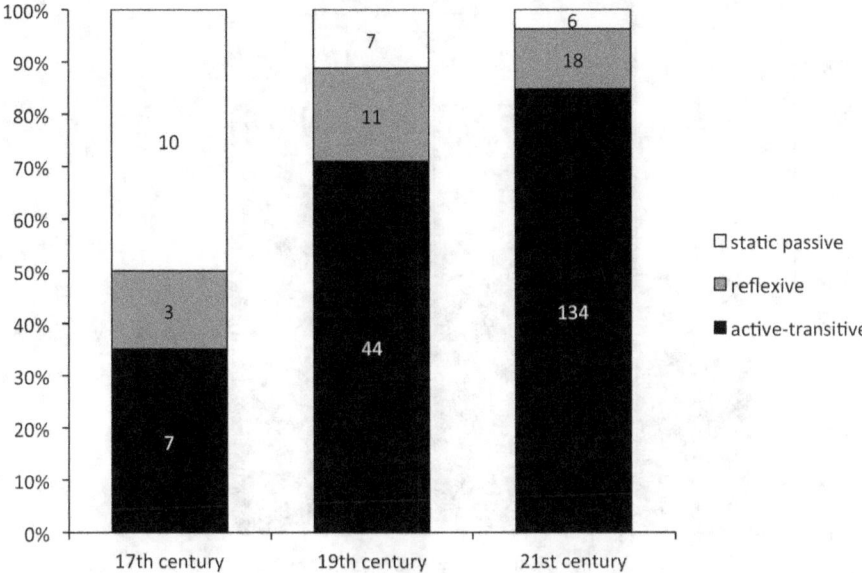

Figure 9: Voice-based constructions with *(be/ver)wonderen* in Modern Dutch

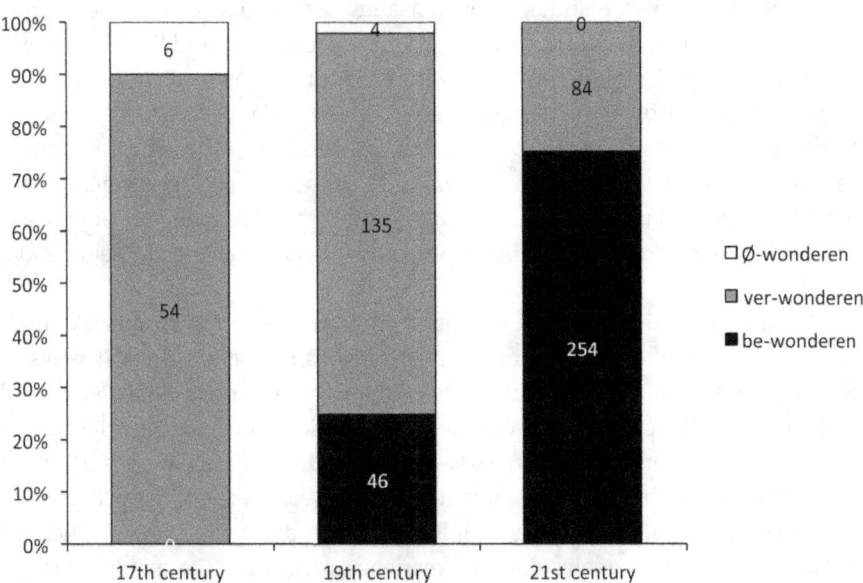

Figure 10: Prefixes in Modern Dutch

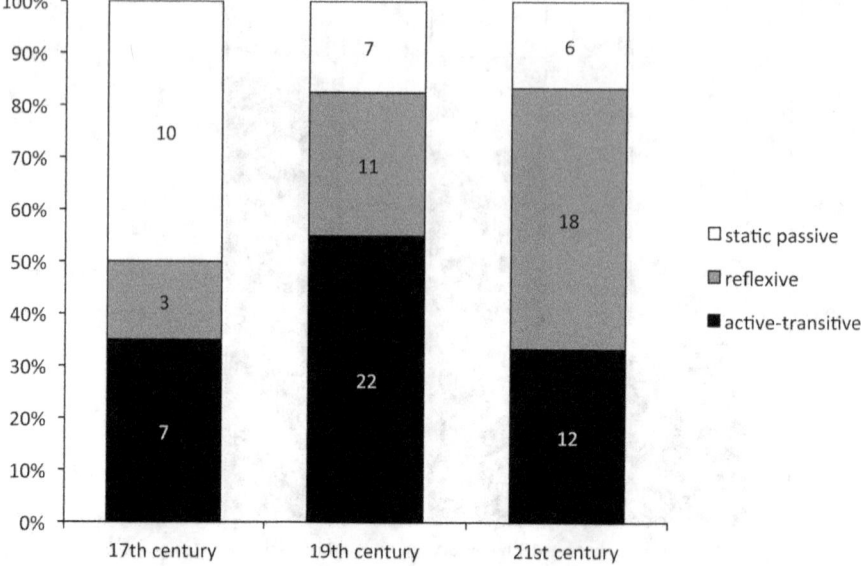

Figure 11: Voice-based constructions with *(ver)wonderen* in Modern Dutch

Another degenerate strategy compensating for the loss of the fine-grained case-based argument realisation for experience processes in Middle Dutch seems to be an increase in the lexical expressions. Next to *(be/ver)wonderen*, present-day Dutch has verbs like *verbazen* 'amaze', *versteld zijn* 'be amazed', *verrassen* 'surprise', which did not occur yet in Middle Dutch. This lexical proliferation can be used to express different meanings. It remains to be seen whether this tendency holds up under a more systematic study, but a similar lexical increase has been observed for Middle Dutch *vergeten* 'forget' (see Van de Velde 2004: 70).

In sum, deflection in Dutch was not as detrimental to the case-based argument realisation of Dutch experience predicates as one might think. Thanks to existing degenerate strategies, the loss of the case system could be sustained without losing the capability of expressing semantic nuances in experience processes. Several alternative strategies were exploited, such as (i) prepositions, (ii) generalisation of the transitive construction, (iii) voice-based distinctions, (iv) applicative prefixes, and (v) lexical differentiation – all of which serve functions outside the argument realisation of experience processes. The actual facts are thus vastly more complex than a simple "transition from cases to prepositions" or a simple "extension of the transitive construction". The multifaceted nature of the diachrony of argument realisation in experience predicates shows how

Dutch, as a complex adaptive system, benefits from degeneracy both in terms of robustness and evolvability: language users can do away with something as central to grammar as case without running into problems.

3.3 Case study 2: Subordination

In the case of subordination, it has been observed that different types of subordinate clauses tend to become more integrated over time (see e.g. Hopper and Traugott 2003: 175–211). Obviously, this undermines one vital part of the system laid out in section 2.3: if concessives have the tendency to become integrated, the criterion of inversion can no longer reliably function as a semantic signal of the degree of integration, and the whole network gets disturbed.[25] Yet this is precisely what has happened and still is happening in Dutch. Example (26) shows that the concessive conjunction *hoewel* did not yet trigger inversion in the 18th century, contrary to what is the case in late 20th century Dutch, see (27). Moreover, the concessive conjunction *(ook) al*, which normally does not trigger inversion, see (10), can occasionally be seen to be used in an integrated construction, triggering inversion in present-day Dutch, see (28). This is still frowned upon in (prescriptive) grammars, but examples can be found even in edited texts.

(26) *Hoewel   ik   haestig   ben,   het   is   aenstonds   gedaen*
     although   I   irascible   am   it   is   immediately done
    'Although I am irascible, it is immediately over.' (18th century, WNT)

(27) *Hoewel   ik   je   invitatie   heel   lief   vind,   zal   ik   niet*
     although   I   your invitation   very   sweet   find   shall I   not
    kunnen   komen.
     can   come
    'Although I find your invitation very sweet, I shall not be able to attend.'
    (20th century, WNT)

(28) *Ook   al   waren   zij   duur   geworden,   had   zij*
     even   though   were   they   expensive become   had   she
    altijd   veel   bloemen   om   zich.
     always   many   flowers   around   herself
    'Even though they had become expensive, she was always surrounded by a lot of flowers.' (20th century, WNT)

---

[25] I want to thank William Van Belle for pointing this out to me in a discussion of Croft (2001).

How does the system of Dutch grammar react to the drift of subordinate clauses towards tighter integration? One strategy that is followed is to make the relations lexically explicit. Indeed, the Dutch language witnesses a considerable increase in the fund of conjunctions. Van der Horst (2008: 984) speaks of a proliferation ("woekering") of subordinating conjunctions in Late Middle Dutch and Early Modern Dutch.[26]

In Middle Dutch, the precise semantic import of a subordinate clause was often left implicit, as can be appreciated from the bewildering set of meanings that the simple subordinator *dat* can convey:

(29) Want **dat** hi enich erchs verdiende, nemmermeer en
for **if** he any bad-GEN achieved nevermore NEG
haddi ons te vriende
had=hi us to friend:DAT
'For if he achieved anything bad, he would not have us as a friend anymore.' (MNW, s.v. dat)

(30) Hi hadde (...) hem selven soe siec ghemaect, **dat** hi
he had him self so sick made **because** he
soe vele hadde ghewaect
so much had stayed_awake
'He had made himself so sick because he had stayed awake so long.' (MNW, s.v. dat)

(31) Ic hebbe in minen droom van hem ghedoghet
I have in my dream of him thought
dat ics vermoeyt bem
so_that (consequence) I=this:GEN tired am
'I thought about him in my dream, so that I am tired because of it.' (MNW, s.v. dat)

(32) Maria brachte haren sone, **dat** menne
Maria brought her son **so_that (goal)** one=him:ACC
besniden soude
circumcise would
'Maria brought her son, so that he could be circumcised.' (MNW, s.v. dat)

---

26 Leuschner and Van den Nest (p.c.) speak about "conjunctional drift".

(33) | Si | dwoughen | sine | voete | met | warmen | borne, |
|---|---|---|---|---|---|---|
| They | washed | his | feet | with | warm | source_water |

dat		ic	wane
as_far_as		I	believe

'They washed his feet with warm water, as far as I know.' (MNW, s.v. dat)

(34) | Nu | es | Brune | die | bere | ghegaen, | **dat** | hi | te | Maupertuus |
|---|---|---|---|---|---|---|---|---|---|
| Now | is | B. | the | bear | gone | **until** | he | to | M. |

es	comen
is	come

'Now Bruin the bear set off, until he reached Maupertuis.' (MNW, s.v. dat)

A more specific subordinating conjunction like *opdat* used to be ambiguous between expressing condition and goal, see (35) and (36), respectively. In present-day standard Dutch, *opdat* unequivocally introduces subordinating clauses of goal.

(35) | **Opdat** | ik | maar | eenigszins | tijd | heb, | zal | ik | het | doen |
|---|---|---|---|---|---|---|---|---|---|
| **if** | I | but | somewhat | time | have, | shall | I | it | do |

'If I have only the slightest amount of time, I will do it.' (18th/19th century, WNT, s.v. opdat)

(36) | Hij ... | hield | de | lamp | omhoog, | **opdat** | zij | des | te | beter |
|---|---|---|---|---|---|---|---|---|---|
| he | held | the | lamp | up | **so_that** | they | all | the | better |

mochten	zien.
might	see

'He held the lamp up, so that they could see (even) better.' (19th century, WNT s.v. opdat)

Still, the view that the grammaticalisation of new conjunctions to make the precise type of subordinate clause more explicit is a "compensatory" strategy for the unstoppable integration of subordinate clauses messing up the iconic system introduced in section 2.3, is incorrect. The reason is that the iconic horizontal network of subordinate clauses developed in sync with the massive grammaticalisation of conjunctions. As shown in Van der Horst (1981, 2008: 538–540, 769–771, 1040–1042), adverbial subordinate clauses of various types, including deeply attached ones, did not yet systematically trigger inversion in the main clause in Middle Dutch, and even later. Weijnen (1971: 13) gives the following example of a non-integrated temporal subordinate clause in Middle Dutch:

(37) | Alsic | dit | horde | ic | was | in | vare
     | when=I | this | heard | I | was | in | fear

'When I heard about this, I was frightened.'

Burridge (1993: 41) says that the systematic use of inversion in the main clause after a sentence-initial subordinate clause only gains momentum after 1650. It is hence more accurate to say that the use of the main verb position and the lexically specific conjunctions are degenerate strategies to express semantic layering. Just as in the case of experience processes, such a situation of degeneracy prevents the system from collapse when one of the degenerate strategies comes under pressure. The other available strategy does not come out of the blue, but its weight is increased. In other words: the grammaticalisation of new, specialised conjunctions was not really a remedy for the integration of higher-order adverbial subordinate clauses, but maybe it has been sped up by the drift towards integration.[27]

An indication that the two processes are still causally related is the observation that adverbial clauses without a specialised conjunction are more likely to resist integration in the main clause: the unambiguous concessive conjunctions *hoewel*, *ofschoon* and *ondanks (het feit) dat* trigger inversion in the main clause in present-day standard Dutch,[28] but concessive clauses without a conjunction like (38) do not, suggesting that they need the syntactic clue of (lack of) inversion in the main clause to indicate their adverbial type. The same argumentation applies to concessive *(ook) al*. This conjunction is not as grammaticalised as *hoewel* and *ofschoon*: *al* retains characteristics associated with its adverbial origin. As shown in (10), *al* clauses do not sport the characteristic verb-final syntax of Dutch subordinate clauses and as shown in (39), *al* does not have to be used subclause-initially.[29] In the latter case, inversion is not possible.

---

[27] This is by no means the only case of degeneracy in Dutch subordination. According to Van der Horst (1981: 182) there is an inverse diachronic correlation between the presence of the expletive default subordinating conjunction *dat* (as in Middle Dutch *hoe dat* 'how (that)' and *soe dat* 'if (that)') and the V-late position of the verb in subordinate clauses.

[28] See example (41) for an exception motivated on semantic grounds.

[29] Admittedly, non-initial *al* features in a restricted constructional context. The exact contours of the licensing construction are not clear, but co-occurrence of *dan* preceding *al* and the presence of the modal auxiliary *mogen* seem to be fairly strong restrictions. Still, *mogen* is not strictly obligatory, as is clear from examples like *Ze was dan al wel 18 jaren oud, maar het bleef toch familie he* 'Even though she was 18 years old already, she was still family' (Internet example, found by Google search).

Concessive meaning can also be expressed by the semi-conjunction 'WH-WORD ... ook', as in (40), again without triggering inversion in the main clause.[30]

(38) | Had | ik | gisteren | nog | hele | doemscenario's | in | mijn | hoofd,
| | had | I | yesterday | still | whole | doom_scenarios | in | my | head

vandaag blijkt maar weer   dat mijn brein dus ikzelf
today   appears once again that my   brain so   myself

mijn ergste vijand op dat gebied ben.
my   worst enemy on that terrain am

'Yesterday I still had full doomsday scenarios in my head, but today my brain – so myself – appears once more to be my own worst enemy.' (Google example)

(39) Want hij mag dan **al** jong multimiljonair zijn, en
for he may then PTC young multimillionaire be and

ambassadeur van Mandela, en de nieuwe God van golf, Ernie
ambassador of M.   and the new   god of golf E.

Els is ook nog steeds een gezonde Hollandse jongen (...).
E. is also still   a   healthy Hollandish boy

'For he may be a multimillionaire at a young age, and the ambassador of Mandela, and the new god of golf, Ernie Els is still a healthy boy from Holland.' (20th century, INL38)

(40) **Hoe** goed ik **ook** kijk, ik zal nooit de bron van het
how well I also look I shall never the source of the

licht kunnen localiseren.
light can   localise

'No matter how well I look, I will never be able to localise the source of the light.' (20th century, INL38)

So although the criterion of inversion in the main clause emerged relatively late, the horizontal network of Dutch subordination patterns is in competition with the tendency of increasing integration of adverbial clauses. It seems that Dutch currently uses the syntactic clue of inversion for the distinction between integration and non-integration in those cases where the conjunction allows for different types of subordinate clauses, like *als*, see (14) vs. (15) and *hoewel*,

---

[30] Van der Horst (2008: 1970) has several 19th century examples of WH-WORD ... ook and al concessive triggering inversion in the main clause, which seem to go against the grain of the integration drift (as Van der Horst points out himself). It is not clear why these concessives enjoyed a period of integration, and later stepped back in line.

see (27) vs. (41), and in those cases where the conjunction is not fully grammaticalised, as in (39)–(40).

(41) NON-INTEGRATION, DUE TO SPECIAL SEMANTICS, C.Q. "ASSERTIVE EMPHASIS" ("MARKED FOCUS", "CONTRASTIVE STRESS") (König and Auwera 1988: 124–125)

Hoewel	ik	Fred	niet	verdragen	kan,	haten	doe	ik	hem
although	I	Fred	not	stand	can	hate	do	I	him

ook niet.
also not
'Although I can't stand Fred, I don't actually hate him.'

In sum, as the tendency for subordinate clauses to get integrated progresses, the semiotic value of main clause inversion risks to break down, as eventually all subordinate clauses may succumb to the integrated construal. This is not happening, though. Thanks to degeneracy in the grammatical system, language users have different cues to assess the semantic level of the subordinate clause.

4 Conclusions

What do the case studies on experiencer predicates and subordination in section 3 tell us about the maintenance of the horizontal relations in constructional networks? Overall, languages, as complex adaptive systems, do not rely on a sole strategy to express abstract syntactic-semantic meaning. Horizontal relations between constructions (V1-V2-Vn; NOM-ACC, DAT-GEN ...; integrated vs. non-integrated subordination) express semantic distinctions that are (partly) expressed by other means as well. In the case of V1 for questions vs. V2 for declaratives, rising intonation is a degenerate way to formulate questions, so that in the absence of V1, clauses can still be interpreted as having interrogative illocutionary force (e.g. *U komt toch ook?* 'You will come as well, won't you?'). Subordination is expressed by Vn as well as by conjunctions, and occasionally also by V1 (*Kom je ook, breng dan een vriend mee* 'If you are coming as well, bring a friend'). The semantic level at which the subordinate clauses operates is expressed by inversion in the main clause and by lexical conjunctions. The agency of the experiencer is expressed by case frames, prepositional objects, applicative morphology and voice-based distinctions. This phenomenon, whereby structurally different elements can express the same function is called "degeneracy", with a technical term from evolutionary biology.

Crucially, degeneracy differs from redundancy in that the different strategies are not fully interchangeable and play a role elsewhere in the system as well. Take for instance the use of the (static) passive with experience predicates: it is not the case that the static passive's only function in Dutch is to express a lower degree of experiencer agency. It is at work in other parts of the grammar as well. The same goes for V1: initial position of the verb can be used to express interrogative illocutionary force, but it can be used for other things as well, such as the expression of conditionals, exclamatives etc. Rather than a one-to-one relationship between form and meaning, or a many-to-one relationship between form and meaning, degeneracy mostly consists of many-to-many relationships between form and meaning. This has implications for diachrony: form-function change seldom consists of "renewal" so that the loss of a grammatical strategy is compensated for by the development of something new. Neither does it consist of the loss of one of several redundant strategies. Rather, form-function changes involve strengthening of already available resources with extension to new domains when a subsystem comes under pressure. This can be visualised as in Figure 12, representing a hypothetical degenerate system in which the full lines stand for strong links and the dashed lines stand for weak links. As is clear from the figure, the loss of forms does not entail loss of functions, even in the case that no new forms are introduced. The only visible change in the forms is a strengthening of formerly weak links. Diachronic degeneracy is in line with the basic tenets of Construction Grammar that grammar, as part of the Construction, is a complex network of constructions.

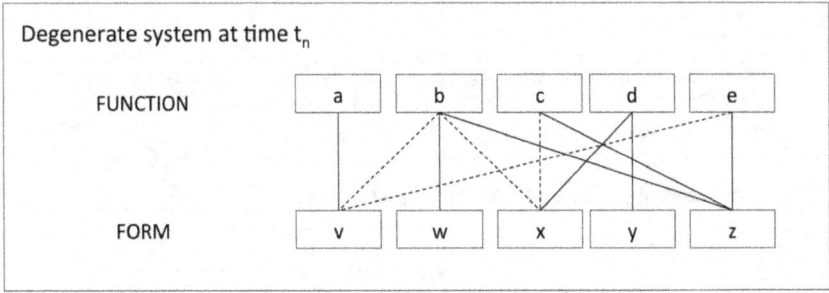

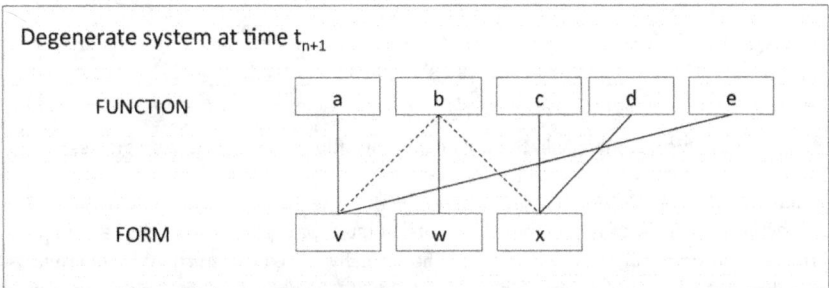

Figure 12: Diachronic form-function change in degenerate systems

In this article, I have looked at two cases studies: the argument realisation of experiencer predicates and the semantic level of subordinate clauses in Dutch. In both cases, there are several indications that we need a network view as in Figure 12 to understand what is going on. A tentative visualisation is given in Figures 13 and 14, respectively.[31] With regard to the expression of the agentivity of the experiencer in Figure 13, there is a loss of one of the formal strategies (c.q. case), leading to a strengthening of other strategies, such as voice-based alternations, the use of prefixes having to do with Aktionsart etc. With regard to the expression of clause relations in Figure 14, there is no loss of formal strategies, but the link between form and function shifts through time: V2 becomes stronger as a marker of main clauses (vs. subordinate clauses), which leads to a further integration of subordinate clauses. This weakens the capacity of V2 in main clauses to serve as a cue for the semantic level of attachment of subordinate clauses. This in turn leads to a stronger link between conjunctions and the semantic level of the attachment of subordinate clauses.

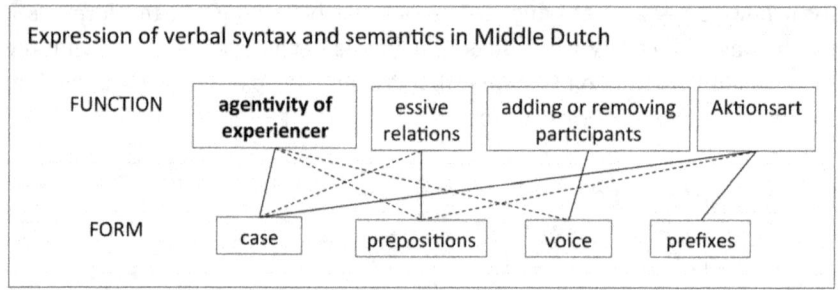

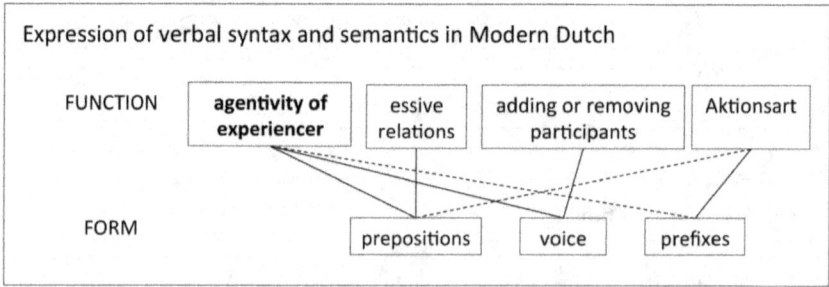

Figure 13: Diachronic degeneracy in the argument realisation of experiencer predicates

---

31 The details are of lesser importance. In Figure 13 the crucial issue is that the "agentivity of experiencer" box (internally made up of a set of horizontally related constructions – not visualised here) is degenerately controlled in both stages of Dutch. The precise relationships between the other forms and the other functions requires additional study. The same goes for Figure 14, mutatis mutandis.

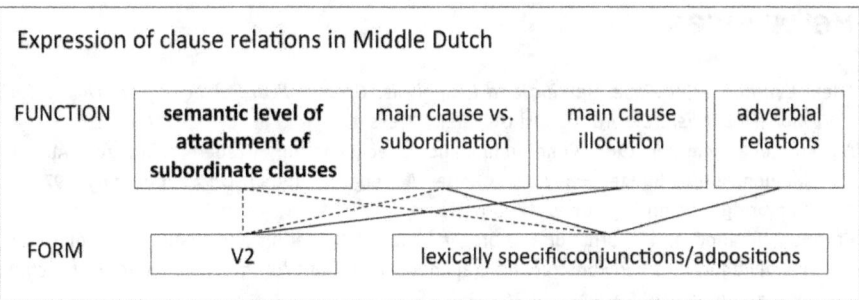
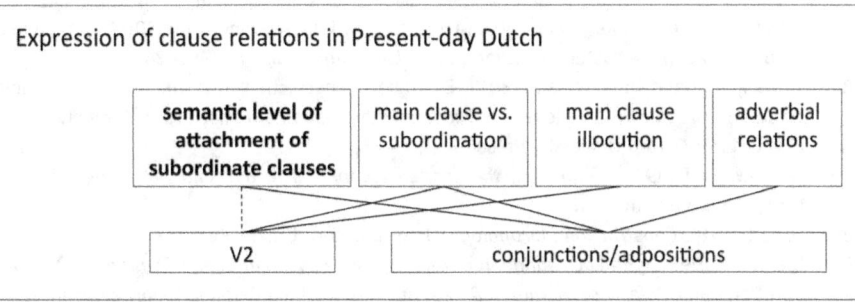

Figure 14: Diachronic degeneracy in the expression of clause relations

Corpora used

INL38: see Kruyt, J. and M. Dutilh 1997 A 38 million words Dutch text corpus and its users. *Lexikos* 7: 229–244.
KLASLIT: *Klassieke literatuur; Nederlandse letterkunde van de Middeleeuwen tot en met de Tachtigers* [Classical literature; Dutch literature from the Middle Ages until the Eightiers] 1999 Cd-rom. Utrecht: Spectrum Electronic Publishing.
LITEROM, see http: //www.knipselkranten.nl/literom. For this corpus study, all material available for the period 2001–2004 was excerpted.
MNW: *Middelnederlandsch woordenboek* [Middle Dutch Dictionary] 1998 's-Gravenhage: Sdu. Cd-rom version of Eelco Verwijs and Jakob Verdam 1885–1952 *Middelnederlandsch woordenboek* [Middle Dutch Dictionary]. 's-Gravenhage: Nijhoff.
WNT: *Woordenboek der Nederlandsche taal* [Dictionary of the Dutch Language] 2003 's-Gravenhage: Sdu. Cd-rom version of Matthias de Vries and Lammert te Winkel 1882–1998 *Woordenboek der Nederlandsche taal* [Dictionary of the Dutch Language]. 's-Gravenhage: Nijhoff.

References

Allen, Cynthia. 1995. *Case Marking and Reanalysis: Grammatical Relations from Old to Early Modern English*. Oxford: Oxford University Press.

Auwera, Johan van der. 1986. Conditionals and speech acts. In: Elizabeth C. Traugott, Alice Ter Meulen, Judith Snitzer Reilly and Charles A. Ferguson (eds.), *On Conditionals*, 197–214. Cambridge: Cambridge University Press.

Barðdal, Jóhanna and Thórhallur Eythórsson. 2012. "Hungering and lusting for women and fleshly delicacies": Reconstructing grammatical relations for Proto-Germanic. *Transactions of the Philological Society* 110: 363–393.

Beckner, Clay, Richard Blythe, Joan Bybee, Morten H. Christiansen, William Croft, Nick C. Ellis, John Holland, Jinyun Ke, Diane Larsen-Freeman and Tom Schoenemann. 2009. Language is a complex adaptive system: position paper. *Language Learning* 59: 1–26.

Bergen, Benjamin and Nancy Chang. 2013. Embodied Construction Grammar. In: Thomas Hoffmann and Graeme Trousdale (eds.), *The Oxford handbook of Construction Grammar*, 168–190. Oxford: Oxford University Press.

Bolinger, Dwight L. 1980. *Language, the Loaded Weapon: The Use and Abuse of Language Today*. London: Longman.

Booij, Geert. 2010. *Construction Morphology*. Oxford: Oxford University Press.

Burridge, Kate. 1993. *Syntactic change in Germanic: Aspects of Language Change in Germanic with Particular Reference to Middle Dutch*. Amsterdam/Philadelphia: John Benjamins.

Bybee, Joan. 2010. *Language, Usage, and Cognition*. Cambridge: Cambridge University Press.

Bybee, Joan and Clay Beckner. 2010. Usage-based theory. In: Bernd Heine and Heiko Narrog (eds.), *The Oxford Handbook of Linguistic Analysis*, 827–855. Oxford: Oxford University Press.

Cinque, Guglielmo. 1999. *Adverbs and Functional Heads: A Cross-Linguistic Perspective*. Oxford: Oxford University Press.

Cristofaro, Sonia. 2003. *Subordination*. Oxford: Oxford University Press.

Croft, William. 2000. *Explaining Language Change: An Evolutionary Approach*. Harlow: Longman.

Croft, William. 2001. *Radical Construction Grammar: Syntactic theory in typological perspective*. Oxford: Oxford University Press.

Croft, William and D. Alan Cruse. 2004. *Cognitive Linguistics*. Cambridge: Cambridge University Press.

Davison, Alice. 1981. Markers of derived illocutionary force and paradoxes of speech act modifiers. *Cahiers de Linguistique Française* 2: 47–73.

Dowty David R. 1991. Thematic proto-roles and argument selection. *Language* 67: 547–619.

Edelman, Gerald M. and Joseph A. Gally. 2001. Degeneracy and complexity in biological systems. *Proceedings of the National Academy of Sciences* 98: 13763–13768.

Evans, Vyvyan. 2007. *A Glossary of Cognitive Linguistics*. Edinburgh: Edinburgh University Press.

Eythórsson, Thórhallur and Jóhanna Barðdal. 2005. Oblique subjects: a common Germanic inheritance. *Language* 81: 824–881.

Foley, William A. and Richard D. Van Valin. 1984. *Functional Syntax and Universal Grammar*. Cambridge: Cambridge University Press.

Goldberg, Adele E. 1995. *Constructions: A Construction Grammar Approach to Argument Structure*. Chicago: University of Chicago Press.

Goldberg, Adele E. 1996. Making one's way through the data. In: Masayoshi Shibatani and Sandra Thompson (eds.), *Grammatical Constructions: Their Form and Meaning*, 27–54. Oxford: Oxford University Press.

Goldberg, Adele E. 2006. *Constructions at Work: The Nature of Generalization in Language*. Oxford: Oxford University Press.

Goldberg, Adele and Alex Del Giudice. 2005. Subject-auxiliary inversion: A natural category. *The Linguistic Review* 22: 411–428.

Grimm, Scott. 2011. Semantics of case. *Morphology* 21: 515–544.

Haeseryn, Walter, Kirsten Romijn, Guido Geerts, Jaap de Rooij and Maarten C. van den Toorn. 1997 *Algemene Nederlandse Spraakkunst* [General Dutch Grammar], 2nd edition. Groningen/Antwerpen: Martinus Nijhoff/Wolters Plantijn.

Haspelmath, Martin. 1998. Does grammaticalization need reanalysis? *Studies in Language* 22: 315–351.

Hengeveld, Kees. 1989. Layers and operators in Functional Grammar. *Journal of Linguistics* 25: 127–157.

Hengeveld, Kees. 1998. Adverbial clauses in the languages of Europe. In: Johan van der Auwera (ed.), *Adverbial Constructions in the Languages of Europe*, 335–419. Berlin/New York: Mouton de Gruyter.

Hengeveld, Kees. 2004. Illocution, mood, and modality. In: Geert Booij, Christian Lehmann, Joachim Mugdan and Stavros Skopetea (eds.), *Morphology. An International Handbook on Inflection and Word-Formation*, vol. 2, 1190–1201. Berlin/New York: Mouton de Gruyter.

Holland John. 1992. Complex adaptive systems. *Daedalus* 121: 17–30.

Hopper, Paul J. 1975. *The Syntax of the Simple Sentence In Proto-Germanic*. The Hague: Mouton.

Hopper, Paul J. and Elizabeth C. Traugott. 2003. *Grammaticalization*, 2nd edition. Cambridge: Cambridge University Press.

Horst, Johannes M. van der. 1981. Onderschikking en de plaats van de persoonsvorm in het Middelnederlands [Subordination and the position of the finite verb in Middle Dutch]. *Tijdschrift voor Nederlandse Taal- en Letterkunde* 97: 161–184.

Horst, Johannes M. van der. 1984. Over vorm en inhoud van bijzinnen [On form and content of subordinate clauses]. In: D.M. Bakker et al. (eds.), *Vorm en funktie in tekst en taal: Bundel opstellen verschenen ter gelegenheid van de voltooiing van het honderdste deel van het Tijdschrift voor Nederlandse Taal- en Letterkunde* [Form and Function in Text and Language: Essays Appearing on the Occasion of the Completion of the Hundredth Issue of *Tijdschrift voor Nederlandse Taal- en Letterkunde*], 154–179. Leiden: Brill.

Horst, Johannes M. van der. 1995. *Analytische Taalkunde* [Analytic Linguistics]. Groningen: Nijhoff.

Horst, Johannes M. van der. 2008. *Geschiedenis van de Nederlandse syntaxis* [History of the Syntax of Dutch]. Leuven: Leuven University Press.

Huffman, Alan. 2001. The linguistics of William Diver and the Columbia School. *Word* 52: 29–68.

Israel, Michael. 1996. The *way* constructions grow. In: Adele E. Goldberg (ed.), *Conceptual Structure, Discourse and Language*, 217–230. Stanford: CSLI.

Jurafsky, Daniel. 1992. An on-line computational model of human sentence interpretation: A theory of the representation and use of linguistic knowledge. Ph.D. dissertation, Computer Science department, University of California at Berkeley.

König, Ekkehard and Johan van der Auwera. 1988. Clause integration in German and Dutch conditional, concessive conditional, and concessive clauses. In: John Haiman and Sandra

Thompson (eds.), *Clause Linking in Grammar and Discourse*, 101–133. Amsterdam/ Philadelphia: John Benjamins.
Lakoff, George. 1977. Linguistic gestalts. *Chicago Linguistics Society* 13: 236–287.
Lehmann, Christian. 1988. Towards a typology of clause linkage. In: John Haiman and Sandra Thompson (eds.), *Clause Combining in Grammar and Discourse*, 181–225. Amsterdam/ Philadelphia: John Benjamins.
Levin, Beth and Malka Rappaport Hovav. 2005. *Argument Realization*. Cambridge: Cambridge University Press.
Levin, Magnus. 2009. The formation of the preterite and the past participle. In: Günter Rohdenburg and Julia Schlüter (eds.), *One Language, Two Grammars? Differences between British and American English*, 60–85. Cambridge: Cambridge University Press.
Michaelis, Laura A. 2009. Sign-Based Construction Grammar. In: Bernd Heine and Heiko Narrog (eds.), *The Oxford handbook of Linguistic Analysis*, 155–176. Oxford: Oxford University Press.
Mufwene, Salikoko S. 2008. *Language Evolution: Contact, Competition and Change*. London: Continuum.
Næss, Åshild. 2007. *Prototypical Transitivity*. Amsterdam/Philadelphia: John Benjamins.
Pagel, Mark. 2007. What is the latest theory of why humans lost their body hair? Why are we the only hairless primate? <http://www.scientificamerican.com/article.cfm?id=latest-theory-human-body-hair>.
Ritt, Nikolaus. 2004. *Selfish Sounds: A Darwinian Approach to Language Change*. Cambridge: Cambridge University Press.
Rosenbach, Anette. 2008. Language change as cultural evolution: Evolutionary approaches to language change. In: Regine Eckardt, Gerhard Jäger and Tonjes Veenstra (eds.), *Variation, Selection, Development: Probing the Evolutionary Model of Language Change*, 23–72. Berlin/New York: Mouton de Gruyter.
Siewierska, Anna. 2004. *Person*. Cambridge: Cambridge University Press.
Smessaert, Hans, Bert Cornillie, Dagmar Divjak and Karel Van den Eynde. 2005. Degrees of clause integration: From endotactic to exotactic subordination in Dutch. *Linguistics* 43: 471–529.
Steels, Luc. 2000. Language as a complex adaptive system. In: M. Schoenauer, K. Deb, G. Rudolph, X. Yao, E. Lutton, J.J Merelo and H.-P. Schwefel (eds.), *Proceedings of the 6th international conference on parallel problem solving from nature*, 17–26. Berlin: Springer.
Steels, Luc. 2011a. Modeling the cultural evolution of language. *Physics of Life Review* 8: 339–356.
Steels, Luc. 2011b. A first encounter with Fluid Construction Grammar. In: Luc Steels (ed.), *Design patterns in Fluid Construction Grammar*, 31–68. Amsterdam/Philadelphia: John Benjamins.
Sweetser, Eve. 1990. *From Etymology to Pragmatics: Metaphorical and Cultural Aspects of Semantic Structure*. Cambridge: Cambridge University Press.
Taylor, John R. 2004. The ecology of constructions. In: Günter Radden and Klaus-Uwe Panther (eds.), *Studies in Linguistic Motivation*, 49–73. Berlin: Mouton de Gruyter.
Trousdale, Graeme. 2008. Words and constructions in grammaticalization: The end of the English Impersonal Construction. In: Donka Minkova and Susan Fizmaurice (eds.), *Empirical and Analytical Advances in the Study of English Language Change*, 301–326. Berlin/New York: Mouton de Gruyter.

Trousdale, Graeme. 2010. Issues in constructional approaches to grammaticalization. In: Ekaterina Stathi, Elke Gehweiler and Ekkehard König (eds.), *Grammaticalization: Current Views and Issues*, 51–71. Amsterdam/Philadelphia: John Benjamins.

Velde, Freek van de. 2004. De Middelnederlandse onpersoonlijke constructie en haar grammaticale concurrenten: Semantische motivering van de argumentstructuur [The Middle Dutch Impersonal Construction and its grammatical competitors: The semantic motivation of argument structure]. *Nederlandse Taalkunde* 9: 48–76.

Velde, Freek van de. 2009. *De nominale constituent: Structuur en geschiedenis* [The Noun Phrase. Structure and History]. Leuven: Leuven University Press.

Verhagen, Arie. 2003. Hoe het Nederlands zich een eigen weg baant: Vergelijkende en historische observaties vanuit een constructie-perspectief [How Dutch creates itself a path. Comparative and historical observations from a constructionist perspective]. *Nederlandse Taalkunde* 8: 328–346.

Verstraete, Jean-Christophe. 2003. Preverbal positions in three Germanic languages: The role of scope as a functional principle. *Languages in contrast* 4: 105–136.

Weerman, Fred. 1988. Moet kunnen: Middelnederlandse zinnen zonder subject [Must can: Middle Dutch sentences without a subject]. *De Nieuwe Taalgids* 81: 289–310.

Weijnen, Antonius. 1971. *Schets van de Geschiedenis van de Nederlandse Syntaxis* [Contours of the History of the Syntax of Dutch]. Assen: Van Gorcum.

Whitacre, James and Axel Bender. 2010. Degeneracy: A design principle for achieving robustness and evolvability. *Journal of Theoretical Biology* 263: 143–153.

Zwart, Jan-Wouter. 2011. *The Syntax of Dutch*. Cambridge: Cambridge University Press.

Gijsbert Rutten and Marijke van der Wal
7 Social and constructional diffusion: Relative clauses in seventeenth- and eighteenth-century Dutch

1 Introduction

In this paper, we discuss a significant change in the morphosyntax of Dutch, arguing that bringing together evidence from (historical) sociolinguistic and constructional analyses advances our understanding of language variation and change. In so doing, we link up with recent developments in cognitive linguistics, where a "social turn" has been argued for (Croft 2000, 2009; Kristiansen and Dirven 2008; Geeraerts, Kristiansen, and Peirsman 2010; Harder 2010; Hoffmann and Trousdale 2011). The change under discussion concerns the rise of *w*-relativizers such as *waar* 'where' at the expense of *d*-relativizers such as *daar* 'lit. there, where'. The change will be introduced in more detail in section 2. In section 3, we discuss previous research, and formulate two hypotheses following suggestions in the literature. First, we hypothesize that the change is a so-called change from above in the social sense, that is a change that spreads from the upper ranks of society to the lower ranks. Second, we hypothesize that the change spreads from construction to construction. We assume, therefore, that the change exhibits diffusion in at least two ways: social and constructional. We will use a socially stratified corpus of seventeenth- and eighteenth-century private letters to investigate this. The corpus will be introduced in section 4. In sections 5 and 6, we argue that both social and constructional diffusion can indeed be found in the change from *d*- to *w*-relativization. Section 5 shows that *w*-relativizers are more in use in letters from the upper ranks of society than in letters from the lower ranks. The private letters in our corpora are characterized by a great number of epistolary formulae. In section 6, we will argue that these formulae can be considered as constructions in the sense of construction grammar, after which we will show that *w*-relativizers appear to spread from formula to formula, that is from construction to construction. In section 7, we discuss the results, and moreover argue that a constructional approach may gain from sociolinguistic analyses.

2 The change from *d-* to *w-*relativizers

In the history of Dutch, relativizers such as relative pronouns, relative adverbs and relative pronominal adverbs have changed or are changing from a *d-*form into a *w-*form. The change from *d* to *w-*relativization constitutes a major shift in the grammar of Dutch, as in other Germanic languages (Romaine 1982; Rissanen 1999: 292–301; von Polenz 1994: 278–279). The change began in the late Middle Dutch period, in the fourteenth or fifteenth century (van der Horst 2008: 603, 703), and is not yet complete. The change affects any kind of relative clause (restricted and appositive relative clauses), any kind of relativizer (pronouns, adverbs and pronominal adverbs), and any kind of syntactic/ semantic context (dependent and independent or free relative clauses). A few examples, taken from the literature and the internet, will illustrate this. In (1–4), the changes in the pronominal system are shown with free relatives (1, 2) and with nominal antecedents (3, 4). The (a)-examples are Middle Dutch, the (b)-sentences are present-day Dutch. In examples (1) and (3), the antecedent is inanimate, in (2) and (4) it is animate. The change represented by (1, 2) is complete. The change in (3) is in progress, with the *w-*form being common in many colloquial varieties of Dutch, while the *d-*form is preferred in the written standard. Only few speakers would accept (4b), but *w-*forms do appear in this position, also in written language.

(1a) *Had ic ghevonden **dat** ic zoeck* (14th c.; van der Horst 2008: 603)
     had I found   that I seek
     'Had I found what I was looking for'

(1b) *Na 5 weken had ik gevonden **wat** ik zocht*[1]
     after 5 weeks had I found   what I sought
     'After five weeks, I had found what I had been looking for'

(2a) ***Die** sine cuusheit uerlieset, die uerlieset sine siele*
     That his chastity looses   that looses   his soul
     'He who looses chastity, looses his soul' (c. 1400; van der Horst 2008: 603)

(2b) ***wie** zijn KUISHEID bewaakt mag door elk deur die hij/zij wil*
     who his chastity guards may through each door that he/she wants
     het paradijs binnentreden![2]
     the paradise enter
     'He who guards his chastity, may enter paradise through any door he/she wants to'

---

[1] http://www.datingwebsites.nl/reviews/second-love/
[2] http://forums.marokko.nl/archive/index.php/t-1459274%2520%253C/t-1703877-p-3.html

(3a) *dat woordt **dat** die heilighe man job sprac*
    that word that that holy   man Job spoke
    'the word that the holy man Job spoke' (14th c.; van der Horst 2008: 377)

(3b) *Neger, ja, dat is het woord **wat** Totti tegen mij zei*[3]
    negro yes that is the word what Totti to me said
    'Negro, yes, that is the word that Totti said to me'

(4a) *vrouwen, **die** ter   merct brengen wouden eyer ende botter*
    women   that to-the market bring would eggs and butter
    'women, who wanted to bring to the market eggs and butter'
    (15th c.; van der Horst 2008: 601)

(4b) *de grote minderheid van de vrouwen **wie** op die manier gebruik*
    the big minority of the women who on that way   use

    maken over internet[4]
    make over internet
    'the vast minority of women who make use of the internet in that way'

Similar changes have affected free relative adverbs (5), relative adverbs (6) and pronominal adverbs (7), all derived from originally locative expressions.

(5a) *Sine es niet **daer** si was tevoren* (13th c.; van der Horst 2008: 477)
    she is not there she was before
    'She is not where she was before'

(5b) *ze is niet **waar** ze eerder was*[5]
    she is not where she earlier was
    'She is not where she was earlier'

(6a) *tot Bruesel, **daer** sy hoer antwoort kreghen*
    in Brussels there they their answer got
    'in Brussels, where they got their answer' (15th c.; van der Horst 2008: 703)

---

3 http://www.voetbalzone.nl/doc.asp?uid=105236
4 http://www.wowforum.nl/viewtopic.php?f=16&t=18006&st=0&sk=t&sd=a
5 https://www.verhalensite.com/info2.php?s=st&ss=r&id=78886

(6b) *te Brussel,* **waar** *zij haar debuut maakte*[6]
    in Brussels where she her debut made
    'in Brussels, where she made her debut'

(7a) *den viere /* **daer** *die bouc in bernende lach*
    the fire there the book in burning lay
    'the fire in which the book lay burning' (12th c.; van der Horst 2008: 498)

(7b) *het vuur* **waarin** *ze branden zal niet doven*[7]
    the fire wherein they burn shall not smother
    'the fire in which they burn will not smother'

The changes exemplified in (5–7) are complete, at least in the majority of Dutch dialects and in standard Dutch.[8] The crucial period were the seventeenth and eighteenth centuries (van der Horst and Storm 1991; de Schutter and Kloots 2000; van der Wal 2002; van der Horst 2008). Therefore, the case studies in the present paper, dealing with relative (pronominal) adverbs, focus on the seventeenth and eighteenth centuries.

3 Background and hypotheses

The change from *d-* to *w*-relativizers has been the topic of a vast body of recent studies in Dutch historical linguistics (van der Horst 1988, 1993; van der Horst and Storm 1991; Schoonenboom 1997, 2000; de Schutter and Kloots 2000; van der Wal 2002, 2003; Rutten 2010; Rutten and van der Wal acc.). It is often assumed or claimed that the change proceeded from indefinite to definite contexts (cf. van der Horst and Storm 1991: 115; van der Horst 1993: 300; van der Wal 2002; de Schutter and Kloots 2000: 327; Schoonenboom 2000: 137–138, 157–158), adopting the following cline of (in)definiteness (van der Horst 1988: 96). The first

---

6 http://www.dutchdivas.net/sopranen/raymonde_serverius.html
7 http://www.allaboutworldview.org/dutch/bestaat-de-hel.htm
8 A recent syntactic atlas of Dutch dialects shows that the locative relative in *De bank waar ze op zaten was pas geverfd* 'The bench that they were sitting on had just been painted' is mostly realized as a *w*-form (267 locations), *d*-forms (33 locations) being largely restricted to the Dutch provinces of North Brabant and Friesland (*SAND* 2005, map 88b). As noted in the commentary to the maps (p. 77), it is striking that there are hardly any dialects with solely *d*-forms. In other words, in dialects where *d*-forms are attested, *w*-forms are often also used.

category would constitute the most indefinite context, whereas definite NP's represent the most definite contexts.[9]

Indefinite   1 the antecedent is absent or implicit: *je moet doen wat ze zegt* 'lit. you must do what she says, you must do as she says'
2 the antecedent is an entire clause: *ze deed erg haar best, wat wij heel flink vonden* 'she really did her best, which we considered very plucky'
3 the antecedent is a word such as *iets* 'something', *niets* 'nothing', *alles* 'everything', *veel* 'much', *weinig* 'little', *genoeg* 'enough': *alles wat hij wil* 'lit. everything what he wants', everything he wants, *is er iets wat/dat ik voor je kan doen?* 'lit. is there something what/that I can do for you?'
4 the antecedent is a nominalized adjective, mostly a superlative: *het vriendelijkste wat/dat Jan heeft gedaan* 'lit. the most friendly what/that Jan has done, the most friendly thing Jan has done'
5 the antecedent is an indefinite NP: *een boek dat (wat) ik mooi vind* 'lit. a book that (what) I like'

Definite   6 the antecedent is a definite NP: *het boek dat (wat) ik gisteren las* 'lit. the book that (what) I read yesterday'

Counterexamples, however, are easily found. There are, for instance, eighteenth-century diaries with *w*-relativizers in category 3 that have *d*-relativizers in other categories (Rutten 2010). Therefore, it has been argued that this cline of (in)definiteness may not be able to explain all empirical facts and that a different approach drawing on construction grammar and frequency may better explain the spread of *w*-relativizers (Rutten 2010).[10]

---

9 The examples are taken from van der Horst (1988: 96), which is a study of the relative pronouns *dat* and *wat*. As to the choice of relative pronoun, Van der Horst distinguishes three options, representing late-twentieth-century standard Dutch: *wat* as in catergories 1 and 2, *wat/dat* as in 3 and 4, indicating that both are possible, and *dat (wat)* as in 5 and 6, which means that *dat* is the norm, while *wat* is often used, too.
10 It has been argued by van der Horst and Storm (1991), van der Horst (1993), de Schutter and Kloots (2000) and Rutten (2010) that in the case of pronominal adverbs the lexical form might be important, either fused into one lexeme (e.g. *het vuur waarin ze branden, zal niet doven* 'the fire where-in/ in which they burn, will not smother') or separated into two lexemes (*het vuur waar ze in branden, zal niet doven* 'lit. the fire where they in burn, will not smother'). This is an important observation. In the present study, we will take into account both fused and separate forms, focusing only on the initial consonant (*d* or *w*). We hope to be able to address the lexical form in subsequent research.

Furthermore, Rutten and van der Wal (acc.) show that some constructions subsumed under the second category are indeed among the first to adopt *w*-forms, but this only applies to so-called continuative relative clauses, not to appositive relative clauses with the preceding clause as antecedent in general. Moreover, continuative relative clauses are ahead of other categories, including the first category. Continuative relative clauses have the form of subordinate clauses while the semantics favors a main clause interpretation (cf. Loock 2007). Considering continuative relative clauses as schematic constructions in the sense of construction grammar, Rutten and van der Wal (acc.) show that an explanation of the spread of *w*-relativizers may gain from a constructionist view of the language system.

As is well-known from variationist studies, changes may also display social and stylistic diffusion, in that some (groups of) speakers may adopt new forms at a faster pace than others. With regard to changes in relativization strategies, it is often assumed that the rise of *wh*-forms in the history of English was a so-called change from above, 'from the formal and literary levels of the language' (Rissanen 1999: 295). Rissanen (1999: 293) also points out that *wh*-forms were well-established in appositive relative clauses in the sixteenth century, though the old form *that* is still found in texts representing the oral mode of discourse (cf. Bergs 2005: 181). Concerning eighteenth-century Dutch, it has been suggested that *d*-relativizers such as *daar* 'there, where' are more frequently found in texts closer to the spoken language such as diaries written by lesser skilled writers (Rutten 2010). Recall in this respect that present-day standard Dutch as well as most dialects only exhibit *w*-relativizers in locative constructions, *d*-forms being restricted to optional usage in a limited number of dialects (section 2).

The present study continues the line of research explained above by focusing on two main issues addressed in the literature. Can a constructionist view indeed further our understanding of the change from *d*- to *w*-relativizers? And can we identify social variation in the spread of *w*-forms? The corpus of seventeenth- and eighteenth-century private letters used for the present study allows us to answer these questions. The corpus is primarily designed for sociolinguistic research (section 4), and we will therefore first investigate possible social effects on the diffusion of *w*-forms. Since it has been suggested that *w*-forms were promoted "from above", we hypothesize that we will establish social variation, with upper ranks using *w*-forms more frequently than lower ranks (see section 5) – despite the fact that most changes qualify as changes from below, particularly when there is no overt metalinguistic discourse on the change nor on the variation it involves, as is the case with *d*- and *w*-relativizers (van der Wal 2003).

Building on previous research, we also hypothesize that the change spreads from construction to construction through a process which might be termed constructional diffusion. We will take the opportunity to investigate this by studying a set of constructions characteristic of the language of private letters and different from the constructions studied before (cf. Rutten 2010; Rutten and van der Wal acc.).

4 The corpus

The corpus used for the present study is part of the so-called *Letters as loot*-corpus compiled at Leiden University for historical-sociolinguistic research.[11] The *Letters as loot*-corpus consists of Dutch seventeenth- and eighteenth-century private letters from a huge collection of Dutch documents, kept in The National Archives in Kew, London. These documents were confiscated by English war ships and private ships (privateers) authorized by the government to attack and seize cargo from enemy ships during frequent times of war from the second half of the seventeenth to the early nineteenth centuries.[12] Among the wide range of material, including plantation accounts, ships' journals and lists of slaves, the collection comprises about 40,000 Dutch letters, both commercial and private. It is the 15,000 private letters, in particular, sent by people of all social ranks, men and women alike, that makes this source so interesting for historical linguists. In order to be able to explore the language of the letters, two cross-sections were made: one for the seventeenth century and the other for the eighteenth century. Not all regions are equally represented in the corpora, the provinces of Holland and Zeeland prevailing due to the origin of the confiscated letters. Many crewmembers and passengers and their families lived in or close to the seaport towns along the coast. This means that the bulk of our letters stem from the western parts of the Northern Netherlands.

For the present study, a corpus of approximately 300,000 words was compiled, consisting of two subcorpora, viz. one for each period. All letters have been transcribed from the original manuscripts and digitized within the project.

---

11 *Letters as loot* (*Brieven als buit*) is a research project at Leiden University, funded by the Netherlands Organisation for Scientific Research (NWO), and directed by Marijke van der Wal. Gijsbert Rutten is a postdoctoral researcher in the project. See www.brievenalsbuit.nl
12 From 1652 till 1813, four Anglo-Dutch Wars were fought and in various other wars England and the Netherlands were on opposite sides.

All letters used are established autographs.[13] The basic figures of the corpus are presented in Table 1.

Table 1: Basic data of the corpus used for the present chapter

	Period	Number of letters	Number of letter writers	Number of words
Subcorpus 1	1660s/1670s	219	168	102,000
Subcorpus 2	1770s/1780s	384	292	196,500

Since the letter collection comprises private letters from various ranks of society, the corpus is fit for sociolinguistic analyses. Reconstructing the social context in order to arrive at a reliable division into social ranks is a notoriously difficult issue, in historical sociolinguistics even more so than in present-day sociolinguistics, and we therefore have to rely gratefully on the work done by social historians (cf. Nevalainen and Raumolin-Brunberg 2003: 30–38; Kiełkiewicz-Janowiak 2012). Following the division into social ranks used by historians of Early Modern Dutch society (Frijhoff and Spies 1999: 190–191), we distinguish between four social strata, viz. lower class (LC), lower middle class (LMC), upper middle class (UMC) and upper class (UC). This division is mainly founded upon the writers' occupation and/or the occupation of family members. The most important exception to the division used by historians is that the highest social level, the so-called patriciate (which includes the nobility, and which is located above the UC) is not represented in our corpus. The LC comprises waged workers, mainly sailors, servants and soldiers. The LMC covers the petty bourgeoisie, including small shopkeepers, small craftsmen and minor officials. To the UMC we allocate the prosperous middle ranks (storekeepers, non-commissioned officers, well-to-do farmers), while the UC mainly comprises wealthy merchants, ship-owners, academics and commissioned officers. Table 2 presents the make-up of the two subcorpora across social rank, giving both the number of letters (Nl) and the number of words (Nw).

---

[13] Corpus compilation involved research into the autograph or non-autograph status of the letters. As part of the seventeenth- and eighteenth-century population was illiterate or semi-literate, we had to establish whether or not the letters were written by the senders themselves. Nobels and van der Wal (2012) explain the procedure followed in order to arrive at an autograph corpus.

Table 2: Social stratification of subcorpora 1 and 2

	Lower		Lower Middle		Upper Middle		Upper	
	Nl	Nw	Nl	Nw	Nl	Nw	Nl	Nw
Subcorpus 1	10	5,500	41	22,000	145	61,000	23	13,500
Subcorpus 2	26	9,000	97	34,000	131	61,000	130	92,500

5 Diachrony and social diffusion

As stated above, we will first look into social effects on the diffusion of *w*-forms. Drawing on both subcorpora, we will also establish diachronic differences. We extracted all relative adverbs and relative pronominal adverbs beginning with *d* and *w* from the two subcorpora, along with their syntactic context. A few ambiguous examples were excluded, mainly because it was impossible to tell if the adverbs introduced a main clause or a subclause for lack of a finite verb. In some cases, a *d*-form such as *daer* 'there' could also be interpreted as a conjunction fulfilling an argumentative function, usually a temporal, adversative or concessive function (*while, whereas, although*), which is a grammaticalized result of the relative adverb. Example (8), taken from subcorpus 1, has the free relative *daer* which contains an "implied antecedent" and could therefore be interpreted as *there where*, but also as a concessive. In example (9) from subcorpus 2, a temporal or adversative interpretation is favored.

(8) god ... dancken ende loeuen voor de genaede die heij aen ons beweijst
    god ... thank and praise for the mercy that he to us shows
    daer   weij sulcke kinderen van verderf sijn
    REL / CONJ we such children of doom are
    '[we should] thank God and praise Him for the mercy which He shows to us there where / although / even though we are such children of doom'

(9) danke inmiddels de Heere voor onze gelukkige behoudenis daar
    thank meanwhile the Lord for our happy safety REL / CONJ
    zoo veel andere haar leeven hebben moeten laaten
    so many others their life have must let
    'meanwhile, I thank the Lord for our happy safety there where / while so many others have lost their lives'

While the concessive interpretation *although, even though* may be preferred in (8), it is still possible to interpret *daer* as a locative expression: it is in the metaphorical position of doom where man finds himself that God nevertheless shows mercy to him. In cases such as (8), *daer* allows the grammaticalized argumentative function but can also be interpreted as the relative adverb. Similarly, in (9), the writer is safe, which is a "location" or position that many others have not been able to reach. The temporal/adversative interpretation is clearly favored, but it is also clear how it has grammaticalized from the locative expression. 6 to 7% of the data are such grammaticalized forms (17 tokens in subcorpus 1, and 44 in subcorpus 2), which we did not exclude from the results.

For the seventeenth century, this procedure resulted in 269 relative clauses, 150 of which beginning with a *d*-relativizer, and 119 with a *w*-relativizer, which amounts to 56% *d*-forms and 44% *w*-forms respectively. In subcorpus 2, we found 598 relative clauses, 169 of which with a *d*-forms, and 429 with a *w*-form, amounting to 28% *d*-relativization and 72% *w*-relativization. See Table 3.

Table 3: Relativization across time in the seventeenth- and eighteenth-century subcorpora

	d-relativizer		*w*-relativizer		Total	
	N	%	N	%	N	%
Subcorpus 1	150	56	119	44	269	100
Subcorpus 2	169	28	429	72	598	100

The corpus results confirm the ongoing spread of the incoming *w*-relativizers, rising from less than fifty percent in subcorpus 1 from the 1660s/1670s to over seventy percent in subcorpus 2 from the 1770s/1780s.

Focusing on the social diffusion of the change, we investigated the distribution across social rank. Figure 1 presents the proportion of *w*-relativizers across social rank and time. The black columns represent the results from subcorpus 1, the grey columns those from subcorpus 2.

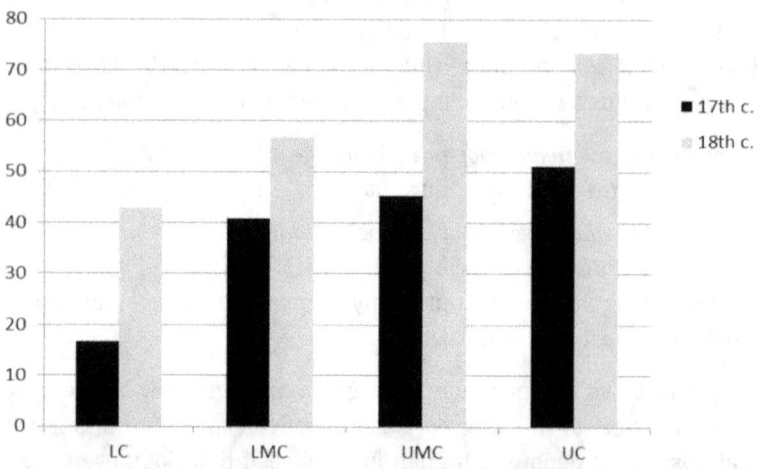

Figure 1: Proportion of *w*-relativizers in subcorpora 1 and 2, across time and social class

Figure 1 shows that the increase in *w*-forms holds when the data are split up by social rank, the grey columns being consistently higher than the black columns. Figure 1 also shows that there are clear social differences with regard to the appropriation of the incoming form. In subcorpus 1, with data from the seventeenth century, the LC are below 20% *w*-forms, whereas the LMC, the UMC and the UC are between 40 and 50%. In the eighteenth-century results based on subcorpus 2, the LC has risen to over 40%, while the other ranks have progressed to almost 60% in the LMC and to approximately 75% in the UMC and the UC. The spread of *w*-relativizers clearly displays social diffusion, the upper ranks of society using the new forms more often than the lower ranks in both periods. In other words, both in the 1660s/1670s and in the 1770s/1780s the change from *d*- to *w*-relativization constitutes a classic example of a change from above in the social sense, confirming our hypothesis about the social diffusion of the change.

6 Epistolary formulae and constructional diffusion

6.1 Epistolary formulae as constructions

The language of private letters, and of our seventeenth-century private letters in particular (Rutten and van der Wal 2012; Rutten and van der Wal 2013) is characterized by a large number of so-called epistolary formulae, that is recurrent expressions mainly or exclusively found in letters. In this respect, the letters in our corpus do not differ from, for example, English, German, Scottish or Finnish correspondence of the Early and Late Modern period (Austin 1973; Tieken-Boon van Ostade 1999; Nevala 2004; Dossena 2007; Elspaß 2012; Laitinen and Nordlund 2012). All these letters bear witness to a pervasive pan-European tradition of letter writing dating back to the medieval rhetorical art of letter writing, the *ars dictaminis*, and Latin and French models for business and legal writings, the *ars notaria* (see Nevalainen 2001; Poster and Mitchell 2007, and the references there).

Epistolary formulae may fulfil various functions and are used throughout letters, though most formulae occur in the opening and closing passages. Some formulae cover intersubjective domains such as greeting and health. Example (10), taken from subcorpus 1, presents an opening formula widely used in seventeenth-century letters. Example (11), taken from subcorpus 2, includes the formulaic expression *fris en gesond* 'fresh and healthy, in good health', repeatedly found in eighteenth-century letters.

(10) *Een Vryendelijcke groetenysse sy gescheuen aen*
    a   friendly   greeting   be written   to
    'a friendly greeting be written to'

(11) *dese diend om UEd te Laten Weten dat ik Nog fris en gesond zyn*
    this serves to you to let know that I still fresh and healthy am
    'this [letter] serves to let you know that I am still fresh and healthy/
    in good health'

Other formulae do not fulfil a concrete intersubjective function, but rather make the structure of the discourse explicit, for instance by announcing a new topic (12) or by preparing the reader to the closure (13). Both (12) and (13) are taken from subcorpus 2.

(12) *Verder heb ik u, myn hertie lief te melden, dat*
    further have I you my heart love to inform that
    'furthermore, I must inform you, my dear love, that'

(13) *Verders niets sonderling meer te melden hebbende als*
    further nothing special more to inform having than
    'furthermore, having/I have nothing special/other to say but/than'

A number of formulae have relative (pronominal) adverbs. In the remainder of section 6, we will focus on two such formulae. Example (14) presents the address of a seventeenth-century letter, taken from subcorpus 1, which includes the formula *waer op Commandeert* 'lit. where on commands, on which commands'. This is a frequently used formula identifying the ship on which the addressee should be found.

(14) *Aen reijnier witte Chirurgijn op 't slands schip de spiegel,*
    to Reijnier Witte barber surgeon on the country's ship De Spiegel
    waer op Commandeert den h^r viceadmirael michiel de ruijter
    REL on commands the Mr vice-admiral Michiel de Ruijter
    To Reijnier Witte, barber surgeon on the country's ship De Spiegel, on which the vice-admiral Mr Michiel de Ruijter commands'

Example (15) gives the opening of a letter from subcorpus 1. It contains the formulaic expression *daer uijt dat ick versta* 'lit. there from that I understand, from which I understand', which is often used to create the transition from reference to a previous letter, to the contents of that letter.

(15) *Gonstige vrient ick hebbe ul   aengenamen wel ontfang daer uijt dat*
     Kind   friend I have your pleasant   well received REL from that

   ick versta   dat ul getrout is
   I   understand that you married is
   'Kind friend, I have well received your pleasant [letter], from which I understand that you have married'

Epistolary formulae such as (10–15) are similar to constructions in the sense of construction grammar (cf. e.g. Croft 2001; Goldberg 1995, 2006). The following well-known table of the syntax-lexicon continuum, consisting of almost entirely schematic constructions on the one hand to fully lexicalized constructions on the other hand, is based on Croft and Cruse (2004: 255).

Table 4: The syntax-lexicon continuum in construction grammar (Croft and Cruse 2004: 255)

Construction type	Traditional name	Examples
Complex and (mostly) schematic	syntax	[Sbj *be*-Tns Verb-Pp *by* Obl]
Complex, substantive verb	subcategorisation frame	[Sbj *consume* Obj]
Complex and (mostly) substantive	idiom	[*kick*-Tns *the bucket*]
Complex but bound	morphology	[Noun-*s*], [Verb-Tns]
Atomic and schematic	syntactic category	[Dem], [Adj]
Atomic and substantive	word/lexicon	[*this*], [*green*]

An important criterion employed in constructionist approaches to grammar is that of non-compositionality, i.e. the observation that constructions may carry meanings independent of the words they consist of (e.g. Goldberg 1995: 1, 2006: 5). The epistolary formulae discussed here, however, appear to be compositional. The meaning of the utterances is easily derived from the individual words making up the utterance. It has also been argued that utterances may be stored as constructions "as long as they occur with sufficient frequency" (Goldberg 2006: 5), resulting in the conventionalization of utterances as idioms (Bybee 2006). The epistolary formulae discussed in the foregoing are all highly frequent sequences in our letter corpora, which in fact leads us to consider them as formulaic. The opening formula in (10), for example, occurs 41 times in subcorpus 1, and never more than once in a letter, which implies that 41/219 or approximately one in five letters begin with this formula.

Most epistolary formulae consist of a string of words, so they are complex, not atomic. They also contain quite some lexical material. Therefore, we may characterize many epistolary formulae as complex constructions with at least one and mostly several substantive elements. A constructionist description of the epistolary formula in (14) would need to take into account not only the grammatical and semantic properties of the formula, but also co- and contextual information (cf. Bergs 2010). If we term the formula the *on which commands-construction*, we can specify its basic syntactic form as [Rel *op commandeert* Subject], meaning that it consists of a relativizer, i.e. a *d-* or *w-*form, the lexicalized string *op commandeert* 'on commands', and a subject identifying the actor who is commanding. These elements can be specified even further. The first variable element, the relativizer, is either *daer* or *waer* (in the most common seventeenth-century spelling), that is either the historic form or the incoming variant. The second variable element, the subject, is always a proper noun, i.e. the name of a captain. Moreover, the entire address as presented in (14) is composed in accordance with certain discourse rules. As to the co-text, the *on which commands-construction*, as a relative clause, is always attached to a noun, i.e. the name of a ship. In (14), this is the ship *De Spiegel* ('The Mirror'). From an even wider perspective, the description of the construction needs to account for the fact that it occurs in the address on a letter, which means that letter writers have control of very specific generic rules.

Describing the *on which commands-construction* as such enables us to cover many examples that we find in our corpus. Diving further into the data, however, we establish that the formula exhibits considerably more variation. In (16–18), taken from subcorpus 1, the meaning COMMAND is not lexicalized by the finite verb form *commandeert*, but by a noun specifying the social role of the person who commands instead. In addition, the subject of the relative clause (*Sijmoen Kerseboom*) occurs immediately following the relativizer in (18). Finally, the use of the formula is extended to other parts of the letter. While most tokens occur in addresses, example (18) is taken from the body of a letter, where the writer indicates the ship with which he has sent his previous letters.

(16) *scheip prinssesse louvijsse   daer Commedeur op is Aert Jansz van es*
    ship   Prinsesse Louvijsse REL commander on is Aert Jansz van Es
    'ship Prinsesse Louvijsse, on which Aert Jansz van Es is commander'

(17) *het schip rotterdam   daer cappetein op is de manachtiggen lendert*
    the ship Rotterdam REL captain   on is the manly   Lendert
    ariiense aeswandt
    Ariiense Aeswandt
    'the ship Rotterdam, on which the manly Lendert Ariiense Aeswandt is the captain'

(18) *het Schip daer Sijmoen kerseboom Schipper op is*
the ship REL Sijmon Kerseboom shipmaster on is
'the ship on which Sijmon Kerseboom is shipmaster'

These examples are not accounted for by the description given above, which means that we have to assume another construction. Semantically and pragmatically, however, examples (16–18) clearly resemble (14). They are likely part of the same family of constructions, as they fulfil exactly the same function as (14). A constructionist description of examples (16–18), which we consider examples of the *where the officer is*-construction, specifies the basic form of the construction as [Rel (Subject) *commandeur/ schipper/ kapitein op is* (Subject)]. Note that in this description the lexicalized part is variable, as it identifies three possible nouns referring to the function of the officer that is in command (commander, shipmaster, captain). As shown in (18), the subject position, as before a proper noun, is variable. The first slot is similar to the first slot of the *on which commands*-construction, i.e. a *d*- or *w*-relativizer. As before, the relative clause always follows the name of a ship. Contrary to the *on which commands*-construction, the *where the officer is*-construction not only occurs in addresses, but also in the body of letters.

As explained in the foregoing, we have two formulae, the *on which commands*-construction and the *where the officer is*-construction, the basic meaning of which is to determine the person commanding a certain ship. From a constructionist perspective, it seems more than likely that these two constructions are connected, in the sense that their resemblance should be accounted for in a representation of letter writers' linguistic resources. Apart from the similar basic meaning, there is the empirical fact that most examples of both constructions occur in letters' addresses. We, therefore, assume an abstract meaning COMMAND, which can be expressed by tokens of two constructions. Both constructions are much more abstract than expected on a first inspection of the data. They are more schematic than the typical idiom that they appeared to be, allowing for variation in wording, syntax and position in the wider discourse. Moreover, the single lexical item that the two subtypes share is the preposition *op* 'on'. In sum, when discussing (14) we stated that the seemingly idiomatic *on which commands*-construction is often found in letters' addresses, but it rather appears that the meaning COMMAND may be lexicalized by a verb (*commandeert*) or by a noun and the verb *is* (*commandeur is, schipper is, kapitein is*). Taking into account examples such as (16–18) forces us to assume a more schematic representation of the epistolary formula at hand, particularly because the meaning COMMAND can be lexicalized in various ways. This schematization co-occurs with increased variability in other areas: the subject can be any high officer, not just a captain; the subject position is variable; the position of the preposition is also variable; the formula is not only used in addresses, but may occasionally turn up in the body of a letter.

Building on Bergs (2010), who proposes an onomasisological analysis of English future constructions as opposed to the predominantly semasiological approach in constructionist work, we consider the two constructions as members of a family of constructions expressing the meaning COMMAND. Bergs (2010) suggests that grouping (sub)constructions from an onomasiological perspective may be visualized by listing a number of semantically related constructions within a box. Note that the boxes and lines-visualization often employed in construction grammar cannot be used here, as these lines usually denote inheritance relationships based on form, whereas we focus on meaning. Figure 2 is merely meant as an illustration of what such an onomasiological approach to constructional representation entails.

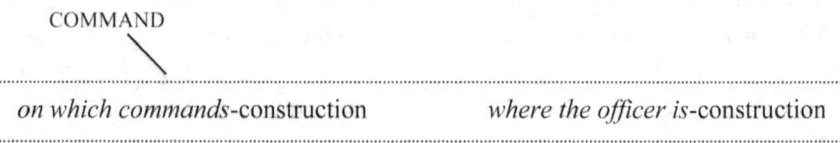

Figure 2: COMMAND constructions

A similar line of reasoning applies to example (15) above. The subcorpora contain many similar examples, and there appear to be clear syntactic, lexical and discourse patterns. The recurrent use of relative clauses with the preposition *uit* 'from' and a form of the verb *verstaan* 'understand' gives the impression of formulaic language, especially because these relative clauses are mostly tied to a noun such as *brief* 'letter' and occur in the opening of a letter. Note that the relative clause is tied to the meaning LETTER, not necessarily to the noun *brief* 'letter'. In (15), for example, the formula follows *ul aengenamen* 'your pleasant', where the noun *brief* 'letter' is omitted. If we term the epistolary formula in (15) the *from which I understand*-construction, we could describe its basic form as [Rel *uit ik verstaan*-Tns]. As before, both *d*- and *w*-relativizers can occupy the first slot. Co-textually, the construction follows the meaning LETTER, and in the wider discourse it is important that it appears in openings. Again, a constructionist description would need to take into account this generic pattern, too.

Also in this case, however, we have to assume a more schematic representation, which we call the UNDERSTAND construction. Passing by concrete examples for reasons of brevity, we confine ourselves to the following observations. The first person subject may be omitted, as was common in letter-writing and diary style. There are also a few examples with a second person subject. A finite verb is also often omitted, writers elliptically restricting themselves to the participle *verstaan* 'understood'. Occasionally, writers use a subclause as in (15), inserting the subordinating conjunction *dat* 'that'. Furthermore, the verb *verstaan* may be replaced by similar verbs such as *vernemen* 'learn, understand' and *zien* 'see, understand'. This lexical variation mainly occurs in the eighteenth century, where moreover some examples are found in the body of letters. In sum, all the slots are variable, including the generic pattern, only the preposition *uit* appearing in all examples of the UNDERSTAND construction.

We have elaborated on the constructional representation of these two epistolary formulae for a number of reasons. Epistolary formulae appear to be complex and (mostly) substantive constructions at first sight. The same lexical material occurs over and over again, and almost always in the same place in the structure of the discourse. The greeting formula in (10), for example, viz. *Een Vryendelijcke groetenysse sy gescheuen aen* 'a friendly greeting be written to', occurs 41 times in subcorpus 1, and is always the first line of a letter. Similarly, examples such as *waer op Commandeert* 'on which commands' (15) are fairly frequent (e.g. 25 tokens in subcorpus 1), and are largely restricted to addresses. Therefore, these formulae show great resemblance to conversational routines and idioms. Actual language use displays too much variation, however, for an interpretation as fixed idiomatic expressions to be plausible.

6.2 Constructional diffusion

Having established that epistolary formulae can be regarded as constructions in the sense of construction grammar, and that they require a fairly schematic description in order to account for the variation in actual usage, the question rises how they interact with the ongoing change in the form of relativizers. At whatever level the formulae are represented, be it substantive or schematic, the relativizer always needs to be rendered schematically, both *d-* and *w-*forms being attested. This suggests that the morphosyntactic change from *d-* to *w-* relativization operates at least partially independently of these constructions. On the other hand, if the language system indeed consists of constructions, and only of constructions, as exemplified in Table 4, a plausible hypothesis would be that language change proceeds through constructions. As sound changes may affect concrete words at different rates, which is often referred to as lexical diffusion, similarly morphosyntactic changes would be expected to affect constructions as in Table 4 at a different pace. This we could term *constructional diffusion*. Specifically, we would expect constructions to behave conservatively due to their being routinized and entrenched by repetition (cf. Bybee 2006, 2010). As stated above (section 3), Rutten (2010) and Rutten and van der Wal (acc.) argue that *w*-relativizers first occur in specific constructions, and these studies therefore provide evidence for the existence of constructional diffusion. In this section, we investigate whether the epistolary formulae discussed in the foregoing confirm the idea of constructional diffusion.

In (14), we presented a COMMAND construction with a *w*-relativizer. (19) is an example with a *d*-relativizer.

(19) *desen bryef aen den eersammen man ijan wijllemse luijtenant op het schep*
     this letter to the honorable man IJan Wijllemse lieutenant on the ship

   de spijegel daer op komder menheer menheer fijes amarael de ruijter
   De Spijegel REL on commands Mr Mr vice admiral De Ruijter
   'This letter to the honorable man IJan Wijllemse, lieutenant on the ship De Spijegel, on which the vice-admiral Mr De Ruijter commands'

As stated above, subcorpus 1 has 25 tokens of such COMMAND constructions, most of which, viz. 17 tokens, are produced by writers from the UMC, who are best represented in subcorpus 1 (Table 2). Recall from Table 3 that the overall proportion of *w*-relativizers in subcorpus 1 is 44%. Figure 1 in section 5 showed that the UMC proportion is in line with the overall proportion, *w*-forms making up 45% of all relative (pronominal) adverbs in the UMC part of subcorpus 1. When investigating the distribution of *d*- and *w*-forms over concrete tokens of COMMAND constructions, it appears striking that only 6/25 or 24% take the incoming *w*-variant, and thus begin with *waer*. Numbers are fairly small here, but still COMMAND constructions seem to be conservative vis-à-vis the change in progress.[14] It may not come as a surprise that epistolary formulae such as the COMMAND constructions appear to behave slightly more conservatively than relative clauses in general, since formulae were probably memorized as a whole, and inserted into discourse as prefabricated strings of words (Rutten and van der Wal 2012).

Interestingly, all 6 *w*-relativizers in the sample are instances of the *on which commands*-construction and thus contain the elements *waer op commandeert*, with the subject in final position. There are 9 tokens of this construction, 3 of which taking a *d*-relativizer. All 16 instances of the *where the officer is*-construction, on

---

14 Comparing the overall results (Table 3) minus the results for the COMMAND formulae to the results of the COMMAND formulae generates a statistically significant result: $\chi^2 = 4.58$, $df = 1$, $p < 0.05$.

the contrary, have a *d*-form.[15] This distribution of *w*- and *d*-relativizers clearly suggests that constructional diffusion is a useful descriptive notion. While one of the two COMMAND constructions already prefers *w*-forms, the other still strictly adheres to *d*-relativizers. This means that COMMAND formulae as such may be conservative, as established above, but also that this conservatism is actually due to only one of the constructions.

In the eighteenth century, COMMAND formulae have nearly disappeared from usage. Subcorpus 2 only provides 4 tokens, all 4 instantiations of the *on which commands*-construction. Interestingly, *d*-forms still occur; see (20–21). Numbers are, however, too low to attach too much value to this.

(20) het Schep de Jonge Jufvrou Margreta War op komandert Schepper
 the ship De Jonge Jufvrou Margreta REL on commands shipmaster
 Tunis Barend
 Tunis Barend
 'the ship De Jonge Jufvrou Margreta, on which shipmaster Tunis Barend commands'

(21) *het schip de Nicolaas en Jan Daar op Commandeerd Captijn frans Reijgert*
 the ship De Nicolaas en Jan REL on commands   captain Frans Reijgert
 'the ship De Nicolaas en Jan, on which captain Frans Reijgert commands'

There are 17 tokens of the UNDERSTAND construction in subcorpus 1. Example (15) above contains a *d*-relativizer. Much more frequent, however, are *w*-relativizers as in (22).

(22) *soo ijst dat ick naer datto van dien een houder van datto uijt Capt*
 so is-it that I after date of that an older of date from captain
 Tange hebbe ontfangen waer uijt verstaen ue grootelijcx verwondert
 Tange have received REL from understood you greatly surprised
 zijt ick soo weijnich rettour ben zendende
 are I so little return are sending
 'So it is [the case] that after the date of that letter I received a [letter] of an older date through captain Tange, from which I have understood that you are greatly surprised that I am returning so little'

---

15 The difference between the two constructions is statistically significant according to the Fisher exact test, $p < 0.05$.

No fewer than 13/17 tokens of the UNDERSTAND construction or 76% have a w-relativizer.[16] In the eighteenth century, there are 16 tokens of the UNDERSTAND construction, all of which begin with a w-relativizer. (23) is an example from subcorpus 2.

(23) myn laaste brief van ue was van den eersten februarij waar uyt
 my latest letter from you was of the first February REL from
 ik heb verstaan
 I have understood
 'my latest letter from you was dated February 1, from which I have understood'

Where COMMAND constructions appear to behave conservatively with regard to the ongoing change, the UNDERSTAND construction seems to behave more progressively. The various epistolary formulae differ greatly in the proportion of w-forms: in subcorpus 1, about a quarter of the COMMAND formulae have a w-form, as opposed to approximately three quarters of the UNDERSTAND formulae. As such, they also diverge from the overall seventeenth-century pattern of 44% w-forms. In subcorpus 2, the few examples of COMMAND constructions still show variation, whereas the UNDERSTAND construction has maintained its progressive behavior and only appears with w-relativizers.

We have discussed a number of epistolary formulae containing a relative clause in some detail. Our main aim was to investigate whether the distribution of d- and w-relativizers over these formulae provided evidence of constructional diffusion, which they did. Somewhat surprisingly, the result is not that epistolary formulae as such are conservative vis-à-vis the ongoing change. On the contrary, the UNDERSTAND construction behaves very progressively, and the *on which commands*-construction also seems to behave progressively, certainly when compared to the *where the officer is*-construction. One complicating factor is the fact that the UNDERSTAND construction is a specific type of relative clause, viz. a continuative relative clause. In the next section, we explain why this is a complicating factor.

7 Discussion and conclusions

We deduced two hypotheses from the literature on changes in relativization systems, viz. that the change from d- to w-relativization exhibits both social

---

[16] Comparing the overall results (Table 3) minus the results for the UNDERSTAND formula to the results of the UNDERSTAND formula gives a statistically significant result: $\chi^2 = 7.64$, $df = 1$, $p < 0.01$.

and constructional diffusion. We were able to demonstrate both types of diffusion, using two subcorpora comprising private letters from the seventeenth and eighteenth centuries.

As noted at the end of section 6, there is a complicating factor in the case of the UNDERSTAND construction, in that this construction is an example of a so-called continuative relative clause. Following Loock (2007), we consider continuative relative clauses syntactically as a subtype of appositives characterized by the discrepancy of form and function. Contrary to other types of appositives, which semantically expand the main clause they are structurally part of, continuative relative clauses usually convey new information, prototypically presented in a main clause, while they have the form of a subordinate clause. As such, continuative relative clauses create coherence with the preceding discourse by employing subordinating syntax, while the information structure would canonically trigger a new main clause. For this discrepancy of form and function, continuative relative clauses should be treated as a separate type of construction, which is corroborated by their behavior with respect to *d*- and *w*-relativization. In Rutten and van der Wal (acc.), we demonstrate that continuative relative clauses appropriate *w*-relativizers at a remarkably fast pace, faster than any other type of relative clause. Using the same collection of seventeenth-century letters, we show that out of 64 continuative relative clauses, no fewer than 53 instances or 83% have a *w*-form. Among these 64 continuative relative clauses are the 17 instances of the UNDERSTAND construction discussed in the present paper. This means that the progressive behavior of instances of the UNDERSTAND construction may be caused by the fact that they behave in accordance with the more general pattern of continuative relative clauses, and need not be explained by constructional diffusion at the level of the UNDERSTAND construction. It is beyond the scope of this paper to clear this matter up, as this would require detailed analyses of many more semantic and (morpho)syntactic aspects of continuative relative clauses. Finally, we wish to point out that an explanation drawing on the progressive behavior of continuative relative clauses in general is not necessarily at odds with the idea of constructional diffusion. It only means that constructional diffusion is at work at a different level, viz. at the level of the continuative relative clause construction.

Another question relates to the probability of the existence of an abstract relative clause construction, of which all examples and constructions discussed here are tokens or subtypes. In section 5, we abstracted away from specific relative clause types, and merely investigated the form of the relativizer. We believe there is, is fact, reason to assume an overarching schematic relative clause construction. One reason is that any relative clause type shows variation of *d*- and *w*-forms, indicating that language users categorize these different relative clause types as subtypes of the relative clause. Constructional diffusion partly determines the degree to which constructions are affected by the ongoing change, yet there is no type of relative clause completely escaping the change. *W*-relativizers already make up 44% of all relative clauses, suggesting that we are dealing with a family of constructions, held together by the very fact that they are relative clause constructions.

Moreover, the neat social distribution as established in Figure 1, with a gradual diachronic rise of *w*-forms in each social rank as well as similar distances between the social classes, also suggests that the abstract relative clause is a valid analytical category. Figure 1 presents a textbook example of gradient stratification by social class (Tagliamonte 2012: 27). If decades of variationist research have shown that linguistic variables often pattern in this way in a language community, we could perhaps turn the line of reasoning upside down, and consider such a pattern, once established, as an indication that we have found a linguistic variable. In other words, and at the risk of circularity, since the distribution of all *d*- and *w*-relativizers taken together in both subcorpora patterns in a way so familiar from sociolinguistic research, we might consider this evidence that language users employ an abstract category "relative clause construction". A major issue in constructional approaches to grammar and to language change is what levels of schematization need to be or can be assumed. How abstract is speakers' knowledge of grammar, and at what level of schematization does language change take place (e.g. Traugott 2008: 35–36)? We have argued that constructional diffusion is a helpful notion when describing the trajectory of change. We also believe that the neat social distribution in Figure 1 suggests that there is, in addition, an overarching category of relative clause constructions within which this change takes place. In other words, Figure 1 provides sociolinguistic evidence that may help decide on the level of schematicity that needs to be assumed for relative clauses in the history of Dutch. If this can be extended to other languages and types of change, it would imply that constructionist approaches to grammar may gain from the results of sociolinguistic research.

References

Austin, Frances. 1973. Epistolary conventions in the Clift family correspondence. *English Studies* 54: 9–22.
Bergs, Alexander. 2005. *Social Networks and Historical Sociolinguistics. Studies in Morphosyntactic Variation in the Paston Letters (1421–1503)*. Berlin/New York: Mouton de Gruyter.
Bergs, Alexander. 2010. Expressions of futurity in contemporary English: a Construction Grammar perspective. *English Language and Linguistics* 14: 217–238.

Bybee, Joan. 2006. From usage to grammar: the mind's response to repetition. *Language* 82: 711–733.
Bybee, Joan. 2010. *Language, Usage and Cognition*. Cambridge: Cambridge University Press.
Croft, William. 2000. *Explaining Language Change. An Evolutionary Approach*. London: Longman.
Croft, William. 2001. *Radical Construction Grammar*. Oxford: Oxford University Press.
Croft, William. 2009. Toward a social cognitive linguistics. In: Vyvyan Evans and Stéphanie Pourcel (eds.), *New Directions in Cognitive Linguistics*, 395–420. Amsterdam/Philadelphia: John Benjamins.
Croft, William and D. Alan Cruse. 2004. *Cognitive Linguistics*. Cambridge: Cambridge University Press.
Dossena, Marina. 2007. "As this leaves me at present". Formulaic usage, politeness, and social proximity in nineteenth-century Scottish emigrants' letters. In: Stephan Elspaß, Nils Langer, Joachim Scharloth and Wim Vandenbussche (eds.), *Germanic Language Histories 'from Below' (1700–2000)*, 13–29. Berlin/New York: Mouton de Gruyter.
Elspaß, Stephan. 2012. Between linguistic creativity and formulaic restriction. Cross-linguistic perspectives on nineteenth-century century lower class writers' private letters. In: Marina Dossena and Gabriella Del Lungo Camiciotti (eds.), *Letter Writing in Late Modern Europe*, 45–64. Amsterdam/Philadelphia: John Benjamins.
Frijhoff, Willem and Marijke Spies. 1999. *1650. Bevochten Eendracht* [1650. A Dearly Won Union]. The Hague: Sdu.
Geeraerts, Dirk, Gitte Kristiansen and Yves Peirsman (eds.). 2010. *Advances in Cognitive Sociolinguistics*. Berlin & New York: Mouton de Gruyter.
Goldberg, Adele E. 1995. *Constructions. A Construction Grammar Approach to Argument Structure*. Chicago/London: University of Chicago Press.
Goldberg, Adele E. 2006. *Constructions at Work. The Nature of Generalization in Language*. New York: Oxford University Press.
Harder, Peter. 2010. *Meaning in Mind and Society. A Functional Contribution to the Social Turn in Cognitive Linguistics*. Berlin/New York: Mouton de Gruyter.
Hoffmann, Thomas and Graeme Trousdale. 2011. Variation, change and constructions in English. *Cognitive Linguistics* 22: 1–23.
Horst, Joop van der. 1988. Over relatief *dat* en *wat* [On relative *dat* and *wat*]. *De nieuwe taalgids* 81: 194–205.
Horst, Joop van der. 1993. Voornaamwoordelijke bijwoorden in 16de-eeuws Nederlands [Pronominal adverbs in sixteenth-century Dutch]. *Spektator* 22: 290–308.
Horst, Joop van der. 2008. *Geschiedenis van de Nederlandse syntaxis* [History of Dutch Syntax]. 2 volumes. Louvain: Leuven University Press.
Horst, Joop van der and R. Storm. 1991. Over de geschiedenis van het betrekkelijk voornaamwoordelijk bijwoord [On the history of the relative pronominal adverb]. *Tijdschrift voor Nederlandse Taal- en Letterkunde* 107: 105–119.
Kiełkiewicz-Janowiak, Agnieszka. 2012. Class, age, and gender-based patterns. In: Juan M. Hernández-Campoy and J. Camilo Conde-Silvestre (eds.), *The Handbook of Historical Sociolinguistics*, 307–331. Oxford: Blackwell.
Kristiansen, Gitte and René Dirven (eds.). 2008. *Cognitive Sociolinguistics. Language Variation, Cultural Models, Social Systems*. Berlin/New York: Mouton de Gruyter.
Laitinen, Lea and Taru Nordlund. 2012. Performing identities and interaction through epistolary formulae. In: Marina Dossena and Gabriella Del Lungo Camiciotti (eds), *Letter Writing in Late Modern Europe*, 65–88. Amsterdam/Philadephia: John Benjamins.

Loock, Rudy. 2007. Appositive relative clauses and their functions in discourse. *Journal of Pragmatics* 39: 336–362.
Nevala, Minna. 2004. *Address in Early English Correspondence. Its Forms and Socio-Pragmatic Functions.* Helsinki: Société Néphilologique.
Nevalainen, Terttu. 2001. Continental conventions in early English correspondence. In: Hans-Jürgen Diller and Manfred Görlach (eds.), *Towards a History of English as a History of Genres*, 203–224. Heidelberg: Universitätsverlag C. Winter.
Nevalainen, Terttu and Helena Raumolin-Brunberg. 2003. *Historical Sociolinguistics. Language Change in Tudor and Stuart England.* London etc: Pearson.
Nobels, Judith and Marijke van der Wal. 2012. Linking words to writers: Building a reliable corpus for historical sociolinguistic research. In: Steffan Davies, Nils Langer, and Wim Vandenbussche (eds.), *Language and History, Linguistics and Historiography*, 343–361. Bern: Lang.
Polenz, Peter von. 1994. *Deutsche Sprachgeschichte vom Spätmittelalter bis zur Gegenwart. Band II. 17. und 18. Jahrhundert.* Berlin/New York: de Gruyter.
Poster, Carol and Linda C. Mitchell (eds.). 2007. *Letter-Writing Manuals and Instruction from Antiquity to the Present. Historical and Bibliographical Studies.* Columbia: The University of South Carolina Press.
Rissanen, Matti. 1999. Syntax. In: Roger Lass (ed.), *The Cambridge History of the English Language. Volume III. 1476–1776*, 187–331. Cambridge: Cambridge University Press.
Romaine, Suzanne. 1982. *Socio-Historical Linguistics. Its Status and Methodology.* Cambridge: Cambridge University Press.
Rutten, Gijsbert. 2010. Vroegmoderne relativa: naar een diachrone constructiegrammatica [Early Modern relativizers: Towards a diachronic construction grammar]. *Nederlandse Taalkunde* 15: 1–32.
Rutten, Gijsbert and Marijke van der Wal. 2012. Functions of epistolary formulae in Dutch letters from the seventeenth and eighteenth centuries. *Journal of Historical Pragmatics* 13: 173–201.
Rutten, Gijsbert and Marijke van der Wal. 2013. Epistolary formulae and writing experience in Dutch letters from the seventeenth and eighteenth centuries. In: Marijke van der Wal and Gijsbert Rutten (eds.), *Touching the Past. Studies in the Historical Sociolinguistics of Ego-Documents*, 45–65. Amsterdam/Philadelphia: John Benjamins.
Rutten, Gijsbert and Marijke van der Wal. Accepted. Discourse continuity and the written channel: Continuative relative clauses in the history of Dutch. In: Hubert Cuykens, Lobke Ghesquiere, and Daniël Van Olmen (eds.), *Aspects of Grammaticalization*.
SAND = *Syntactische Atlas van de Nederlandse Dialecten* [Syntactic Atlas of Dutch Dialects]. Volume I. 2005. Edited by Sjef Barbiers, Hans Bennis, Gunther De Vogelaer, Magda Devos and Margreet van der Ham. Amsterdam 2005: Amsterdam University Press.
Schoonenboom, Judith. 1997. De geschiedenis van *dat, wat* en *hetgeen* in bijbelvertalingen [The history of *dat, wat* and *hetgeen* in Bible translations]. *Nederlandse Taalkunde* 2: 343–369.
Schoonenboom, Judith. 2000. Analyse, norm en gebruik als factoren van taalverandering. Een studie naar veranderingen in het Nederlands onzijdig relativum [Analysis, norm and use as factors of language change. A study of changes in the Dutch neuter relativizer]. Ph.D. dissertation, University of Amsterdam.
Schutter, Georges de and Hanne Kloots. 2000. Relatieve woorden in het literaire Nederlands van de 17e eeuw [Relative words in 17th-century literary Dutch]. *Nederlandse Taalkunde* 5: 325–342.

Tagliamonte, Sali A. 2012. *Variationist Sociolinguistics. Change, Observation, Interpretation*. Oxford: Wiley-Blackwell.

Tieken-Boon van Ostade, Ingrid. 1999. Of formulas and friends: Expressions of politeness in John Gay's letters. In: Guy A.J. Tops, Betty Devriendt and Steven Geukens (eds.), *Thinking English Grammar to Honour Xavier Dekeyser*, 99–112. Louvain: Peeters.

Traugott, Elizabeth Closs. 2008. The grammaticalization of *NP of NP* patterns. In: Alexander Bergs and Gabriele Diewald (eds.), *Constructions and Language Change*, 23–45. Berlin/New York: Mouton de Gruyter.

Wal, Marijke van der. 2002. Relativisation in the history of Dutch: Major shift or lexical change? In: Patricia Poussa (ed.), *Dialect Contact and History on the North Sea Littoral*, 27–36. München: Lincom.

Wal, Marijke van der. 2003. Relativiteit in de grammaticale traditie. Tussen norm en descriptie? [Relativity in the grammatical tradition. Between norm and description?] In: Els Ruijsendaal, Gijsbert Rutten and Frank Vonk (eds.), *Bon jours Neef, ghoeden dagh Cozyn! Opstellen voor Geert Dibbets*, 361–375. Münster: Nodus Publikationen.

Muriel Norde, Bernard De Clerck, & Timothy Colleman
8 The emergence of non-canonical degree modifiers in non-standard varieties of Dutch: A constructionalization perspective

1 Introduction

Degree modifying adverbs have been subject to extensive linguistic discussion as they constitute a class that is very prone to language change: in studies with a (historical-) sociolinguistic perspective, the class is often portrayed as being in more or less constant flux, as initially hyperbolic new members are subject to rapid pragmatic wear-and-tear and in their turn give way to even newer members (see, e.g., Bolinger 1972; Partington 1993; Peters 1994; Paradis 2000; Lorenz 2002; Ito and Tagliamonte 2003; Macaulay 2006). While it remains to be seen whether all instances of degree modifiers are truly the result of hyperbole, what is for certain is that new members to the class are recruited from various linguistic sources. Cross-linguistically, typical source expressions for the development of new degree modifiers include words meaning 'true' (e.g. French *vraiment*, English *very* or *truly*) or 'terrible' (e.g. German *furchtbar*, English *awfully*), for instance, but also *quantifying* expressions (e.g. Italian *molto*, Portuguese *muito*, Czech *velmi* and Swedish *mycket*, all of which mean 'very' as well as 'much').

The extent to which quantifying expressions may be used to fulfil modifying functions differs widely between languages, however. In Dutch, according to Klein (1998: 31–39), expressions of high quantity do *not* double up as boosters, i.e. modifying adverbs which scale a property upwards: whereas prototypical low quantity expressions such as *weinig* 'few' and *een beetje* 'a bit' can function as downtoners – i.e., modifiers scaling a property downwards (e.g. *Hij is weinig intelligent* 'He is not very intelligent', *Ik was een beetje dronken* 'I was a bit drunk') – the prototypical high quantity expression *veel* 'many' cannot be used as a booster (e.g. **Ze is veel mooi* 'She is very pretty'). Instead, Dutch boosters are recruited from a variety of other lexical sources, including expressions of completeness (e.g. *heel* lit. 'wholly'), modal adverbs (e.g. *echt* 'really', *bepaald* 'definitely'), deictics (e.g. *zo* 'so') and, especially, qualitative adjectives (e.g. *erg* lit. 'awful', *knap* lit. 'handsome'/'tight', *vet* lit. 'fat', *zwaar* lit. 'heavy', *vreselijk* lit. 'gruesome', *ongelooflijk* lit. 'unbelievable', *verbluffend* lit. 'baffling', etc.) (see Klein 1998: 25–62 for extensive discussion). While the above observation on *veel* 'many' is correct, the generalization purported by Klein is too strong, as there are several (admittedly, less prototypical) high quantity expressions which do seem to be developing into degree modifiers.[1] Norde (2006) and De Clerck and Colleman (2013) noted the emergence of intensifying uses of the indefinite quantifier *tig* 'umpteen' in informal Netherlandic Dutch and of the quantifier noun *massa's* 'masses' in western non-standard varieties of Belgian Dutch, respectively, see (1) and (2) for attested examples in which the items in question are used to grade qualitative adjectives. Additional instances of expressions of high quantity which double up as degree modifiers in (non-standard varieties of) present-day Dutch include *duizend* 'thousand' and *een partij* 'a set, a batch, a lot', as illustrated in (3) and (4), respectively.[2]

(1) *Die   van   mij   zijn   nu   4   maanden   oud,   en   zijn   ook*
    those   of   me   are   now   4   months   old   and   are   too

   *al   **tig**   groot.*
   already umpteen   big
   'Mine are four months old now, and they're already real big, too.'
   [www.venividivissie.org]

(2) *Maar   dat   van   die   prophecy   vind   ik   wel   maar   **massa's***
    but   that   of   that prophecy   find   I   PRTC   PRTC   masses

   belachelijk   hoor.
   ridiculous   PRTC
   'But I think the prophecy thing is bloody ridiculous, you know.'
   [www.fkserv.ugent.be]

---

[1] A note on terminology is in order here. There are in fact two subtypes of modifiers which denote a scale upwards from an assumed norm: next to *boosters*, which indicate a high point on a scale, there are also *maximizers*, which denote the upper extreme of a scale (e.g. *completely, utterly*). *Amplifiers* is sometimes used as a cover term for both subclasses (e.g. in the Quirk et al. 1985 grammar). The converse of amplifiers are *downtoners*, which scale a property downwards and which, since Bolinger (1972), have been divided in three subtypes: *compromisers* (e.g. *rather*), *diminishers* (e.g. *a little, slightly*), and *minimizers* (e.g. *barely*). *Intensifier* and *degree modifier* are two overarching terms for all subtypes of boosters and downtoners, which will be used interchangeably in this article.

[2] In the absence of similar modifiers deriving from quantifying expressions in English, we will often use informal boosters such as *totally, dead, damn*, or *bloody* in the English translations.

(3) Zo   forum was   even   **duizend**   traag.
    so   forum was   a while thousand   slow
    'So, the forum was damn slow for a while.'
    [forum.scholieren.com]

(4) Hot moddefokking DAMN! Dat is   me   toch   **een** **partij** vet, zeg!
                           that is   me   PRTC   a   plot   cool PRTC
    'Hot motherfucking damn, now that's totally cool!'
    [forum.fok.nl]

The present paper offers a detailed comparison of the formal and functional properties of these four emerging modifiers, which, from a construction grammar point of view, can be seen as constituting distinct *micro-level constructions* (see Traugott 2008a, 2008b; Trousdale 2010). In addition to laying bare similarities and differences between these cases as different instantiations of the quantifier to degree modifier pathway of change, we will also reflect on the repercussions of the observed micro-constructional changes on higher levels of the constructional hierarchy, i.e. at the *macro-* and/or *meso-level*. We will argue that all cases are examples of grammatical constructionalization (Traugott and Trousdale 2013).

The empirical data for the investigation will be mainly drawn from online discussion forums and message boards such as the discussion forums of some 15 to 20 different Ghent University student organizations at <fkserv.ugent.be> and the Dutch forums <forum.scholieren.nl> and <forum.fok.nl>. These data sources are particularly suited to this kind of investigation as they contain large amounts of highly informal language, a large majority of which is contributed by people in their teens or early twenties. The examples above are pretty representative for the kind of linguistic contexts in which we typically find these emerging modifiers. By comparison, none of the modifying uses in (1) to (4) is represented in conventional corpora of written Dutch, such as the 38-million-word-corpus of the Institute for Dutch Lexicology and the CONDIV corpus, which are (mostly) made up of texts representing more formal registers of language. In addition, these corpora date back to the 1990s or ever earlier and simply fail to grasp recent developments in the class of degree modifiers. The latter drawback also applies to the Corpus of Spoken Dutch, the data for which were compiled in the period 1998–2004. What is more, even informal corpora sometimes fail to provide sufficient examples for these constructions. Constructions featuring *tig* as a degree modifier, for instance, are even difficult to find in gigatoken web corpora such as COW (Schäfer and Bildhauer 2012). The Dutch section of this corpus contains over 2.47 billion tokens in randomly selected sentences from

1.6 million documents, yet the number of hits for *tig* as degree modifier in this corpus is substantially lower than the number of hits using specific Google queries (see section 2.5).[3] While the latter method does allow retrieval of a fair number of relevant constructions, one of the obvious restrictions of this approach is that data drawn from a non-restricted corpus impedes the use of advanced statistical methods (as applied to constructional changes in Hilpert 2013, for instance), nor does it allow to trace diachronic developments that underlie synchronic variation and collocational scatter.

2 Four case studies

2.1 Introduction

In order to account for the degree modifying uses of *massa's, duizend , een partij en tig*, we will trace and document their development from their purely lexical uses to the currently attested instances of modification. It will be argued that, despite the different origins of these elements (a plural size noun, a numeral, a singular size noun and a suffix, respectively) they all go through similar stages in their development from quantifier to degree modifier. *Massa's* and *een partij* go through a similar shift from binominal construction to quantifying construction: lexical uses tick over into quantifying uses which in turn lead to subsequent degree modifying functions. The first part of this development, i.e. from lexical to quantifying is a well-documented process of grammaticalization, which, especially in the case of size nouns, has been attested in many a language (see Keizer 2001; Brems 2003, 2007a, 2007b, 2010; Denison 2005; De Smedt, Brems, and Davidse 2007; Traugott 2008a, 2008b; Langacker 2009: 60–80; De Clerck and Colleman 2013, to name a few). In these cases, a semantic extension or delexicalization motivates changes in the distribution which can eventually lead to a complete syntactic reanalysis, involving rebracketing (reversal of head positions), functional shifts of the first noun in the binominal construction (in what follows: N1) into modifier, host-class expansion from concrete to abstract second nouns (in what follows: N2s), synchronic layering and cross-linguistic replication (cf. Traugott 2008a). Within this context Brems (2011) distinguishes two major functions in English of these non-lexical uses: a quantifier use (as in *loads of people*) and a valuing(-quantifying) use in which the referent is evaluated

---

[3] For example, of the collocations mentioned in Tables 4 and 5, most do not occur in COW at all, and the token frequency of the most common ones is much lower (e.g. 25 for *tig meer* 'much / many more' or 5 for *tig veel* 'very much' as opposed to 382 and 186 in our own data set).

rather than quantified (as in *a load of crap* or *a bunch of liars*). In Dutch, too, similar uses and similar processes can be attested. Doetjes (1997: 99), for instance, observes a process in which the size noun, e.g. *een hoop* ('a heap'), *een berg* ('a mountain'), *tonnen* ('tonnes'), *een paar* ('a pair'), etc.) "turns from an expression indicating a specific amount only [...] into an expression which can also be used to indicate a non-specific quantity, which is either relatively big ('a lot') or small ('a bit')" (see also Joosten 2003; Joosten et al. 2007). In addition to purely hyperbolic quantifying uses, valuing quantifying uses are attested as well: non-lexical, diminutive uses of *stelletje* (originally 'couple') and *zoo(i)tje* (originally 'stew'), for instance, are subject to "functional crystallization" (Brems 2007a: 215) and only function as valuing-quantifiers with a negative semantic prosody in binominal constructions, e.g. *een stelletje amateurs* ('a bunch of amateurs'), *een zootje flauwe moppen* ('a bunch of lame jokes'). Since all of our cases involve quantifiers, each of the sub-sections below will first of all briefly sketch this development from lexical to (valuing)-quantifying uses.

Most of the attention, however, will be devoted to the second stage in the development, i.e. the further development from quantifying to degree modifying uses. Actual frequencies and contexts of use (e.g. possible host class expansion from adjective to adverb and verb, or vice versa) of the attested degree modifying uses of *massa's*, *een partij*, *tig* en *duizend* will be examined more closely and subjected to individual comparison. This general trend in which quantifiers develop into degree modifiers (a trend which can also be observed in colloquial English, e.g. *heaps funny*, *loads better* as shown in De Clerck and Brems in press) will be captured within a construction grammar framework. Following De Clerck and Brems (in press), who show that the degree of expansion of modifying uses is partially influenced by the degree of grammaticalization of quantifying uses (cf. *piles* vs. *loads* as degree modifiers), individual differences will be explained on the micro-constructional level resulting from differences in grammatical constructionalization (see section 3 for a more elaborate discussion).

2.2 *Massa's*

As shown in De Clerck and Colleman (2013), *massa's* features in both lexical and quantifying uses as the result of ongoing grammaticalization processes. In the latter uses, the fully lexical meaning of the noun *massa* 'mass', i.e. 'a body or quantity of matter, usually considerable in size or volume, but without a determinate or specified shape' is semantically bleached and lends itself easily for quantitative interpretations in binominal constructions, in which N1 expresses a large quantity of N2. Lexical uses are shown in (5) and (6) and illustrate that the body of matter itself can either be a coherent body or lump of (pliable or malleable) raw material (e.g. jelly), not yet moulded into a definite shape; or it can consist of a dense aggregation of objects (and even human beings) having the appearance of a single, continuous body. The singular concord in (5) also illustrates the head status of *massa* in the noun phrase. The quantifying uses illustrated in (7) to (12) show that there seem to be very few restrictions on the noun filling the N2 slot, which may be countable, uncountable, concrete, abstract and human. This may partially be caused by the original meaning of *massa*, whose semantically vague nature – unlike *stelletje* (a pair of matching items), *zooitje* (a stew), *pile* or *bunch*, it neither expresses a specific quantity nor a specific shape – may have facilitated processes of delexicalization.

(5) *Jam is een geleiachtige **massa** van met suiker gekookte vruchten.*
'Jam is a jelly-like mass of fruit boiled with sugar.'
[www.datisjammie.nl/page/2]

(6) *Veelal moeten clematissen worden gesnoeid omdat ze anders nogal vlug een wilde **massa** hout vormen.*
'In many cases, clematises need pruning because they have a tendency to turn into a wild mass of wood.'
[www.groen.net/Article.aspx?id=7612]

(7) *Een **massa** mensen was getuige van de show, maar niemand viel iets buitengewoons op.*
'A mass of people witnessed the show, but no one noticed anything out of the ordinary.'
[www.kloptdatwel.nl]

(8) *Allez, ze krijgt er toch **massas** stress van.*
'Well, it does give her loads/?masses of stress.'[4]
[fkserv.ugent.be]

---

[4] The literal translation in English does not sound very idiomatic which may point to the fact that collocational broadening of English *masses* is more limited than Dutch *massa's*. English multimillion word corpora (such as the BNC and COCA) present only few examples of quantifier uses with the non-countable abstract nouns *fear, hope, pain, grief, misery*, etc., instances of which did occur in the considerably smaller sets of Dutch data we have analyzed. In other words, quantifier uses of some N1 N2 combinations in Dutch may have reached a higher degree of standardization than their English equivalents.

(9) *De periode 1874–1914 kende **massa's** aanslagen (ook in België)*
'The 1874–1914 period witnessed loads of attacks (also in Belgium)'
[fkserv.ugent.be]

(10) *Wat een dilemma, ik ga al **massa's** activiteiten hebben volgend schooljaar én eu hopelijk een thesis enzo.*
'What a dilemma, I'll already have masses of activities next academic year and uhm hopefully a Master thesis and such.'
[fkserv.ugent.be]

(11) *[…] en heb ik wraak genomen door het laatste uur **massa's** drank weg te geven en mensen gelukkig te maken.*
'[…] and I took revenge by giving loads of free booze during the last hour and making people happy.'
[fkserv.ugent.be]

(12) *Ik hoop dat er door de crisis **massa's** scholieren en studenten keihard buizen, zodat ik deze zomer dik betaald bijles kan gaan geven.*
'I hope the crisis will cause masses of students to fail miserably so I can earns loads by teaching extra lessons.'
[fkserv.ugent.be]

However, uses of *massa* and *massa's* are not restricted to pure quantification within the binominal size noun construction. Closer analysis of the data reveals other contexts of use, outside the size noun construction, in which *massa* and *massa's* function as degree modifiers. When used as degree modifiers, their meaning is still associated with and can still be paraphrased as 'much' or 'a lot' but now pertains to the degree to which a quality described is present (in combination with comparative adjectives and adverbs as in 13 and 14), or to the frequency of an action in combination with verbs, as in 15 and 16).

(13) *Uhu, het kapsel is ook **massas** beter nu ze!*
'Uhu, the haircut is loads better now, believe me!'
[fkserv.ugent.be]

(14) *Toen ik extra uitleg vroeg, kreeg ik enkel als antwoord dat iedereen **massa's** meer moest betalen.*
'When I asked for further explanation, the only answer I got was that everyone had to pay loads more.'
[fkserv.ugent.be]

(15) *Heb ik in de grote vakantie nog **massas** naar gekeken toen ik thuis bij mijn vader in Aruba was (Amerikaanse zenders en al).*
'I watched it loads during summer holidays while staying with my father on Aruba (American channels and all)'.
[fkserv.ugent.be]

(16) *We knuffelen toch al **massa's**.*'
'We do hug loads, don't you think?'
[fkserv.ugent.be]

In addition to these degree modifying uses which are still quantificational, in a sense, a fair number of unambiguously intensifying uses can be attested where *very* or *really* rather than *much* – or in Dutch *erg* rather than *veel* – is the best paraphrase. Such uses have been attested with verbs, adjectives and adverbs, even in non-comparative form, as illustrated in (17)–(20) below. Note that in examples (19) and (20), focus is on the intensity of the event expressed by the verb, not the frequency of it (as in examples 15 and 16). Also, it should be noted that such unambiguously intensifying uses are limited to the plural form *massa's*: building on Brems's (2007a) account of English *loads* etc., De Clerck and Colleman (2013: 158) attribute this to the fact that the plural number adds to *massa's* hyperbolic value.

(17) *hihi een vriendin van mij werkt daar ook, zo interviews regelen en zo, en die heeft et **massas** druk, maar ze doet het indd ook graag ...*
'Hihi a friend of mine also works there, setting up interviews and such, and she is really busy, but, indeed, she likes doing it. ...'
[fkserv.ugent.be]

(18) *Die dudes die gewonnen hebben waren **massa's** cool.*
'Those dudes that won were really cool.'
[fkserv.ugent.be]

(19) *Donderdagen en vrijdag suckn **massas** tzal wè kerl.*
'Thursdays and Fridays totally suck, you bet.'
[fkserv.ugent.be]

(20) *Nog volk da **massa's** gaat buizen?*
'More people that are going to fail big time?'
[fkserv.ugent.be]

While some other Dutch size nouns also allow for degree modifying uses with comparative adjectives or adverbs, as in *bakken/hopen/tonnen/stukken + meer/beter/mooier* ('loads/heaps/tons/lots' + 'more/better/nicer'), uses in which these size nouns are combined with *non*-comparative adjectives etc. are much rarer if not absent. In English, too, uses with *loads, bunch, a lot* and *heaps* have been reported on with comparative adjectives (cf. Quirk et al. 1985; Traugott 2005; Brems 2007a; Langacker 2010), though not with *masses*. Table 1 below gives an overview of the degree modifying and intensifying uses (as opposed to purely quantificational uses in the N1N2 size noun construction) in the different formal contexts as attested in the Ghent University student weblogs and discussion boards at <fkserv.ugent.be> (see De Clerck and Colleman 2013 for more information on data retrieval).

Table 1: Quantifying and intensifying uses of *massa's* in Ghent University student weblog data

	#	%
Lexical uses	13	8,1
Ambiguous lexical/quantifying uses	6	3,8
Quantifying uses	68	42,5
Ambiguous quantifying/intensifying[5]	13	8,1
Intensifying uses	66	41,3
Modifying a verb	7	4,4
Modifying an adjective	39	24,4
Modifying an adverb (incl. *veel* 'much')	16	10,0
Unclassified	4	2,5
Total	**160**	**100**

The table shows that degree modifying uses are by no means a marginal phenomenon in these data (unlike the fairly rare uses attested for English size nouns, or for any of the other size nouns in Dutch for that matter). With 66 out of 160 instances, intensifying uses account for no less than 41% of the *massa's* instances culled from the Student weblogs, which testifies to the frequent and productive use of such instances in the represented language variety. In addition, uses such as (21) below where *massa's* modifies *weinig* 'few' – which, obviously, does not tally well with the original lexical semantics of *massa's* – underscore the substantial semantic bleaching and advanced grammaticalization as a degree modifier.

---

[5] These are constructions such as examples (13) to (16).

(21) *Verbruikt **massa's** weinig, heeft overschot van power en is ook nog eens exclusief!*
'Consumes very little, has loads of power and is exclusive on top of that.'
[http://www.bimmerboard.be/forum/index.php?topic=4805.205;wap2]

However, while these uses are entrenched in the idiolects of the language users in our data, they are generationally and regionally restricted. While more sociolinguistic research will need to throw more light on amplitude and possible expansion, our data suggest that such uses are typical of the language of the western part of Dutch-speaking Belgium, i.e. the province of West Flanders and large parts of the neighbouring province of East Flanders. They are mainly used by young speakers in informal language, but instances have been reported of a knock-on effect on parents' language as well (see De Clerck and Colleman 2013). This actual spread outside the peer group may trigger its actual demise as routinization and frequency affect both the hyperbolic nature of new degree modifying expressions as well as their exclusive nature as markers of group identity. In passing, no such uses were attested in Netherlandic Dutch <fok.nl> data at all, so it seems to be a strictly Belgian Dutch phenomenon.

2.3 *Duizend*

The example in (22), where the speaker clearly does not want to associate Burundi with literally one thousand problems and opportunities, illustrates the frequent use of the word form *duizend* 'thousand' as an indefinite quantifier denoting an unspecified (very) large quantity rather than as a cardinal numeral.[6]

(22) *Ik vertrek morgen naar Burundi ... Land van de totale chaos en dus van **duizend** mogelijkheden, **duizend** problemen en **duizend** kansen.*
'I'm leaving for Burundi tomorrow, the land of total chaos and hence of a thousand opportunities, problems and chances.'
[http://www.corduwener.nl/weblog/?m=200804]

---

6 A comparable example, which cannot be discussed in this paper for reasons of space, is the use of *nul* 'zero' as a downtoner, as in (i) below:

(i) *Ik heb een vriend die ik al jaren ken en die ik **nul** aantrekkelijk vind.*
'I've got a friend whom I have known for years and whom I find zero attractive.'
[silly73.blogspot.com/2010/08/vriendschap.html]

This *duizend* presents another example of a high quantity expression that has been recruited as a degree modifier in informal varieties of Dutch. Examples can easily be found through Google queries for the exact string of the word form *duizend* immediately followed by a frequent adjective or adverb. *Duizend* grades a comparative adjective in (23), adjectives in the positive degree in (24) and (25), and a qualitative adverb in (26).

(23) *[A]lleen vond ik de kits altijd **duizend** mooier dan de merchandise figuurtjes.*
'It's just that I've always found the kits loads nicer than the merchandise figures.'
[aniway.nl/forum]

(24) *Ik was echt **duizend** blij toen ze zei: "…"*
'I really was totally glad when she said: "…"'
[ikbenkarelpti.blogspot.com/2007_12_01_archive.html]

(25) *En zoals je ziet ben ik vrij curvey, dus dit is **duizend** moeilijk voor me haha.*
'And as you can tell I'm quite curvy, so this is damn difficult for me, haha.'
[forum.girlscene.nl]

(26) *Ik weet heus wel dat dat Wikkie de Viking is, dat keek ik vroeger **duizend** vaak*
'I know very well that it is Wicky the Viking, I used to watch that programme very often.'
[forum.scholieren.com]

In addition, *duizend* is used to grade the quantifier *veel* 'many' (27) and, like *massa's* and *tig*, it is even found with *weinig* 'few' (28), a combination which testifies to the high degree of semantic bleaching *duizend* has undergone.

(27) *Het is geen ongelofelijk schone citytrip naar het buitenland geweest, waar ik **duizend** veel foto's heb getrokken.*
'It wasn't an unbelievably nice city trip abroad during which I took loads of pictures'
[laviedunereveuse.blogspot.com/2012_03_01_archive.html]

(28) *Ik heb ook **duizend** weinig zin in school de laatste tijd.*
'Also, I totally don't feel like going to school lately.'
[forum.scholieren.com]

We have also found a small number of examples of *duizend* grading verbs, as in (29), but such uses are quite marginal, it seems. Google queries for *duizend* in combination with a number of usual suspects of verbs which are prone to being modified in this way – e.g. *meevallen* 'turn out better than expected', *zich amuseren* 'to have a good time', *dansen* 'dance', *slapen* 'sleep', *schrikken* 'be startled', etc. – produce no more than a handful of examples.

(29) *Borrel was mooi, heb echt **duizend** geslapen daarna!*
'The drink was nice, I really slept very well afterwards.'
[damestwaalf09.mygb.nl/]

Unlike *massa's* and *tig*, the use of *duizend* as a degree modifier does not appear typical of either Belgian or Netherlandic Dutch. If the URLs of the attested examples are anything to go by, the intensifier *duizend* has pockets of use in both Belgium and the Netherlands: the examples in (24) and (27) are taken from Belgian weblogs, the remaining of the above instances appeared on Dutch forums. In this respect, we can point towards an interesting metalinguistic discussion on <http://kringbabylon.be/forum> on 19–20 October 2009 (last accessed 25/03/2011), the discussion board of language students at the University of Leuven, where a student who, according to his profile, is based in Alkmaar in the west of the Netherlands expresses his surprise at the use of *duizend* as an intensifier in a post from a fellow student based in Wuustwezel, in the Belgian province of Antwerp, as he was under the impression that intensifying *duizend* was typical of the language of student fraternities in Groningen, in the north of the Netherlands. The Belgian student replies that she has taken over intensifying *duizend* from a friend and now uses it all the time, and another student joining the discussion says that he knows quite a lot of Belgians who use *duizend* in that way and thinks that it may originally be a Ghent thing. All of this suggests that intensifying *duizend* is a typical group language phenomenon, which has pockets of use in several regions of the Dutch language area. It also suggests that we may be dealing with a phenomenon that is very much above the level of consciousness, i.e. a kind of lexico-grammatical stereotype in the Labovian sense (Labov 1972), though we must of course not lose sight of the fact that the participants in the online discussion are students of *linguistics*.

Many of the occurrences found on Belgian websites use the non-standard forms *duust* or *duusd*, spellings which are meant to reflect the typical monosyllabic pronunciation found in south-western dialects (i.e., in West Flemish and East Flemish), with a monophthong /y/ rather than the standard diphthongic pronunciation /œy/ and with a reduced final syllable. (30) and (31) are cases in point.⁷,⁸ Note that (31) displays several lexical, morphological and phonological features of West Flemish dialect. The verb in question, for instance, is *zich jeunen*, a typically West Flemish expression for 'to have a good time'.

(30) Ik wil ook keigraag een kat. Maar ik ben **duust** allergisch aan alles, dus ook aan katten.
'I would very much like to have a cat, too. But I'm highly allergic to everything, including cats.'
[www.fkserv.ugent.be]

(31) Ken me **duust** gejeund, mo 'k peizen dak te vele gezopen en.
'I had a really good time, but I think that I drank too much.'
[club.studiant.be/moedergietut/db/galspuwer.asp]

The very high frequency of *duizend* as a cardinal numeral precludes a preliminary quantitative investigation of this form along the lines of the other case studies in this paper, but this is less of an obstacle in the case of the south-western regional variant *duust*. In order to get some sense of the relative frequency of the various uses, we used the same source as we did for *massa's*, viz. the Ghent University student weblogs and discussion boards at <fkserv.ugent.be>. The manual filtering of the results from a query for all occurrences of the exact word forms *duust* and *duusd* on this website launched on 08/12/2010 produced 387 instances, only nine of which are unambiguous instances of degree modifier use – by comparison, indefinite quantifier uses similar to the use of *duizend* in (22) above account for 362 out of 387 instances. The set of nine intensifying uses includes five cases where *duust* grades an adjective, three cases in which it grades the comparatives *meer* 'more' or *minder* 'less' and one case of *duust veel* 'very much'. In addition, there is one ambiguous example in which *duust* either functions as an indefinite quantifier or as a degree modifier (32). As in the case

---

7 Note that the first part of example (30) features another degree modifier that is typical of southern varieties of Dutch (including the South of The Netherlands), viz. the prefix *kei-* (originally the noun 'boulder').
8 Occasionally, we also find the spelling *duzend* or *duuzend*, which reflects a pronunciation with a more general southern and eastern regional distribution, viz. with the monophthong vowel but without the reduction of the final syllable, as in example (i) from the website of a ladies' football team based in the North Brabantian town of Bergen op Zoom, in the southern part of the Netherlands.
(i) Ik ben morgen van de partij, lekker ballen word echt **duuzend** lekker weer!!!
<www.doskodames.nl>
'Count me in for tomorrow, nicely playing ball, it will be really nice weather!'

of *tig* (see 2.5), such uses may have provided a bridging context for the development of intensifying from quantifying uses.

(32) *Muse heeft toch **duusd** betere nummers dan dit, ik snap het niet.*
'Muse has a lot of songs that are better than this, I don't get it.'
'Muse has songs that are a lot better than this, I don't get it.'
[fkserv.ugent.be]

The conclusions that can be drawn from this small-scale quantitative investigation are (i) that the use of *duust* as a degree modifier is much less widespread among students at Ghent University than the use of *massa's* as a degree modifier, as shown by the difference in token frequency (cf. the 66 occurrences of intensifying *massa's* in the same material, see section 2.1) and (ii) that *duust* is still much more frequently used as a quantifier than as a degree modifier.

As a final observation, consider the instances in (33) and (34), which show that *duizend* was used as a degree modifier in 18th and early 19th century Dutch, too.

(33) *"Zie Hendrik", zeide hij "het is een aardig meisje [...] Jammer, **duizend** jammer! dat zy niet van ons Geloof is.*
'"See, Hendrik", he said, "she is a nice girl ... It is a shame, a dire shame, that she is not of our faith."'
[Wolff & Deken, *Historie van mejufvrouw Sara Burgerhart*, 1782]

(34) *Hoor nu eens, wat hij van u zeide: "'T is wel **duizend** 'jammer, THOMAS, dat zulk een knappe jongen een' pennelikker, en geen braaf Soldaat is."*
'Now hear what he said about you: "It is a dire shame, Thomas, that such a smart boy is a pen-pusher and not a brave soldier."'
[Anonymous, *De gevallen van Rudolf Reybridge*, 1815]

Exactly how widespread this use was at the time is still an open question: there is no mention of it in the extensive discussion of *duizend* in the *Dictionary of the Dutch Language* [Dictionary of the Dutch Language] (in what follows: WNT), and, so far, we have been able to find examples for the specific combination *duizend jammer* (lit. 'thousand shameful') only, mostly from plays or from quoted speech passages in novels.[9] Anyhow, it is clear from these examples that the potential of *duizend* as an intensifier has been tapped into in earlier language stages as well. The present-day instances found on the Internet might

---

9 For information on WNT see http://www.inl.nl/onderzoek-a-onderwijs/lexicologie-a-lexicografie/wnt.

be relics from this older language stage. However, given that the intensifying use of *duizend* was apparently not frequent or productive enough in 18th and 19th century language to be noticed by the compilers of the WNT and given the kind of web sources the modern examples spring from (weblogs and discussion boards rather than genres with a tendency for archaic language), it seems much more likely that we are dealing with a case of what Geeraerts (1997: 64) labels *semantic polygenesis*, i.e., "[the phenomenon in which] a particular reading of a word may crop up several times in the history of the item, on independent grounds, and with a remarkable temporal hiatus". The discussion in Geeraerts (1997: 62–68) stresses that semantic polygenesis involves the application of general mechanisms of semantic extension: typically, polygenesis involves transient metaphorical readings which do not subsist over time, while the readings which served as the source for the metaphorical extension do subsist over time. Applied to the phenomenon under discussion here, the extension from *duizend*'s well-established use as an indefinite quantifier to its novel use as a degree modifier use seems to have occurred several times in the history of the item. As such, *duizend*'s history lends added proof to the hypothesis that the development of degree modifiers from indefinite quantifiers presents a natural pathway of change in Dutch.

2.4 Een partij

In its original lexical meaning *een partij* (derived from French *partie*, which in itself is related to the verb *partir/partager*, i.e. 'to share') refers to 'a part of something', 'a part of a larger whole' or 'something that was divided into several parts', as shown in (35). Other and related shades of meaning that fall under the umbrella of purely lexical uses include uses in which *partij* refers to 'a group of people forming a unit', 'a group of people that share the same political views', 'a celebration organized by a group of people', 'a part of a musical composition', 'one sequence of a particular game' (e.g. *een partijtje schaak*, 'a game of chess') or 'one of two in a married/engaged couple'.

(35) *De stadt Veronis ..., zynde met eenen houten muur omringt, maer verdeelt in drie **partyen**.*
 'The city of Veronis..., surrounded with a wooden wall, but divided into three parts.'
 [V. RIEBEECK, Dagverh. 1, 21 [1652]]

All of these lexical uses share the "partitive" meaning which provides fertile soil for the development of quantitative uses in those cases where *partij* is followed by an N2 denoting what the part actually consists of. In (36) below, *partij* still refers to a part of a larger whole but gets an additional quantitative interpretation as 'a set of X number of items/a quantity of something available as one unit' (normally in a sales situation). Fed by frequent collocations with N2s referring to 'bulk' – or spatial N2s (such as land, property, etc.) as shown in (37), the partitive/quantitative lexical meaning also fuelled expressive quantitative readings in which the expression of pure quantity or a large part of something is "subjectified" into a reading that labels the attested quantity as 'a lot'. Expressive uses of this kind allow for collocational scattering and a spread from concrete (un)countable to abstract (un)countable N2s, as shown in (38) to (41).

(36) *Ik heb me vorige week **een partij** onderbroeken op de markt gekocht:15 stuks in de aanbieding in mijn normale maat.*
'Last week I bought a batch of knickers on the market: 15 items on offer, my size.'
[FOK.nl]

(37) *Wie er geinteresseerd is in **een partij** diamanten graag ff hier posten.*
'Anyone who's interested in a batch of diamants, please post here.'
[FOK.nl]

(38) *We schrijven bijna half november en ze staan er nog steeds, hele **partijen** mai*
'It's almost mid November, and there they still are: large plots of corn.'
[http://melancholia.typepad.com/melancholia/2012/11/mais.html]

(39) *Afijn, ik trek dat ding open, GVD **EEN PARTIJ** RANZIGHEID!*
'Anyway, I pull the thing open, Jesus Christ, a load of filth!'
[FOK.nl]

(40) *Waar krijgt deze gozer GVD voor betaald? Omdat ie **een partij** dreunen aan elkaar kan draaien, zonder enige melodie?*
'What the heck is this guy getting paid for? For mixing a load of beats without any melody whatsoever?'
[FOK.nl]

(41) *Maar tijdens het googlen werd ik spontaan misselijk, wat **een partij** schotwonden op het internet zeg, GADVERDAMME MAN*
'While surfing I got nauseous spontaneously, what a load of bullet wounds on the internet! JESUS!'
[FOK.nl]

As was the case for *massa's*, the trajectory leading to these grammaticalized quantitative uses is not a very long one: first, as opposed to other size noun constructions (e.g. *pile, bunch*, etc.) the original lexical meaning of *partij* needs to shed little semantically specific meaning that might hamper quantitative readings. Second, the N2s in its original meaning could either be countable, non-countable, human or non-human. Once spread to abstract uses, both "positive" (e.g. *lol* 'fun') and "negative" N2s (e.g. *pijn* 'pain') can be attested, so there seems to be no clear manifestation of obvious semantic prosody.

As a next step, reference can be made to those uses in N1 N2 constructions that display a fairly ambiguous reading between quantifying ('a lot') and intensifying ('very') readings, especially in those cases where Dutch allows both *erg (e)* en *veel* as modifiers of these N2s, as in (42) to (44), where the gradable gravity of a condition is modified. Another ambiguous instance is (45), where *een partij zweetvoeten* could either refer to 'a set/pair of smelly feet', which would be similar to the lexical uses in (36) to (41) above, or to 'very smelly feet', i.e. an intensifying use.

(42) Zeg ik heb er toch **een partij** zin in!
      'Hey, I am very much/really/so in the mood for it!'
      [FOK.nl]

(43) Yo, ik heb me toch **een partij** pijn in me oor!
      'Yow, my ear freakin' hurts/hurts a lot.'
      [FOK.nl]

(44) Dat moet toch wel **een partij** herrie gegeven hebben.
      'That must have produced heaps of noise.'
      [FOK.nl]

(45) Ik heb me **een partij** zweetvoeten, heerlijk ik zit echt te genieten hier.
      'What an awesome pair of smelly feet I have. Lovely, I am having such a great time.'
      [FOK.nl]

Unambiguously intensifying uses are illustrated in (46) to (50). Such intensifying uses are by no means rare and occur in combination with adjectives and adverbs in the positive degree as well as with verbs, as shown in the examples. Table 2 below provides an overview of the attested uses and presents the actual proportion of quantifying, degree modifying and intensifying uses, as gleaned from the <FOK.nl> student discussion forum (accessed 16/03 2011).

(46) Ik ben me toch **een partij** moe.
      'I am so freakin' tired'
      [FOK.nl]

(47) Wow! Het is toch **een partij** donker buiten!
'Wow! It's really pitch dark outside!'
[FOK.nl]

(48) Ik zie op de stoep een meisje staan met een kind van een jaar of vier. Die kijkt niet en steekt zo over. Bijna onder onze fiets. Dus ik roep nog van Hey kijk uit. Word die griet mij toch een partij giftig. En **een partij** moeilijk doen.
'I see a girl with a four year old child on the pavement. She is not looking and just crosses the street. Almost hit by our bicycles. So I go like 'Hey, look out'. My, she gets very pissed. And gives us a hard time.
[FOK.nl]

(49) in de bus naar A'dam Noord zat er een vrouw voor mij die rijstwafels aan het eten was en het vervolgens wegspoelde met yogidrink. Dat stonk me toch **een partij**!
'In the Amsterdam North bus there was a lady eating them rice waffles which she washed down with a yoghurt drink afterwards. What a stench that was.'
[FOK.nl]

(50) tjeziz gisteren bij mijn ex geweest (kinderen hé) maar die zat me toch **een partij** te zeiken snap niet waarom ben een hele aardige kerel wat mot ik nou met z'n k*twijf.
'Djesus had to go to my ex yesterday (kids, you know) and she was nagging like hell, don't know why, am a nice guy; what am I going to do with such a b*tch.'
[FOK.nl]

Table 2: Quantifying and intensifying uses of *een partij*

	#	%
Lexical uses	327	67,4
Ambiguous lexical/intensifying uses	6	1,2
Quantifying uses	37	7,6
Ambiguous quantifying/intensifying	13	2,7
Degree modifying uses	71	14,6
Modifying a verb	27	5,6
Modifying an adjective	33	6,8
Modifying an adverb	5	1,0
Modifying a noun	1	0,2
Ambiguous	5	1,0
Total	485	100,0

A number of interesting tendencies are revealed. First, lexical uses still account for most of the data, which, in view of *partij*'s polysemous nature (even if used in a purely lexical sense) is probably not surprising. In addition, a lot of the data stem from discussions on political topics with references to political parties. Second, degree modifying uses with comparative adjectives are rare in the data we examined (as opposed to *massa's* for instance), though examples do occur, as shown in an example from additional web queries in (51). Third, quantifying uses are outnumbered by degree modifying uses, many of which – and contra the *massa's* and *duizend* data – occur with verbs as well.

(51) wat word dit fietsje toch **een partij** mooier zonder die tudbuster.
 'This bike really is a lot nicer without the tudbuster.'
 [www.mountainbike.nl, accessed 7 October 2013]

Again, these data show that such uses are very much entrenched for these language users, i.e. uses of non-standard varieties of Northern Dutch. They have not standardized yet, nor have instances of such uses been attested in non-standard varieties of Belgian Dutch (at least not in the data we consulted). As a fourth observation, special attention should also be drawn to the frequent co-occurrence of intensifying *een partij* with the discourse marker *toch* and/or the ethical dative construction with *me*, both of which are markers of expressive language. *Toch* occurs no less than 64 times in total, 51 of which occur with degree modifying uses, 13 of which occur with quantifying and ambiguous uses. The ethical dative construction with *me* occurs no less than 61 times, 59 of which in combination with degree modifying uses. Interestingly, the occurrence of the ethical dative and *toch* in combination with *een partij* seems to trigger or favour a degree modifying interpretation. In fact, one could actually raise the question which portion of the expressive force of the entire utterance is actually covered by the ethical dative, by *toch*, and by the use of *een partij*, respectively. Pushing the envelope even further, one may even argue that both the ethical dative and *een partij* belong to a larger constructional pattern that triggers this hyperbolic, expressive meaning (see also the comment on *boel* below), further fuelled by *toch*, which has often been described as a reinforcing modal particle, expressing surprise, fear or counterexpectation (see Vismans 1994; Snel 2011).[10] Ethical datives, too, are known to add emotional colouring by introducing a "non-argument affectee" (Horn 2008: 188; also see Lamiroy and Delbecque

---

[10] Interestingly, such uses of the ethical dative often occur in combination with the historical present, as in (48), which adds to the liveliness of the account. See Janssen (2002) for an elaborate account on the praesens historicum.

1998; Cuervo 2003). In fact, the addition of the extra argument in the ethical dative construction and the additional expressive emphasis it imports is not unlike the effect of "intensifying ditransitive constructions" such as *zich een aap/bult/hoedje schrikken, zich blauw betalen* (lit. 'to scare oneself a monkey/bump/hat', 'to pay oneself blue') discussed in Cappelle (this volume), which also add an extra argument and intensify the degree to which the added argument (co-referring with the subject) is affected by the state of affairs. In these cases, the element filling the non-reflexive object slot normally carries negative semantic prosody and triggers a degree modifying reading (as 'a lot' or 'very').[11]

Summing up, *een partij* is a clear example of "synchronic divergence" (see Hopper 1991: 23–24) with both lexical, quantitative and intensifying uses, the latter of which have fairly easily developed out of a lexical meaning that particularly welcomes quantitative interpretations and hence constitutes a useful resource for innovative quantitative N1 N2 uses and subsequent developments.

As a final remark, it should be noted that *een partij* is not unique in this sense and similar uses of, for instance *een boel* 'a lot', *een potje* 'a (little) jar' or *stapels* 'heaps' can be attested as well, as shown below:

(52) *Soms is een beetje ordinair **een boel** lekker.*
'Sometimes a little tacky can be very hot.'
[FOK.nl]

(53) *Dat gezicht van Rooney is me **een potje** lelijk, maar met een Manchester shirt aan lijkt zelfs Rooney minder lelijk.*
'My, that face of Rooney's is really ugly, but in a Manchester shirt even Rooney looks less ugly.'
[www.fmbel.be]

(54) *Ik ben er nog steeds **stapels** blij mee.*
'I am still really happy with it.'
[www.nl.facebook.com]

---

[11] Even uses of diminutives (cf. *hoedje*) in the resultative *zich (een) X schrikken*, do not affect the hyperbolic interpretation. Attested examples on the web also include *zich een apenootje/een rotje schrikken*, while instances like *zich dood/een ongeluk/een hartaanval schrikken* (lit. 'to scare oneself to death/an accident/a heart attack') emphasize the hyperbolic expressiveness of the construction. In most cases one would find illnesses in this slot (especially in Northern Dutch); *de tyfus* (typhoid), *de klere* (cholera), *de pleuris* (pleurisy), *het lazarus* (referring to the Biblical character Lazarus who had leprosy). See Cappelle (this volume) for elaborate discussion.

However, the data do seem to show a special preference for *een partij* with intensifying uses, especially in combination with the ethical dative construction: additional queries (17 January 2013) on "*me toch een partij*" yielded 1,749 hits, whereas "*me toch een boel*" only yielded 28 hits, most of which were quantitative uses. This may be due to a blocking effect of the more fashionable *een partij*, and/or *een boel* may not have reached the same degree of collocational scatter and semantic expansion. We leave it to future research to verify this.

2.5 Tig

Dating back to Proto-Indo-European **dékm̥* 'ten', Dutch *tig* 'very' boasts a long and complex history, which can be schematized as in (55) below (Norde 2006: 33). In Proto-Germanic, the PIE numeral had developed into a noun, **texu-/ *teʒu-*, which inflected as an u-stem (Ross and Berns 1992: 602–613).[12] This noun, meaning 'unit of ten', could be used in complex numerals, e.g Gothic *fimf tigjus* 'five units of ten > fifty' (Van Hamel 1923: 114), from which it gradually developed into a numeral suffix, e.g. Dutch *vijftig* or English *fifty*. In German, Frisian and Dutch, this suffix came to be used independently as a context-dependent, indefinite quantifier comparable to English *umpteen*, or *zillion*. These changes were accompanied by an increase in phonetic substance: as quantifying *tig*, unlike the suffix *–tig*, is invariably stressed, its pronunciation changes from [təx] to [tɪx]. Such a shift from bound to free morpheme is quite rare cross-linguistically, and has been characterized as a case of degrammaticalization in Norde (2009: 213–220). Language users appear to be aware of the suffixal origin of *tig*, because they sometimes spell it <-tig>, both in quantifying and intensifying contexts. This instance of degrammaticalization appears to be largely confined to Netherlandic Dutch, but a handful of examples occur in the Belgian part of the CONDIV corpus nevertheless (cf. Table 3 below).

(55) PIE 'ten' > PGmc 'unit of 10' > PGmc 'x10' > Du 'umpteen' > Du 'very'
     free   > free   > bound   > free   > free

The history of *tig* has not been discussed at great length in the literature, with the exception of two brief papers dating from 20 years ago or more (Hamans 1993; Van Marle 1985) and a more recent, empirical study by Norde (2006). Its origin has been disputed – it is generally assumed that independent *tig* was borrowed from German in the second half of the 20th century (Van der Sijs

---

[12] This noun is still found in Old Icelandic as *tigr, tegr*, meaning 'group of ten'.

2001: 266, 505), but according to Van Marle (1985: 147n.) this is unlikely, as none of his informants using *tig* were aware of the German equivalent. We disagree with Van Marle on this point however, because it is of course perfectly possible that his informants adopted the usage from other speakers who did know the German construction. As this is informal usage, it is not inconceivable that independent *tig* is (much) older than has been assumed thus far, but the age of the construction is a topic that falls outside of the scope of this paper and will not be addressed further.

Data for this case study were partly drawn from the same sources as *duizend* and *massa's* (cf. section 1). For *tig* we used the CONDIV corpus as well as *Scholierenforum*, an internet discussion forum for secondary school pupils, and *Studentenforum*, a similar forum aimed at students in tertiary education.[13] From the *Scholierenforum*, all postings containing *tig* were excerpted on December 14th, 2010, using the forum's own search tool. This resulted in a very coarse list of data, from which all irrelevant constructions and doubles (in quotations of earlier postings) were deleted manually. This yielded only three unambiguous examples of *tig* as a degree modifier, so in order to find more examples of *tig* as a degree modifier, a Google search was performed on March 10–11, 2011. Because of the sheer size of the Google corpus, we chose to search for collocations of *tig* and a specific list of adjectives and adverbs, both positive and comparative.[14] This list consisted of 39 adjectives and adverbs that had been found to collocate with the "vanilla" intensifiers *heel* 'very' and *erg* 'very' most frequently in the USENET subcorpus of CONDIV (on the CONDIV corpus, see Grondelaers et al. 2000). In these queries, we only used the base form of the adjective (both positive and comparative). The inflected form of the adjective in Dutch, with the suffix *–e*, would have yielded too many ambiguous examples. For example, the form in *–e* is used with plural nouns, which also frequently co-occur with *tig* as a quantifier. Thus, in the examples (56) and (57) below, it is not possible to

---

[13] URLs: http://forum.scholieren.com/ and http://www.studentenforum.nl
[14] As *tig* also appears to be the name of a welding technique, pages were selected that did not contain the word *lassen* 'to weld' or *lasser* 'welder'. Another thing one has to bear in mind is that *tig* may be a misspelling for *tog* (i and o are adjacent on the qwerty keyboard after all), which in turn is an erroneous spelling of the adverb *toch* 'still, yet, anyway' that appears to be popular in informal writing of younger users. Thus, a sentence like *Amsterdam is tig leuker* could mean 'Amsterdam is much nicer', but it is perhaps more likely to be misspelled *Amsterdam is toch leuker*, in which case it would mean 'Amsterdam is nicer anyway'. Such cases, where <tig> could be interpreted as <toch>, have been excluded from the analysis.

establish whether *tig* functions as a quantifier or a degree modifier. Given that *tig* as a quantifier is very frequently used on the internet, it would be very time-consuming to disambiguate all examples, because in each case the (larger) context would have to be considered. We will return to these ambiguous constructions below. In all, we made 76 separate Google queries, and again, the irrelevant constructions were removed.[15]

(56) tig   mooie   foto's
      tig   nice   pictures
      'many nice pictures / really nice pictures'

(57) tig   mooiere   foto's
      tig   nicer   pictures
      'many nicer pictures / much nicer pictures'

Table 3: Total number of relevant *tig* constructions in the corpora used

			CONDIV				
	Scholierenforum	Studentenforum	NL:IRC	NL:Krant	NL: usenet	FL: IRC	FL: Usenet
Quantifier	288	21	30	4	60	1	4
Ambiguous	2	1					
Degree Modifier	3						
Noun	1						
Adjective	1					2	
Total	295	22	30	4	62	1	4

As was mentioned above, the use of *tig* as a quantifier appears to be a relatively recent phenomenon, at least as far as written recordings go. For example, *tig* is not mentioned as an independent morpheme in the *Woordenboek der Nederlandsche Taal* (WNT) [Dictionary of the Dutch Language]; it would have

---

[15] The 39 adjectives and adverbs were: *goed* 'good', *veel* 'many', *leuk* 'nice', *mooi* 'beautiful', *lang* 'long', *duur* 'expensive', *populair* 'popular', *groot* 'big', *moeilijk* 'difficult', *tevreden* 'pleased', *hoog* 'high', *handig* 'handy', *belangrijk* 'important', *weinig* 'few', *benieuwd* 'curious', *snel* 'fast', *ver* 'far', *jammer* 'sorry', *simpel* 'simple', *slecht* 'bad', *laag* 'low', *duidelijk* 'clear', *sterk* 'strong', *lekker* 'delicious', *blij* 'happy', *graag* 'willingly', *makkelijk* 'easy', *hard* 'hard', *vaak* 'often', *erg* 'very', *anders* 'different', *klein* 'small', *ander* 'other', *eenvoudig* 'simple', *kort* 'short', *gemakkelijk* 'easy', *normaal* 'normal', *goedkoop* 'cheap', *aardig* 'kind'. Of these, *ander* 'other' and *anders* 'different' do not have a comparative form, hence there were 76 queries, not 78.

had to be included in volume XVII, which was written between 1941 and 1960. The second most extensive dictionary (the 14th edition of the *Van Dale Groot Woordenboek van de Nederlandse Taal* [Van Dale's Comprehensive Dictionary of the Dutch Language], Den Boon and Geeraerts 2005) does have an entry for *tig* (both as quantifier and as degree modifier), but notes that it is informal.

Tig as a quantifier has focalizing function, expressing that the amount of the NP it quantifies is exceptionally high. Thus, the meaning of *tig* ranges from (approximately) less than five in (58), to billions, as in (59). It is also frequently used to express annoyance, as in example (60) (for usage of *tig* as a quantifier see further Norde 2006 and Norde 2009: 213–220).

(58) *Studenten zijn ook wel weer een luie bevolkingsgroep en daarbij zijn onze keukentjes vaak klein, dus geen plek voor **tig** afvalverzamelingsdingen.*
'Students are admittedly a lazy part of the population, and moreover our kitchens are often small, so [there is] no room for dozens of garbage thingies.'
[forum.scholieren.com]

(59) *ik vind liever geen vieze beesten met **tig** bacterieen en virussen in hun lijf tussen mijn food.*
'I'd rather not find dirty bugs with dozens of bacteria and viruses in their bodies among my food.'
[forum.scholieren.com]

(60) *Dat heb ik die mensen al **tig** keer uitgelegd.*
'I have explained it to those people dozens of times already.'
[CONDIVNL_KRANT]

The use of *tig* as an intensifier was first noted in Van Marle (1985: 146) and, as we saw above, it has been included in the *Van Dale* dictionary. In Norde's (2006) study of *tig* in newspaper texts, no examples were found in national newspapers, and only three examples were found in the regional newspapers (from three different regions), the oldest dating from 1999. All examples involved the phrase *tig meer* 'many more'.

In the corpus used for this study, it is extremely rare as well – it only occurs three times in *Scholierenforum*, all in combination with the quantifying adjective *veel* 'many'. The Google searches produced more examples, which are given in (61) to (65). Adjectives or comparatives that did not co-occur with *tig* as degree modifier have been excluded from these tables (see note 15 for a full list of queries).

Table 4: Google results of *tig* + adjective / adverb collocations

Type	#	Type	#
veel	186	duur	2
lang	20	moeilijk	2
vaak	14	duidelijk	1
ver	4	erg	1
groot	3	hard	1
weinig	3	leuk	1
anders	2	mooi	1
blij	2	tevreden	1
Total			244

As far as adjectives and adverbs in the positive degree are concerned, it is clear that the quantifying adjective *veel* 'many' is by far the most frequent collocate: *tig veel* may be followed by a plural count noun as in (61), or by a mass noun as in (62). It may also be followed by a comparative, e.g. *tig veel meer* 'very many more' in (63), or *tig veel leuker* 'very much nicer' in (64). Finally, *veel* can be used as a head, with *tig veel* meaning 'very much' (example 65). Apart from *veel*-collocations, the Google search produced examples with other gradable adjectives (examples 66–67), adverbs (example 68), or the quantifying adjective *weinig* 'little, few' (example 69).

(61) *Het eerste winkeltje wat we in gingen had **tig** veel schoenen van alle bekende merken.*
'The first shop we entered had very many shoes of all known brands.'
[www.roberto-online.nl/?p=163]

(62) *Het ligt vast aan je pc dan, ik heb er ook **tig** veel muziek in en geen probleem.*
'It must be your pc then, I have very much music on it as well and no problem.'
[http://www.wmcity.nl/forum_topic.php?id=509087&ppp=20&page=2]

(63) *de mensen die dit leuk vinden kopen het toch wel. Al helemaal als er **tig** veel meer liedjes bij zitten.*
'People who like this will buy it anyway. Especially if it comes with very many more songs.'
[www.gamer.nl/review/1790/singstar-pop]

(64) *"De nederlandse Abercrombie" maar dan nog **tig** veel leuker!*
'"The Dutch Abercrombie, but very much nicer!'
[http://webstore.scotch-soda.com/. http://www.nickyroeg.com]

(65) want heb net **tig** veel van je zitten lezen maar ik ga niet overal commentaar opgeven.
'because I have just been reading very much of yours but I am not going to comment on everything.'
[www.verhalensite.com/index.php?s=st&ss=r&id]

(66) Ze zijn **tig** duur, maar van een geweldige kwaliteit.
'They are really expensive, but of great quality.'
[http://jegsynesblog.wordpress.com/2006/04/26/hanami-en-nooit-afgeleerde-jongensstreken/]

(67) Nee maar ik vind duits **tig** moeilijk en heb met me mentor besproken dit maand nog proberen en als het niet lukt dan kan ik ermee stoppen.
'No, but I think German is really difficult and have agreed with my mentor that I try this month and if I do not succeed I can quit.'
[http://www.gamersnet.nl/phpBB/viewtopic.php?p=377520]

(68) Voor het laatst dronken: Lang geleden. **'Tig'** lang geleden.... Ik drink nooit.
'Last time drunk: "Long ago. Really long ago .... I never drink.'
[http://www.dekrant-info.nl/persoonlijk/21601-persoonlijk.html]

(69) Maar geloof me het het zijn er maar **tig** weinig.
'But believe me there is only very few of them.'
[http://www.ed.nl/regio/7265062/%27Bureaucratie%27-rond-ex-straatprostituee.ece]

Table 5: Google results of *tig* + comparative collocations

Type	#	Type	#
meer	382	harder	4
beter	62	moeilijker	4
minder	32	sterker	4
duurder	18	verder	4
groter	17	liever[16]	3
mooier	10	kleiner	2
sneller	10	lager	2
goedkoper	8	lekkerder	2
belangrijker	7	eenvoudiger	1
hoger	7	gemakkelijker	1
langer	5	slechter	1
leuker	5	korter	0
vaker	5	normaler	0
erger	4	aardiger	0
Total			600

---

[16] Note that the attested instances of *liever* are not comparatives of the adjective *lief* 'sweet', but of the adverb *graag* 'eager'.

As shown in Table 5, the Google queries involving comparatives yielded far more tokens, which might be taken to imply that comparative constructions were the bridging context for the reanalysis of *tig* as a degree modifier (we will return to this issue below). Perhaps unsurprisingly, the most frequent collocate was *meer* 'more' (the comparative of *veel* 'many'). Just like *tig veel*, *tig meer* may modify different types of NPs – the plural form of count nouns as in (70), the singular of mass nouns as in (71), or it may be used independently (i.e. without an NP head) as in (72). Example (73), finally, is of particular interest because it contains a kind of pleonastic comparative.[17]

(70) *Je hebt **tig** meer wapens zoals een weerwolf catapult die weerwolven recht op je vijand afschiet.*
'There are many more weapons such as a werewolf catapult that launches werewolves straight to the enemy.'
[www.bol.com › Home › Games › PC]

(71) *Tiens, ik meende altijd dat er '**tig** meer gevaar uitgaat van neo-fascisten en neo-liberalen.*
'Right, I always thought that neo-fascists and neo-liberals posed much more danger.'
[forum.politics.be/showthread.php?p=496377]

(72) *Ik heb nog maar een paar minuutjes gezocht, maar er zullen er vast nog **tig** meer zijn.*
'I have only been searching for a couple of minutes, but there will surely be many more.'
[www.singsnap.com/snap/forum/topic/ac27d98]

(73) *Het is vlak in de buurt waar wij naar toe zouden gaan alleen **tig** meer luxer en mooier, kijk dat is niet mis.*
'It is close to the area where we would be going, only much more grander and better-looking, look that's not bad.'
[www.reismee.nl/reisblogs/.../costa-rica/]

As regards other collocation types there is clearly more variation than with positive adjectives. Some examples are given in (74)–(78):

---

[17] As in English, there are two types of comparative constructions in Dutch – one synthetic by adding the suffix *-er*, one analytic involving the adverb *more* 'meer'. Example (73) appears to be a contamination of both types, possibly for emphatic purposes.

(74) *en dat zegt een BMW freak ja, spijt me maar hij is gewoon **tig** mooier dan X3.5.*
'Says a BMW freak, yes, I'm sorry but it is just much better-looking than X3.5.'
[www.autojunk.nl/2008/07/audi-q5-in-valencia]

(75) *Doe anders gewoon een tafelkleed over je tafel (heb ik ook) ziet er **tig** beter uit.*
'Otherwise, just put a table cloth on your table (I have one too), looks a lot better.'
[www.licht-geluid.nl/forum/.../3571-bovenbouwfeest-20-6-2002-a-3.html]

(76) *Resultaat: de treinkaartjes worden **tig** duurder.*
'Result: the train tickets will be far more expensive.'
[www.nujij.nl/betaalt-u-straks-vier-euro-voor-een-liter-benzine.11567369.lynkx]

(77) *Dit is **tig** belangrijker dan wat belastinggeld, jullie geloofwaardigheid staat op het spel.*
'This is much more important than a bit of tax money, your credibility is at stake.'
[mickbook.blogspot.com/2007/.../pepijn-versus-nederland.html]

(78) *Huntelaar had -**tig** minder kansen nodig dan Luis.*
'Huntelaar needed much fewer chances than Luis.'
[www.ajaxshowtime.com/.../-barcelona-volgt-suarez-.html&page=10]

As we have shown above, quantifying *tig* does not merely refer to an unspecified large amount, it also underscores that the quantity is exceptionally large in the given context. This emphatic function may have facilitated the reanalysis from quantifier to intensifier. In what follows we will discuss three constructional contexts in which the shift from quantifier to degree modifier may have occurred: ellipsis, reanalysis in bridging contexts and contamination.

The first scenario is rooted in the observation that as a quantifier, *tig* is most frequently found in the phrase *tig keer* 'dozens of times' (cf. example 60). This phrase, in turn, can be used to intensify comparatives, as in *tig keer beter* 'umpteen times better'. A possible path of development, then, would be from the comparative construction in (79) to the elliptical construction in (80a). Once the elliptical construction has become entrenched, speakers may cease to regard it as elliptical and reinterpret *tig* alone as degree modifier.

(79) het origineel is **tig** keer beter
the original is umpteen times better
[http://www.axclub.net/phpbb3/viewtopic.php?p=210272]

(80) a. het origineel is **tig**   (keer)   beter
       the original   is umpteen times   better

   b.' het origineel is **tig** beter
       the original   is much   better
       [http://forums.marokko.nl/archive/index.php/t-3655390.html]

Secondly, as suggested by Norde (2006, 2009: 218), the use of *tig* as a degree modifier may have originated in so-called "bridging contexts" (Heine 2002), i.e. ambiguous constructions where *tig* precedes a comparative adjective and a plural noun, as in example (81). In this construction, *tig* can either be interpreted as a quantifier (reading a) or a degree modifier (reading b). Note that the hierarchical structure of the noun phrase is different – in (81a), *tig* takes scope over the following NP, whereas in (81b) it only takes scope over the adjective. This reinterpretation was possible because in Dutch, the adverb *veel* is used both as a quantifier meaning 'many' and as a degree modifier of comparatives.[18] As a result, the semantic extension and categorial reanalysis of *tig* may have been modelled on the two functions of its near-synonym *veel*, as an example of proportional analogy (Hock and Joseph 1996: 160), as shown in (82):

(81) *Emigreren naar dubai en dan nog een vent vanuit hier meenemen in je koffer?? Hell no!! Daar heb je **tig** leukere mannen...!!*
   'Emigrating to Dubai and then taking a guy from here with you in your suitcase? Hell no!
   a. 'There are dozens of nicer men over there!!'
   b. 'There are much nicer men over there!!'
   [http://www.maroc.nl/forums/wie-schrijft-blijft/287061-zakelijke-aanbieding-2.html]

(82) veel oplossingen : tig oplossingen
   veel beter(e)   : X   (>tig betere)

In constructional terms, the *tig* and *veel* micro-constructions already share a link to the higher level abstract schema (the quantifier construction) which invites an analogical link (see Figure 1 in section 3 below). On the basis of this analogy, the *tig* micro-construction also forms a link with the degree modifier

---

[18] In this respect Dutch differs from English, which uses *many* as a quantifier and *much* to grade comparatives.

of comparatives construction, which is the second abstract schema that the *veel* micro-construction may be sanctioned by. In other words, because of analogical alignment on the micro-level, *tig*-constructions are attracted to the schematic degree modifier construction. We will return to this issue in section 3.

It seems likely that, once reanalysed as a degree modifier, *tig* spread to comparative constructions with singular noun phrases, where there is no such ambiguity. It might appear that the occurrence of *tig* as degree modifier of positive adjectives and adverbs cannot be the result of analogy with *veel* constructions, as pointed out by Doetjes (2008).

> Norde assumes that the first step of the change was the analogy between *veel* and *tig*, both of which can modify plurals. As *veel* is also used with comparatives, the use of *tig* would have been extended to that context via syntactic reanalysis of [*tig* [*betere oplossingen*]] 'a very large number of better solutions' to [[*tig betere*] *oplossingen*] 'far better solutions.' This, in turn, might have been the source of the use of *tig* as an intensifier. As shown above, degree modification of adjectives and of comparatives is not similar in Dutch, so a change from a modifier of comparatives into a modifier of adjectives is not based on an analogy similar to the one causing the first step in the change. (Doetjes 2008: 133)

However, Doetjes is not quite correct in assuming that positive and comparative adjectives cannot select the same degree modifier in Dutch. This may be the case for traditional degree modifiers (cf. **heel** leuk 'very nice' vs. **veel** leuker 'much nicer'), but it is not true of degree modifiers deriving from quantifiers. As we have shown in this paper, *massa's*, *duizend*, *een partij* and *tig* can all be used with both positives and comparatives. The same is true by the way for downtoners – it is possible to say, for instance, *een beetje dom* 'a bit stupid', as well as *een beetje dommer* 'a bit more stupid', or *enigszins intelligent* 'somewhat intelligent', as well as *enigszins intelligenter* 'somewhat more intelligent'. This suggests that these degree modifiers are sanctioned by a more schematic construction which does not distinguish between positive and comparative forms (cf. Figure 1 in section 3). Therefore, there is no reason to assume that usage as a degree modifier cannot spread from comparative to positive constructional contexts.

Doetjes herself (2008: 133) offers a third analysis, which is that the phrase *tig veel* is probably rooted in a contamination of *tig* 'terribly many' and *ontzettend veel* 'terribly much / many'. For example, the constructs *tig mensen* 'dozens of people' and *ontzettend veel mensen* 'very many people' may have "blended" into a construct *tig veel mensen*. Thus, Doetjes suggests that the intensifying usage of *tig* may have spread from *tig veel* collocations to other gradable adjectives, such as *leuk* 'nice', or comparatives such as *sneller* 'faster'.[19] However, it is not immediately clear why and how such a contamination should have arisen, or indeed why a construction involving another intensifier such as *ontzettend* 'terribly' would have to be presupposed at all. It is also conceivable that *tig veel mensen* is simply a contamination of *tig mensen* and *veel mensen*, possibly rooted in a kind of emphatic tautology similar to constructions as *never nooit niet* 'never never not'. Such tautological constructions are not uncommon in the quantifier/intensifier domain. For example, *een boel* 'a lot' (cf. example 52) may also collocate with *veel*, as in example (83), sometimes with deletion of the indefinite article, as in example (84):[20]

(83) *Ik heb alle paarden vanaf 2002, en nog **een boel veel** oudere paarden.*
'I have got all horses from 2002 up till now, and still a lot of many older horses / a whole lot of older horses.'
[http://www.everyoneweb.com/schleichverzameling]

(84) *Joene kent **boel veel** mensen van fok*
'Joene knows many a lot of people from Fok forum / Joene knows a whole lot of people from Fok forum.'
[forum.fok.nl/topic//1488]

To conclude, on the basis of the available data it is not possible to establish exactly how *tig* developed into a degree modifier. Based on the frequencies of *tig*-collocations however, which show that *tig keer meer* 'tig times more' is by far the most frequent collocation, coupled with the observation that *tig* +

---

19 Doetjes also notes that the collocation *tig bedankt* 'thanks a whole lot' might be an example of intensifying *tig*. However, it is difficult to find convincing examples of this, as *tig* in those cases might be interpreted as a misspelling for the adverb *toch* (see footnote 14), e.g. in example (i) below, where the use of the adversative conjunction *maar* 'but' actually makes the second interpretation more plausible.

(i) *Eigenlijk morgen pas maar **tig bedankt** jonge*
  1: 'Tomorrow, actually, but thanks a lot pal.'
  2: 'Tomorrow, actually, but thanks anyway pal.'
  [rheren3.mygb.nl/?page=26]

20 It should be noted that this kind of contamination is possible only if both quantifiers are relatively schematic and productive; very specific quantifier constructions with low type frequency hardly ever combine with *veel* in constructions similar to (83) and (84). For example, *lots of rain* can be translated into Dutch as, for instance, *veel regen* 'much rain' (515,000 raw Google hits), or *bakken regen* 'cisterns of rain' (33,400 raw Google hits), but *bakken veel regen* occurs only once. (Search performed November 1, 2012.)

comparative is far more frequent than *tig* + corresponding adjective, it seems likely that the reanalysis as a degree modifier occurred in both these contexts. Spread to non-comparative adjectives may have been facilitated by tautological constructions, but that would require a more fine-grained empirical analysis, and seeing that these constructions are very informal it is questionable whether sufficient diachronic data is available.

3 Theoretical discussion

In this section, we will outline how the empirical observations in the preceding sections can be accounted for using a Diachronic Construction Grammar (DCxG) approach. Diachronic Construction Grammar (DCxG), like any diachronic linguistic approach, is dynamic by definition. In very general terms, the basic research question in DCxG is: "How do languages acquire constructions?" (Noël 2007: 178), which paraphrases the basic research question in usage-based approaches to grammaticalization, which is: "How do languages acquire grammar?" (Bybee 2003: 145–146). Thus, the alignment of grammaticalization studies and construction grammar (Langacker 2005; Noël 2007; Traugott 2007, 2008a, 2008b; Booij 2008, 2013; Trousdale 2008a, 2008b, 2010, 2012; Trousdale & Norde 2013) seemed only a matter of time, because they have similar views on grammar. To be sure, constructions have featured as input for grammaticalization at least since Givón (1979), as pointed out by Traugott (2008a: 23), but they were often not clearly defined, if at all. For the most part, "construction" was used more or less as a synonym of "collocation", "string" or "context". However, with the arrival of construction grammars of various kinds, it has become possible to refine the notions of "construction" and "constructional change" in current theorizing about grammaticalization and lexicalization (Traugott 2008a: 23).

In the functional-typological approach which prevails in most grammaticalization theorizing, language change is typically regarded as gradual. On this view (e.g. Brinton & Traugott 2005: 6; Hopper and Traugott 2003: 49), a change typically looks like (85). This cline acknowledges that change is not the abrupt substitution of one structure for another, but always involves variation, with older and newer forms coexisting side by side. In other words, change is gradual, and this may result in (synchronic) gradience (Traugott & Trousdale 2010). We find gradience in the case studies discussed in this paper as well: *een partij* and *massa's* still function as both lexical noun phrase heads and quantifying constructions, and *duizend* and *tig* continue to be used as quantifiers.

(85) A > {A / B} > (B)

One of the basic concepts in DCxG is *constructionalization*, i.e. the rise of new form-meaning pairings. Such new signs arise through a series of small-step neo-analyses of formal and semantic features. This results in new nodes in a constructional network as well as new links between those nodes. In Traugott and Trousdale's (2013) definition:

> Constructionalization is the creation of form$_{new}$-meaning$_{new}$ (combinations of) signs. It forms new type nodes, which have new syntax or morphology and new coded meaning, in the linguistic network of a population of speakers. It is accompanied by changes in degree of schematicity, productivity, and compositionality. The constructionalization of schemas always results from a succession of micro-steps and is therefore gradual. New micro-constructions may likewise be created gradually, but they may also be instantaneous. (Traugott and Trousdale 2013: 22)

Constructionalization may affect a single construction or entire networks of related constructions (on networks see below). There are basically two kinds of constructionalization: *grammatical constructionalization* and *lexical constructionalization* (Trousdale 2012). In grammatical constructionalization, constructions come to serve a more procedural function. For example, some [*NP of NP*] constructions in English have developed into complex determiners/quantifiers (Traugott 2008a): *(a) kind of a problem, a bit of a liar, (not) a shred of honour*. In lexical constructionalization, constructions come to serve a more referential function, e.g. the development of monomorphemic forms from historically complex forms involving productive suffixes (*winsome* 'attractive' < OE *wynn* 'joy' + OE *-sum*, or *buxom* 'plump and comely' < OE *bug(an)* 'bow' + OE *-sum*) (Trousdale and Norde 2013).[21]

A second important concept in DCxG is the concept of *taxonomic hierarchy* (Croft 2001: 25), a network which connects constructions at different levels of schematicity. Traugott (2008a: 30, 2008b: 236) has coined the following terms for constructional levels, at decreasing degrees of schematicity:[22]

(i) *macro-constructions*: form- meaning pairings that are defined by structure and function;
(ii) *meso-constructions*: sets of similarly behaving constructions; often there is more than one meso-level (see below);
(iii) *micro-constructions*: individual construction types
(iv) *constructs*: the empirically attested tokens

---

21 It is important to recognize that the terms grammatical and lexical constructionalization are not synonymous with grammaticalization and lexicalization respectively. Grammatical constructionalization does not only encompass grammaticalization, but some types of degrammaticalization as well. In the same way, lexical constructionalization encompasses lexicalization, but some (other) types of degrammaticalization too (for examples of the latter see Trousdale and Norde 2013).
22 Note that Traugott and Trousdale (2013) use the terms *schema* and *subschema* instead of *macro-* and *meso-construction*.

For example, the ditransitive is a macro-construction which is maximally schematic (Traugott 2008c). Meso-constructions are sets of similarly behaving, partially substantive constructions, e.g. [<V> <subj, obj1 *to* obj2>] or [<V> <subj, obj1 *for* obj2>]. Micro-constructions are individual construction types, e.g. *give* <subj, obj1 *to* obj2>] or [*buy* <subj, obj1 *for* obj2>]. Constructs, finally, are individual tokens (spoken or written).

Applying this four-level model to the degree modifiers discussed in this paper, we note the following. The constructs are the attested tokens in our corpus, as represented in Table 6. These tokens are instantiations of micro-constructions, or types. For example, there are 382 instances of the construct *tig meer* 'much more', and there is only one of *tig eenvoudiger* 'much simpler'. These constructs are instantiations of partially schematic micro-constructions, which in turn are instantiations of a higher level of schematic meso-constructions, where the part of speech of the intensified item is not specified. The macro-construction, finally, is the *Degree Modifier Construction*, which is the parent construction of the degree modifiers that feature in this paper, but also of other degree modifiers, such as *erg* 'very', *heel* 'very', *enorm* 'enormously', or *vreselijk* 'terribly'.

Table 6: Examples of meso-constructions, micro-constructions and constructs

meso-construction	micro-constructions	constructs
[*massa's* X]	[*massa's* <ADJ$_{POS}$>]	*massa's cool* 'really cool'
	[*massa's* <ADJ$_{COMP}$>]	*massa's beter* 'loads better'
	[*massa's* <V>]	*massa's buizen* 'to fail big time'
[*duizend* X]	[*duizend* <QUANT>]	*duizend veel* 'very many'
	[*duizend* <ADJ$_{POS}$>]	*duizend allergisch* 'really allergic'
	[*duizend* <V>]	*duizend slapen* 'to sleep very well'
[*een partij* X]	[*een partij* <ADJ$_{POS}$>]	*een partij moe* 'really tired'
	[*een partij* <ADJ$_{COMP}$>]	*een partij mooier* 'much more beautiful'
	[*een partij* <V>]	*een partij stinken* 'to stink a lot'
[*tig* X]	[*tig* <QUANT>]	*tig veel* 'very much'
	[*tig* <ADJ$_{POS}$>]	*tig moeilijk* 'really difficult'
	[*tig* <ADJ$_{COMP}$>]	*tig duurder* 'much more expensive'

Collectively, the constructions of variable degrees of schematicity form a constructional network, a tiny part of which is represented in Figure 1 below. This figure illustrates constructions involving the noun phrase *betere films* 'better movies', which can be either quantified 'many better movies', or intensified 'much better movies'. Assuming that [QUANTIFIER <ADJ$_{COMP}$>] constructions function as bridging contexts, we hypothesize that the existing ambiguity of *veel betere films* 'many/much better movies' coerces a similar ambiguity in other [QUANTIFIER <ADJ_COMP>] constructions, e.g. [*tig* <ADJ_COMP>] with the result that several other quantifiers come to serve an intensifying function.

Figure 1 reads as follows. The Quantifier Construction and the Degree Modifier Construction are macro-constructions. They are maximally schematic, i.e. the quantifier c.q. degree modifier and other elements in the NP are unspecified. For reasons of space, Figure 1 only features part of the taxonomic hierarchy, but of course there are many more quantifiers (e.g. numerals) and degree modifiers (e.g. *erg*, 'very' or *ontzettend* 'terribly'). One level to the right are the partially schematic meso-constructions, in which the quantifier or degree modifier is specified, but not the other elements in the noun phrase. On this level, too, only a few possible meso-constructions are given, namely meso-constructions in which the noun phrase contains an adjective. In addition, quantifiers nor degree modifiers exclusively occur in noun phrases, so there are of course other meso-constructions, too. In the quantifier meso-constructions in Figure 1, *veel* and *tig* quantify the noun phrase, whereas in the degree modifier meso-construction *tig* is an adverb modifying the following adjective.[23] On the micro-constructional level, all parts of speech have been specified for their grammatical properties (in this case, whether the adjective is positive or comparative) but they have not yet been lexically specified. On the level of constructs, finally, all elements have substantive form – these are maximally specific constructions. The nodes in this network are not only hierarchically related; some of them are also connected to sister nodes on the same level. For example, some nodes may be analogically linked on the basis of semantic/functional similarity, as explained above, this is indicated by the accolades on the micro-level. Bridging contexts are represented by brackets.

Obviously, it also possible to extend and refine this network and complement it with constructions whose meanings are compatible with the quantifying and degree modifying potential of constructions under discussion. In the case of *een partij*, for instance, which turned out to be an easy bedfellow with the ethical dative construction, one could present the degree modifying construction as a slot in this larger construction, the combination of which would then underscore the expressive nature of the utterance. The ethical dative construction, in its turn, could then be linked to other expressive constructions with an extra argument (e.g. *zich een aap schrikken* 'to be scared out of one's wits') and possibly to a shared macro-construction of intensifying added argument constructions with a form-function fit between the extra arguments that are expressed and

---

[23] Note that there is no [[*veel* [ADJ]]_AP [N]]_NP meso-level, because *veel* can only collocate with comparative adjectives, not positive ones.

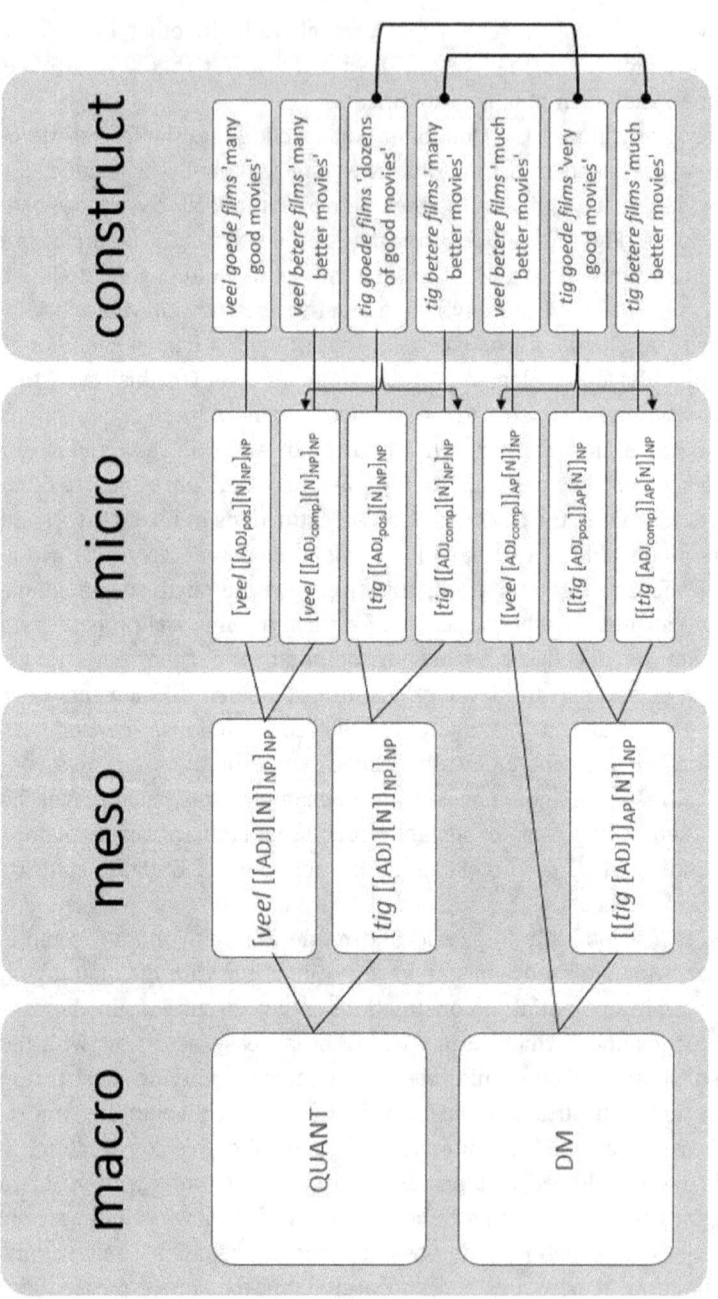

Figure 1: Part of the constructional network of Dutch Quantifier and Degree Modifier constructions

affectedness. The architecture of such a network, however, is something we will explore in further research. On the view that constructions of various degrees of complexity, and various degrees of schematicity, are essentially the same (i.e. symbolic form-meaning pairings, see e.g. Croft 2001: 17), constructional change can, in principle, occur on all levels. An interesting question is, therefore, at which level(s) quantifiers came to be used as degree modifiers. On the basis of our data, we suggest the following scenario: because of the existing double inheritance of the quantifier/degree modifier *veel*, some constructs involving other quantifiers aligned with *veel* in that they likewise became ambiguous. Token frequency suggests that the first bridging contexts involved comparatives (notably *meer* 'more'), followed by host-class expansion (Himmelmann 2004). This may lead to entrenchment of the collocation, with the result that its upper level micro-construction becomes more productive, attracting fully substantive members. Initially, these were probably other comparative forms of adjectives and adverbs, but positive forms came to be recruited as well. This resulted in an increase in frequency (and hence entrenchment) at both construct and micro-construction level. Further, whenever a new link between a micro-level quantifier construction and a micro-level degree modifier construction has been established, this also strengthens the association between the two macro-levels, so that other quantifiers are reanalysed as degree modifiers as well. This may explain why a number of quantifier constructions are going through similar changes more or less simultaneously. In addition, as we have seen in the discussion of *duizend*, the same extension from well-established quantifier uses to novel degree modifier uses may occur several times in the history of an item and *need* not always lead to the entrenchment of the latter: while we found several instances of the construct *duizend jammer* 'such a shame' in texts from around the year 1800, there is as yet no sign that there was a productive *duizend* degree modifier construction at the time.

A last issue that remains to be resolved concerns the "birth" of the actual construction, i.e. when constructionalization actually took place. We propose to consider the emergence of non-ambiguous degree modifier constructions as unequivocal evidence of a new node in the constructional network. In the case of *tig*, for instance, predicative constructions such as *ze zijn tig duur* 'they are very expensive' or collocations with adverbs such as *tig vaak* 'very often' *only* allow for a degree modifier interpretation, so that their occurrence serves as a kind of terminus ante quem: constructionalization of *tig* as a degree modifier must have occurred in order for such intensifying uses to be sanctioned. While we have no diachronic data which document the hypothesized spread of the new intensifiers to various syntactic contexts, it can be observed that all four of them have reached the crucial stage of occurring in adjectival or adverbial phrases. (86) to (89) below repeat a number of instances in which they modify a predicative adjective in the positive degree, for instance.

(86) *Die dudes die gewonnen hebben waren **massa's** cool.*
'Those dudes that won were really cool.'
[fkserv.ugent.be]

(87) *Ik was echt **duizend** blij toen ze zei: "..."*
'I really was totally glad when she said: "..."'
[ikbenkarelpti.blogspot.com/2007_12_01_archive.html]

(88) *Ik ben me toch **een partij** moe.*
'I am so freakin' tired'
[FOK.nl]

(89) *Ze zijn **tig** duur, maar van een geweldige kwaliteit.*
'They are really expensive, but of great quality.'
[http://jegsynesblog.wordpress.com/2006/04/26/hanami-en-nooit-afgeleerde-jongensstreken/]

4 Conclusions and outlook

Degree modifiers, as we stated in the introduction, form a very productive class of adverbs. While there are several sources speakers can tap from, the current paper focused on expressions of high quantity in present-day Dutch and how these expressions develop into degree modifiers. Four of them were singled out for closer examination, each of which had its own specific features: *massa's* as a plural noun, *duizend* as a cardinal numeral, *een partij* as a singular noun phrase, and *tig* originally as a numeral suffix (cognate with English *-ty* as in *sixty*). Despite the different nature of the source lexical items, the study shows that they all function as hyperbolic quantifiers in quantifying constructions, denoting an indefinite amount, but one that is exceptionally large in the given context. The study further showed that degree modifying uses are attested as well for each of these items, as well as for several other quantifiers (cf. examples 52–54, and the example of *nul* 'zero' as a downtoner in note 6). We have argued that degree modifier uses may have come about through processes of reanalysis in (bridging) contexts in which the quantifier that precedes a full noun phrase no longer highlights the amount of the head noun, but the degree of the quality expressed by the adjective modifying the head noun. In other words, scope decreases from the full noun phrase to the adjective (cf. the meso-constructions in Figure 1). Adopting a constructional approach to the changes observed, we have argued that the use as a degree modifier arose in specific constructs (reflected by high token frequency), which lead to the emergence of a partially schematic micro-construction. As these micro-constructions become increasingly entrenched, new constructs (collocations) come to be sanctioned by the micro-construction, but we also hypothesized that it likewise resulted in the formation of similar micro-constructions, in which the degree modifier derives from a quantifier. As intensifiers, all four constructions discussed in this paper acquire a more procedural function, which makes them instances of grammatical constructionalization (Trousdale 2012). We propose to consider the emergence of non-ambiguous degree modifier uses, such as their use in combination with predicative adjectives in the positive degree, as unequivocal evidence of the creation of a new node in the constructional network.

It is interesting to note that recruitment of quantifiers as degree modifiers is not restricted to Dutch. For instance, a degree modifier construction corresponding to *massa's* is found in Swedish (example 90), the use of 'thousand' as a degree modifier is found in both Swedish and German (examples 91 and 92),[24] and German *zig* can be found in constructions similar to Dutch *tig* (example 93).

(90) Resan hem var **massor** trevlig.
      'The journey home was really nice.'
      [http://www.frida.se/blogg/blogginlagg.php?entry_id=12469]

(91) jag hoppas att hon har **tusen** kul därnere.
      'I hope she has it really cool down there -> I hope she's having a great time down there.'
      [http://xannax.blogg.se/2007/june/is-it-yees-its-friday.html]

(92) Und das kuscheln im Auto war **tausend** schön.
      'And snuggling up in the car was really nice.'
      [http://classic.uboot.com/glicerine/board/profile/3/0]

---

24 Note also that the degree modifying use of 'thousand' is not restricted to Germanic languages. Modern Greek, for instance, features a prefix *xilio-* with intensifying function, e.g. in *xilioforeménos* (lit. thousand worn) 'much worn' (Gavriilidou 2013).

(93) *Die Hotline hat leider nie etwas bewirkt obwohl ich **zig** oft angerufen habe.*
'Unfortunately, the hotline never achieved anything, although I called them really often.'
[http://forum.digitalfernsehen.de/forum/sky-technik-allgemein/241918-hilfe-sky-veraeppelt-mich-4.html]

The productivity of this kind of degree modifier construction at both micro- and meso-level, in several languages, calls for empirical investigations across larger data sets. It would also be interesting to see whether any of the degree modifiers we discussed will eventually spread to the entire language community, or whether they will be substituted for by new means to express a very high degree.

References

Bolinger, Dwight. 1972. *Degree Words*. The Hague: Mouton.
Booij, Geert. 2008. Constructional idioms as products of linguistic change: The *aan het* + infinitive construction in Dutch. In: Alexander Bergs and Gabriele Diewald (eds.), *Constructions and Language Change*, 79–104. Berlin/New York: Mouton de Gruyter.
Booij, Geert. 2013. Morphology in Construction Grammar. In: Thomas Hoffmann and Graeme Trousdale (eds.), *The Oxford Handbook of Construction Grammar*, 255–273. Oxford: Oxford University Press.
Boon, Ton den and Dirk Geeraerts. 2008. *Van Dale Groot Woordenboek der Nederlandse Taal* [Van Dale's Comprehensive Dictionary of the Dutch Language], 14th edition. Utrecht/Antwerpen: Van Dale Lexicografie.
Brems, Lieselotte. 2003. Measure noun constructions: An instance of semantically-driven grammaticalization. *International Journal of Corpus Linguistics* 8: 283–312.
Brems, Lieselotte. 2007a. The synchronic layering of size noun and type noun constructions in English. Ph.D. dissertation, Department of Linguistics, University of Leuven.
Brems, Lieselotte. 2007b. The grammaticalization of small size nouns: Reconsidering frequency and analogy. *Journal of English Linguistics* 35: 235–293.
Brems, Lieselotte. 2010. Size noun constructions as collocationally constrained constructions: Lexical and grammaticalized uses. *English Language and Linguistics* 14: 83–109.
Brems, Lieselotte. 2011. *Layering of Size and Type Noun Constructions in English*. Berlin/New York: Mouton De Gruyter.
Brinton, Laurel J. and Elizabeth Closs Traugott. 2005. *Lexicalization and Language Change*. Cambridge: Cambridge University Press.
Bybee, Joan. 2003. Cognitive processes in grammaticalization. In: Michael Tomasello (ed.), *The New Psychology of Language: Cognitive and Functional Approaches to Language Structure*. Volume 2, 145–167. Mahwah, NJ: Erlbaum.
Clerck, Bernard de and Lieselotte Brems. In press. Size nouns matter: A closer look *at mass(es) of* and extended uses of SNs. To appear in *Language sciences*.

Clerck, Bernard de and Timothy Colleman. 2013. From noun to intensifier: *Massa* and *massa's* in Flemish varieties of Dutch. *Language Sciences* 36: 147–160.
Croft, William. 2001. *Radical Construction Grammar: Syntactic Theory in Typological Perspective*. Oxford: Oxford University Press.
Cuervo, Maria Cristina. 2003. Datives at large. Ph.D. dissertation, Massachusetts Institute of Technology.
Denison, David. 2005. The grammaticalization of *sort of*, *kind of* and *type of* in English. Paper Presented at the NRG 3 conference (New Reflections on Grammaticalization 3), Santiago de Compostela, 17–20 July 2005.
Doetjes, Jenny. 1997. *Quantifiers and Selection: On the Distribution of Quantifying Expressions in. French, Dutch and English*. The Hague: Holland Academic Graphics.
Doetjes, Jenny. 2008. Adjectives and degree modification. In: Louise McNally and Christopher Kennedy (eds.), *Adjectives and Adverbs: Syntax, Semantics, and Discourse*, 123–155. Oxford: Oxford University Press.
Gavriilidou, Zoe. 2013. Intensifying prefixes in Greek. Paper presented at the Conference on Morphology and its interfaces, Lille, 13-09-13.
Geeraerts, Dirk. 1997. *Diachronic Prototype Semantics: A Contribution to Historical Lexicology*. Oxford: Clarendon Press.
Givón, Talmy. 1979. *On Understanding Grammar*. New York/San Francisco/London: Academic Press.
Grondelaers, Stefan, Katrien Deygers, Hilde van Aken, Vicky van den Heede and Dirk Speelman. 2000. Het CONDIV-corpus geschreven Nederlands [The CONDIV corpus of written Dutch]. *Nederlandse Taalkunde* 5: 356–363.
Hamans, Camiel. 1993. Van epicentrum tot episch centrum: enige notities over distinctieve morfologie [From epicenter to epic centre: some notes on distinctive morphology]. *Tabu* 23: 63–73.
Hamel, A.G. van. 1923. *Gotisch handboek* [Handbook Gothic]. Haarlem: H.D. Tjeenk Willink & Zoon.
Heine, Bernd. 2002. On the role of context in grammaticalization. In: Ilse Wischer and Gabriele Diewald (eds), *New Reflections on Grammaticalization*, 83–101. Amsterdam/Philadelphia: John Benjamins.
Hilpert, Martin. 2013. *Constructional Change in English: Developments in Allomorphy, Word Formation, and Syntax*. Cambridge: Cambridge University Press.
Himmelmann, Nikolaus P. 2004. Lexicalization and grammaticalization: Opposite or orthogonal? In: Walter Bisang, Nikolaus P. Himmelmann and Björn Wiemer (eds.), *What Makes Grammaticalization? A Look from its Fringes and Components*, 21–42. Berlin/New York: Mouton de Gruyter.
Hock, Hans Henrich and Brian D. Joseph. 1996. *Language History, Language Change and Language Relationship: An Introduction to Historical and Comparative Linguistics*. Berlin/New York: Mouton de Gruyter.
Hopper, Paul J. 1991. On some principles of grammaticalization. In: Elizabeth Closs Traugott and Bernd Heine (eds.), *Approaches to Grammaticalization*, Vol. I., 17–36. Amsterdam/Philadelphia: John Benjamins.
Hopper, Paul. J. and Elizabeth Closs Traugott. 2003. *Grammaticalization*, 2nd edition. Cambridge: Cambridge University Press.
Horn, Laurence R. 2008. *I love me some him*. The landscape of non-argument datives. *Empirical Issues in Syntax and Semantics* 7: 169–192.

Ito, Rika and Sali Tagliamonte. 2003. Well weird, right dodgy, very strange, really cool. *Language in Society* 32: 257–279.
Janssen, Theo A.J.M. 2002. Deictic principles of pronominals, demonstratives and tenses. In: Frank Brisard (ed.), *Grounding: The Epistemic Footing of Deixis and Reference*, 151–193. Berlin/New York: Mouton de Gruyter.
Joosten, Frank. 2003. Collectiva en aggregaatsnamen in het Nederlands: Begripsbepaling en typologie [Collective and aggregate nouns in Dutch: definition and typology]. Ph. D. dissertation, Department of Linguistics, University of Leuven.
Joosten, Frank, Gert De Sutter, Denis Drieghe, Stefan Grondelaers, Robert J. Hartsuiker and Dirk Speelman. 2007. Dutch collective nouns and conceptual profiling. *Linguistics* 45: 85–132.
Keizer, Evelien. 2001. A classification of *sort/kind/type*-Constructions. Ms., University College London.
Klein, Henny. 1998. *Adverbs of Degree in Dutch and Related Languages*. Amsterdam/Philadelphia: John Benjamins.
Labov, William. 1972. *Sociolinguistic Patterns*. Philadelphia: University of Pennsylvania Press.
Lamiroy, Beatrice and Nicole Delbecque. 1998. The possessive dative in Romance and Germanic languages. In: Willy van Langendonck and William van Belle (eds.), *The Dative. Vol. 2: Theoretical and Contrastive Aprroaches*, 29–74. Amsterdam/Philadelphia: John Benjamins.
Langacker, Ronald W. 2005. Construction grammars: Cognitive, radical and less so. In: Francisco J. Ruiz de Mendoza and Sandra Peña Cervel (eds.), *Cognitive Linguistics: Internal Dynamics and Interdisciplinary Interaction*, 101–159. Berlin/New York: Mouton de Gruyter.
Langacker, Ronald W. 2010. A lot of quantifiers. In: Sally Rice and John Newman (eds.), *Empirical and Experimental Methods in Cognitive/Functional Research*, 41–57. Stanford: CSLI.
Langacker, Ronald W. 2009. *Investigations in Cognitive Grammar*. Berlin/New York: Mouton de Gruyter.
Lorenz, Gunter. 2002. *Really worthwile* or *not really significant*? A corpus-based approach to the delexicalization and grammaticalization of intensifiers in Modern English. In: Ilse Wischer and Gabriela Diewald (eds.), *New reflections on grammaticalization*, 143–161. Amsterdam/Philadelphia: John Benjamins.
Macaulay, Ronald. 2006. Pure grammaticalization: The development of a teenage intensifier. *Language Variation and Change* 18: 267–283.
Marle, Jaap van. 1985. Bij de woordvorming van *tig* [On the word formation of *tig*]. *De Nieuwe Taalgids* 78: 145–148.
Noël, Dirk. 2007. Diachronic construction grammar and grammaticalization theory. *Functions of Language* 14: 177–202.
Norde, Muriel. 2006. Van suffix tot telwoord tot bijwoord: degrammaticalisering en (re)grammaticalisering van *tig* [From suffix to numeral to adverb: degrammaticalization and (re)grammaticalization of *tig*]. *Tabu* 35: 33–60.
Norde, Muriel. 2009. *Degrammaticalization*. Oxford: Oxford University Press.
Paradis, Carita. 2000. It's well weird: Degree modifiers revisited: The Nineties. In: John M. Kirk (ed.), *Corpora Galore: Analyses and Techniques in Describing English*, 147–160. Amsterdam: Rodopi.
Partington, Alan. 1993. Corpus evidence of language change: The case of the intensifier. In: Mona Baker, Gill Francis and Elena Tognini-Bonelli (eds.), *Text and Technology: In honour of John Sinclair*, 177–192. Amsterdam/Philadelphia: John Benjamins.
Peters, Hans. 1994. Degree adverbs in Early Modern English. In: Dieter Kastovsky (ed.), *Studies in Early Modern English*, 269–288. Berlin/New York: Mouton de Gruyter.

Quirk, Ronald, Sidney Greenbaum, Geoffrey Leech and Jan Svartvik. 1985. *A Comprehensive Grammar of the English Language*. London/New York: Longman.

Ross, Alan S.C. and Jan Berns. 1992. Germanic. In: Jadranka Gvozdanović (ed.), *Indo-European Numerals*, 555–715. Berlin/New York: Mouton de Gruyter.

Schäfer, Roland and Felix Bildhauer. 2012. Building large corpora from the web using a new efficient tool chain. In: Nicoletta Calzolari, Khalid Choukri, Thierry Declerck, Mehmet Uğur Doğan, Bente Maegaard, Joseph Mariani, Jan Odijk and Stelios Piperidis (eds.), *Proceedings of the Eight International Conference on Language Resources and Evaluation*, 486–493. Istanbul: ELRA.

Sijs, Nicoline van der. 2001. *Chronologisch woordenboek: De ouderdom en herkomst van onze woorden en betekenissen* [Chronological dictionary: The Origin and Age of our Words and Meanings]. Amsterdam/Antwerpen: L.J. Veen.

Smet, Hendrik de, Lieselotte Brems and Kristin Davidse. 2007. NP-internal functions and extended uses of the 'type' nouns *kind*, *sort*, and *type*: Towards a comprehensive, corpus-based description. In: Roberta Facchinetti (ed.), *Corpus Linguistics 25 Years on*, 225–255. Rodopi, Amsterdam.

Snel, Barbara. 2011. Het lemma 'toch': Een corpusgebaseerde partikelstudie [The lemma *toch*: A corpus-based study of a particle]. MA Dissertation, University of Leiden.

Traugott, Elizabeth Closs. 2005. Lexicalization and grammaticalization. In: Alan D. Cruse, Franz Hundsnurscher, Michael Job and Peter Rolf Lutzeier (eds.), *Lexikologie/Lexicology: Ein Internationales Handbuch Zur Natur und Struktur Von Wortern und Wortschatzen*, vol. 2, 1702–1712. Berlin/New York: Mouton de Gruyter.

Traugott, Elizabeth Closs. 2007. The concepts of constructional mismatch and type-shifting from the perspective of grammaticalization. *Cognitive Linguistics* 18: 523–557.

Traugott, Elizabeth Closs. 2008a. The grammaticalization of *NP of NP* patterns. In: Alexander Bergs and Gabriele Diewald (eds.), *Constructions and Language Change*, 23–45. Berlin/New York: Mouton de Gruyter.

Traugott, Elizabeth Closs. 2008b. Grammaticalization, constructions and the incremental development of language: Suggestions from the development of degree modifiers in English. In: Regine Eckhardt, Gerhard Jäger and Tonjes Veenstra (eds.), *Variation, Selection, Development: Probing the Evolutionary Model of Language Change*, 219–250. Berlin/New York: Mouton de Gruyter.

Traugott, Elizabeth Closs. 2008c. "All that he endeavoured to prove was...": On the emergence of grammatical constructions in dialogic contexts. In: Robin Cooper and Ruth Kempson (eds.), *Language in Flux: Dialogue Coordination, Language Variation, Change and Evolution*, 143–177. London: Kings College Publications.

Traugott, Elizabeth Closs. 2010. Revisiting subjectification and intersubjectification. In: Hubert Cuyckens, Kristin Davidse and Lieven Vandelanotte (eds.), *Subjectification, Intersubjectification and Grammaticalization*, 29–70. Berlin/New York: Mouton de Gruyter.

Traugott, Elizabeth Closs and Graeme Trousdale. 2010. Gradience, gradualness and grammaticalization: How do they intersect? In: Elizabeth Closs Traugott and Graeme Trousdale (eds.), *Gradience, gradualness and grammaticalization*, 19–44. Amsterdam/Philadelphia: John Benjamins.

Traugott, Elizabeth Closs and Graeme Trousdale. 2013. *Constructionalization and constructional changes*. Oxford: Oxford University Press.

Trousdale, Graeme. 2008a. Constructions in grammaticalization and lexicalization: evidence from the history of a composite predicate construction in English. In: Graeme Trousdale and Nikolas Gisborne (eds.), *Constructional Approaches to English grammar*, 33–67. Berlin/New York: Mouton de Gruyter.

Trousdale, Graeme. 2008b. A constructional approach to lexicalization processes in the history of English: evidence from possessive constructions. *Word Structure* 1: 156–177.

Trousdale, Graeme. 2010. Issues in constructional approaches to grammaticalization in English. In: Katerina Stathi, Elke Gehweiler and Ekkehard König (eds.), *Grammaticalization: Current Views and Issues*, 51–71. Amsterdam/Philadelphia: John Benjamins.

Trousdale, Graeme. 2012. Grammaticalization, constructions and the grammaticalization of constructions. In: Kristin Davidse, Tine Breban, Lieselotte Brems and Tanja Mortelmans (eds.), *Grammaticalization and Language Change: New Reflections*, 167–198. Amsterdam/Philadelphia: John Benjamins.

Trousdale, Graeme and Muriel Norde. 2013. Degrammaticalization and constructionalization: two case studies. *Language Sciences* 36: 32–46.

Vismans, Roel. 1994. *Modal particles in Dutch directives. A study in functional grammar.* Amsterdam: IFOTT.

WNT = Matthijs de Vries, L.A. te Winkel et al. 1882–1998. *Woordenboek der Nederlandsche Taal* [Dictionary of the Dutch Language]. 29 volumes. The Hague: Nijhoff etc.

Bert Cappelle

9 Conventional combinations in pockets of productivity: English resultatives and Dutch ditransitives expressing excess

1 Introduction[1]

Google hits for *sneezed the napkin off the table* run into the thousands. The sequence of words has become common good, to the extent that we see it quoted with a range of different subjects (*Adele*(!), *Alex, Bob, Donna, Frank, Fred, Jack, Joan, Joe, John, Mary, Paul, Pat, Rachel, Sally, Sue, Tom, I, He, She, The baby...*) and often without reference to Goldberg's (1995) original *sneeze* example.[2] The example is captivating to anyone who first hears or reads it, because in its simplicity it manages to capture the essence of the constructionist movement, in which argument structure constructions still adopt a central place. In true constructionist spirit, one might even consider [X *sneezed the napkin off the table*] a construction all by itself, with (i) an open slot preferentially filled by a mono- or bisyllabic, somewhat old-fashioned, all-American proper name,[3] (ii) a specific genre restriction (viz. academic writing related to linguistics or cognitive science) and (iii) a conventionalized interpretation: 'a verb may be plugged in larger syntactic frames which provide arguments not directly associated with the verb itself'. On a more serious note, however, this key example in present-day linguistics may have given rise to the idea that, provided there are no semantic clashes between word-level lexical constructions and the more

---

[1] Earlier versions of this paper were presented at the fourth International Conference of the French Association of Cognitive Linguistics (AFLiCo) and subsequently during seminars for students and colleagues at the University of Lille 3. I have benefited from various comments by members of my audiences on these occasions. Obviously, all shortcomings are mine only.

[2] There *is* no one single original example, as Goldberg actually used it herself with a variety of subjects, objects and resultant positions in her 1995 book: "Pat sneezed the napkin off the table" on p. 3, "Sally sneezed the napkin off the table" on p. 6, "He sneezed the napkin off the table" on pages 9, 55 and 224, "Sam sneezed the napkin off the table" on p. 29, "Frank sneezed the napkin off the table" on p. 154, "Frank sneezed the tissue off the table" on p. 152 and "Frank sneezed the tissue off the nightstand" on p. 161.

[3] However, I did find some more "peripheral" examples in which the subject used was *Gogol*, *Kim* or *Regina*.

schematic phrasal constructions which provide slots to them, "anything goes" in grammar. And Goldberg (2003: 221) does little to nuance such a conception when she writes that "[c]onstructions can be combined freely to form actual expressions as long as they are not in conflict".

This paper argues against this view, extending some of the corrective perspectives advanced by, among others, Boas (2003), Iwata (2008), Croft (2012), Kay (2013) and Welke (2011) and drawing on corpus-based and web-collected data about English and Dutch intensifying argument structure constructions. My argumentation is rather complicated, which is why I give a preview of the different steps here. In section 2, I will discuss the caused-motion pattern in English (of which the now-famous *sneeze* example is an illustration), claiming that it is idiosyncratically constrained and that novel uses may be analysed as the result of analogical extensions from conventional three-argument verbs and hence do not prove that there is a productive, Goldbergian (i.e. maximally schematic) caused-motion construction. In section 3, I will turn to a pattern in English which does seem to be very productive, namely the Body Part *Off* Construction (henceforth BPOC, e.g. *work one's head off*). Here, I will argue that instances of this pattern are *not* understood by means of a pragmatic reasoning process which ought to allow us to infer that the literal scenario cannot be meant by the speaker. This pattern may share the syntax of the caused-motion pattern (and, more generally, of the resultative pattern), but its semantics is action-intensifying rather than resultative. Speakers of English have to "learn" the BPOC as a form-meaning pattern in its own right. It is therefore a distinct pattern and cannot serve to prove the productive nature of the caused-motion pattern, let alone of the even more general resultative pattern. In section 3, I will use data from Dutch to support my claim that instances of the English BPOC are not formed or interpreted pragmatically, i.e. on the basis of the caused-motion pattern and general expressive or reasoning skills. If they were, we would have to find formally similar instances in Dutch. What we find in this neighbouring language, instead, is a set of syntactically rather different patterns expressing excess, including a ditransitive one. In section 4, I will take a more in-depth look at the BPOC, showing that it may best be analysed in terms of high-frequency learned instances and some creative extensions from these. In section 5, I will show that the same kind of analysis should be adopted for Dutch intensifying double-object cases. Section 6 provides some contrastive observations about the two patterns, revealing more conventionality. Section 7 discusses the findings in the light of the tension between stored linguistic information and free application of constructional templates. Section 8 sums up the main points.

2 Absentees and occasional visitors in the English caused-motion pattern

2.1 The caused-motion pattern seen as an argument structure construction

There are some very persuasive arguments for the existence of a caused-motion construction (henceforth CMC) in English. Goldberg (1995), referring to an observation made earlier by Aske (1989), notes that several verbs which can be used in the CMC do not evoke change of location outside of the construction, which makes it implausible to posit a distinct motion sense for such verbs:

(1) a. *Frank squeezed the ball.* (no implication of change of location)
   b. *Frank squeezed the ball through the crack.* (implication of change of location)

It is apparently due to an independently existing CMC that the Path prepositional phrase is added, along with the interpretation of change of location. Besides, my own research on verb-particle constructions in English (e.g. Cappelle 2005) has not failed to convince me of the possibility of, indeed, *squeezing* words into a transitive verb-particle construction, thereby imparting it with a caused-motion sense that it doesn't have by itself. Here is an authentic example, in which the quality of a household cleaning product is promoted:

(2) *Cif Actifizz. Fizzes Stains Away Fast.*

The verb *fizz* is not even a motion verb, so the force-dynamic scenario evoked in (2) must be attributed to the CMC that the transitive phrasal verb construction can be an instantiation of.

Goldberg and Jackendoff (2004) describe the CMC as a member of the *resultative* "family" of constructions:

(3) a. Causative property resultative
       e.g. *Bill watered the tulips flat.*

   b. Noncausative property resultative
       e.g. *The pond froze solid.*

c. Causative path resultative (caused-motion construction)
e.g. *Bill rolled the ball down the hill.*

d. Noncausative path resultative (intransitive motion construction)[4]
e.g. *The ball rolled down the hill.*

By using the term "family", Goldberg and Jackendoff (2004) aim to point out that there is no such thing as "*the* resultative", conceived of as a unified, undiversified category. Instead, they treat the patterns in (3) as individual subconstructions of a general "resultative" pattern, "sharing important properties but differing in certain specifics, including their degree of productivity" (Goldberg and Jackendoff 2004: 535).

2.2 The caused-motion pattern as a "pattern of coining" (Kay 2013)

Despite the relative ease with which one might find occurrences of verbs whose syntactic behaviour in specific usage instances seems to be expanded beyond what could be readily expected on the basis of their inherent semantics, there is a feeling among some linguists working within the constructionist framework that schematic argument-structure constructions of the sort proposed by Goldberg (1995, 2006) are too general to account for unexpected gaps in their potential output. In a paper called "The limits of (Construction) Grammar", which has circulated on the web since 2002 as the manuscript titled "Patterns of coining", Kay (2013) casts doubts on the productivity or even existence of the CMC. The same strong reservations have been formulated in Kay (2005). Below I refer to Kay (2013) because it conveniently brings together some counterarguments on just a couple of pages, but similar ideas have been formulated in a detailed and careful way by Boas and by Iwata in a number of publications on the resultative and other argument structure constructions (e.g. Boas 2003, 2005, 2010, 2011; Iwata 2002, 2008). In fact, Goldberg and Jackendoff (2004) themselves acknowledge that "there is also a great deal of idiosyncrasy involved in the resultatives, especially the property resultatives" (p. 564). For example, while it is grammatically perfectly fine to say that *Amy ran herself to exhaustion*, one wouldn't say that **Amy ran herself exhausted* (Goldberg and Jackendoff 2004: 560).

---

[4] This construction is also sometimes referred to as the "self-motion construction" or the "self-agentive motion construction".

Kay (2013) notes that many verbs which appear with a direct object and a prepositional phrase do not require a CMC, since such expressions can be licensed by two independently existing constructions. For example, (4d) may be just the combination of a transitivizing construction, which is needed anyhow to produce (4b), and of a construction which adds a path argument to an intransitive verb, needed to produce (4c):

(4) a. *The top was spinning.*

   b. *Kim was spinning the top.* (licensed by the Agent Adding Construction (AgAC))

   c. *The top was spinning off the table.* (licensed by the Path Argument Adding Construction (PAAC))

   d. *Kim was spinning the top off the table.* (licensed by a combination of AgAC and PAAC)
   (After Kay 2013)

As Kay points out, these two constructions obviate the need for a caused-motion construction, but not vice versa: even if the grammar of English were to have a caused-motion construction, which directly contained structural positions for agent, theme and path arguments, then a construction providing an extra agent would still be needed for many non-motion verbs such as *boil, evaporate, freeze, grow, melt*, etc.; we would also clearly need a construction which furnishes a path to intransitive motion verbs that do not necessarily express motion from one location to another, such as *hop, jump, roll, topple*, etc.

Moreover, Kay (2013) argues that the caused-motion pattern, conceived of as a productive construction as in Goldberg's (1995) treatment, inevitably overgenerates:[5]

(5) a. **He bragged her out of the room.*

   b. **She screamed him under the bed.*

   c. **She smiled him to her.*

   d. **He screeched her hands over her ears.*
   (Kay 2013)

---

[5] Goldberg (1995: 164–174) does however constrain the CMC in a number of ways and while I assume that Kay is aware of these general constraints, I have checked whether they might explain away Kay's examples of overgeneration. As far as I can see, they do not.

Kay then suggests that verbs whose occurrence in this pattern cannot be explained on the basis of the constructions producing (4b) and (4c) should be analysed as either by themselves subcategorizing for a theme and path argument (e.g. {*laugh* / *snore} *somebody off the stage*, {*let* / *allow / *leave} *something* (e.g. *water*) *somewhere* (e.g. *out of the pool*), {*show* / *demonstrate / *reveal} *someone to the door*, etc.) or as being given existence as nonce formations, created by analogy with existing caused-motion verbs. In the former case, verbs are by lexical convention associated with certain argument-structural configurations, the caused-motion pattern possibly being one of their conventionalized configurations. In the latter case, a verb is being used just for once with the argument structure that a semantically close verb is conventionally associated with. That caused-motion pattern is therefore not a regular, productive construction in the grammar of English, according to Kay, but a "pattern of coining".

The example in (2) above might illustrate such an analogical extension, even though one would not immediately consider *fizz* to be close in meaning to *wash*. Nevertheless, the formation of small bursting bubbles can make us think of the way a tablet dissolves in water, until the solid structure of the tablet is no longer there as such; a similar "disappearing act" is also present in the semantics of *wash*, by which dirt is removed from a surface, often involving frothing foam of soap which resembles the gas bubbles on the surface of a fizzing liquid. So, clearly, there *is* some semantic overlap between *fizzing* and *washing*, which then provides the ground for analogy. Note that it is commercially quite clever to use *fizz* in a pattern which is lexically associated with *wash*: we know that *washing* something *away* typically requires force on the part of an external agent (often a human), while *fizzing* is a kind of self-instigated activity. The intended interpretation, which we naturally arrive at, is that the removal of stains will not require brute, mechanical force but will happen automatically, by some kind of microscopic chemical process, if we use the advertised cleaning product.

Similarly, the use of *sneeze* in the caused-motion pattern is made possible by its semantic resemblance with verbs such as *blow*, which can conventionally take the caused-motion pattern (cf. Boas 2005; Pulvermüller, Cappelle and Shtyrov 2013).[6] Such an analogical extension from *blow* to *sneeze* is not neces-

---

[6] It is possible that *laugh NP off the stage* was initially also created analogically, before becoming a sequence listed in the lexicon. After all, *laugh* is also an air-emission verb. The overlap in frame-semantic information is larger for *laugh* and *blow* than for *snore* and *blow*, since *snore* produces most sound when air is being inhaled, not exhaled. So, in *laugh NP off the stage*, we can easily picture the situation, because it is as if the exhaled air impacts directly on the affected entity. The same is true for *boo NP off the stage*.

sarily accepted by all speakers of a language. In a survey among 223 undergraduates, Boas found that the sentence *Frank sneezed the napkin off the table* was rated by most participants towards the bottom end of the acceptability scale, indicating that "*sneeze* is not (yet) conventionally associated with the [NP V NP PP] frame for the majority of the population" (Boas 2005: 450, fn. 6). This is also how Herbst (2010: 244) looks at this and similar nonce formations: "Most (if not all) of the examples given of such creative uses seem to have a special stylistic effect, which can be interpreted as a conscious violation of linguistic norms."

Nonetheless, there is one subpattern of the caused-motion pattern which *is* very productive, the so-called *Body Part Off Construction* (henceforth BPOC, as in *John worked his head off*). I'll turn to this pattern in the next section. My strategy is to show that this pattern is not just an expected instance of the CMC but should be treated as an altogether distinct pattern.

3 The Body Part *Off* Construction: a pattern distinct from the caused-motion pattern

3.1 Some semantic properties of the Body Part *Off* Construction

The Body Part *Off* Construction (or BPOC), exemplified in (6a–b), is a pattern which superficially looks like the CMC but which does not involve the idea of actual displacement of the object NP:[7]

(6) a. *Susan worked / swam / danced her head off last night.*

  b. *Fred talked his head / his ass / his butt off, but to no avail.*
  (Jackendoff 1997a: 551)

---

[7] The BPOC is not the only pattern with the syntax of the CMC but with specific semantics. Another such idiomatic pattern is the "A hole through Y" construction (AHTY), discussed by Boas (2008). In *Joe knocked a hole through the wall*, the direct object argument does not refer to an affected but to an effected entity: the hole doesn't move anywhere but is brought into being by the action of knocking the wall. Note also that the object of the preposition *through* in the AHTY is not just a Landmark but a patient argument, which gets unified with the patient role associated with *knock*.

This pattern has received quite some attention in the literature (Cappelle 2005: 46–65; 453–455; 2007; 2008; Culicover and Jackendoff 2005: 32–38; Espinal and Mateu 2010; Glasbey 2003; 2007; Goldberg and Jackendoff 2004: 560; Jackendoff 1997a: 551; 1997b: 171; 2002a: 86–87; 2002b: 173–74; Kudo 2011; Sawada 2000). As I argued elsewhere (Cappelle 2005), the idiomaticity of the pattern involved can be appreciated if we consider the following web-attested examples:

(7) a. *They work their ass off.* (www)

b. *It's ten degrees and snowing its ass off.* (www)

c. *I laughed my proverbial ass off at that movie.* (www)

In (7a), the head of the object NP has no plural suffix, which it should take if it literally referred to the buttocks of the multiple agents involved (cf. subject *they*). In (7b), the subject *it* refers to the weather, so the object NP *its ass* obviously cannot be given a literal interpretation. In (7c), the speaker makes it explicit that the word *ass* is part of an idiom (perhaps to mitigate the taboo value of this word).

It has also been noted (e.g. Jackendoff 1997a: 551) that the BPOC construction has different aspectual properties from regular resultatives. Compare:

(8) a. *… we've developed a whole new set of exercises that tone every part of your body, and **blowtorch the fat off in no time**.* (www)

b. *I have been **exercising my ass off for the past 3 weeks** and I think I have lost oh about ONE POUND!!!! Discouraging much!!!!* (www)

In (8a), *blowtorch* is used in the resultative (caused-motion) pattern, by analogy of such verbs as *burn* and *melt*. The direct object (*the fat*) is really a theme argument which is claimed to undergo motion (i.e. removal) off of one's body. The situation is therefore an "accomplishment" in Vendler's (1957) terminology: a telic event allowing the use of an *in X time* adverbial adjunct. In (8b), *exercising* is used without a true theme argument. The postverbal sequence *my ass off* means "intensely" and/or "excessively". The (excess fat of the) subject referent's *ass* has not been significantly removed from her body: the one pound mentioned can hardly count as the intended result expressed by the verb phrase, which is an "activity" in Vendler's terminology. Such an event type allows the use of a *for X time* adverbial adjunct as in this example, but not of an *in X time* adverbial adjunct.

3.2 On Kudo's (2011) pragmatic model of mental representation

In spite of these differences, Kudo (2011) analyses the BPOC as a pattern whose interpretation is parallel to that of (other) resultatives (e.g. *He cried his eyes red*; *She ate herself sick*). That is, Kudo suggests that sentences such as (6a–b, 7a–c, 8b) are made sense of by hearers as referring to intense events *only* because their literal interpretation (on which they refer to events in which a body part actually comes off as a result of the action) would not be feasible in the real world. The BPOC, according to Kudo, is thus interpreted by means of a general interpretive mechanism, one which we also use to interpret an utterance such as *The joggers ran the pavement thin* (Goldberg 1995: 184), whose form is that of a causative property resultative, as having an intensifying postverbal sequence.

It would seem, then, that we are dealing here with what Croft (1998) calls the "pragmatic model of mental representation", which he defines as follows: "There is one independently represented unit in the mind with a general meaning U, [a/U]; (a/U1) and (a/U2) are derived from the general meaning U and general cognitive principles relevant to the specific context of use" (Croft 1998: 154). In the case of Kudo's proposal, [a/U] is then a general resultative construction, from which a literal reading and an excessive-event reading can be derived pragmatically, both for the caused property resultative and for the BPOC.

Croft (1998) proposes a fairly straightforward means of excluding this pragmatic model for any given linguistic unit. A linguist should check whether the translation equivalent of a supposedly pragmatically accountable use of that unit in another language is (*mutatis mutandis*, i.e. taking into account more general structural differences as well as trivial lexical differences) formally equivalent; if there is no formal equivalence, then the use of that unit must be considered to be stored as such in the first language, rather than being computed "on-line". As an example, Croft gives the noun-noun (NN) compound *water tower*, which in essence is indeed a tall structure supporting a tank of water. In French, however, such structures are referred to as "water castles" (*châteaux d'eau*). Croft (1998: 159) concludes: "This cross-linguistic difference is strong evidence that the pragmatic model is not appropriate for the derivation of this particular noun compound; otherwise speakers of both languages would come to the same solution to the naming of this object". Of course, one might object that the French term is in fact a rather special and unexpected combination while *water tower* is a fully transparent NN combination, so that it is only the French term, not the English one, which requires storage in the mental lexicon. One might also point out, as Croft is in fact aware one might, that castles may have been culturally more salient (i.e. frequently occurring) structures in France when water towers made their appearance, so that when they were first dubbed *châteaux d'eau*, this made perfect sense, given the fortress-like appearance of the earliest water towers. The point is, though, that for present-day speakers of French and English, one cannot plausibly assume that *water tower* and *château d'eau* are coined anew on each occasion a term referring to the object in the world is called for; more likely, speakers in a given speech community, French or English, just re-use the conventional expression available to them to denote this object.

Crucially, Croft (1998: 159) further suggests that "[t]he same argumentation can be applied to more general grammatical patterns." In the next section (section 3.3) I will indeed apply Croft's "test" to the BPOC. For one anonymous reviewer, Croft's translatability test fails to convince as an argument against a purely pragmatic approach: "Why would 'pragmatic' constructions *necessarily* be the same in all languages?" I nevertheless believe that the test can be usefully applied to languages which otherwise provide their speakers with comparable encoding possibilities. So, even though *water tower* may look as though it is a purely "pragmatic" choice, there is nothing, except the blocking effect triggered by *water tower* itself, which in principle prevents speakers of English from producing alternative terms for this object. Among other imaginable possibilities, we could have had terms similar to French *château d'eau*, such as *water castle*, *water fortress* or *water keep*, given that there was also a Gothic architecture revival in England and the United States. The crucial idea here is that the existence of a rather different encoding choice in another language may alert one to the not-so-obviousness of a given lexical choice in the language under study. Note, moreover, that speakers of English could just as well have modeled the term for the object in question on the familiar word *light house*, and thus have coined *water house*, which indeed is actually a now obsolete term for *water tower*. Still other terms could have been *water tank tower*, *hydrotower*, *water building*, *water pillar*, *water silo* or *cistern tower*. English does in fact have an alternative: water towers are sometimes referred to as *standpipes*. In short, alternative encodings in other languages – or in (older stages of) the same language – may help us realize that a complex expression which seems transparently compositional is actually conventionalized and thus listed as a learned language item. And the further claim made here is that if a combination is conventionalized, it is no longer assembled from scratch each time it is used, nor is it decoded inferentially ("it definitely can't be a tower *made* of water, so it must be a tower that *contains* water"...) each time it is used.

For now, let me point out that from the early days of construction grammar, it has been suggested that constructions can be stored along with specific "pragmatic" properties beyond their so-called "literal" meaning. For example, in their classic paper on the *let alone* construction, Fillmore, Kay and O'Connor (1988) explicitly link up pragmatic instructions on the use of this construction with the construction itself. Likewise, Fillmore and Kay (1999) argue that the *What's X doing Y?* construction comes with rich semantic information, which includes instructions for its conventional pragmatic usage. As a result, an utterance such as *Waiter, what's that fly doing in my soup?* is – or should be – understood as expressing that the situation described is judged to be incongruous rather than as being a straightforward question for information. The well-known joke ("I believe that's the backstroke, Sir") hinges on the waiter blatantly ignoring this pragmatic part of the construction. Conventionalized indirect speech acts of the type exemplified in *Can you pass me the salt?* have also been discussed from a construction grammar perspective by Stefanowitsch (2003).[8]

In the present paper, too, the position defended is that the "non-literal" reading of the BPOC construction has become conventionalized as part of the semantic component of a separate construction. Even though the literal reading clearly keeps on lingering in the background, it is not *via* this reading and Gricean or other general rules of communication that the intended, "non-literal" reading is arrived at. This position does not blur the traditional distinction between semantics (or "literal meaning") and pragmatics ("typical usage"). It merely requires that for some complex language items, the stored semantic information be backgrounded and the stored pragmatic information be foregrounded.

3.3 Excessive-semantics patterns in Dutch

As we mentioned above, Kudo (2011) proposes a parallel analysis for causative property resultatives and instances of the BPOC: both can be used literally (although this is extremely unlikely for the BPOC) and if they acquire an excessive reading, this interpretation is mediated by general rules of inference. But if this were all there was to the BPOC, its correct interpretation would be merely a matter of applying language-independent, hence cognitively universal, reasoning principles. One might then be tempted to conclude that the grammar of English does not need to stipulate the existence of this pattern and what it conventionally means. Such a conclusion would be wrong. While we will concede in

---

8 "The problem a hearer is faced with when hearing strings like [*Can you close the window?*; *Would you mind telling me the time?*; *I would like a cheeseburger*] is *not* to process its "literal" meaning, determine that the utterance does not lend itself to a literal interpretation, and then infer possible "non-literal" meanings. [...] Instead, the problem faced by the hearer is to realize that each of these expressions is ambiguous in terms of the conventional meanings attached to the constructions they instantiate, and to use context in order to determine which of their conventionalized meanings is the one intended by the speaker. [...]" (Stefanowitsch 2003: 122–123)

section 4 that the hyperbolic interpretation of BPOC instances could perhaps be figured out on the basis of commonsensical reasoning – nobody ordinarily loses a body part in the process of, say, laughing or dancing – there is no obvious reason why it should be the case that activities performed to excess can be expressed by the BPOC construction. Adopting Croft's (1998) argument explained in section 3.2, if the BPOC's excessive interpretation were merely a pragmatic effect, we would have to find a similar construction cross-linguistically. That is, the derivational rule linking the general meaning of the resultative to its intensification-expressing use would then be language-independent, rendering it unnecessary to store literal and excessive usages separately. This means that, *mutatis mutandis* (i.e., taking into account obvious but irrelevant differences in lexis and grammar between languages), any other language would have an almost exact counterpart to the BPOC, employed for the expression of events carried out intensively. As it turns out, however, even closely related languages can exhibit highly specific conventions in how resultatives or other patterns can be exploited for excessive-event semantics.

Dutch, like English, contains many conventionalised excessive cases of causative property resultatives, illustrated in (9a–c), but it does not have a perfect counterpart to the English BPOC.

(9) a. *Het vriest de stenen uit de grond.*
    it freezes the stones out the ground
    'It's freezing very hard.'

  b. *We betalen ons blauw.*
    we pay us blue
    'We're paying an awful lot of money.'

  c. *Ik lach me rot!*
    I laugh me rotten
    'I'm rolling on the floor laughing!'

The closest Dutch equivalent of the BPOC is a caused-motion pattern allowing a more restricted set of body part object NPs and, instead of a standalone particle as in English, a full PP with the prepositions *van* 'off' or *uit* 'out of' taking an NP expressing source:

(10) a. *Ze zong haar longen uit haar lijf.*
    she sang her lungs out-of her body
    'She was singing her lungs out.'

b. *Hij huilde zijn ogen uit zijn kop.*
   he cried his eyes out-of his head
   'He cried his eyes out.'

c. *Die jongen traint zijn ballen van zijn lijf.*
   That boy trains his balls off-of his body
   'That boy is training his ass off.'

In addition, Dutch has a ditransitive variant of this caused-motion pattern with a "possessor" reflexive, illustrated in (11).[9] In this pattern, the two post-verbal noun phrases (the one functioning as direct object and the other as prepositional complement) do not contain a possessive determiner but the definite article:

(11) a. *Ze zong zich de longen uit het lijf.*
      she sang her-REFL the lungs out-of the body
      'She was singing her lungs out.'

b. *Hij huilde zich de ogen uit de kop.*
   he cried him-REFL the eyes out-of the head
   'He cried his eyes out.'

c. *Die jongen traint zich de ballen van het lijf.*
   that boy trains him-REFL the balls off-of the body
   'That boy is training his ass off.'

---

9 This reflexive pronoun has a similar function to what is expressed by a so-called "ethic(al)", "free" or more specifically "maleficiary" dative pronoun in German (cf. Abraham 1973; Lee-Schoenfeld 2006; Welke 2011; cf. also various chapters in Hole, Meinunger and Abraham 2006). Perhaps an even closer correspondence is the French inalienable possession construction with a reflexive, as in *Jean s'est gratté le nez* (litt. John him-REFL scratched the nose, 'John scratched his nose'). In fact, Dutch uses this construction (i.e., reflexive pronoun and definite article) for inalienable possession in certain figurative expressions, as in (i) (Van Belle et al. 2005: 217):

(i) *Hij rukte zich de haren uit het hoofd.*
   He tore him-REFL the hairs out-of the head
   'He was tearing his hair out'

Though hyperbolically expressing a situation of excessive anger or desperation and thus not to be taken quite literally, this utterance is actually an instance of the caused-motion pattern. This is clear from the fact that the verb *rukken* is transitive and so it is this verb, not the construction, which is responsible for licensing *de haren* as a direct object NP. I am ignoring here a possible reading of (i) where the verb *rukken* is taken to be an intransitive one, meaning 'to wank'. In that case, this utterance would be a case of the Dutch BPOC. Since it would lack a *conventionalized* combination of a NP and PP, (i) could in that sense only be used as a language joke.

A somewhat common instance of this pattern is *zich de ogen uit het hoofd schamen* (literally: *to shame oneself the eyes out of the head*, i.e. 'to be terribly ashamed'), where the pronoun *zich* is best analyzed as a reflexive pronoun expressing inalienable possession required by the construction rather than as the reflexive pronoun regularly used with the verb *schamen*.

Not all instances of the English BPOC construction can be rendered in Dutch by means of one or both of these related caused-motion patterns, which are all in all not very frequent. I have not looked into their usage frequency but one thing is certain: they are much less commonly used than a third Dutch pattern expressing excess, one which has ditransitive rather than resultative syntax. Unlike English, Dutch abounds with conventionalised excessive double-object expressions with a reflexive pronoun and a full noun phrase (Cappelle 2011), illustrated in (12a–c):[10]

(12) a. *Ik schrik me een hoedje.*
    I start me a little-hat
    'I'm startled out of my wits.'

 b. *We vervelden ons de tering.*
    we bored us the phthisis
    'We're bored to death.'

 c. *Ik lach me een bult!*
    I laugh me a hunch
    'I'm rolling on the floor laughing!'

English does not have such excessive ditransitives.[11] Given that excessives find different realizations in Dutch and English, we should posit them as distinct con-

---

10 As an anonymous reviewer pointed out, the fact that Dutch has as one of its options a (reflexive) ditransitive syntactic pattern to encode a meaning which English conveys with a caused-motion syntactic pattern is nicely paralleled in another area of grammar, namely the *way*-construction (cf. Verhagen 2002, 2007). Compare:

(i) He made his way to the door.

(ii) *Hij baande zich een weg naar de uitgang.*
    He made him-REFL a way to the exit

(Note that the Dutch verb *banen* is a bound word, not occurring outside this construction, so that I see no harm in glossing it with a light verb like *make*, even though the noun *baan* from which it is zero-derived actually also means 'way'.) Sentence (ii) makes use of a ditransitive structure if the PP *naar de uitgang* is treated as a postmodifier to the noun *weg*. Another possible parse for this PP is as a sister to *een weg*, in which case (ii) has the same trivalent verb syntax, but of course again not the semantics, as the alternative BPOC in Dutch illustrated in (11a–c) with post-verbally a reflexive pronoun, an NP and a PP.

11 An apparent exception like *Cry me a river* is best analysed as a non-excessive transfer ditransitive involving an "act of symbolic dedication" (Pinker 2007: 63):

structions in each of these two otherwise closely related languages. Figures 1 and 2 represent simplified constructional networks involving excessives in English and Dutch, respectively.[12]

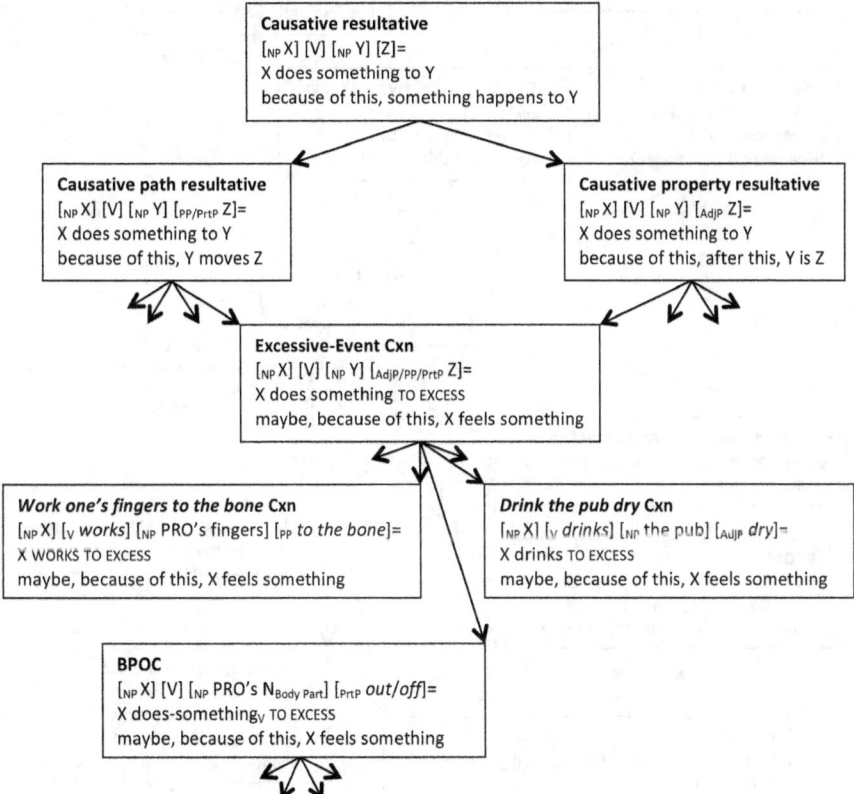

Figure 1 Simplified and partial constructional network of the English Excessive-Event Construction, together with some constructions from which it inherits its syntax (at the top of the figure) and with some more specific constructions it generalizes over (towards the bottom), including the BPOC. Not shown in detail here are true (path and property) resultatives which also inherit their syntax from the two three-argument 'resultative' patterns. Multiple arrows departing from a construction indicate that this construction is instantiated by several more specific patterns.

(i) a. *If you want my hand in marriage, first you'll have to kill me a dragon.*
   b. *Cry me a river!*
   c. *God said to Abraham, "Kill me a son."*
      (Pinker 2007: 63)

12 The semantics of the constructions are rendered in natural semantic metalanguage (NSM) (cf. Goddard and Wierzbicka 2002; Wierzbicka 1996). Nothing crucial depends on the choice of this format for my analysis. No attempt has been made, moreover, to explicate "TO EXCESS", which in NSM may perhaps be explicated as "much more than someone else would do".

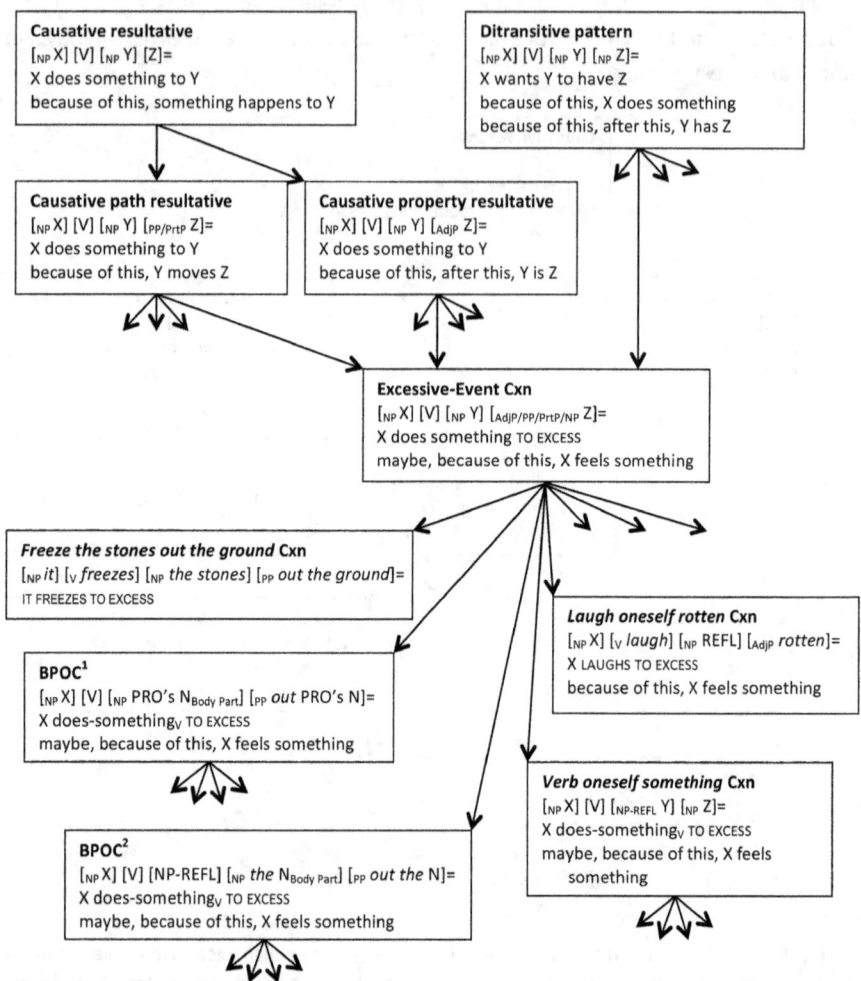

Figure 2 Simplified and partial constructional network of the Dutch Excessive-Event Construction (shown in the middle), some constructions from which it inherits its syntax (at the top of the figure) and some more specific constructions it generalizes over (towards the bottom). Not shown in detail here are true (path and property) resultatives and true transfer-expressing constructions, which also inherit their syntax from the two three-argument 'resultative' patterns and from the ditransitive pattern, respectively. The example sentences are direct English translations from Dutch. Multiple arrows departing from a construction indicate that this construction is instantiated by several more specific patterns.

In Figures 1 and 2, the Excessive-Event Construction is represented as inheriting the syntax but not the semantics of other constructions existing in the grammar. In English, these existing constructions are the two subtypes of the

Causative Resultative Construction only; in Dutch, the Ditransitive Construction is a third construction that shares its syntax with the Excessive-Event construction.[13] In sum, the diagrammatic figures aim to represent the idea that excessives constitute a constructional pattern all by themselves in both English and Dutch, distinct from the constructions whose syntax they share. The reason is that their form is language-specific, while their semantics, involving the notion of "excess" is constant across languages.[14] Following Croft (1998), I argue that the cross-linguistic differences observed here exclude, *contra* Kudo (2011), a pragmatic, derivational model of mental representation. I will come back to this conclusion in the next section.

In the next two sections (sections 4 and 5), I will argue with Kay (2013) and especially Boas (2003, 2005) that many instances of these excessive patterns in English and Dutch are conventionalized word sequences.

4 Conventionalization in the BPOC: evidence from the Corpus of Contemporary American English

Commenting on the BPOC, as well as on *V up a storm* (e.g. {*cook / curse / dance / party / sing / sweat / talk / tweet /...} up a storm*), Jackendoff (2002a: 86) writes that the "the choice of verb seems totally open, whereas by contrast, the choice of NP is totally fixed". Elsewhere I have shown that in actual language usage, there is quite a bit of variation in the choice of NP: every possible alternative word for *ass* and *butt* can make its appearance in the pattern, including *behind, fanny, rear, tail, tush* and any other term one could find in a good thesaurus. As for the verbs used in this pattern, Goldberg and Jackendoff (2004: 560) are more careful when they write that "the choice of verb is quite broad". To examine *how* broad, I have conducted a corpus study, using the Corpus of Contemporary American English (COCA, Davies 2008–). Ten search strings were used, each time consisting of an open position (for a verb), followed by a possessive pronoun, a body part noun known to occur in the pattern (including a couple of the less frequently used alternatives for *ass* and *butt*) and the particle *off* or *out*. Table 1 shows the twenty most frequently used verbs in this pattern, with token frequencies for each post-verbal sequence.

---

[13] In addition, the Possessor Dative Construction or the Ethical Dative Construction may be extra sources for instances with an extra reflexive pronoun in the BPOC (i.e. BPOC² in Figure 2).
[14] Cf. Leino (2010) for similar reflections about how syntactically different constructions across languages may nonetheless be characterized as being semantically equivalent.

Table 1: Token frequencies for the twenty most frequently used verbs and ten common post-verbal sequences appearing in the BPOC in the Corpus of Contemporary American English.

	one's ass off	one's heart out	one's head off	one's eyes out	one's butt off	one's tail off	one's guts out	one's lungs out	one's balls off	one's tush off	
work	66	19	1		69	43			1		199
cry		17	4	80			2	1			104
scream	2	2	44				3	13			64
laugh	25		30					1			56
bawl	1	2	4	39			1				47
sing	1	43	1				1				46
freeze	24				8	1			8	1	41
play	2	16			5		3		1		27
puke							19				19
dance	8	8			1	1					18
run	4	5			3						12
bark	1		10								11
sob		9		2							11
fight		5			2		2				9
talk			8					1			9
sweat	2				1		1	4			8
cough	1						6				7
lie	3		4								7
yell			5					2			7
cheer	1	1					3				5
hapaxes	22	14	13	6	11	4	9	5	2	1	87
total tokens	162	145	136	129	100	47	43	31	14	1	807
hapaxes per tokens	14%	10%	10%	5%	11%	9%	21%	16%	14%	100%	11%

Grey-shade legend

tokens		1	2	≥ 3	≥ 5	≥ 8	≥ 11	≥ 17	≥ 26	≥ 38	≥ 57
hapaxes/tokens (in %)	0	1–3	4–6	7–9	10–12	13–15	16–18	19–21	22–24	25–27	≥ 28

Note: the bottom row gives the hapax/token ratio for each post-verbal sequence, thus providing an indication of its productivity. Darker shades are used for easy identification of high token frequencies or high number of hapaxes as well as high hapax/token ratios (cf. legend).

Table 1 contains detailed information about the distribution of individual verbs and post-verbal sequences in the BPOC. It allows us to see (i) for each frequently used verb which post-verbal intensifier it takes and (ii) for each post-verbal sequence which high-frequency verbs may precede it and with how many verb tokens it is used. Verbs and post-verbal sequences are ordered by frequency from top to bottom and from left to right, respectively. Thus, *work* is the most frequently used verb in the BPOC and it is followed mainly by *one's butt off*, *one's ass off*, *one's tail off* and *one's heart out* in the corpus. Conversely, the "subpattern" of the BPOC with the post-verbal sequence *one's ass off* is used most frequently: it has the highest number of verb tokens (165), for which *work* (66 tokens), *freeze* (27 tokens) and *laugh* (25 tokens) are mainly responsible.

For each subpattern, Table 1 also gives the number of *hapax legomena*, or *hapaxes*, verbs which combine with that postverbal sequence only once in the corpus. The more hapaxes appear in the open slot of a pattern, the more lexical items may in fact be expected to be used on a one-off basis in this pattern *outside the corpus*. That is why hapaxes have been used as a measure of productivity of a pattern. One such measure, proposed by Baayen (1989) for morphological processes but perfectly applicable for above-word-level patterns as well, is formulated as the proportion of hapaxes in a corpus to the total number of words in the corpus used in that pattern. Of all verb tokens used in the investigated subpatterns of the BPOC in COCA, it appears that 11% occur in a particular subpattern only once. So, on average, every tenth verb in a subpattern will be a hapax. This can be taken as evidence that the BPOC is indeed a "pocket of productivity" within the more general caused-motion construction or the yet more general resultative construction.[15] The subpattern [V one's *butt off*] is a representative one within the BPOC: 11 of the 100 occurrences of this subpattern contain a verb which is used just once in it, for instance *dance, sweat* and (not shown in the table) *bike, coach, compete* and *lip-sync*. If we ignore [V one's *tush off*], which is found only once in the corpus (with the verb *freeze*) and which accordingly has full productivity, the subpattern [V one's *guts out*] has the highest degree of productivity, with one fifth of the verb tokens found in it being hapaxes.

At the same time, it can also be appreciated that there is a high degree of conventionality within this productive area of English grammar. For example, while [V one's *guts out*] is indeed quite productive, there is one verb, *puke*, which accounts for almost half of its occurrences in the corpus; besides, no other intensifying post-verbal sequence appears to be used with that verb, which tells us that *puke one's guts out* is a strong collocation. Note, furthermore, that only one in twenty of the verb tokens used in the subpattern [V one's *eyes out*] are hapaxes. This subpattern is used practically exclusively with *cry* and *bawl*.

Of course, there is some motivation why *puke* combines with *guts* and *cry* and *bawl* with *eyes*, rather than vice versa. The motivation is, of course, that if one pukes, contents of one's guts are ejected, and that if one cries, tears flow from one's eyes. Similarly, [V one's *lungs out*] naturally attracts verbs denoting an activity of forceful air expulsion, such as *scream, cough, cheer* and *yell*. In

---

[15] By comparison, the suffixes *-able, -ful* ('measure'), *-ful* ('property'), *-ize, -ness* and *-wise*, all of them said to be productive, have lower hapax/token ratios (Plag et al. 1999).
  While this may be an indirect indication of how productive the BPOC is, I am for now very hesitant to compare morphological and phrasal constructions with respect to this measure, especially across different corpora.

each of these cases, the metonymical construal (container for contained), may be supported by a conceptual metaphor according to which an intense activity can be represented as an excessive change of location, *in casu* the exhaustion or detachment of a body part (Mateu and Espinal 2007; Espinal and Mateu 2010). An utterance such as *John cried his eyes out* may therefore be paraphrased most accurately not just as 'John cried intensely' (cf. Jackendoff 1997a, b, 2002a, b) but as 'John cried so much that his eyes almost came out', as represented in Figure 3.

Figure 3: Pictorial representation of a hyperbolic reading of *John cried his eyes out*, from Mateu and Espinal (2007)

The existence of a hyperbolic reading, in which the literal interpretation of a BPOC utterance is conceived of as depicting the actual event in an exaggerated (and therefore realistically unfeasible way), is compatible with Kudo's (2011) analysis mentioned in section 3.2 above. Crucial to that analysis is that BPOC utterances *could* in principle receive a literal interpretation, referring to an actual event in the real world. The encyclopaedic relatedness of the verb's meaning and the denotation of the head noun helps explain why certain combinations have become strong collocations while other combinations (e.g. *cough one's butt off*) have not. Most of these conventionalized sequences are therefore not "idioms of decoding" in Makkai's (1972: 47) sense: their meaning could easily be guessed on the basis of what we know about the words used, the meaning of the resultative pattern, the function of a possessive pronoun etc. I would like to claim that they are still "idioms of encoding" (Makkai 1972: 57), however, since a speaker can't be expected to realize that *cry one's eyes out* is a conventional figure of speech in English without having learned that fact. In support of this, note again that in Dutch, whose grammar also provides its speakers the opportunity to make use of the resultative pattern, one doesn't say **Jan huilde z'n ogen uit*, the direct translation of *John cried his eyes out*.

There are some further surprising observations to be made on the basis of Table 1. First, note that while the subpattern [V one's *head off*], with its hapax/token proportion of 9%, is about as productive as the BPOC pattern in general, it occurs with the verb *work* only once in the corpus, although this verb accounts for almost one fourth of all verb tokens in the BPOC. This suggests that the use of *work one's head off* may be blocked by the frequent occurrence of e.g. *work one's butt off* and *work one's ass off*. Second, while *ass* and *butt* are synonyms, there are 25 occurrences of *laugh one's ass off* but no occurrences of *laugh one's butt off* in the corpus.[16] (Remarkably, occurrences of *laugh one's ass off* are *not* blocked by the common use of *one's head off* as a post-verbal intensifier with this verb.)

In sum, what the corpus data reveal is (i) that subpatterns of the BPOC show varying degrees of productivity; (ii) that motivations based on the physical involvement of a certain body part and the nature of the activity expressed by the verb exist but that these motivations do nothing to diminish the *conventionality* of some of the high-frequency combinations; and (iii) that some verbs occur with a range of post-verbal intensifying sequences but may still exhibit unexpected "gaps" in this range, apparently due to blocking effects – though exactly *when* a blocking effect occurs is itself an unpredictable matter. In short, the usage patterns found in COCA suggest that native speakers of English make use of a great deal of knowledge about conventional combinations of individual verbs and particular post-verbal sequences. Native speakers apparently also know which combinations are to be avoided, even though they could have been perfectly possible given full productivity of the BPOC. Apparently, not anything goes.

5 Conventionalization in the Dutch intensifying ditransitive: web-based evidence

Table 2 below provides co-occurrence data for verbs frequently used with double-object intensifiers in Dutch. These data are based on an extensive web search carried out in the search engine Google in December 2011, restricted to a year leading up to the time of search. As the first object, *me* 'myself' was invariably

---

16 Near-rhyme (*laugh* – *ass*) could be a factor in the conventionalization of this combination. Reporting findings based on dictionaries of idioms, Boers and Stengers (2008) note that almost one fifth of the English idiom repertoire contains some sort of "catchy" sound pattern, involving alliteration and/or assonance.

Table 2: Token frequencies for the twenty most frequently used verbs (see verb stems, column left) with fifteen common intensifying double-object sequences (see top row) in the search result pages obtained from a Google search (December 2011) in web pages from the Netherlands spanning one year

	me een ongeluk	me een hoedje	me de pleuris	me de tering	me een breuk	me een slag in de rondte	me de tyfus	me een bult	me een kriek	me het apezuur	me het schompes	me het apelazerus	me het leplazerus	me de pest	me een aap	
schrik 'be startled'	101	327	106	122	1		35	34		28		22	12	3	15	806
lach 'laugh'	20	8	16	13	96	7	3	20	69	6		5		1	3	267
zoek 'look for'	83	10	32	10	30	17	3	12		5	11	7	3	1	1	225
werk 'work'	3		39	10	3	53	14			4	14	2	3	6		151
verveel 'be bored'	7	3	37	38			19			1		2		8		115
sjouw 'carry; drag'	1			1	42			2								46
zweet 'sweat'	12	1	2	6			1	1		3		1	2	2		31
verschiet 'be startled'	5							13								18
hoest 'cough'	6		4	3			2	1			1					17
lees 'read'	8		1		1	3	1				1					15
loop 'run'	2		5	2	1	1		1				2	1			15
vecht 'fight'						1						12	1			14
poets 'scrub'	3		1	1	2	3						2				12
google 'google'	2				1	4				4					1	12
betaal 'pay'			3	3	1		2	1		1		1				12
erger 'be irritated'	2		1	4			1	1				2				11
ren 'run'	3		2			1	2	2				1				11
sleep 'drag'	2				3							4				9
eet 'eat'	1				1	4	1					1				8
klik 'click'	4			1		2						1				8
Hapaxes	50	4	17	18	19	46	10	8		11	10	7	11	6	5	222
Tokens	365	354	263	231	225	176	90	89	69	61	61	50	38	25	23	2120
hapaxes per tokens (in %)	14	1	6	8	8	26	11	9	0	18	16	14	29	24	22	5

Grey-shade legend

Tokens		1	2	≥3	≥6	≥10	≥19	≥34	≥61	≥110	≥198
hapaxes/tokens (in %)	0	1-3	4-6	7-9	10-12	13-15	16-18	19-21	22-24	25-27	≥28

Note: the bottom row gives the hapax/token ratio for each intensifying sequence, thus providing an indication of its productivity. Darker shades are used for easy identification of high token frequencies or high number of hapaxes as well as high hapax/token ratios (cf. legend). See main text for translations and some explanation of the intensifying sequences.

chosen; fifteen different fake direct object NPs were selected, based on my own intuitions about which of these NPs occur with some frequency in Dutch (cf. also Cappelle 2011) and on data found in Hagers and Schutz's (s.d.) online *Woordenboek van Nederlandse intensiveringen*. Searches were restricted to pages from the Netherlands, as many of the intensifications are not common in Flanders (the Dutch-speaking part of Belgium) at all.[17] A subset of these NPs consists of colloquialisms for (formerly) life-threatening infectious diseases such as *de pleuris* 'pleurisy', *de tyfus* 'typhoid fever' or 'consumption', *de tering* 'tuberculosis', *de pest* '(bubonic or pneumonic) plague'. Some terms refer to fictitious diseases (*het apezuur* 'monkey acid', *het schompes*) or are related to leprosy via the Biblical figure Lazarus (*het leplazerus*, in which *lep-* may be a shortening of *lepra* 'leprosy' and *het apelazarus* 'monkey leprosy'). Yet others refer to physical damage or deformations (*een breuk* 'a fracture', *een bult/kriek* 'a hunch'), to a general mishap (*een ongeluk* 'an accident') or, in a nonsensical way, to a random entity (*een hoedje* 'a little hat', *een slag in de rondte* 'a smash all around', *een aap* 'a monkey').[18]

For each search, all pages with search results returned by the Google search engine were carefully screened so as to retrieve relevant examples only. (Sometimes, this required consulting the actual website.)

As can be seen, *schrikken* 'to be startled' is the most frequently used verb and it occurs with most of the patterns, with some notable exceptions, namely *me een breuk* and *me een kriek*, both of which combine most frequently (or even exclusively) with *lachen* 'to laugh', and *me een slag in de rondte*, which combines most frequently with *werken* 'to work'. Some other verbs also combine with most of the subpatterns, such as *lachen* 'to laugh', *zoeken* 'to look for' and *werken* 'to work'. Other verbs are much more 'picky'; this is especially clear for *vechten* 'to fight'. Individual subpatterns also show considerable variation in productivity (measured here again using the hapax per token ratio). With some subpatterns, more than a fourth of the verb occurrences are one-offs ([V + *me het*

---

17 This is especially true for patterns with diseases (cf. infra). One pattern which is rather frequent in Belgian Dutch, however, is one with *een indigestie* 'an indigestion' as second postverbal NP, after verbs like *eten* 'eat', *schransen* 'engorge, eat immodestly' and *drinken* 'drink'. That there is a great deal of regional variation can also be observed for the BPOC (Cappelle and Dewinter 2013).

18 Less frequent NPs not included in the subset of fake direct object NPs are *een beroerte* ('a stroke') and *een liesbreuk* ('inguinal hernia'), both of which can be used with a variety of verbs. There are also completely novel and hence highly infrequent creations, such as *zich een polsbreuk applaudisseren* 'applaud oneself a wrist fracture', which were not considered for inclusion either.

leplazerus], [V + *me een slag in de rondte*]) while others have zero or near-zero productivity ([V + *me een kriek*], [V + *me een hoedje*]).

The pattern is syntactically ditransitive, which is semantically speaking in fact always a kind of resultative as well, insofar as the prototypical meaning is 'cause NP_1 to receive NP_2', with the reception being the intended result. The intensifying ditransitive pattern under investigation here allows the hyperbolic interpretation 'V so intensely/excessively that one gets a NP_2 (as a result of doing so)'. This literal meaning is hardly ever motivated by an inherent relation between the nature of the activity and the NP referring to an unwanted condition caused by it. An exception may be that an excessive case of *sjouwen* 'carry, drag' could in principle result in *een breuk* 'a fracture', more so than in an infectious disease. This may explain why *een breuk* is the favoured NP_2 with this verb. However, the rule seems to be that there is no obvious relationship whatsoever between the activity and the result. For instance, being startled never actually results in the subject obtaining a little hat. Some of the subpatterns can therefore be considered true "idioms of decoding": supposing one did not have any general familiarity with other subpatterns of the intensifying ditransitive, then one wouldn't normally guess their meaning on the basis of the meaning of the verb and the meaning of the noun in NP_2.

Note that the high frequency of some combinations may have given rise to analogical extensions. For instance, speakers may have been aware of the high frequency of *zoeken* 'look for' in a wide variety of intensifying ditransitive subpatterns and on the basis of these combinations have been inclined to use some of the subpatterns also with closely related verbs such as *googelen* 'google' and *klikken* 'click'. Still, one may wonder why *verschieten* 'be startled', which is a (somewhat regionally restricted) alternative to *schrikken* does not occur with *me een hoedje*, which combines so frequently (327 tokens) with the latter verb. It may be the case that the combination *zich een hoedje schrikken* 'be frightened out of one's wits' is such a strong collocation that it practically blocks the use of *zich een hoedje* (i.e. the two complements) with other verbs than *schrikken*. As was mentioned above, there are hardly any hapaxes in this subpattern, although there are many tokens for it.[19]

In sum, what emerges from Table 2 is that while the intensifying ditransitive is generally quite productive (one in twenty of all verb tokens appears only once

---

[19] Practically all the tokens for [V + *me een hoedje*] are accounted for by *schrikken*. Oddly enough, in my paper (three-volume) edition of the Van Dale dictionary (Geerts and Heestermans 1992), I find *zich een hoedje lachen* (litt. 'laugh oneself a little hat') s.v. *hoedje*, while *lachen* is comparatively very infrequent in this subpattern. In the latest edition, however (Den Boon and Geeraerts 2011), the combination *zich een hoedje schrikken* is also given.

in a given subpattern, suggesting a fairly high degree of productivity overall for the pattern), individual subpatterns differ widely in how readily they combine with verbs to form novel sequences. Again, we have found loci of convention within a productive area in the grammar.

6 Further contrastive observations

A comparison of the data for the English BPOC and the Dutch intensifying ditransitive is also revealing of the language-specificity and conventionality of each of these constructions. Of course, there *are* some commonalities, not just semantically (which is why they are investigated here together in the first place) but also syntactically: both constructions involve two complements, one of which is a direct object; in neither construction can this argument appear as the subject of a related passive construction (**my ass was worked off*; **een ongeluk werd me gezocht* 'an accident was looked for to me'). There are also some crucial differences: the BPOC involves an inalienable body part – I'm leaving out of the discussion cases like *laugh one's socks/pants off* – followed by the particle *off* or *out*, while the Dutch intensifying ditransitive involves a reflexive pronoun followed by a full NP. This difference in how the same notion (intensification) is expressed in the two languages allowed us to exclude the possibility that the English BPOC is merely pragmatically derived from the caused-motion construction: if it were, we would also have to find it in Dutch.

The tables presented in the preceding sections allow us to compare the constructions in more detail. We can see that only five of the top twenty most frequently used verbs in the BPOC find their direct translation equivalent among the top twenty most frequently used verbs in the Dutch intensifying ditransive: *work/werken*, *laugh/lachen*, *run/lopen*, *fight/vechten* and *sweat/zweten*. These are verbs whose semantics easily allows for intensification, but this can be said for many of the other verbs as well. Surprisingly, for three of the top five most frequently used Dutch verbs, there is not even an equivalent in Table 1, nor in fact in the entire data set: *schrikken* ('be startled'), *zoeken* ('look for') and *(zich) vervelen* ('be bored'). A likely reason for this is that the English equivalents lack the required syntactic structure: they are used with *be* or with a fixed preposition.

Note that the presence of a preposition does not appear to pose a problem in Dutch. Compare:

(13) a. ?*I've been looking my ass off for a solution.

    b. Ik   heb   me   een ongeluk   gezocht   naar een oplossing
        I   have me   an   accident   searched   to   a   solution
        'I've been looking everywhere for a solution.'

Apparently, the use of a prepositional complement in English hinders the use of intensifying complements (especially, I presume, the particle, which shares many similarities with PPs (cf. Cappelle 2004)).

In any case, a comparison of the two tables allows us to see that, despite some overlap, the two different languages appear to intensify different kinds of verbs in the two patterns investigated. Not all differences can be attributed to selection restrictions or voice of the verbs involved. In the entire Dutch dataset, no verbs of forceful air expulsion such as *krijsen* 'shriek', *roepen* 'call, shout' or *schreeuwen* 'shout, scream' are used, while the counterparts to these verbs are frequent in the English dataset and could in principle have been used in the Dutch intensifying ditransitive pattern. In short, this brief contrastive analysis again supports my claim that there is considerable conventionality in both patterns.

7 Discussion

Communication systems need to meet two conditions to allow successful transfer of rich and varied messages. On the one hand, they have to provide their users with a sufficiently large number of agreed-upon or otherwise mentally shared form-function pairs, without which individual users would be trapped in their own private world of ideas. On the other hand, efficient communication systems need to have in-built flexibility so that senders can give audible substance to new entities and previously undescribed states or events. All languages (i.e. the human communication systems studied in linguistics, as opposed to forms of animal communication) meet these two conditions, as indeed any first-year student of linguistics is supposed to realize after the first few classes of an introductory course in the field. The reason I am re-pointing out this obvious insight here is that it puts the finger on one the most crucial as well as hardest tasks for linguists: determining just how much of language use has to be analysed as part of the established form-meaning pairings, and how much of it can be treated as derived from grammar-internal combinatory rules and/or grammar-independent "pragmatic" principles of generalization, reasoning, discourse and the like. In other words, linguists need to face this constant challenge: How can we know whether a part of an utterance is retrieved as such from the mental lexicon (or "construct-i-con") or whether it is assembled "on the fly" (cf. Jackendoff 2010: 226)?

The present paper has provided evidence for the assumption that much of what could possibly have been created productively may already have been stored in the mind of the speaker. Both the BPOC and the Dutch intensifying ditransitive allow the insertion of any verb whose performance can vary in degree of intensity (provided, as we have seen in section 6, that it is not used in the passive or that it does not already take a prepositional complement, in which case it is not compatible with the BPOC).

A crucial finding is that some of the subpatterns, within either construction, are hardly productive or not productive at all. As for the BPOC, for instance, speakers know that one wouldn't ordinarily use *cough one's tail off*, *lie one's guts out*, or *sob one's butt off*. Such combinations *are* attested on the web, but using them is flouting convention. As for the intensifying ditransitive in Dutch, speakers also know that *zich een kriek* only combines with *lachen*. The two general patterns are therefore halfway between productive and semi-productive constructions: new combinations are allowed but it might be safe to use some well-worn combinations rather than combine verbs and intensifying sequences at will.

8 Conclusion

This paper started out by arguing that Goldberg's famous *sneeze* example does not convincingly prove that there is a general caused-motion argument structure construction which allows any verb, within certain general semantic constraints, to fuse with it. A verb's lexical entry may already subcategorize for a path argument or, if not, it may only be coerced into an argument-structure pattern *by analogy of* semantically related verbs which do subcategorize for the relevant type of argument(s) (Boas 2011). In the case of *sneeze*, the basis of analogy might be a verb such as *blow*, which commonly selects a theme and a path.

The chapter then focused on the Body Part *Off* Construction (BPOC), a pattern which is considered to be an area of productivity within the caused-motion construction – and hence, more generally, within the resultative "family" of constructions (Goldberg and Jackendoff 2004). I argued against the assumption (cf. Kudo 2011) that making sense of instances of this construction (e.g. *laugh one's ass off, cry one's eyes out*) involves a "pragmatic" interpretive process aimed at deriving the excessive reading from the hearer's realization about the unfeasibility of the event actually taking place in the real world (i.e. a body part literally coming off). Following Croft (1998), I take the non-occurrence of a direct translation of the BPOC in Dutch, a closely related Germanic language which also has the caused-motion pattern, to be an argument against a purely pragmatic representation of the English BPOC. Its occurrence in English is not a given – speakers must *know* that it exists.

I then provided the results of an in-depth corpus-based and web-based investigation of the usage of the BPOC and of a semantically related but formally different construction in Dutch, namely intensifying ditransitives (whose direct English translations would sound like, e.g., *laugh oneself a fracture*). The results suggested that knowing that these constructions exist is not sufficient either to use them appropriately, as there are some highly conventional combinations which may prevent the use of combinations that *could* have been possible.

I fully agree with Jackendoff's (2010: 34) statement that "[i]nsofar as productivity is an issue not only for phonology and morphology but also syntax, in my opinion it must take a place as one of the central issues of linguistic theory for the coming years." The present study suggests that within generally productive constructions there may be semiproductive subpatterns where conventionality reigns supreme.

References

Abraham, Werner. 1973. The ethic dative in German. In Kiefer, Ferenc and Nicolas Ruwet (eds.), *Generative Grammar in Europe*, 1–19. Dordrecht: D. Reidel.
Aske, Jon. 1989. Motion predicates in English and Spanish: A closer look. *BLS* 15: 1–14.
Baayen, R[olf] H[arald]. 1989. A corpus-based approach to morphological productivity: Statistical analysis and psycholinguistic interpretation. Ph.D. dissertation, Free University of Amsterdam.
Boas, Hans C. 2003. *A Constructional Approach to Resultatives*. Stanford: CSLI Publications.
Boas, Hans C. 2005. Determining the productivity of resultative constructions: A reply to Goldberg & Jackendoff. *Language* 81(2): 448–464.
Boas, Hans C. 2008. Resolving form-meaning discrepancies in Construction Grammar. In: Jaako Leino, (ed.), *Constructional Reorganization*, 11–36. Amsterdam/Philadelphia: John Benjamins.
Boas, Hans C. 2010. The syntax-lexicon continuum in Construction Grammar: A case study of English communication verbs. *Belgian Journal of Linguistics* 24, 54–82.
Boas, Hans C. 2011. Coercion and leaking argument structures in Construction Grammar. *Linguistics* 49(6): 1271–1303.
Boers, Frank and Hélène Stengers. 2008. Adding sound to the picture: An exercise in motivating the lexical composition of metaphorical idioms in English, Spanish and Dutch. In: Mara Sophia Zanotto, Lynne Cameron and Marilda C. Cavalcanti (eds.), *Confronting Metaphor in Use: An Applied Linguistic Approach*, 63–78. Amsterdam: John Benjamins.

Cappelle, Bert. 2004. The particularity of particles, or why they are not just "intransitive prepositions". *Belgian Journal of Linguistics* 18: 29–57.
Cappelle, Bert. 2005. Particle patterns in English: A comprehensive coverage. Ph.D. dissertation, Leuven University.
Cappelle, Bert. 2007. When "wee wretched words" wield weight: The impact of verbal particles on transitivity. In: Marja Nenonen and Sinikka Niemi (eds.), *Collocations and Idioms 1: Papers from the First Nordic Conference on Syntactic Freezes, Joensuu, Finland, May 19–20, 2006*, 41–54. Joensuu: Joensuu University Press.
Cappelle, Bert. 2008. What should stockings look like? On the storage of linguistic units. In: Jean-Rémi Lapaire, Guillaume Désagulier and Jean-Baptiste Guignard (eds.), *Du fait grammatical au fait cognitif / From Gram to Mind: Grammar as Cognition*, 171–189. Bordeaux: Presses Universitaires de Bordeaux.
Cappelle, Bert. 2011. Er verder op los intensifiëren [intensifying away some more]. *Over Taal* 53 (3), 66–67.
Cappelle, Bert and Annelien Dewinter. 2013. British heads and American asses: Regional, register and recent variation in the Body Part *Off/Out* Construction. Paper presented at the 12th International Cognitive Linguistics Conference, University of Alberta, Edmonton, Canada, 23–28 June 2013.
Croft, William. 1998. Linguistic evidence and mental representations. *Cognitive Linguistics* 9(2): 151–173.
Croft, William. 2012. *Verbs: Aspect and Causal Structure*. Oxford: Oxford University Press.
Culicover, Peter W. and Ray Jackendoff. 2005. *Simpler Syntax*. Oxford: Oxford University Press.
Davies, Mark. 2008–. *The Corpus of Contemporary American English: 425 million words, 1990–present*. Available online at http://corpus.byu.edu/coca/.
Den Boon, C.A. and D[irk] Geeraerts. 2011. *Groot Woordenboek van de Nederlandse Taal. Veertiende uitgave als downloadproduct 2010–2011. Versies 14.6 en 14.7 ["Dikke Van Dale online"] [Large Dictionary of the Dutch Language; Fourteenth edition as download product 2010–2011. Versions 14.6 and 14.7 ["Thick Van Dale online"]]*. Utrecht: Van Dale Uitgevers.
Espinal, M. Teresa and Jaume Mateu. 2010. On classes of idioms and their interpretation. *Journal of Pragmatics* 42(5): 1397–1411.
Geerts, Guido and H. Heestermans. 1992. *Groot Woordenboek der Nederlandse Taal. Twaalfde druk in de nieuwe spelling [Large Dictionary of the Dutch Language. Twelfth edition in the new spelling]*. Utrecht/Antwerpen: Van Dale lexicografie.
Glasbey, Sheila R. 2003. Let's paint the town red for a few hours: composition of aspect in idioms. In A.M. Wellington (ed.), *Proceedings of the ACL Workshop: The Lexicon and Figurative Language*, Sapporo, Japan, 42–48.
Glasbey, Sheila R. 2007. Aspectual composition in idioms. In: Louis de Saussure, Jacques Moeschler and Genoveva Puskás (eds.), *Recent Advances in the Syntax and Semantics of Tense, Aspect and Modality*, 71–87. Berlin/New York: Mouton de Gruyter.
Goddard, Cliff and Anna Wierzbicka. 2002. *Meaning and Universal Grammar: Theory and Empirical Findings* (2 vols.). Amsterdam/Philadelphia: John Benjamins.
Goldberg, Adele E. 1995. *Constructions: A Construction Grammar Approach to Argument Structure*. Chicago/London: The University of Chicago Press.
Goldberg, Adele E. 2003. Constructions: a new theoretical approach to language. *Trends in Cognitive Science* 7(5): 219–224.
Goldberg, Adele E. 2006. *Constructions at Work: The Nature of Generalizations in Language*. Oxford: Oxford University Press.

Goldberg, Adele E. and Ray Jackendoff. 2004. The English resultative as a family of constructions. *Language* 80(3): 532–568.

Hagers, Marlies and Rik Schutz. s.d. *Woordenboek van Nederlandse Intensiveringen [Dictionary of Dutch intensifications]*. Available online at http://www.onderwoorden.nl/intensiveringen/.

Herbst, Thomas. 2012. Valency constructions and clause constructions or how, if at all, valency grammarians might sneeze the foam off the cappuccino. In: Hans-Jörg Schmid and Susanne Handl (eds.), *Cognitive Foundations of Linguistic Usage Patterns*, 225–255. Berlin/New York: Mouton de Gruyter.

Hole, Daniel, André Meinunger and Werner Abraham (eds.). 2006. *Datives and Other Cases: Between Argument Structure and Event Structure*. Amsterdam/Philadelphia: John Benjamins.

Iwata, Seizi. 2002. Does MANNER count or not? Manner-of-motion verbs revisited. *Linguistics* 40(1): 239–292.

Iwata, Seizi. 2008. *Locative Alternation. A Lexical-Constructional Approach*. Amsterdam/Philadelphia: John Benjamins.

Jackendoff, Ray. 1997a. Twisting the night away. *Language* 73(3): 534–559.

Jackendoff, Ray. 1997b. *The Architecture of the Language Faculty*. Cambridge, MA: The MIT Press.

Jackendoff, Ray. 2002a. English particle constructions, the lexicon, and the autonomy of syntax. In: Nicole Dehé et al. (eds.), *Verb-Particle Explorations*, 67–94. Berlin/New York: Mouton de Gruyter.

Jackendoff, Ray. 2002b. *Foundations of Language: Brain, meaning, Grammar, Evolution*. New York: Oxford University Press.

Jackendoff, Ray. 2010. *Meaning and the Lexicon: The Parallel Architecture 1975–2010*. New York: Oxford University Press.

Kay, Paul. 2013. The Limits of (Construction) Grammar. In: Graeme Trousdale and Thomas Hoffmann (eds.), *The Oxford Handbook of Construction Grammar*, 32–48. Oxford: Oxford University Press.

Kudo, Shun. 2011. A comparative study between Resultative Constructions and Body Part *Off* Constructions. *Tsukuba English Studies* 29: 169–185.

Lee-Schoenfeld, Vera. 2006. German possessor datives: raised *and* affected. *The Journal of Comparative Germanic Linguistics* 9(2): 101–142.

Leino, Jaakko. 2010. Results, cases, and constructions: Argument structure constructions in English and Finnish. In: Hans C. Boas (ed.), *Contrastive Studies in Construction Grammar*, 103–136. Amsterdam/Philadelphia: John Benjamins.

Makkai, Adam. 1972. *Idiom Structure in English*. The Hague: Mouton & Co.

Mateu, Jaume and M. Theresa Espinal. 2007. Laughing our heads off: When metaphor constrains aspect. Handout for a paper presented at the 33rd Annual Meeting of the Berkeley Linguistics Society, University of California, Berkeley, February 9–11, 2007.

Pinker, Steven. 2007. *The Stuff of Thought: Language as a Window into Human Nature*. London: Penguin Books.

Plag, Ingo, Christiane Dalton-Puffer and Harald Baayen. 1999. Morphological productivity across speech and writing. *English Language and Linguistics* 3(2): 209–228.

Pulvermüller, Friedemann, Bert Cappelle and Yury Shtyrov. 2013. Brain basis of words, constructions and grammar. In: Graeme Trousdale and Thomas Hoffmann (eds.), *The Oxford Handbook of Construction Grammar*, 397–416. Oxford: Oxford University Press.

Sawada, Shigeyasu. 2000. The semantics of the 'Body Part *Off*' Construction. *English Linguistics* 17(2): 361–385.

Stefanowitsch, Anatol. 2003. A construction-based approach to indirect speech acts. In: Panther, Klaus-Uwe and Linda L. Thornburg (eds.), *Metonymy and Pragmatic Inferencing*, 105–126. Amsterdam/Philadelphia: John Benjamins.

Van Belle, William, Beatrice Lamiroy, Willy Van Langendonck, Karen Lahousse, Peter Lauwers, Ingrid Van Canegem-Ardijns and Kristel Van Goethem. 2005. *Nederlandse Grammatica voor Franstaligen [Dutch Grammar for Francophones]*. K.U.Leuven. Downloadable at http://wwwling.arts.kuleuven.be/NGF_N/NGF_NL.htm.

Vendler, Zeno. 1957. Verbs and Times. *The Philosophical Review* 66(2), 143–160.

Verhagen, Arie. 2002. From parts to wholes and back again. *Cognitive Linguistics* 13: 403–439.

Verhagen, Arie. 2007. English constructions from a Dutch perspective: Where are the differences? In: Mike Hannay and Gerard J. Steen (eds.), *Structural-functional studies in English grammar. In honour of Lachlan Mackenzie*, 257–274. Amsterdam/Philadelphia: John Benjamins.

Welke, Klaus. 2011. *Valenzgrammatik des Deutschen: Eine Einführung*. Berlin/New York: de Gruyter.

Wierzbicka, Anna. 1996. *Semantics: Primes and Universals*. Oxford: Oxford University Press.

IV **Constructions in interaction**

Jörg Bücker
10 *Und mit der Party, wie wollen wir das organisieren?* Tying constructions with the preposition *mit* in German talk-in-interaction

1 Introduction[1]

As various studies have shown, German uninflectable word classes have a strong dialogical bias inasmuch as their functions cannot be separated from concrete conditions and requirements of situated interaction. Auer (2006), Deppermann (2009) and Imo (2010b), for example, argue convincingly that the use of adverbs and particles has to be related consistently to the temporal and dialogical emergence of structure and meaning in spoken discourse (see also Auer 2000, 2005, 2007). Furthermore, several German conjunctions have been shown to establish connections between discourse segments as conversational actions rather than between propositions of clauses; the German concessive conjunction *obwohl* 'although', for example, can be used as a repair device in spoken conversation in order to revise a prior "speech act"[2] (Günthner 1999; see also Günthner 2000b).

While adverbs, particles, conjunctions and discourse markers (cf. Schiffrin 1988; Gohl and Günthner 1999; Auer and Günthner 2005) are rather well-studied from a *dialogical* point of view, other uninflectable categories still need to be opened up as a field of study for a "theory of *linguistic praxis*" (Linell 2009b: 280) which takes the impact of dialogical language use on language structure into consideration. For instance, prepositions have not yet been analyzed as a word class with a dialogical bias. Hence, it is the objective of this study to show that prepositions can be analyzed as crucial discourse-structuring devices.

---

[1] This study arises from the project "Grammatik und Dialogizität: Retraktive und projektive Konstruktionen im interaktionalen Gebrauch" (head: Prof. Dr. Susanne Günthner) supported by the German Research Foundation (Deutsche Forschungsgemeinschaft, DFG). I would like to thank Susanne Günthner, Wolfgang Imo, Henrike Helmer, and the participants of the conference "Grammar and Dialogism: Sequential, syntactic and prosodic patterns between emergence and sedimentation" (held June 13–15, 2012, at the University of Münster) for helpful comments and suggestions. Thanks to Beate Weidner for an example from her data.
[2] I'm using the notion "speech act" in an informal way in this study and not in the restricted, technical and rather monological sense of Speech Act Theory (Searle 1969).

The example which will be taken here is the preposition *mit* 'with', which, apart from its canonical functions, can be used in spoken conversation to tie topically related stretches of talk together (see section 2). Since such instances of *mit* cannot be analyzed in terms of adding a certain context to one of the canonical types of *mit*, they represent a dialogical construction in its own right (see section 3).[3]

2 Forms and functions of *mit*$_{tying}$ + NP in German talk-in-interaction

The German preposition *mit* 'with' has a wide range of functions, especially if it is not part of a fixed verb-particle combination such as *abrechnen mit* 'to settle up with'. Its canonical non-attributive instances are usually classified as comitative (*Ich ging mit meiner Nachbarin ins Kino* 'I went to the cinema (together) with my neighbor'), temporal (*Mit 18 Jahren begann ich zu studieren* 'At the age of 18 I started to study'), instrumental (*Ich zerstörte die Wand mit einem Hammer* 'I smashed the wall with a hammer') and modal (*Du solltest die Entscheidung mit Sorgfalt treffen* 'You should make the decision with care'). Furthermore, *mit* can signal relationships such as "affiliation/part-whole" (*Er fiel mit dem Gesicht auf den Boden* 'He fell to the floor on his face') or "identification" (*Mit dem Oetker-Konzern entstand einer der größten Nahrungsmittelhersteller Europas* 'The Oetker group emerged as one of the largest food producers in Europe').[4] This classification holds true for the majority of attributive instances with *mit* as well. For example, one can distinguish between comitative (*unsere Fahrt mit den Eltern* 'our journey with the parents'), instrumental (*die Brandbekämpfung mit chemischen Stoffen* 'the firefighting with chemical substances'), modal (*das Fahren mit hoher Geschwindigkeit* 'the driving with high speed') and "affiliation/ part-whole" (*der Aufprall mit dem Kopf auf dem Boden* 'the collision with the head on the floor') attributes with *mit*.[5]

---

[3] This study is based on the analysis of 134 examples of *mit* from spoken talk-in-interaction which are taken from the "linguistischen Audio-Datenbank (lAuDa)" in Münster and the "Archiv für gesprochenes Deutsch (AGD)" in Mannheim. The examples in this study are transcribed following the "Gesprächsanalytisches Transkriptionssystem (Gat) 2" (Selting et al. 2009, Barth-Weingarten and Couper-Kuhlen 2011; see also section 5). The transcript lines always start with 1; relevant context information will be given in the text.
[4] See Zifonun, Hoffmann, and Strecker (1997, III: 2135ff) and Hilpert (2009). The last example is taken from Hilpert (2009: 30).
[5] Cf. Droop (1977), Teubert (1979), Lehmus (1983), Lauterbach (1993: 126ff) and Schierholz (2001, 2004) with regard to prepositional attributes in German.

In German talk-in-interaction, however, *mit* can also be used in other ways: It can take a nominal phrase as its complement which, in the given context, functions as a *metapragmatic index* (Silverstein 1993) and refers back to a *topical antecedent* (a discourse topic which is considered to be intersubjectively accessible by the speaker) in order to establish it as a part of the context for adjacent turn-constructional units (cf. sections 2.1 and 2.2).[6] I will refer to such tying instances of *mit* by means of *mit*$_{tying}$ + NP (cf. the following excerpt from example 1 which is analyzed more comprehensively in section 2.1.1):

Example (1) Concert [excerpt]

10 → H: °h Aber **mit dem konZERT?**
           but regarding the concert

11 →   dAs WEISS ich ja nich.
           I don't know

12 →   ob DAS klAppt.
           if that will work

(*Source*: Archiv für Gesprochenes Deutsch, Interaction PF026)

Here, Helga (H) establishes an upcoming concert as the local topic by means of the turn-constructional unit in line (10) – a topic which has already been talked about in the preceding course of talk but which was not the local conversational business-at-hand anymore.

Since the tying instances of *mit* cannot be explained compositionally in terms of adding a certain context and an indexical topical keyword to one of the canonical types of *mit*, they can be classified as constructs of a construction in its own right (see section 3). This construction can be characterized as a *dialogical construction* inasmuch as it cannot be sufficiently described in terms of semantic, morphological and syntactic features which completely abstract from dialogue-constituting aspects such as sequential positions and communicative practices.

Just like their canonical counterparts, the instances of *mit*$_{tying}$ + NP can be subdivided into attributive and non-attributive occurrences. Since the functions and meanings of *mit* manifest themselves more clearly in a non-modifying syntactic environment, the non-attributive *mit*$_{tying}$ + NP will be addressed first. They

---

[6] Thus, *mit*$_{tying}$ + NP is comparable to "the topicalizer/cleft construction *was X betrifft*" which is mentioned in Auer (1996: 299). See also Goodwin (1995: 127) with regard to "prospective indexicals" and Gundel, Hedberg and Zacharski (1993) and Gundel (2010) with regard to reference and accessibility.

can be found in the initial ("left") (2.1.1) and the final ("right") periphery of turn-constructional units (2.1.2) or integrated into a turn-constructional unit (2.1.3).

2.1 Non-attributive *mit*$_{tying}$ + NP

2.1.1 Non-attributive *mit*$_{tying}$ + NP in the initial periphery

Non-attributive instances of *mit*$_{tying}$ + NP in the pre-front field of a subsequent turn-constructional unit are usually prefaced by conjunctions such as *und* 'and' or *aber* 'but':

Example (1) Concert

1	H:	°h pAssen_se AUF.
		just wait
2		DA is wieder AUsverkauft.
		it will be sold out again
3		(0.3)
4		LAchen wOllen_se;
		they want to laugh
5		aber ERNste sachen wollen_se nich hÖren.
		but they don't want to hear serious things
6		(1.5)
7	G:	na wOlln_wa HOFfen.
		well let's hope
8		dAss es SO wird.
		that it will be that way
9	H:	Aber SIcher.
		you bet
10 →		°h Aber **mit dem konZERT**?
		but regarding the concert
11 →		dAs WEISS ich ja nich.
		I don't know
12 →		ob DAS klAppt.
		if that will work
13		(1.0)

14	°h also MEI:ne bekannten sind begEIstert.
	well my friends are enthusiastic
15	(.)
16	die sonst NICHT hingehen in die brOnshalle.
	those who otherwise don't go to the Bronshalle
17	HIER gehen se alle hIn.
	that's where they all want to go

(*Source*: Archiv für Gesprochenes Deutsch, Interaction PF026)

Example (1) is taken from a conversation between Helga (H) and Gerd (G), who are talking about cultural events in Emden (a German town in Lower Saxony). In the preceding course of their conversation, Helga and Gerd talked about a recent symphony concert (which was not successful and did not attract much attention) and an upcoming concert in the "Bronshalle" (a festival hall in Emden). After that, Helga and Gerd changed the topic and talked about the theatre in Emden and one of the pieces which is going to be enacted there, the comédie-ballet "The Imaginary Invalid" by Molière.

The excerpt starts at a point when "The Imaginary Invalid" is still the conversational subject: Helga expects "The Imaginary Invalid" to be successful in Emden because "LAchen wOllen_se; aber ERNste sachen wollen_se nich hÖren." ('they want to laugh but they don't want to hear serious things', cf. lines 1–6). After Helga and Gerd agreed that they wish Molière's "The Imaginary Invalid" to be successful (lines 7–9), she returns to the topic of the upcoming concert, i.e. she re-establishes a topic which has been talked about in the preceding course of talk but which is not the local conversational business-at-hand anymore (lines 10–17). Thus, Helga deals with three conversational tasks at this point of the conversation:

(i) She closes or at least suspends the local topic (= the theatre in Emden with a focus on the upcoming play "The Imaginary Invalid").
(ii) She explicitly establishes a "new" topic (= the upcoming concert).
(iii) She marks the "new" topic as intersubjectively accessible.

Helga accomplishes these three tasks by means of the turn-constructional unit "Aber mit dem konZERT?" ('but regarding the concert') in line (10), which is followed by the complex clause "=dAs WEISS ich ja nich. ob DAS klAppt." ('I don't know if that will work') in lines (11–12). "Aber mit dem konZERT?" is a topical *"misplacement marker"* (Schegloff and Sacks 1973) which indicates that the topic change takes place in a sequential position in which it is not necessarily expectable for the addressee. Syntactically and prosodically, it can be classified as a *hanging topic*:[7] It occupies a position in the pre-front field[8] of the subsequent syntagma, it is prosodically independent, and the subsequent syntagma does not contain an anaphoric pronoun which refers to the hanging topic as its antecedent.[9] Furthermore, it is initiated by the adversative conjunction "Aber" ('but'), which marks a contrastive caesura with regard to the preceding turn-constructional unit(s). Note that canonical prepositional phrases with *mit* (i.e. instrumental, modal, temporal etc. adverbials), in contrast, usually cannot occupy the pre-front field in terms of a hanging topic.

The prepositional phrase "mit dem konZERT?" ('regarding the concert') not only differs from canonical prepositional phrases with *mit* for syntactic and prosodic reasons, but semantically and pragmatically as well. First, this can be shown *retrospectively* (sequentially backward-pointing) with regard to the complement of *mit*, which, in the given context, is not a symbolic part of a proposition but functions as an *indexical topical keyword* (or "conversational deictic" 'Gesprächsdeiktikum') that marks a prior stretch of talk in Helga's and Gerd's conversation as its *topical antecedent*.[10] This makes it possible for Helga to employ the hanging topic as a *tying rule* in the sense of Sacks. Sacks (1964–1972/2005, I: 322) defines tying rules as

> a means by which one piece of conversation is tied to another. If conversation simply consisted of A-B-A-B in alternation, then one might, for example, be perfectly well able to disorder all the parts, as long as the alternation is preserved, and still have a recognizable conversation, or even the same conversation. What these "tying rules" do is radically restrict that possibility, and provide for very local control over the relationship between utterances.

---

7 I am following Altmann's (1981: 48ff) and Selting's (1993) studies of hanging topics. See also Ochs and Schieffelin (1976) and Duranti and Ochs (1979). It would also be possible to analyze the prepositional phrase in line 10 as a left-dislocated attribute to the correlative pronoun "dAs" in line 11, but I prefer to classify it as a hanging topic due to its pragmatic salience and prosodic independence. This goes well with Selting's (1993) observation that hanging topics tend to indicate a more or less significant break instead of smooth progression.

8 In German, declarative non-dependent sentences are topologically defined by the position of the finite and non-finite parts of the verb which separate the *front field* (position before the finite verb), the *middle field* (position between the finite and non-finite parts of the verb) and the *end field* (position after the non-finite parts of the verb). The *pre-front field* is positioned before the front field. It can be occupied by conjunctions, discourse markers (see Auer 1996) and hanging topics.

9 The direct object "dAs" in line (11) has a vague anaphoric reading which gets specified by the turn-constructional unit in line (12).'

10 The notions "retrospective" and "prospective" are used here in the sense of Lenk (1998: 52). See also Goodwin (2006).

Sacks shows that conversational tying can be accomplished by means of repetitions, or *locational tying techniques* as he calls them (see Sacks 1964–1972/2005, I: 722ff).[11] Locational tying techniques have the advantage that they allow for *skip-tying* (Sacks 1964–1972/2005, I: 734), i.e. they can tie two distant stretches of discourse together while skipping utterances between them. This is exactly what is happening in example (1): The complement "konZERT" ('concert') – a "thematic" lexeme with a high recognition value which has often been used in the preceding course of talk – makes it possible to connect a preceding stretch of talk (the topical antecedent) to the local context even though there are several turns in between.

Secondly, the prepositional phrase "mit dem konZERT?" ('regarding the concert') does not have a phrasal or a clausal scope, but a wider scope from a *prospective* (sequentially forward-pointing) point of view: Since Helga establishes the topical antecedent as an integral part of the topical presuppositions of subsequent speech acts (thereby restricting their possible readings), the prepositional phrase functions as a *pragmatic operator* with a pragmatically driven scope that is not tied to syntactical boundaries.[12] This operator is part of a *self-initiation of topic talk*: Helga establishes the topical antecedent in order to carry on with topic-related talk herself. Canonical prepositional phrases with *mit*, in contrast, specify the verb phrase or at most their syntactic host-clause as a whole, but not a complex sequence of speech acts.

Example (1) shows that mit_{tying} + NP in the pre-front field is structurally and semantically different from the canonical uses of the preposition *mit*. It is both *context shaped* (i.e. "built in response to the frameworks of intelligibility and action" created by prior utterances) and *context renewing* (i.e. providing "the contextual point of departure for the action(s) that will follow"; see Heritage 1984: 242; Goodwin 2006: 443). Hence, it can be characterized as a dialogical *inter-act* in the sense of Linell (2001: 207). In example (1), this inter-act is being used as a means to self-initiate topic talk, but there are also examples in which mit_{tying} + NP *other-initiates topic talk*. In these cases, the turn-constructional unit after the hanging topic is a question or an invitation to talk followed by turn-taking:

---

[11] See also Tannen (1989), Aitchison (1994), Anward (2005) and Du Bois (2010) as concerns the communicative functions of repetitions in language use.
[12] Bücker (i.Pr.) suggests calling such a scope an *adlocutionary scope*. See also Fiehler, Barden, Elstermann, and Kraft (2004) concerning "Operator-Skopus-Strukturen" ('operator-scope-structures') in German spoken interaction and Imo's (2010a) study of "Mein Problem ist/mein Thema ist".

Example (2) Educational curricula

```
1      B:   es IST (–) im allgemeinen (–) dOch zu sagen,
            in general it can be said
2           dass die schüler nach: (.) KURzer zEIt,=
            that the pupils after a short while
3           vielleicht EInem mOnat; (.)
            a month maybe
4           der neuen schule gAnz_äh geWACHsen sind?=
            are able to cope with the new school
5           und AUFfällige lücken (–) geschlOssen haben.
            and have filled remarkable knowledge gaps
6  →   H:   °h und mit den schUlPLÄ:nen.
            and regarding the educational curricula
7  →        °h gelten DIEse für eine längere zEIt?
            do they hold for a longer period of time
8  →        oder_äh finden häufig ÄNderungen solcher schUlpläne
            statt?
            or are there many revisions of these educational curricula
9      B:   °h die SCHULpläne werden in der regel in einem\
            reglemENT
            the educational curricula are usually scheduled by regulations
10          der einzelnen schulen festgelegt,
            of the particular schools
```

(*Source*: Archiv für Gesprochenes Deutsch, Interaction PF397)

In this example, Herbert (H) talks with Bernd (B), a teacher, about Bernd's job. After Bernd told Herbert that pupils usually do not need much time to get used to a new school (lines 1–5), Herbert changes the topic and asks Bernd for information concerning the educational curricula which structure the teaching in school (see lines 6–8).

Just like in example (1), the new topic is being introduced by means of a hanging topic which is initiated by a conjunction (*und* 'and') and which features an indexical topical keyword ("den schUlPLÄ:nen." 'the educational curricula') as the complement of a prepositional phrase with *mit* (see line 6).[13] Sequentially

---

13 In example (2), the referent of the hanging topic is taken up in the subsequent clause by a coreferential pronoun. However, since the turn-constructional units in lines (6) and (7) are separated prosodically (they both feature a focus accent and they are both embraced by an initial inbreath and an independent final pitch movement), the turn-constructional unit in line (6) can be classified as a hanging topic.

and topically, example (2) is slightly different in comparison to example (1), though. First, the accessibility of the new topic is not linked to a preceding stretch of talk (Herbert and Bernd had not talked about educational curricula before, at least not in the data available) but is based on pragmatic inferences in combination with contextual knowledge and world knowledge: Since Herbert knows that Bernd is a teacher, he can assume that the topic "educational curricula" is accessible to him. Secondly, Herbert does not carry on with topic-related talk himself but invites Bernd to talk by means of an alternative question (cf. lines 7–8). Accordingly, the hanging topic with *mit* in line (6) can be classified as a means to other-initiate topic talk which is pre-structured by the pragmatic scope of the operator in the pre-front field.

In examples (1) and (2), the prepositional hanging topics with mit_{tying} + NP are employed for *mid-scale* or *large-scale topic tying*: They are used when a topic is regarded to be accessible to the addressee but

(a) has not been opened up before or has already been closed explicitly (= large-scale topic tying), or
(b) has been opened up before but is not being dealt with in the preceding turn-constructional unit(s) (= mid-scale topic tying).[14]

The reason seems to be that the explicit establishment of an accessible topic – especially in the pre-front field as a syntactically and pragmatically prominent position (see Auer 1996 and Auer and Günthner 2005, for example) – makes sense primarily when the topic is "misplaced" inasmuch as it cannot necessarily be considered to be "active" or the local conversational business-at-hand.

However, hanging topics with mit_{tying} + NP can also be used for *small-scale topic tying*, i.e. with regard to a topic which has not been closed yet and is also being dealt with in the preceding turn-constructional units. One such context is the use of mit_{tying} + NP as a means to compete for the floor in order to express disagreement, as in the following example, which is taken from the German TV cooking show "Lanz kocht!":

---

14 Hence, they have characteristics of "second-level discourse markers" (see Siepmann 2003: 266): "[T]ypically, second-level discourse markers, hereafter SLDMs, are restricted medium frequency collocations composed of two or more printed words and having a definably pragmatic function. They act as single units establishing local linkage between adjacent elements, sequences or text segments and/or global linkage between text segments further apart."

Example (3) Salad

```
1      S:   ALso?=
            well
2           =dIr SCHMECkter.
            you like it
3      L:   ja SEHR gUt.=
            yes very good
4           =SEHR gUt.
            very good
5      S:   und DAzu gibts_en kartOelsalat?
            and additionally we're going to have a potato salad
6           (das) is ein kartOel VOgerlsalat,
            that's a potato and lamb's lettuce salad
7           was ja auch (.) tYpisch ÖSterreichisch is,
            which is typically Austrian actually
8      L:   SUper.
            great
9      S:   °h u:nd beim FELDsalat müssen wa sAgn,
            and concerning lamb's lettuce we have to say
10          der fEldsalat hat von dem vitamin CE her,
            lamb's lettuce has, in respect of vitamin C,
11          DOPpelt so vIEl?
            twice as much
12          °h als JEder kOpfsalat.=
            as any garden salad
13     L:   Aber KOMM.
            but come on
14     S:   sEhr viel [BEtakarotine?]
            a lot of beta-carotene
15  →  L:             [aber mIt mIt ] dem saLAT,=
                      but regarding the salad
16  →       =ich hab NEUlich wieder\ eine_eine stUdie äh_äh gehör
            I heard of a study recently again
17  →       oder das erGEBnis einer stUdie,
            or of the results of a study
```

18	→		da KAM im grUnde raus,
			basically, the results say
19	→		dass\ salAt is einfach nur für karNICkel.
			that salad is just something for rabbits
20		S:	NEIN.=
			no
21			=Is a SCHMARRN.=
			that's nonsense
22			[=Is DAS.]
			is that
23		L:	[DOCH.]
			yes
24		S:	JA.=
			yes
25			=Aber-=
			but
26		L:	[=da is nix DRIN,]
			there is nothing in it
27		A:	[( )]
28		L:	da is nix DRIN,
			there is nothing in it

(*Source*: Example from Beate Weidner)

The host of the cooking show, Markus Lanz (L), talks with Alfons Schuhbeck (S), a cook who is a regular guest on "Lanz kocht!", about the meal Schuhbeck is currently preparing. After Lanz has confirmed that he enjoys Schuhbeck's meal (lines 1–4), Schuhbeck comments on the side dish, a kind of Austrian potato salad (cf. lines 5–8), and he takes the view that lamb's lettuce is healthier in comparison to garden salad due to its wealth of vitamins (lines 9–12), but Lanz, the host of the show, indicates upcoming disagreement (line 13). Since Schuhbeck keeps on talking (line 14), Lanz interrupts him by means of an overlapped hanging topic with *mit* in order to refer to the results of a study which differ from Schuhbeck's point of view since they indicate that salad is not very healthy at all because "there is nothing in it" (cf. lines 15–28). This point of view – which is also held by Andreas Studer (A), another guest cook – does not convince Schuhbeck, though (cf. lines 20–22).

In this example, the prepositional hanging topic "[aber mIt mIt] dem saLAT," ('but regarding the salad') in line (15) is used as a means for *small-scale topic tying*: its topical antecedent is a part of the local conversational business-at-hand which is not only accessible but even active at the time of Lanz's turn. Thus, it actually does not need to be reactivated. However, the prepositional hanging topic makes it possible for Lanz to indicate the topical relevance (or relatedness) of his turn in the exposed initial position that gets overlapped (Jefferson 2004) and to stop the topic progression in Schuhbeck's turn while holding back dissent until he has successfully occupied the turn himself.

Another context in which prepositional hanging topics with mit_{tying} + NP can be employed for small-scale topic tying are list-like (Jefferson 1991; Selting 2004) topical structures in the preceding turn(s). It can be useful, then, to tie follow-up turn-constructional units explicitly to one of the preceding list items:

Example (4) Baking

1	W:	tirOler hut NÄ:hen.
		sew a Tyrolean hat
2		JEder bewohner soll EInen hut anfertigen.
		every resident ought to make a hat
3	C:	ph:::
		phhh
4	W:	<<while other discourse participants are talking simultaneously> WEIter.
		furthermore
5		(-)
6		am dOnnerstag wird um ZEHN uhr ein hau den lukas in den garten gehoben.>
		on Thursday at ten o'clock a strength tester will be carried into the ga
7		°h BUCHstaben backen.
		bake letters
8		den teig für buchstaben (.) könnt ihr nach dem beidigen[15] rezept,=
		you can [prepare] the batter for the letters using the enclosed recipe
9		ham wir HIER?
		[which] we have here

---

15 Probably an unclear pronunciation of *beiliegenden* 'enclosed'.

10		(0.5) zubereiten.
		[...]
11	C:	ph:::
		phhhh
12	S:	( )
13	W:	BUCHsta:ben müssen ungefähr in der größe vIErzig,
		letters ought to be [shaped] about the size of forty
14		auf ACHTnzwanzig zentimEter geformt werden.
		on twenty-eight centimeters [...]
15	S:	hm,
		hm
16		es is aber nIch so LEICHT.=
		but that's not so easy
17		=also äh [von DAher,]
		well eh hence
18	W:	[ja.]
		yes
19 →	S:	grAd **mit dem BACken**.
		especially regarding the baking
20 →		ich glaub [dAs:] gibt die MEISten probleme.
		I think that will cause the most problems
21	W:	[ja.]
		yes
22 →	S:	weil das brIcht ausnANder,
		because that breaks apart
23 →		oda du mUss was [( )]
		or you have to
24	W:	[( )] lAUgen,
		[made] lye
25		lAUgengebäck gemacht?
		lye bread [...]

(*Source*: linguistische Audio Datenbank (lAuDa), Interaction 25)

This excerpt is taken from the German adaption of the TV reality show "Big Brother", which films a group of people who live together in a large isolated house and have to do certain tasks every week. Walter (W), Christian (C) and Stefanie (S) are talking here about the tasks they have to do this week, and Walter reads out a list they have received from the "Big Brother" organizers: The housemates have to sew Tyrolean hats (lines 1–2), use a strength tester (line 6) and bake letters (lines 7–14). After Walter read out the list (accompanied by several commentaries by the other discourse participants), Stefanie expresses her opinion that it won't be easy for them to complete these tasks (cf. lines 16–17). Stefanie finishes her turn-constructional unit in line (17) by means of the "topic-tag" "von DAher," ('hence'), a frequent construction in spoken German talk-in-interaction which marks the topical and argumentative coherence and completeness of the turn-so-far by signaling that a conclusive continuation would be possible in principal but does not necessarily need to be realized at the moment.[16] Then Stefanie carries on and specifies her point: She refers to the preceding topical list item "baking letters" (line 19) in order to characterize this task as the most difficult task because baked letters easily break apart (lines 20–22). Then she is interrupted by Walter (lines 23–25).

The hanging topic with mit_{tying} + NP (line 19) is being used in example (4) as a means for small-scale topic tying which focuses on a certain item (baking) within a list of items (sewing, striking a strength tester and baking). So, just like in example (3), there is a concrete sequential reason here to make use of a hanging topic with mit_{tying} + NP even though the topic is not only accessible but active at the time of the utterance.

2.1.2 Non-attributive mit_{tying} + NP in the final periphery

While examples (1–4) featured non-attributive examples of mit_{tying} + NP in the initial periphery, (probably) non-attributive instances of mit_{tying} + NP can also be found in the final ("right") periphery. Since these examples are syntactically, prosodically and functionally quite similar, it is sufficient to discuss only the following example from a private conversation:

---

[16] Stefanie's "von DAher," gets overlapped by Walter's back-channel in line (18) since it is not projected by the preceding turn-constructional unit. See Bücker (in print) for a comprehensive analysis of the forms and functions of *von daher* in German spoken interaction.

Example (5) Shitty history stuff

1	A:	sEkt is NICH so geil.
		champagne is not that great
2	S:	DOCH.=
		yes it is
3		=sEkt is GEIL.
		champagne is great
4	A:	proSECCO.=
		prosecco
5		=JA.
		yes
6	S:	BAH.
		ugh
7	A:	<<smile voice> Is SPRUdeliger.> [((laughs))]
		it is more sparkling
8	S:	[NE;]
		nope
9	?:	<<p> BAH.>
		ugh
10	A:	ja.=kEIne AHnung.
		well dunno
11		ja.=das Is am SAMStag.
		well it's on Saturday
12		aber das sind NICH dA-
		but that ain't
13		WEISS nIch,=
		dunno
14		=das geht dann [von SAMStag irgendwie elf-]
		it goes from Saturday somewhat eleven
15	s:	[aber_wieso-=SAMStag Is doch-]
		but what's the matter, on Saturday the stress will be
16		äh_is doch [stress wieder vorbei erstmal.]
		eh the stress will be over for the moment
17	A:	[°hhh]
18		hhh° JA.
		yes

19		ja.=ja.ja.=
		yes yes yes
20	→	ja.=ich bin auch SO: frOh,
		well I'm so glad as well
21	→	dass ich das jEtzt geREgelt hab?=
		that I managed it/that now
22	→	=**mit dem schEIss geSCHICHTskram** da.
		regarding the shitty history stuff there
23		(1.2)
24	S:	nur noch EIN thEma.
		just one more subject
25		dU SCHWEIN.
		you pig
26	A:	JA.
		yes
27		VOLL.
		indeed

(*Source*: linguistische Audio Datenbank (lAuDa), Interaction 161)

First, the two friends Andrea (A) and Sandra (S) talk about the question of whether they like champagne or not (lines 1–9). This question is a sub-topic of a conversation about a promotional film which will be shot on Saturday. After Andrea closed the champagne side sequence (Jefferson 1972) and returned to the issue of the promotional film as the main topic (see lines 10–11), she produces two truncated turn-constructional units (cf. lines 12, 14). Sandra's reaction to these disfluencies in Andrea's turn indicates that she perceives them as a display of concern: she emphasizes that the stress will be over after Saturday (lines 15–16); note that Andrea has agreed to participate in the promotional film, but she and Sandra also have to prepare for an upcoming presentation and a test. Andrea, in return, agrees with Sandra by means of a series of agreement tokens and breathing (lines 18–19). Then she emphasizes that she finally managed to do "something" (note that the anaphoric/deictic pronoun "das" 'it/that' in line 21 is referentially vague) and immediately carries on with the turn-constructional unit "mit dem schEIss geSCHICHTskram da" ('regarding the shitty history stuff there', line 22) in order to provide further information which specifies the topical background of her preceding turn-constructional unit and, hence, restricts its possible readings. After a notable pause of over one second (line 23), Sabine takes over the turn and underlines that there is not much work left (line 24).[17] Then Andrea agrees emphatically by means of "JA" ('yes') in combination with the affirmative intensifier "VOLL." ('indeed').[18]

The turn-constructional unit "mit dem schEIss geSCHICHTSkram da" ('regarding the shitty history stuff there', line 22) ties the preceding turn-constructional unit back to the issue of the upcoming presentation (the presentation has to deal with a historical issue) – a topic Andrea and Sandra did not talk about in the preceding course of talk (at least as far as it has been recorded) but which is well known to Sandra since she has to prepare the presentation together with Andrea. Syntactically and prosodically, "mit dem schEIss geSCHICHTSkram da" in line (22) is realized after a point of possible syntactic and prosodic completion: the sentence brace has been closed, all argument positions are filled and the turn-constructional unit has its own focus accent and a terminal pitch movement. There is no inter-turn gap, though, which might be treated as a transition relevance place by Sandra. Since Andrea neither carries on talking herself nor motivates Sandra to talk with regard to the topical antecedent, "mit dem schEIss geSCHICHTSkram da" cannot be analyzed as a dislocated constituent in the initial periphery of the subsequent turn-constructional unit which is meant to initiate topic talk. It could be classified as an *insertable* instead – i.e. an element that does not "properly fit the end of the prior unit but belong[s], canonically speaking, somewhere within it" (Couper-Kuhlen and Ono 2007: 515) – if "dem schEIss geSCHICHTSkram da" were to be analyzed as an extraposed attributive modifier (cf. "das ↔ mit dem schEIss geSCHICHTSkram da" 'that ↔ with the shitty history stuff there'). In that case, it could be characterized as a "quasi-attributive" mit_{tying} + NP which oscillates between the categories "attributive mit_{tying} + NP" and "non-attributive mit_{tying} + NP".

2.1.3 Integrated non-attributive mit_{tying} + NP

Non-attributive instances of mit_{tying} + NP which are syntactically and prosodically fully integrated are rare in my data. I will discuss just one example here:

---

[17] It is not clear if the address term "Schwein" ('pig', line 25) is a means for teasing or an allusion to the German idiomatic expression "Glücksschwein" ('lucky pig'; in Germany, pigs are known as a symbol for good luck). Cf. Eisenberg (1986), Miller (1986), Drew (1987) and Günthner (2000a: 155ff) as regards teasing in everyday conversation.
[18] See Imo (2011) concerning post-positioned intensifiers in spoken German talk-in-interaction.

Example (6) Rechargeable battery and slippers

1	J:	<<smile voice; Sabrina is laughing> die SCHLA:Ppen hEr
		give the slippers to me
2		Und das AKku.
		and the rechargeable battery
3		aber GANZ schnEll;>
		and be quick about it
4		[°hhh hhh°] °h
5	S:	[<<innocent voice> ich HAB das nich hIEr drin.>]
		I don't have it in here
6		(0.6)
7	J:	HÄH?
		heh
8	S:	ich HAB das [nich hIEr.]
		I don't have it in here
9 →	J:	[**mi(m) AK_AKku?**]
		regarding the rechargeable battery
10		(.)
11 →	J:	KRIEste Ärger.=ne,
		you will get into trouble
12	S:	mIt WEM?
		with whom
13 →	J:	**mit den sch** <<all> ja.=**mim Akku** krieste von DEn(en) ärger?
		regarding the s(lippers) well regarding the rechargeable battery you will get into trouble with them
14 →		[und **mitn schlAppen** kries mit MIR ärger.> ((laughs briefly))]
		and regarding the slippers you will get into trouble with me
15	S:	[((laughing))]
16		(1.5)
17	?:	( )
18	S:	KALT?
		cold
19		GANZ [kAlt.]
		very cold
20	J:	[hm.]
		hm

(*Source*: linguistische Audio Datenbank (lAuDa), Interaction 2)

Just like example (4), this excerpt is taken from the German adaption of the TV reality show "Big Brother". Jürgen (J) suspects Sabrina (S) to have hidden a pair of slippers and a rechargeable battery which he wants back (lines 1–4). The interaction is playful and humorous, though; both participants smile and laugh while they talk. Since Sabrina pretends to be innocent (lines 5–8), Jürgen announces that she will get into trouble regarding the rechargeable battery (lines 9–11). Sabrina, however, still pretends to be innocent by asking "mIt WEM?" ('with whom', line 12). Hence, Jürgen repeats that concerning the rechargeable battery, she will get into trouble with "them" (= other housemates) while concerning the slippers, she will get into trouble with him (lines 13–14). After that, Jürgen and Sabrina enter into some sort of "pot hitting" game: Jürgen starts to search for the rechargeable battery and the slippers while Sabrina indicates by means of "cold" and "very cold" that Jürgen is not searching in the right place (lines 18–20).

The instances of mit_{tying} + NP in lines (9), (13) and (14) are structurally and prosodically fully integrated and occupy the front field. However, they are neither a canonical part of the propositional content nor are they subcategorized by the verb. Instead, the complete "host speech acts" are within their scopes as they point back to a certain conversational issue in the prior context (two missing articles of daily use) by means of the complements "rechargeable battery" and "slippers" (note that Jürgen by no means wants to say that the trouble he talks about will involve the "instrumental" use of the battery and the slippers). From a sequential point of view, the instances of mit_{tying} + NP are means for small-scale topic tying since Jürgen and Sabrina talked about this issue immediately before. The small-scale topic tying is triggered by the list-like topical structure of the preceding turn (see example 4 in section 2.1.1, too): On a sub-topical level, the issue of the rechargeable battery needs to be distinguished from the issue of the slippers since Jürgen expects that Sabrina will get into trouble with different persons concerning each issue (see lines 13–14). Furthermore, example (6) resembles example (5) inasmuch as mit_{tying} + NP does not initiate a multi-unit stretch of talk which presupposes the topical antecedent. Its scope as a pragmatic operator remains restricted to the host turn-constructional unit instead.

2.2 Attributive mit_{tying} + NP

The preceding examples all featured non-attributive instances of mit_{tying} + NP in spoken talk-in-interaction. However, mit_{tying} + NP can also be used as an attributive modifier of an abstract noun (for example, *Sache* 'matter' or *Ding* 'thing')[19] or a pronoun. This type of *mit*_tying + NP has already been mentioned by Droop (1977: 215f).[20] Droop does not take the indexical character of the *mit*-complement into consideration, though – just like their non-attributive counterparts, the attributive instances of *mit*_tying + NP are first and foremost a means to establish a topical antecedent as a part of the local context for adjacent turn-constructional units. They have to be, in fact, because otherwise it would be impossible to assign a referent to the abstract modificand. For example, "dAs hab ich eben nich: ERNST gemeint?" ('I was not serious about that') in line (6) would be opaque without "mit den äh liedern" ('concerning the eh songs'):

Example (7) Songs

1	B:	wie_wie grOß is mariettas PARtytauglichkeit so,
		how how big is Marietta's capability to party
2	A:	WAHNsinnich.
		incredibly
3		marietta is Echt_n PARtylöwe.=
		Marietta really is a party animal
4		[=FIND Ich?]
		I think
5	M:	[((laughs))]
6 →	A:	[deshalb also **dAs mit den äh liedern** hab ich eben nich: ERNST gemeint?]
		thus well I was not serious about that concerning the eh songs
7	M:	[((laughs)) °hhh]
8	A:	weil ich hab marietta nur SINgen [und] tAnzen und sonstwas sehen?
		since I have always seen Marietta singing and dancing and whatever
9	M:	[hh°]

(*Source*: linguistische Audio Datenbank (lAuDa), Interaction 95)

---

19 Since these nouns are very abstract, they are not prototypical "Rektionssubstantive" (nouns which govern the preposition of their attributes) such as "Einladung zu einer Feier" ('invitation to a party'). See Schierholz (2001) for a recent discussion of prepositional attributes in German.
20 Droop considers this type different from other patterns such as the "Merkmal-'mit'" ('feature-'mit'", for example "der Mann mit dem Hut" 'the man with the hat'). Teubert (1979: 159) cites Droop's example "die Geschichte mit Klaus" ('the story/matter with Klaus') and paraphrases it in terms of "die Geschichte, in der Klaus vorkommt" ('the story/matter in which Klaus occurs'). Teubert's paraphrase and his analysis show that he does not consider the indexical character of the *mit*-complement either.

This example is taken from a TV conversation between the German journalists and friends Anne Will (A) and Marietta Slomka (M) with Reinhold Beckmann (B), the host of the German TV talk show "Beckmann". After Beckmann asked Anne Will if Marietta Slomka is capable of partying (line 1), Anne Will emphasizes that, in her opinion, Marietta Slomka is a real "PARtylöwe" ('party animal', lines 2–4). She is acknowledged by Marietta Slomka by means of laughter (line 5), and then she relates to one of her prior claims by means of the complex nominal phrase "dAs mit den äh liedern" ('that with the eh songs') in order to reassess this claim as "not serious" (lines 6–8).

Syntactically, the nominal phrase "dAs mit den äh liedern" ('that concerning the eh songs') fills the position of the direct object which is required by the verb "meinen" ('mean'). This shows that the attributive affiliation with a modificand makes it possible for mit_{tying} + NP to be part of an argument of a verb. Regarding its functions and its sequential embedding, "dAs mit den äh liedern" is a means for mid-scale topic tying and the self-initiation of topic talk: In the preceding course of talk, Anne Will had claimed that she knows more carnival songs than Marietta Slomka, but now she picks her claim up again in order to relativize it.

At first view, this might look like the kind of topic tying which occurs in the previous examples, but there is an important difference. Note that the non-attributive instances of mit_{tying} + NP in section (2.1) did not metapragmatically deal with speech-act-related characteristics of the topical antecedent (its validity claims, informational value, appropriateness or argumentative weight, for example) but established it as an explicated and restrictive part of the presupposed "background" of the local interaction; in example (7), in contrast, a certain speech act is being picked up as the topical antecedent in order to reassess its validity claims. This is characteristic of the other attributive instances of mit_{tying} + NP in my data as well – they refer to a certain piece of *talk* or *information* as the topical antecedent in order to deal with its characteristics. This can be part of a problematization sequence such as a correction, a defense, a justification or an apology:

Example (8) History of art

1   S: JA:;=wIr sind hier bei (.) dAs (.) SOFA,
                  well here we are with "Das Sofa"

2   <<all> und NEben mir sitzt herr ulrich wEIgel,
                  and Mister Ulrich Weigel is sitting beside me

3   wie wir gerAde schon im portrait geHÖRT haben,>
                  as we just have heard in the portrait

4   halLO,=hErr WEIgel,
                  hello Mister Weigel

5		schön dass sie heute Abend geKOMmen [sind?]
nice that you came here tonight
6	W:	[JA:.]
yeah
7		gUten Abend;=
good evening
8		=frau DI donAto;°h
Miss Di Donato
9	S:	°h gUten Abend,
good evening
10		(0.5)
11		ÄHM,
ehm
12		JA;=EIn kleiner FEHler hat sich eingeschlichen;
well a little mistake slipped in
13		wir wf\ <<all> WISsen durch das kUrzportrait,
we know thanks to the short portrait
14		dass sie wissenschaftlicher MITarbeiter sind,>=
that you are a lecturer
15		=am Institut für SPORTwissenschaften,=
at the department of sports science
16		=hIEr in MÜNster,
here in Münster
17 →		°h Aber **das mit der KUNSTgeschichte** stimmt nicht so ganz genau.
but that concerning the history of art is not really correct
18		°h DENN (.) sIE haben n anach ihrem abitur n:icht kunstgeschichte,
since you didn't [study] history of art after your A-Levels
19		sondern kunsterZIEHung studiert.
but art education

(*Source*: linguistische Audio Datenbank (lAuDa), Interaction 29)

After Sarah (S), the host of the talk show, and her guest Ulrich Weigel (W) heard a short portrait of Weigel for the "overhearing audience" (Hutchby 2006), Sarah welcomes the audience and her guest (lines 1–9). Then she initiates a dispreferred repair (Pomerantz 1984; Auer and Uhmann 1982; Kotthoff 1993; Schegloff, Jefferson, and Sacks 1977) with regard to one of the claims in the portrait (note that the pause, the particles "ÄHM," and "JA;", the explicit notification of a repair and the repetition of correct information in lines 10–16 significantly delay the actual repair starting in line 17): Weigel is a lecturer at the department of sports science, but he did not study history of art but art education (cf. lines 12–19). Sarah makes use of an attributive instance of mit_{tying} + NP in line (17) in order to locate the reparandum (= the wrong claim that Weigel studied history of art) precisely in the context. The attributive mit_{tying} + NP is a part of the nominal subject of the clause, and it helps to establish a concrete speech act as a topical antecedent which needs to be corrected.

The examples (1–8) indicate that attributive instances of mit_{tying} + NP tend to establish the topical antecedent as *an accessible piece of talk (usually a certain speech act) or information to deal with on a metapragmatic level (for example, correcting or modifying)* while the non-attributive instances of mit_{tying} + NP tend to establish the topical antecedent as *an explicated topical presupposition of and restrictive topical frame for local speech acts*. This observation can be linked to the lexical features of the modified (pro)noun and to the question of whether the topical antecedent is being established as a part of the predicate or not:

(i) Modificands such as "Sache" ('matter'), "Ding" ('thing') and "das" ('that') indicate a high degree of "identifiability" and categorical "boundedness" of their referents. Ascribing these features to a topical antecedent makes it easier to deal with it as a concrete piece of talk or information which can be reassessed or modified on a metapragmatic level.

(ii) In order to reassess or modify a concrete piece of talk or information, it is necessary to place it within the predicate in terms of an argument of the verb which becomes affected and specified by its semantics.[21] However, only the attributive mit_{tying} + NP can establish a topical antecedent non-anaphorically in the predicate as a part of a constituent with a verb-driven thematic role. The non-attributive mit_{tying} + NP, in contrast, can only indirectly establish its topical antecedents as a part of the predicate, namely by means of a dislocated instance of mit_{tying} + NP and an integrated phoric pro-form in the predicate.

Despite their differences, the attributive and the non-attributive mit_{tying} + NP share their tying function and a restrictive semantics – while the non-attributive mit_{tying} + NP restricts the possible readings of the local speech acts it is attached to, the attributive mit_{tying} restricts the number of possible referents which could be assigned to its abstract modificand.

---

[21] Cf. Hopper's (1979: 240) observation that "[t]he verb is the location of new, narrative-advancing information."

3 A usage-based model of *mit*~tying~ + NP as a construction

Up to this point, it has been shown how non-attributive and attributive instances of *mit*~tying~ are used to tie the local context to a topical antecedent. This section aims to show that the occurrences of *mit*~tying~ + NP can be analyzed by means of a *construction* in the sense of a usage-based approach to Construction Grammar.

3.1 Construction Grammar from a usage-based point of view

In a series of seminal studies, Fillmore, Goldberg, Croft and other advocates of Construction Grammar (CxG) argue that the primary units of the linguistic competence are surface-near *constructions* rather than atomic units and abstract autonomous rules (see Fillmore 1988, Fillmore, Kay, and Catherine O'Connor 1988, Goldberg 1995, 2006 and Croft 2001, amongst others). Constructions are considered to be entrenched symbolic pairings of *form* (phonological, morphological and syntactical representations) and *meaning* (usually both semantic and pragmatic representations) which can differ with regard to internal complexity and specification and which are created and shaped by actual language use. Most of the branches of Construction Grammar are usage-based (cf. Langacker 2000, Barlow and Kemmer 2000, Bybee and Hopper 2001, Tomasello 2003 and Bücker 2012, for example) and reject the distinction between autonomous structure- and rule-based parts of grammar (substantially brought about by an innate universal grammar) on the one hand and the lexicon (as the host of all idiosyncrasies in a certain language) on the other. Instead, language is seen as constantly emerging within and through the actual use of symbolic pairings of form and meaning.

Recent usage-based studies in Construction Grammar have shown that the use of constructions as *constructs* (Fried and Östman 2005: 18) in talk-in-interaction is both complex and context-driven since it strongly interacts with sequential positions, genres and sometimes also social registers (cf. Selting and Kern 2009). For example, Günthner (2010, 2011a) notes that *dense constructions* are particularly common in conversational narrative genres, while Imo (2010a) considers German *mein Problem ist/mein Thema ist* 'my problem is/my topic is' to be a conventionalized means to initiate topic talk in German radio phone-ins. Such studies reveal that constructions can emerge in virtually every "ecological niche" of language use – such "niches" being sequential positions, genres and other sociolinguistic constellations of all kinds – as the result of specific communicative conditions and particularities which characterize these "niches".

Due to this, it is by no means unlikely that there are still many patterns in talk-in-interaction which have not been recognized yet as corresponding to entrenched pairings of form and meaning.[22] In my opinion, one of these patterns is mit_{tying} + NP. However, in order to avoid a naïve exemplar-based approach with a behavioristic bias, not every pattern of language use should directly be identified with a construction (see Bücker 2014). It needs to be shown instead that the degree of structural and functional "autonomy" a certain pattern of language use has is really high enough to justify the postulation of a cognitively entrenched construction.

3.2 A construction model of mit_{tying} + NP

For our discussion of the question of whether the instances of mit_{tying} + NP correspond to one construction (or even more constructions) or not, it needs to be considered that we came across two patterns of mit_{tying} + NP in the data which have slightly different structural and functional properties. The following two tables summarize the typical features of these patterns:

Table 1: Pattern I (prototypical non-attributive mit_{tying} + NP)

Form	– mit_{tying} + NP is placed in the pre-front field of a subsequent turn-constructional unit, in the end field of a preceding turn-constructional unit or even syntactically integrated (front field or middle field) into a host turn-constructional unit – mit_{tying} + NP is neither subcategorized by a verb nor a part of a constituent which is subcategorized by a verb – The complement of mit_{tying} is a noun which is marked as definite
Function	– mit_{tying} is not a canonical symbolic part of the propositional content of the subsequent, preceding or host turn-constructional unit but rather an index (or topical keyword) – mit_{tying} + NP does not have a phrasal or a clausal scope but is a pragmatic operator with a pragmatically driven (and hence potentially far-reaching) scope – Retrospective: The complement of mit_{tying} points (back) to a topical antecedent which is considered to be intersubjectively accessible – Prospective: mit_{tying} + NP establishes the topical antecedent as an explicated topical presupposition of local speech acts in order to restrict their possible readings

---

[22] See Birkner (2006), Imo (2007), Günthner (2009) and Bücker (2009) with regard to further examples of constructions which have not been discussed as entrenched form-meaning pairings before.

Table 2: Pattern II (prototypical attributive mit_{tying} + NP)

Form	– mit_{tying} + NP is an attributive modifier of a nominal phrase as its modificand
	– The modificand of mit_{tying} + NP is both subcategorized by a verb and syntactically integrated into the front or middle field of the host turn-constructional unit
	– The complement of mit_{tying} is a noun which is marked as definite
Function	– The modificand of mit_{tying} + NP denotes an abstract concept
	– The complement of mit_{tying} is not a canonical symbolic part of the propositional content of the host turn-constructional unit but rather an index (or topical keyword)
	– Retrospective: Together, mit_{tying} + NP and its modificand point (back) to a topical antecedent which is considered to be intersubjectively accessible; this is possible because mit_{tying} + NP restricts the number of possible referents which could be assigned to the abstract modificand
	– Prospective: Together, mit_{tying} + NP and its modificand establish the topical antecedent as an accessible piece of talk (for example, a certain speech act) or information to deal with on a metapragmatic level (for example, correcting or modifying)

As one can see, the differences between these two patterns basically affect the syntactic position of mit_{tying} + NP and the question of whether the topical antecedent is being established as an explicated restrictive topical presupposition or metapragmatically assessed as a certain piece of talk or information. As far as I can see, these differences can be explained fully compositionally by the interaction of *one* tying and restrictive mit_{tying} + NP-pattern with different field positions (pre-front field, front field, middle field, end field) and different types of phrasal embedding (attributive, non-attributive):

– The integration of mit_{tying} + NP into a nominal phrase with an abstract head makes it possible to establish the topical antecedent in the predicate where it can be assessed on a metapragmatic level. As a constituent which is integrated in the predicate, the nominal phrase with mit_{tying} + NP usually occupies the front-field or the middle field and is prosodically integrated. However, the attributive use of mit_{tying} + NP blocks the capability of the topical antecedent to become a restrictive part of the presuppositions of one or more speech acts – since the scope of an attributive mit_{tying} + NP is restricted to the phrasal boundaries of the nominal phrase it is embedded in, it can only restrict the extension of the phrasal head (i.e. the number of its possible referents) but not the possible readings of complete utterances.
– The non-attributive use of a mit_{tying} + NP makes it possible to establish the topical antecedent as a restrictive part of the presuppositions of one or more speech acts since non-attributive instances of mit_{tying} + NP are neither

subject to the phrasal boundaries of a nominal phrase nor subcategorized by a verb. This explains why the pre-front field is a preferred position for the non-attributive mit_{tying} + NP – as the typical and prominent position for elements with a complex pragmatic scope (cf. Schiffrin 1988; Gohl and Günthner 1999; Auer and Günthner 2005 with regard to discourse markers, for example), the pre-front field supports the far-reaching scope of the non-attributive mit_{tying} + NP the most. However, the non-attributive use of mit_{tying} + NP blocks or at least impedes the capability of the topical antecedent to be assessed on a metapragmatic level since a non-attributive mit_{tying} + NP cannot be integrated in the verbal domain as "the location of new, narrative-advancing information" (Hopper 1979: 240).

This shows that only one mit_{tying} + NP-construction[23] needs to be assumed which can be realized either as a non-attributive constituent with a low degree of syntactic and prosodic integration (Pattern I) or as an attributive modifier with a high degree of syntactic and prosodic integration (Pattern II).[24]

4 Summary and conclusions

In this study, it has been shown that not all prepositional instances of *mit* in spoken German talk-in-interaction can be classified as instantiations of the canonical comitative, temporal, instrumental, modal, "affiliating" or "identifying" preposition *mit*. Instead, the preposition *mit* can also be used together with a nominal complement that, in the given context, refers back to a topical antecedent which is considered to be intersubjectively accessible and which is being established as a topical context for adjacent turn-constructional units. An

---

23 See also Bührig and House (2007: 349ff) who classify "extraposed prepositional phrases" (for example, "In doing this,...", "In fact,...") as "linking constructions" within a "systemic-functional" and "functional-pragmatic" approach.
24 Ronny Boogaart makes me aware of the fact that Dutch has a constructional counterpart with *met* which is only rarely used non-attributively (hence, it can be represented in terms of "NP + met_{tying} + NP"). In my opinion, this shows that in Dutch, the modificand is a fixed part of the constructional pattern while in German it is not. Accordingly, the Dutch construction usually emerges as a noun or pronoun with met_{tying} + NP as an attributive modifier while the German construction is free to be used both non-attributively and attributively. This indicates that even similar-looking constructions in closely related languages are language-specific "corners of convention in pockets of productivity" (Cappelle, this volume) which are associated with each other in terms of cross-linguistic family resemblances rather than cross-linguistic identity.

antecedent of such "topic navigating" (Chafe 2003) instances of mit_{tying} + NP can either be a preceding stretch of topic talk within the actual conversation or shared contextual, situational and encyclopedic knowledge.

Concerning the sequential distance between instances of mit_{tying} + NP and their topical antecedents, it has been possible to distinguish between small-scale topic tying (the topic is both accessible and active), mid-scale topic tying (the topic is accessible, but not necessarily active anymore) and large-scale topic tying (the topic is accessible, but definitely not active since it has either not been opened yet or it has already been closed). While the main reason for mid-scale and large-scale topic tying is the (re-)activation of a topical antecedent which is "misplaced" inasmuch as it is neither active nor expectable, this cannot be the primary reason for small-scale topic tying since it affects a topical antecedent which is still active. Instead, small-scale topic tying by means of mit_{tying} + NP can be employed as a resource to compete for the floor (mit_{tying} + NP in the pre-front field can interrupt the topical progression of the current speaker's turn and allows the indication of topical relevance within overlap while more important parts of the turn can be held back until the turn is occupied successfully) or to accomplish a list-like topical structure (it allows adjacent turn-constructional units to be tied to exactly one list item as the relevant topical antecedent).

Furthermore, this study has shown that mit_{tying} + NP can be combined with initial conjunctions and particles such as *und* 'and', *aber* 'but' or *gerade* 'especially'. With regard to such co-occurring functional items, the position in the pre-front field proves to be useful since it makes it possible to integrate mit_{tying} + NP into the scope of a preceding conjunction while the follow-up turn-constructional unit is excluded.[25] By this means, the topical antecedent of mit_{tying} + NP can be marked exclusively as a local caesura (for example, *aber*), continuation (for example, *und*) or focus (for example, *gerade*) with regard to prior turns while the subsequent speech act does not need to have the same relation to the context. This shows that co-occurring conjunctions and particles strongly interact with the syntactic position of mit_{tying} + NP and efficiently integrate it into its sequential and contextual position.

Finally, it has become obvious that mit_{tying} + NP not only ties its local context to a certain topical antecedent (in terms of a retrospective operation) but also pre-structures the subsequent course of conversation in a characteristic way. Used attributively, it helps to establish the topical antecedent as a concrete conversational action (i.e. not only as a topical antecedent but as a fully-fledged speech act antecedent, for example) or piece of information to deal with on a metapragmatic level, while its non-attributive instances establish the topical

---

25 If mit_{tying} + NP were in the front field of a host turn-constructional unit, the scope of a conjunction would not only include mit_{tying} + NP but the whole turn-constructional unit.

antecedent as an explicated topical presupposition of local speech acts in order to restrict their possible readings and localize them within the overall topical organization of the conversation.

Since the non-attributive and attributive instances of mit_{tying} + NP differ from the canonical prepositional types of *mit* both structurally and functionally, they not only belong to systematic patterns of language use but can also be regarded as constructs of a cognitively entrenched construction in the sense of Construction Grammar. This construction can be characterized as a *dialogical construction* for two reasons:

(i) Since it is a discourse-structuring resource, its characteristics cannot be sufficiently reconstructed by means of features which completely abstract from dialogue-constituting aspects. Instead, the abstract constructional body of the mit_{tying} + NP-construction contains slots which, in situated talk-in-interaction, correspond to complex conversational actions which have neither a fixed category nor a (fixed) argument role.
(ii) The instantiations of the mit_{tying} + NP-construction are neither completely pre-structured by nor completely independent from their local contexts. Instead, they are "dynamic construals" (Linell 2006) which emerge as flexible local phenomena that not only perfectly fit into "real coherent sequences of sense-making in talk (or text)" (Linell 2009a: 106) but are also major reasons for cohesion and coherence themselves.

The complex, tight and dynamic interplay between situation-transcending constructional features on the one hand and situational conditions on the other demands a linguistic approach that treats mit_{tying} + NP both as a cognitively entrenched constructional unit and an "interactional achievement" in the sense of Schegloff (1982: 75), i.e. "as something 'produced' over time, incrementally accomplished, rather than naturally born out of the speaker's forehead". Especially its nature as an "interactional achievement" makes it necessary to stick to empirical data consistently and to treat instances of mit_{tying} + NP as phenomena which demand "a grammatical analysis rooted in an understanding of all the factors underlying the use of language to accomplish social work among real people interacting with each other in real time" (Hopper and Thompson 2008: 118). For this reason, mit_{tying} + NP is a genuine object of study for a dialogical grammar which not only analyzes its "inner syntax" but also takes its "outer syntax" (i.e. antecedent and subsequent structures as well as characteristically co-occurring elements) into account (see Linell 2006: 165).[26]

---

[26] See also Auer (2000, 2005, 2007), Günthner (2011b, 2012), Linell (2009b) and Du Bois (2010). Hartung (1987: 109) postulated the need for a "Dialog-Grammatik" in the 1980s already.

References

Aitchison, Jean. 1994. "Say, say it again Sam": The treatment of repetition in linguistics. In: Andreas Fischer (ed.), *Repetition*, 15–34. Tübingen: Narr.
Altmann, Hans. 1981. *Formen der "Herausstellung" im Deutschen. Rechtsversetzung, Linksversetzung, Freies Thema und verwandte Konstruktionen*. Tübingen: Niemeyer.
Anward, Jan. 2005. Lexeme recycled. How categories emerge from interaction. *Logos and Language* 2: 31–46.
Auer, Peter. 1996. The pre-front field in spoken German and its relevance as a grammaticalization position. *Pragmatics* 6/3: 295–322.
Auer, Peter. 2000. On Line-Syntax – oder: was es bedeuten könnte, die Zeitlichkeit der mündlichen Sprache ernst zu nehmen. *Sprache und Literatur* 31/1: 43–56.
Auer, Peter. 2005. Projection in interaction and projection in grammar. *Text – Interdisciplinary Journal for the Study of Discourse* 25/1: 7–36.
Auer, Peter. 2006. Construction Grammar meets conversation: Einige Überlegungen am Beispiel von "so"-Konstruktionen. In: Susanne Günthner and Wolfgang Imo (eds.), *Konstruktionen in der Interaktion*, 291–314. Berlin/New York: Mouton de Gruyter.
Auer, Peter. 2007. Syntax als Prozess. In: Heiko Hausendorf (ed.), *Gespräch als Prozess. Linguistische Aspekte der Zeitlichkeit verbaler Interaktion*, 95–142. Tübingen: Narr.
Auer, Peter and Susanne Günthner. 2005. Die Entstehung von Diskursmarkern im Deutschen – ein Fall von Grammatikalisierung? In: Torsten Leuschner, Tanja Mortelmans and Sarah de Groodt (eds.), *Grammatikalisierung im Deutschen*, 335–362. Berlin/New York: Mouton de Gruyter.
Auer, Peter and Susanne Uhmann. 1982. Aspekte der konversationellen Organisation von Bewertungen. *Deutsche Sprache* 10: 1–32.
Barlow, Michael and Suzanne Kemmer. 2000. A schema-based approach to grammatical description. In: Suzanne Kemmer and Michael Barlow (eds.), *Usage-based Models of Language*, 19–42. Stanford: CSLI Publications.
Barth-Weingarten, Dagmar and Elizabeth Couper-Kuhlen. 2011. A system for transcribing talk-in-interaction: GAT 2. *Gesprächsforschung – Online-Zeitschrift zur verbalen Interaktion* 12: 1–51.
Birkner, Karin. 2006. (Relativ-)Konstruktionen zur Personenattribuierung: "ich bin n=mensch der…". In: Susanne Günthner and Wolfgang Imo (eds.), *Konstruktionen in der Interaktion*, 205–238. Berlin/New York: Mouton de Gruyter.
Bücker, Jörg. 2009. Quotativ-Konstruktionen mit *Motto* als Ressourcen für Selbst- und Fremdpositionierungen. In: Susanne Günthner and Jörg Bücker (eds.), *Grammatik im Gespräch: Konstruktionen der Selbst- und Fremdpositionierung*, 215–247. Berlin/New York: de Gruyter.
Bücker, Jörg. 2012. *Sprachhandeln und Sprachwissen: Grammatische Konstruktionen im Spannungsfeld von Interaktion und Kognition*. Berlin/New York: Mouton de Gruyter.
Bücker, Jörg. 2014. Konstruktionen und Konstruktionscluster: Die Zirkumposition *von XP her* im gesprochenen Deutsch. In: Alexander Lasch and Alexander Ziem (eds.), *Grammatik als Inventar von Konstruktionen? Sprachliches Wissen im Fokus der Konstruktionsgrammatik*, 117–135. Berlin/New York: Mouton de Gruyter.
Bührig, Kristin and Juliane House. 2007. "So, given in this theme…" Linking constructions in discourse across languages. In: Jochen Rehbein, Christiane Hohenstein and Lukas Pietsch

(eds.), *Connectivity in Grammar and Discourse*, 345–365. Amsterdam/Philadelphia: John Benjamins.

Bybee, Joan L. and Paul Hopper. 2001. Introduction to frequency and the emergence of linguistic structure. In: Joan Bybee and Paul Hopper (eds.), *Frequency and the Emergence of Linguistic Structures*, 1–24. Amsterdam/Philadelphia: John Benjamins.

Cappelle, Bert. this volume. Conventional combinations in pockets of productivity: English resultatives and Dutch ditransitives expressing excess.

Chafe, Wallace. 2003. The analysis of discourse flow. In: Deborah Schiffrin, Deborah Tannen and Heidi E. Hamilton (eds.), *The Handbook of Discourse Analysis*, 673–687. Oxford: Blackwell.

Couper-Kuhlen, Elizabeth and Tsuyoshi Ono. 2007. "Incrementing" in conversation. A comparison of practices in English, German and Japanese. *Pragmatics* 17/4: 513–552.

Croft, William. 2001. *Radical Construction Grammar. Syntactic Theory in Typological Perspective*. Oxford: Oxford University Press.

Deppermann, Arnulf. 2009. Verstehensdefizit als Antwortverpflichtung: Interaktionale Eigenschaften der Modalpartikel "denn" in Fragen. In: Susanne Günthner and Jörg Bücker (eds.), *Grammatik im Gespräch: Konstruktionen der Selbst- und Fremdpositionierung*, 23–56. Berlin/New York: de Gruyter.

Diewald, Gabriele. 1999. Die dialogische Bedeutungskomponente von Modalpartikeln. In: Bernd Naumann (ed.), *Dialogue Analysis and the Mass Media*. Proceedings of the International Conference, Erlangen, April 2–3, 1998, 187–199. Tübingen: Niemeyer.

Drew, Paul. 1987. Po-faced receipts of teases. *Linguistics* 25: 219–253.

Du Bois, John W. 2010. *Towards a Dialogic Syntax*. Manuscript.

Duranti, Alessandro and Elinor Ochs. 1979. Left-dislocation in Italian conversation. In: Talmy Givón (ed.), *Syntax and Semantics 12: Discourse and Syntax*, 377–418. New York: Academic Press.

Eisenberg, Ann R. 1986). Teasing: Verbal play in two Mexicano homes. In: Bambi B. Schieffelin and Elinor Ochs (eds.), *Language Socialization across Cultures*, 182–197. New York: Cambridge University Press.

Fiehler, Reinhard, Birgit Barden, Mechthild Elstermann, and Barbara Kraft. 2004 *Eigenschaften gesprochener Sprache*. Tübingen: Narr.

Fillmore, Charles J. 1977. Scenes-and-frames semantics. In: Antonio Zampolli (ed.), *Linguistic Structures Processing*, 55–81. Amsterdam/New York/Oxford: North Holland Publishing Company.

Fillmore, Charles J. 1978. On the organization of semantic information in the lexicon. In: Donka Farkas, Wesley M. Jacobsen and Karol W. Todrys (eds.), *Papers from the Parasession on the Lexicon*, 148–173. Chicago: Chicago Linguistic Society.

Fillmore, Charles J. 1988. The mechanisms of "Construction Grammar". *Proceedings of the Annual Meeting of the Berkeley Linguistics Society* 14: 33–55.

Fillmore Charles. 2008. The merging of "frames". In: Rema Rossini Favretti (ed.), *Frames, Corpora and Knowledge Representation*, 1–12. Bologna: Bononia University Press.

Fillmore, Charles J., Paul Kay and Mary Catherine O'Connor. 1988. Regularity and idiomaticity in grammatical constructions: The case of "Let Alone". *Language* 64/3: 501–538.

Fried, Mirjam and Jan-Ola Östman. 2005. Construction Grammar. A thumbnail sketch. In: Mirjam Fried and Jan-Ola Östman (eds.), *Construction Grammar in a Cross-Language Perspective*, 11–86. Amsterdam/Philadelphia: John Benjamins.

Gohl, Christine and Susanne Günthner. 1999. Grammatikalisierung von "weil" als Diskursmarker in der gesprochenen Sprache. *Zeitschrift für Sprachwissenschaft* 18/1: 39–75.
Golato, Andrea. 2005. *Compliments and Compliment Responses. Grammatical Structure and Sequential Organization*. Amsterdam/Philadelphia: John Benjamins.
Goldberg, Adele E. 1995. *Constructions: A Construction Grammar Approach to Argument Structure*. Chicago: Chicago University Press.
Goldberg, Adele E. 2006. *Constructions at Work: The Nature of Generalization in Language*. Oxford: Oxford University Press.
Goodwin, Charles. 1995. The negotiation of coherence within conversation. In: Morton Ann Gernsbacher and Talmy Givón (eds.), *Coherence in Spontaneous Text*, 117–137. Amsterdam/Philadelphia: John Benjamins.
Goodwin, Charles. 2006. Retrospective and prospective orientation in the construction of argumentative moves. *Text & Talk* 26/4–5: 443–461.
Günthner, Susanne. 1999. Entwickelt sich der Konzessivkonnektor "obwohl" zum Diskursmarker? Grammatikalisierungstendenzen im gesprochenen Deutsch. *Linguistische Berichte* 180: 409–446.
Günthner, Susanne. 2000a. *Vorwurfsaktivitäten in der Alltagsinteraktion. Grammatische, prosodische, rhetorisch-stilistische und interaktive Verfahren bei der Konstitution kommunikativer Muster und Gattungen*. Tübingen: Niemeyer.
Günthner, Susanne. 2000b. Grammatik im Gespräch: Zur Verwendung von "wobei" im gesprochenen Deutsch. *Sprache und Literatur* 85/31: 57–74.
Günthner, Susanne. 2009a. "Adjektiv + 'dass'-Satz"-Konstruktionen als kommunikative Ressourcen der Positionierung. In: Susanne Günthner and Jörg Bücker (eds.), *Grammatik im Gespräch: Konstruktionen der Selbst- und Fremdpositionierung*, 149–184. Berlin/New York: de Gruyter.
Günthner, Susanne. 2010. Grammatical constructions and communicative genres. In: Heidrun Dorgeloh and Angelika Wanner (eds.), *Syntactic Variation and Genre*, 195–217. Berlin/New York: Mouton de Gruyter.
Günthner, Susanne. 2011a. The construction of emotional involvement in everyday German narratives – interactive uses of "dense constructions". *Pragmatics* 21/4: 573–592.
Günthner, Susanne. 2011b. Dass-Konstruktionen im alltäglichen Sprachgebrauch – Facetten ihrer "interaktionalen Realität" (= GIDI Arbeitspapierreihe, No. 35).
Günthner, Susanne. 2012. Eine interaktionale Perspektive auf Wortarten: das Beispiel "und zwar". In: Björn Rothstein (ed.), *Nicht-flektierende Wortarten*, 14–47. Berlin/New York: de Gruyter.
Gundel, Jeanette K. 2010. Reference and accessibility from a Givenness Hierarchy perspective. *International Review of Pragmatics* 2: 148–168.
Gundel, Jeanette K., Nancy Hedberg and Ron Zacharski. 1993. Cognitive status and the form of referring expressions in discourse. *Language* 69: 274–307.
Hartung, Wolfdietrich. 1987. Das Dialogische als Prinzip des Sprachlichen: Positionen zwischen Kontinuität und Diskontinuität. In: Werner Neumann and Bärbel Techtmeier (eds.), *Bedeutungen und Ideen in Sprachen und Texten*, 93–111. Berlin: Akademie-Verlag.
Heritage, John. 1984. *Garfinkel and Ethnomethodology*. Cambridge: Polity Press.
Hilpert, Martin. 2009. The German *mit*-predicative construction. *Constructions and Frames* 1/1: 29–55.
Hopper, Paul. 1979. Aspect and foregrounding in discourse. In: Talmy Givón (ed.), *Syntax and Semantics 12: Discourse and Syntax*, 213–241. New York/San Francisco/London: Academic Press.

Hopper, Paul and Sandra A. Thompson. 2008. Projectability and clause combining in interaction. In: Ritva Laury (ed.), *Crosslinguistic Studies of Clause Combining: The Multifunctionality of Conjunctions*, 99–124. Amsterdam/Philadelphia: John Benjamins.
Hutchby, Ian. 2006. *Media talk: Conversation Analysis and the Study of Broadcasting*. Glasgow: Open University Press.
Imo, Wolfgang. 2007. *Construction Grammar und Gesprochene-Sprache-Forschung*. Tübingen: Niemeyer.
Imo, Wolfgang. 2010a. "Mein Problem ist/mein Thema ist" – how syntactic patterns and genres interact. In: Heidrun Dorgeloh and Angelika Wanner (eds.), *Syntactic Variation and Genre*, 141–166. Berlin/New York: Mouton de Gruyter.
Imo, Wolfgang. 2010b. Das Adverb "jetzt" zwischen Zeit- und Gesprächsdeixis. *ZGL* 38/1: 25–58.
Imo, Wolfgang. 2011. *Ad hoc-Produktion oder Konstruktion? Verfestigungstendenzen bei Inkrement-Strukturen im gesprochenen Deutsch* (= GIDI Arbeitspapierreihe, No. 29).
Jefferson, Gail. 1972. Side sequences. In: David Sudnow (ed.), *Studies in Social Interaction*, 294–338. New York: Free Press.
Jefferson, Gail. 1991. List construction as a task and resource. In: George Psathas (ed.), *Interactional Competence*, 63–92. New York: Irvington Publishers.
Jefferson, Gail. 2004. A sketch of some orderly aspects of overlap in natural conversation. In: Gene H. Lerner (ed.), *Conversation Analysis: Studies from the First Generation*, 43–59. Amsterdam/Philadelphia: John Benjamins.
Kotthoff, Helga. 1993. Disagreement and concession in disputes: on the context sensitivity of preference structures. *Language in Society* 22: 193–216.
Langacker, Ronald W. 2000. A dynamic usage-based model. In: Suzanne Kemmer and Michael Barlow (eds.), *Usage-based Models of Language*, 1–63. Stanford: CSLI Publications.
Lauterbach, Stefan. 1993. *Genitiv, Komposition und Präpositionalattribut – zum System nominaler Relationen im Deutschen*. München: Iudicium.
Lehmus, Ursula. 1983. *Attribut oder Satzglied? Untersuchungen zum postnominalen Präpositionalausdruck unter einem syntaktischen, semantischen und kommunikativ-pragmatischen Aspekt*. Helsinki: Suomalainen Tiedeakatemia.
Lenk, Uta. 1998. *Marking Discourse Coherence. Functions of discourse markers in spoken English*. Tübingen: Narr.
Linell, Per. 2001. *Approaching Dialogue: Talk, Interaction and Contexts in Dialogical Perspectives*. Amsterdam/Philadelphia: John Benjamins.
Linell, Per. 2006. Towards a dialogical linguistics. In: Mika Lähteenmäki, Hannele Dufva, Sirpa Leppänen and Piia Varis (eds.), *Proceedings of the XII. International Bakhtin Conference, Jyväskylä, Finland, 18–22 July, 2005*, 157–172. Finland: Department of Languages, University of Jyväskylä.
Linell, Per. 2009a. Grammatical constructions in dialogue. In: Alexander Bergs and Gabriele Diewald (eds.), *Context and Constructions*, 97–110. Amsterdam/Philadelphia: John Benjamins.
Linell, Per. 2009b. *Rethinking Language, Mind, and World Dialogically*. Charlotte: Information Age Publishing.
Miller, Peggy. 1986. Teasing as language socialization and verbal play in a white working class community. In: Bambi B. Schieffelin and Elinor Ochs (eds.), *Language Socialization across Cultures*, 199–212. New York: Cambridge University Press.

Ochs Keenan, Elinor and Bambi Schieffelin. 1976. Foregrounding referents: A reconsideration of left dislocation in discourse. *Proceedings of the Second Annual Meeting of the Berkeley Linguistics Society*: 240–257.
Pomerantz, Anita. 1984. Agreeing and disagreeing with assessments: Some features of preferred/dispreferred turn shapes. In: Maxwell Atkinson and John Heritage (eds.), *Structures of Social Action*, 57–101. Cambridge: Cambridge University Press.
Schegloff, Emanuel A. 1982. Discourse as an interactional achievement. In: Deborah Tannen (ed.), *Analyzing discourse: Text and talk*, 71–93. Washington: Georgetown University Press.
Schegloff, Emanuel, Gail Jefferson, and Harvey Sacks. 1977. The preference for self-correction in the organization of repair in conversation. *Language* 53: 361–382.
Schegloff, Emanuel and Harvey Sacks. 1973. Opening up closings. *Semiotica* 7: 289–327.
Schierholz, Stefan J. 2001. *Präpositionalattribute. Syntaktische und semantische Analysen*. Tübingen: Niemeyer.
Schierholz, Stefan J. 2004. Valenzvererbung? Präpositionalattributskonstruktionen und ihre Herleitung. In: Speranta Stanescu (ed.), *Die Valenztheorie. Bestandsaufnahme und Perspektiven*, 79–96. Frankfurt: Lang.
Schiffrin, Deborah. 1988. *Discourse Markers*. Cambridge: Cambridge University Press.
Searle, John R. 1969. *Speech Acts: An Essay in the Philosophy of Language*. Cambridge: Cambridge University Press.
Selting, Margret. 1993. Voranstellungen vor den Satz: Zur grammatischen Form und interaktiven Funktion von Linksversetzung und Freiem Thema im Deutschen. *Zeitschrift für Germanistische Linguistik* 21: 291–319.
Selting, Margret. 2004. Listen: Sequenzielle und prosodische Struktur einer kommunikativen Praktik – eine Untersuchung im Rahmen der Interaktionalen Linguistik. *Zeitschrift für Sprachwissenschaft* 23/1: 1–46.
Selting, Margret and Friederike Kern. 2009. On some syntactic and prosodic structures of Turkish German in talk-in-interaction. *Journal of Pragmatics* 41/12: 2496–2514.
Selting, Margret, et al. 2009. Gesprächsanalytisches Transkriptionssystem 2 (GAT 2). *Gesprächsforschung – Online-Zeitschrift zur verbalen Interaktion* 10: 353–402.
Siepmann, Dirk. 2003. Second-level discourse markers across languages. *Languages in Contrast* 3/2: 253–287.
Silverstein, Michael. 1993. Metapragmatic discourse and metapragmatic function. In: John Arthur Lucy (ed.), *Reflexive Language: Reported Speech and Metapragmatics*, 33–58. Cambridge: Cambridge University Press.
Tannen, Deborah. 1989. *Talking voices: Repetition, Dialogue, and Imagery in Conversational Discourse*. Cambridge: Cambridge University Press.
Teubert, Wolfgang. 1979. *Valenz des Substantivs*. Düsseldorf: Schwann.
Tomasello, Michael. 2003. *Constructing a Language: A Usage-Based Theory of Language Acquisition*. Harvard: Harvard University Press.
Zifonun, Gisela, Ludger Hoffmann, and Bruno Strecker (1997): *Grammatik der deutschen Sprache*. Drei Bände. Berlin/New York: de Gruyter.

Appendix: Transcription conventions

The examples cited in this study are transcribed according to the standards set out in the "Gesprächsanalytisches Transkriptionssystem 2" (GAT 2; cf. Selting et al. 2009 and Barth-Weingarten and Couper-Kuhlen 2011 for an English translation). The following list comprises only those transcription conventions which occur in the samples:

(i) Sequential features

[ ]	Two or more pairs of square brackets mark a temporal overlap among turns produced by two or more speakers
( )	A pair of round brackets marks an incomprehensible stretch of talk
=	The equal sign marks the end and the beginning of two intonation units which follow each other without an intervening gap ("latching")

(ii) Pauses

(1.8)	Time specifications enclosed in parentheses indicate a timed pause measured in seconds and deciseconds
(.)	A period enclosed in parentheses indicates a micropause of less than 0.25 seconds
(-)	One or more hyphens enclosed in parentheses indicate a pause ranging from 0.25 to 0.75 seconds (the length of the pause is indicated by using one, two or three hyphens)

(iii) Pitch contour and pitch change

,	A comma indicates a slightly rising pitch contour at the end of an intonation unit
?	A question mark indicates a rising pitch contour at the end of an intonation unit
;	A semicolon indicates a slightly falling pitch contour at the end of an intonation unit
.	A period indicates a falling pitch contour at the end of an intonation unit
-	A hyphen indicates a neither rising nor falling pitch contour at the end of an intonation unit

(iv) Accentuation and volume

GRANDfather	Capitalization of a syllable indicates that the syllable carries the primary accent within the respective intonation unit
grAndfather	Capitalization of the nucleus of a syllable indicates that the syllable carries the secondary accent within the respective intonation unit

(v) Further conventions

°h	A degree sign followed by an "h" indicates an audible inhalation of breath (the length of the inhalation is indicated by using one, two or three "h's")
h°	An "h" followed by a degree sign indicates an audible exhalation of breath (the length of the exhalation is indicated by using one, two or three "h's")
:	Colons indicate a sustained enunciation of a syllable (the length of the sustained syllable is indicated by using one, two or three colons)
<< operator> scope>	Angle brackets are used to define an operator which is valid for a stretch of talk within its scope; the operator "dim", for example, indicates a voice which is continuously decreasing in loudness ("diminuendo")
(( ))	A pair of doubled round brackets marks non-verbal actions and events
_	An underscore character indicates two turn-constructional units which follow each other without an intervening gap within an intonation unit
→	Horizontal arrows indicate important lines in the transcript

Wolfgang Imo

11 Appositions in monologue, increments in dialogue?
On appositions and apposition-like patterns in spoken German and their status as constructions

1 Introduction[1]

Typically, so-called wide appositions of the pattern *NP + NP* are used to provide additional information about a newly introduced referent. In written, monologically oriented language this pattern is fairly common, but it is also used in monological settings in spoken language, as the following example shows:[2]

Example 1: radio interview

5	H	→	*mIr gegenüber sitzt nun markus ERtel,*
			'opposite of me is now sitting Markus Ertel'
6		→	*einer der verANstalter dieses projEkts. (1.0)*
			'one of the organizers of this project'
7			*markus ERtel,*
			'Markus Ertel'
8			*die HEUrige bürgermesse hat ein motto das lAUtet, (-)*
			'this year's citizens' fair has got a motto that says'
9			*was ALle Angeht können nur alle lÖsen. (-)*
			'what concerns everybody can only be solved by everybody'

The example is taken from a radio interview. The host of the radio program (H) has just started greeting the audience and, beginning in line 5, he introduces his guest and interview partner, Markus Ertel. In lines 5 to 6 the radio host uses a traditional wide apposition, linking the name "markus ERtel" with the co-referential noun phrase "one of the organizers of this project", which helps his audience identify the interviewee.

---

[1] I would like to thank Daniel Ross for proofreading the text.
[2] The transcription conventions are listed on the last page. All names were anonymized. The proper name of the citizens' fair in line 8 has been replaced by the words "citizens' fair".

If one compares monologically and interactionally oriented spoken data, a striking observation can be made. In monological sequences such as in example 1, where the host can talk without fearing interruption, typical wide appositions occur, while in interactional sequences, such as in example 2, where a constant change of speaker turns occurs, a different structure is used:

Example 2: private phone call

03	S2		*von wo rufst DU denn an;*
			'where are you calling from'
04			(–)
05	S1	→	*äh von SKYPE weil unser tElefon so rAUscht die Anlage, (-)*
			'erm via Skype because our telephone is so noisy the system'
06	S2		*ach SO; (-)*
			'oh all right'
07	S1		*wieso WEIL äh::- (-)*
			'why because erm'
08			*(ma) keine NUMmer angezeigt wurde oder warUm.*
			'(my) no number was shown (on the display) or why'
09	S2		*NE: weil; (.)*
			'no because'
10			*keine NUMmer angezeigt wurde;*
			'no number was shown'

Transcript 2 is taken from a private telephone conversation between two sisters (S1 and S2). S2 asks her sister where she is calling from, because her telephone display does not show the caller's telephone number. S1 replies that she is using the computer software Skype and not her telephone because she has technical problems with her telephone. The noun phrase "our telephone" is expanded by the vaguely co-referential noun phrase "the system". This second noun phrase could have been placed next to the first one to create an – albeit slightly odd-sounding – "monological" wide apposition (e.g. "our telephone, the system, is so noisy") but here it is placed *after* the finite verb ("rauscht / is noisy"). Therefore, in terms of *Interactional Linguistics*, the phrase "the system" rather resembles an increment (e.g. Couper-Kuhlen and Ono 2007) and not an apposition.

The aim of this paper is to show how a combination of *Interactional Linguistics* (Couper-Kuhlen and Selting 2001) with *Construction Grammar* (e.g. Goldberg 1996; Croft 2002) can be used to create an approach that may be called *Interactional Construction Grammar* (see also Deppermann 2006) that is able to explain the constructional status and network relations of both of the patterns presented here.

2 (Interactional) Construction Grammar

The term *Construction Grammar* does not denote a single theory but rather – in the sense of the plural form *Construction Grammars* (Östman and Fried 2005) – refers to what Fischer and Stefanowitsch (2006: 3; my translation) call a "family of theories that all share the conviction that human language consists of signs (i.e. form-meaning pairings) on all linguistic levels". This focus on the sign-based nature of language goes back to the very foundations of *Construction Grammar*. Fillmore (1988: 36), for example, defines grammatical constructions as syntactic patterns which are "assigned one or more conventional functions in a language". For Croft (2002: 21), too, what is decisive about *Construction Grammar* is the fact that it "treats grammatical units as fundamentally symbolic, that is, pairings of grammatical form and the corresponding meaning or semantic structure".

This extension of the (Saussurean) sign to all linguistic levels, such as phonology, morphology, syntax, text and discourse,[3] is not just shared by those approaches that include the words *Construction Grammar* in their name (e.g. Croft's 2002 *Radical Construction Grammar*, Bergen and Chang's 2005 *Embodied Construction Grammar*, Sag's 2011 *Sign-based Construction Grammar* or Van Trijp's 2008 and Steels's 2011 *Fluid Construction Grammar*) but also by many of those within the field of *Cognitive Grammar*. Langacker's (1987) *Cognitive Grammar* is indeed so similar to *Construction Grammar* approaches that Goldberg (1998: 205) opts for an interchangeability of both terms: "*Construction Grammar* (also *Cognitive Grammar*)". In a textbook about *Cognitive Grammar*, Taylor (2002: 20–21) provides the following basic definition of what *Cognitive Grammar* is about:

> *Cognitive Grammar* is driven by the idea that language is essentially and inherently symbolic in nature. Linguistic expressions symbolize, or stand for, conceptualizations. I shall refer to this basic assumption as the symbolic thesis. [...] The symbolic thesis actually amounts to little more than the claim that language is in essence a means for relating sound and meaning. [...] What is special about the *Cognitive Grammar* approach is that syntax itself is regarded as inherently symbolic, and is therefore handled in terms of symbolic relations between phonological and semantic structures. (Taylor 2002: 20–21)

---

[3] For an extension of the range of *Construction Grammar* to text and discourse patterns see Östman (2005) and to genres Günthner (2006b; 2010) and Imo (2010).

Despite some recent criticism (e.g. Jacobs 2008) of attempts at viewing the whole of language as signs, the "symbolic thesis" (Taylor 2002: 38–60) is still one of the mainstays of both *Construction* and *Cognitive Grammar*.

The reason why the idea of treating everything from morphemes to texts or discourse patterns as constructions appears so attractive to many linguists is that the concept of *meaning* has been extended considerably in *Construction Grammar*. While for Saussure signs simply consist of *form* and *meaning*, constructions consist of pairings "of form with meaning/use" (Goldberg 1996: 68). This extension implies that a construction not only contains information about its semantic (and maybe functional) properties, but also includes every relevant fact about the context it usually occurs in. In other words, "facts about the use of entire constructions, including facts about registers, restricted dialect variation etc., are stated as part of the construction" (Goldberg 1996: 69).

Especially for empirically oriented linguists, for whom most theories of syntax are problematic because of their tendencies to attempt maximally context-free descriptions of rules and patterns, *Construction Grammar* may offer a way to include any type of information into a construction that empirical analyses prove important. Because of this advantage, there have been some attempts in recent years within the field of *Conversation Analysis* and *Interactional Linguistics* to establish an approach within *Construction Grammar* which could be called *Interactional Construction Grammar* (Auer 2006b; Deppermann 2006; Günthner 2006a, b, c, Günthner and Imo 2006; Imo 2006, 2007a, b, 2008, 2009, 2011a, b, 2012; Zima and Brône 2011). In an article published in 2006, for example, Deppermann (2006: 1) asks whether *Construction Grammar* could be expanded into a "grammar for interaction". The reason why *Construction Grammar* might indeed be a useful theory of syntax for *Interactional Linguistics* is that three basic tenets are shared by both approaches. First, the idea of viewing the basic units of language as holistic gestalts – i.e. constructions – which include all relevant information about their morphological, syntactic, prosodic, functional, sequential, situational and genre-related properties. Second, the symbolic thesis, which claims that there are no merely formal structures but that there is always a combination of formal and functional aspects. Third, the usage-based approach that both *Construction Grammar* and *Interactional Linguistics/Conversation Analysis* share, i.e. the idea that constructions emerge out of repeated use in interactions via routinization processes. Drawing on converging interests between these approaches, Deppermann (2006: 43) arrives at the following conclusion:

> Commonalities of *Construction Grammar* and *Conversation Analysis* with respect to these three claims are sketched. As a conclusion, the paper argues for the combination of detailed sequential analysis in a CA mode with corpus-linguistic methods, and it pleads for the integration of cognitive and interactive perspectives on the meaning and use of grammatical constructions.

With *Construction Grammar*, it is possible to reformulate the findings of *Interactional Linguistics/Conversation Analysis* – which are always based on detailed, highly qualitative, sequential and context-sensitive analyses – within the framework of a theory of syntax that, in turn, opens up new vistas for *Interactional Linguistics/Conversation Analysis*. These new vistas concern the morphological, semantic and general cognitive aspects of constructions about which the strictly empirical approach of *Interactional Linguistics/Conversation Analysis* has to be silent for methodological reasons:

> On the other hand it is clear that Conversation Analysis is not able to explain quite a lot of properties of constructions. [...] Most of all, this concerns morphological and semantic aspects that only rarely provide the basis for conversation, and if they do, they do it only in a very superficial way. Therefore, it is necessary to draw on cognitive concepts [...].
> (Deppermann 2006: 61; my translation)

Many of the cognitive concepts mentioned by Deppermann can be provided by *Construction Grammar*. One important concept that allows for many of the aforementioned aspects to be explained is the idea of a network of constructions, which is taken as the repository of the organization of the grammatical (i.e. constructional) knowledge of a language (see, for example, Boas 2010). Usually, the inventory of constructions is conceptualized as some kind of a "structured inventory" that contains – in a very broad sense – the "speaker's knowledge of the conventions of their language" (Croft 2002: 25). Croft's wide focus on the "conventions" of a given language has the advantage that it is possible to include any kind of information that is necessary to describe the form and function of a given construction as well as all types of relations to more or less similar neighboring constructions into the description of a construction.

The concept of a structured network has another great advantage. It makes it possible to explain processes of the "blending" (Fauconnier 2004) or "amalgamation" (Günthner 2006c; Imo 2007b) of constructions as well as processes of grammaticalization, pragmaticalization and lexicalization. All of these phenomena can be viewed as results of a shifting of positions of single constructions within the whole network, the construct-icon. It is important to keep in mind this constantly emerging structure of the construct-icon and not to fall into the trap of viewing this network as a permanently fixed inventory: "Our characterization of schematic networks has emphasized their 'static' properties, but it is important to regard them as dynamic, continually evolving structures. A schematic network is shaped, maintained and modified by the pressures of language use." (Langacker 1987: 381)

In spite of the commonalities between *Interactional Linguistics* and *Construction Grammar* – the focus on processes of routinization as a driving force of language and the demand for sign-based, holistic descriptions including information about prosody, context etc. – many questions still remain unanswered. One of the most important problems that emerges when *Construction Grammar* and *Interactional Linguistics* are combined is how to reconcile the rather schematic, pattern-based approach of *Construction Grammar* with the process-oriented approach of *Interactional Linguistics*, in which syntax is viewed as an open, temporally emergent structure: Auer (2000) uses the term "on-line syntax" to refer to the fact that much of language is produced incrementally and that these increments are often triggered by factors outside of "syntax proper". For example, a sentence can be expanded by adding new material in a piecemeal fashion if the recipient does not react or shows a lack of understanding (e.g. Auer 2007b and the whole special issue of Pragmatics 2007 edited by Couper-Kuhlen and Ono on "Turn continuation in cross-linguistic perspective"). The problem of incremental utterance expansion will be addressed in this paper by contrasting the use of wide appositions in monological stretches of talk and incremental, apposition-like structures in interactional stretches of talk.

3 Appositions in German

Appositions are a syntactic phenomenon that is extremely difficult to describe. The reason is that a wide variety of very different patterns are grouped under the heading of *appositions*, which leads to attempts to differentiate at least between so-called *wide* and *narrow* appositions (i.e. between structures such as *König Wilhelm* ['King William'] and *Wilhelm, der König* ['William, the king']). The Duden reference grammar (2005: 990; my translation), for example, stresses the fact that the term *apposition* is used to refer to "a range of different constructions" which share the following features: They are noun phrases that refer to another noun or a noun phrase, they either have the same case as the noun phrase they are modifying or the neutral nominative case and they are not introduced by some special marker such as a preposition or a conjunction. The "Grammatik der Deutschen Sprache" (Zifonun, Hoffmann, and Strecker 1997: 2042) takes this basic definition as its starting point, but the authors then differentiate between what they call "loose/wide/slack apposition" and "narrow/rather narrow apposition" (1997: 2043). They argue that the latter type of apposition – which includes structures such as *King John, John Brown* or *my friend John* – ought not to be called appositions but "expanded nouns" ("Erweiterungsnomen"). Only wide appositions such as *I met John, my old friend, in London.* are treated as appositions proper in this view. In his "Grundriss der deutschen

Grammatik", Eisenberg (2004: 254; my translation) explicitly states the problems that arise when describing appositions: "There is no consensus about what 'apposition' may mean and, furthermore, there are a lot of emerging and changing constructions. With appositions, it becomes much more complicated than with other syntactic structures to draw a line between grammatical and ungrammatical expressions."[4] Eisenberg (2004: 255; my translation) uses a selection of made-up sentences to illustrate these problems:

a. *Ronald – er ist der berühmte Kammersänger – tritt in Berlin auf.*
   'Ronald – he is the well-known singer – will perform in Berlin.'

b. *Ronald – berühmter Kammersänger – tritt in Berlin auf.*
   'Ronald – well-known singer – will perform in Berlin.'

c. *Ronald, der berühmte Kammersänger, tritt in Berlin auf.*
   'Ronald, the well-known singer, will perform in Berlin.'

d. *Ronald der berühmte Kammersänger tritt in Berlin auf.*
   'Ronald the well-known singer will perform in Berlin.'

e. *Der berühmte Kammersänger Ronald tritt in Berlin auf.*
   'The well-known singer Ronald will perform in Berlin.'

Eisenberg (2004: 255) excludes the first two examples (a and b) from his list of potential candidates for appositions because he claims that in those sentences the noun phrases "he is a well-known singer" (example a) and "well-known singer" (example b) are parenthetical utterances which are independent of and not integrated into the surrounding sentence.

The examples c, d and e, in contrast, are classified as appositions because, according to Eisenberg (2004: 255), appositions have to combine with another unit (usually a noun phrase) to form a larger, unified noun phrase that is to be treated as a single constituent. In all three cases, the complete appositional structure (*Ronald, the well-known singer* in example c, *Ronald the well-known singer* in example d and *The well-known singer Ronald* in example e) can be replaced by the single pronoun *he* while in examples a and b this would not be possible, according to Eisenberg (2004: 255).[5]

While it is marginally possible to differentiate between appositions and related structures such as parentheses or relative clauses on syntactic or orthographic/

---

[4] See also Molitor (1977: 19).
[5] This test is problematic, in my opinion, as it seems to rely more on information structure (given/new; backgrounded/foregrounded) than on syntactic structure. It has to suffice here, though, as there are no better tests available.

prosodic grounds,[6] the differentiation between wide and narrow appositions is much more difficult. Eisenberg (2004: 255; my translation) proposes calling example c a wide apposition but examples d and e narrow appositions. He concedes, though, that "it is not really clear what wide and narrow means" (Eisenberg 2004: 255) and tries to argue – although not with a lot of conviction – that wide appositions are marked off orthographically or prosodically while narrow appositions are integrated. There are no empirical studies concerning these hypotheses, so I would rather follow Duden (2005: 990) and Zifonun, Hoffmann, and Strecker (1997: 2042) and classify d as a wide apposition and e as a narrow apposition (Duden) or expanded noun (Zifonun, Hoffmann, and Strecker).

For my analysis, I will focus mainly on wide appositions, namely appositions of the type *NP + NP* (or types c and d in Eisenberg's list of examples cited above). One important criterion for these appositions is that in those cases where one of the two NPs is a proper name, the noun phrase containing the proper name usually comes first and is then followed by a noun phrase including additional information.

4 The data

The corpus I searched for candidate appositions contains about twenty hours of spoken German. Among the communicative genres that are represented in the data are both very informal interactions (telephone as well as face-to-face conversations between friends or family members) and more formal interactions (radio talk programs, psychological counseling on the radio, radio and TV interviews, and TV talk shows). These data are part of the *linguistische Audio Datenbank (lAuDa)* of Susanne Günthner (Münster). The spoken data were transcribed according to the GAT 2 standards developed by Selting et al. (2009).[7] The transcripts were searched "by hand" (the reason for this was that, first, these data are not annotated and, second, I was interested in all possible related structures besides prototypical wide appositions) for candidate structures that

---

[6] In his analysis of appositions in English, Meyer (1992) avoids the problems of a formal classification by treating relative clauses or discourse structuring phrases (*I've got to ask you two things: First,... Second...*) as appositions, too. The advantage of this approach is to avoid detailed definitions, while the disadvantage is a very heterogeneous collection of phenomena.
[7] For an English translation of the transcription conventions see Couper-Kuhlen/Barth-Weingarten (2011).

fulfill the criteria of two noun phrases that may be said to form a single constituent and where one noun phrase provides additional information about the other.[8] It turned out that wide appositions are an extremely rare phenomenon in spoken German, as the total number within those twenty hours was a mere 23 instances (including those repair-like cases discussed at the end of the paper). Of these, six were produced in monological circumstances and the rest in interactional settings.

5 Analysis

What became obvious after I had searched the transcripts and classified the possible appositions is a strong bias for prototypical wide appositions to be restricted to those passages of talk where a monological speaker situation prevails. Wide appositions typically occur within newscasts – where there is only one speaker anyway – or at the beginning of radio or TV programs, where a new interviewee is introduced to the audience and where the radio or TV host is sure of not being interrupted by any invited guest (interviewee, talk partner etc.). In interactional passages, on the other hand, where speaker change is always possible, I could not find a single instance of a traditional wide apposition. Instead, a kind of repair or incrementing structure can be found in these interactional data that loosely resembles an apposition. It, too, consists of two noun phrases which belong closely together, but this structure has a different syntactic format as well as partly different functions compared to "monological" appositions.

5.1 Appositions in monological passages of talk

A very typical place for appositions is radio and TV newscasts. The following example is taken from the middle of a radio news program. The news presenter (NP) is talking about the death of the former Argentine president Néstor Kirchner:

---

[8] Sometimes, as Eisenberg (2004: 255) shows, there are cases where it is no longer clear which part is appositive and which is the core. Both noun phrases are both mutually appositive and provide the core for each other. In these cases it might be more appropriate to assume a symmetrical relationship between both noun phrases.

330 — Wolfgang Imo

Example 3: radio newscast

0089	NP	.hh (.) *der frühere argentinische präsident KIRCHner ist tot.*
		'the former Argentine president Kirchner is dead'
0090		*.hh nach berichten örtlicher MEdien;*
		'according to local news agencies'
0091		*starb er im alter von sechzig JAHren,*
		'he died sixty years of age'
0092		*an einem HERZinfarkt.*
		'from a heart attack'
0093	→	*.hh kirchner galt neben seiner FRAU,*
		'Kirchner was considered alongside his wife'
0094	→	*der amtierenden staatschefin chrisTIna kirchner;*
		'the current head of state Christina Kirchner'
0095		*.hh als einflussreichster poLItiker des südamerikanischen landes.*
		'to be the most influential politician of the South American country'

This short transcript contains three appositions. First, in line 0089, there is a narrow apposition (or expanded noun) of the type *title/function + proper name*: "der frühere argentinische präsident KIRCHner / the former Argentine president Kirchner". As I will only focus on wide appositions here, I will not analyze this pattern in detail. The function of this type of narrow apposition is to provide the listeners with relevant information about the status, profession, function, titles and gender together with the (usually newly introduced) proper name of a person that is talked about.[9] Often, honorific functions are important, too, but in this example the information about the profession of the former president is the central piece of information that is added to the proper name *Kirchner*.[10]

What is more important for my analysis here is the wide apposition in lines 093 and 094. There are two noun phrases – "seiner FRAU / his wife" and "der amtierenden staatschefin chrisTIna kirchner / the current head of state Christina Kirchner" – which belong closely together and might be said to form one unified

---

9 E.g. *His Excellency Jones* (status/title/gender), *Professor Jones* (status, profession, title), *actor/actress Jones* (profession, gender), *linesman Jones* (function/profession/gender) etc.
10 This information is very important here because the name Kirchner is not widely associated with the former president of Argentina and, furthermore, it is also an ordinary German name, so a German audience might be at a loss concerning the referent of the name. With an uncommon name such as Barack Obama the additional information *President Barack Obama* would not be as vital.

constituent. Both phrases together could be replaced by the pronoun *her* and both have the same case marking. What is difficult here, though, is to decide which noun phrase provides the core and which the appositional phrase. Both constellations would work. Either "the current head of state Christina Kirchner" modifies "his wife" or vice versa. This is one of the cases Eisenberg (2004: 255) would classify as a mutually appositive, symmetrical structure. If the "on-line" (i.e. temporal) structure of these utterances is taken into account, though, it seems more plausible to view "the current head of state Christina Kirchner" as the appositional element. The noun phrase "seiner FRAU / his wife" is prosodically strongly integrated into the utterance in line 0093 and, therefore, fills the argument slot of the preposition "neben / next to", while the noun phrase "the current head of state Christina Kirchner" is realized within a separate intonation phrase and is therefore prosodically isolated from the rest of the utterance in lines 0093 and 0095. Furthermore, the noun phrase in line 0094 contains an additional narrow apposition, i.e. "der amtierenden staatschefin / the current head of state", which provides the relevant piece of information about the function and profession of Christina Kirchner, setting off the whole noun phrase even further from "seiner FRAU / his wife". What, then, is the function of the apposition in line 0094? According to Weinrich (2005), "wide" post-positioned appositions are often used to provide additional pieces of information which characterize a newly introduced person: "When an apposition follows a reference to a person or a proper name [...], it is often used to highlight a certain aspect of the biography of the person named" (Weinrich 2005: 362; my translation). This is in line with Meyer's (1992: 74) findings. In an empirical study of the use of appositions in English and American written and spoken language he comes to the conclusion that the main semantic function of appositions (about 59%) is to give more specific information about a previously mentioned unit. Among the functional sub-classes of *specification*, Meyer (1992: 74) lists "identification", "appellation", "particularization" and "exemplification". *Identification* refers to the function of providing recipients with enough further information to help them understand which person or concept one is referring to, *appellation* concerns post-positioned proper nouns which provide the name of a person or an object mentioned before, with *particularization* Meyer refers to processes of narrowing down the choice of things or persons one is referring to and with *exemplification* an example is given after a previously mentioned noun phrase to ease understanding. The wide apposition in example 3 can be categorized both as providing additional identification (Christina Kirchner is not just the wife of former president Néstor Kirchner but has also twice been elected as president of Argentina herself) and appellation (her name is Christina Kirchner).

The use of the two narrow appositions and one wide one in this short news broadcast allows for a tight and very economic packing of information, which is made possible by the planning time a news presenter has. Usually, the text is written before the newscast and then read. Complex syntactic structures are no problem, therefore, because the written manuscript helps the presenter keep track of what he already said and how to finish his sentence.

The next example of a typical wide apposition has already been presented in the introduction. It is taken from a radio interview. An Austrian radio host (H) talks with Markus Ertel, who organizes an exhibition/fair about the future of civil society. The program has just started and the radio host introduces his guest and interviewee:

Example 4: radio interview

5   H   →   *mIr gegenüber sitzt nun markus ERtel,*
            'opposite of me is now sitting Markus Ertel'
6   →   *einer der verANstalter dieses projEkts. (1.0)*
            'one of the organizers of this project'
7   *markus ERtel,*
            'Markus Ertel'
8   *die HEUrige bürgermesse hat ein motto das lAUtet, (-)*
            'this year's citizens' fair has got a motto that says'
9   *was ALle Angeht können nur alle lÖsen. (-)*
            'what concerns everybody can only be solved by everybody'

Again, the basic communicative situation is monological, although much less so than in example 3, where a written manuscript is read. Nevertheless, the radio host, too, had enough time to think beforehand about how to introduce his guest and he knows that there is little opportunity for interruption until his introduction is finished. The basic structure of this wide apposition is prototypical insofar as the first noun phrase consists of a proper name ("markus ERtel"; line 5) which is followed by a complex noun phrase giving additional information about this person ("einer der verANstalter dieses projEkts / one of the organizers of this project"; line 6). This ties in quite well with Weinrich's (2005: 362) claim that wide appositions often provide information about the properties of a newly introduced referent. In Meyer's (1992: 74) terms, the semantics of this apposition can again be placed within the wider area of "specification", with its sub-functions of "identification", "appellation", "particularization" and "exemplification". More specifically, it concerns the specifications necessary for the proper "identification" of the referent. It helps those of the radio audience who have heard about the upcoming citizens' fair to identify Markus Ertel as its organizer.

Again, by using the construction of a wide apposition, the radio host is able not just to pack a lot of information into a given syntactic structure, but he can also use the special properties of wide appositions for structuring information. According to Meyer (1992: 93), in English and American appositions new information is given in between 71 and 93% of all cases. In written texts as well as monological spoken passages this percentage is higher because there the writer/speaker has the necessary time to plan his utterances carefully and, therefore, make full use of the information structuring properties of appositions.

So far, prototypical wide appositions have been analyzed. The following transcript contains two rather unusual appositions that oscillate between narrow and wide appositions. Example 5 is taken from a radio talk program where listeners can call and get free astrologic counseling by the invited astrologer Walter (W). The function of the radio host (H) is to introduce every new caller and provide the astrologer as well as the radio audience with the relevant background information about the callers, which he receives from his team working in the background. Caller Stefan (S) is the second caller during that day's program:

Example 5: radio talk (psychological counseling)

152	H	*WALter jetzt gehts um ne pArtnerschaftsgeschichte.*
		'Walter now it's about partnership troubles'
153	T	*ja::?*
		'yes'
154	H	*und zwar (.) äh HAbe ich,*
		'well ehm I have'
155		*ich WEIß nicht entweder den stefan,*
		'I don't know either the Stefan'
156		*oder die ANna am tElefon,*
		'or the Anna in the line'
157		*hallo ihr BEIden,*
		'hello both of you'
158	S	*äh ICH bins-*
		'ehm it's me'
159		*[MOIN-]*
		'hi'

160	H		[STEfan.]
			'Stefan'
161	S		jo.
			'yes'
162	H		HI::::;
			'hi'
163			so [ich] ich-
			'so I I'
164	S		[ja;]
			'yes'
165	H	→	deine FREUNdin,
			'your girlfriend'
166		→	die ANna,
			'the Anna'
167			ist die AUCH in der nÄhe?
			'is she near, too'
168	S		jA die liegt im BETT;
			'yes she's lying in bed'
169			hört ZU;
			'listening'
170	H		na okay dann können wir ja bisschen inTImer über die anna sprechen,
			'well okay then we can have a more intimate talk about the Anna'
171	S		geNAU;
			'right'
172			sie HÖRTS ja nich.
			'because she cannot hear it'
173	H		ich ich sAge ganz kurz DU bist ähm jAhrgang neunzehnhundertsechsundsiebzig,
			'I I quickly say you were ehm born in 1976'
174	S		mhm.
			'mhm'

---

11 It is not clear why the radio host comes to that conclusion. My guess is that he didn't listen properly to what Stefan said and therefore missed Stefan's "hört ZU / listening" in line 169. He probably only heard that Anna is in bed and so inferred that she is not listening to the radio program. Interestingly enough, Stefan does not correct the host but confirms his intention to have a "more intimate talk" (line 170) about Anna.

175	H	→	*und deine FREUNdin die Anna ist jahrgang nEUnundsiebzig-*
			'and your girlfriend the Anna was born in 79'
176			*du bist in BREmen geboren-*
			'you were born in Bremen'
177			*und sie in SACHsen in mUsterstadt.*
			'and she in Saxony in Musterstadt'
178	S		*JA genau.*
			'yes right'

What is remarkable here is the strong preference of the radio host to use the definite article *der/die* in front of a proper name. This feature is usually associated with "southern German and partially middle German colloquial speech" (Zifonun, Hoffmann, and Strecker 1997: 1932) but the radio host is from northern Germany, which indicates that it seems to be a more common colloquial German pattern. During the whole of the radio talk program a total of four callers were counseled by the astrologer Walter. All callers were introduced by the radio host with a combination of definite article and proper name and the host even refers to the invited astrologer as "der Walter / the Walter" several times.

So, when the host introduces "den stefan / the Stefan" and "die ANna / the Anna", the use of the article is not very remarkable in the given context. It becomes important, though, in lines 165 and 166 as well as in line 175, because the definite article prevents the utterance "your girlfriend *the* Anna" to be analyzed as a narrow apposition (i.e. expanded noun), which would have to be realized as "your girlfriend Anna". In lines 165 and 166 the separation between the two noun phrases is further marked by the fact that both "deine FREUNdin" ('your girlfriend') and "die ANna" ('the Anna') are realized in separate intonation phrases. So, while the apposition in line 175 – "deine FREUNdin die Anna / your girlfriend the Anna" – might still be classified as a narrow apposition – albeit a rather unusual one – because of the prosodic integration of both noun phrases, this is not possible with "deine FREUNdin, die ANna" (lines 165–166). This supports Eisenberg's (2004: 255) claim that a neat separation into different classes of appositions is not possible but that there are gliding scales between "more wide" and "more narrow" appositions.

Concerning the functions of the two appositions in lines 165/166 and 175, things become even more complicated. Again, the first case can be explained quite well by the fact that so far the radio host has only informed his audience that he expected either caller Stefan or caller Anna or maybe both (see lines 155 to 157). At that point he does not mention that Stefan and Anna are a couple (although this might be inferred by the host's announcement that the next astrologic counseling would be about a "pArtnerschaftsgeschichte" (line 152), i.e. about partnership troubles.) Nevertheless, in lines 165 and 166 he provides the "identification" (Meyer 1992: 74) of Anna by calling her Stefan's girlfriend.

Why he also uses an apposition in line 175 is much less clear. The relationship between Stefan and Anna has been established by now. The fact that Anna is Stefan's girlfriend is known to the audience. It seems that the phrase *deine Freundin die Anna* is almost used as a set phrase in much the same way as "rosy-fingered dawn" and "swift-footed Achilles" were used in Homer's epic. Meyer (1992: 109) also refers to possible "stylistic reasons" that sometimes trigger the use of appositions, although he only found this use in literary texts. I would argue that stylistic reasons, too, may be a force that triggers the use of appositions in everyday speech. The reason for using this construction could be that a personalized atmosphere can be created for both the callers and the audience by repeating the names of the callers and the people they talk about.

One further observation can be made on the basis of the data in my corpus. Prototypical wide appositions seem to occur with noun phrases denoting persons (either proper names or general terms referring to persons such as "his wife" in example 3). Of the six wide appositions found in monological settings there is only one wide apposition where the second appositional noun phrase modifies a previous noun phrase that semantically refers to a *concept* and not a *person*. Interestingly enough, this example is taken from a TV newscast for kids. The news presenter (NP) is talking about Germany's attempts to gain a permanent seat in the UN Security Council. After having mentioned the Security Council, he explains what it is:

Example 6: TV newscast for kids

0021	NP	*der weltsicherheitsRAT,*
		'the World Security Council'
0022		*ist eine gruppe von fünfzehn LÄNdern.*
		'is a group of fifteen countries'
0023	→	*und gehört zu den vereinten naTIOnen.*
		'and belongs to the United Nations'
0024	→	*.hh also der vereinigung der meisten STAAten dieser welt. (.)*
		'.hh i.e. the union of most of the world's states'
0025		*.h die AUFgabe des sicherheitsrates ist es,*
		'the job of the Security Council is'
0026		*dafür zu sorgen dass es FRIEden auf der welt gibt.*
		'to provide for peace on earth'

In lines 0021 to 0022, the news presenter explains what the Security Council is and uses a copula clause for this purpose: "der weltsicherheitsRAT, ist eine gruppe von fünfzehn LÄNdern / the World Security Council is a group of fifteen countries". Copula clauses are supposed to be closely related to appositions (see Eisenberg 2004: 258) and are indeed the preferred structure when a *thing* or *concept*, and not a *person*, has to be specified by adding further information. The problem the news presenter has here is that he has to explain parts of his explanation, too. When he says that the Security Council is part of the United Nations (line 0023), he also has to explain what the United Nations is. At that point, the news presenter uses not a copula clause but an apposition: "den vereinten naTIOnen. .hh also der vereinigung der meisten STAAten der welt / the United Nations .hh i.e. the union of most of the world's states" (lines 0023–0024). The advantage of an apposition over a copula clause is that with an apposition the information is rather backgrounded while with a copula clause it gains more weight (salience) and is therefore foregrounded. The fact that the explanation of what the United Nations are is an explanation within an explanation may explain why the backgrounding structure of an apposition is chosen. Weinrich (2005: 364; my translation) refers to that use when he lists the use of appositions to provide "explanatory asides" as one possible function. The back grounding effect is further promoted by the fact that the apposition is not a "true"apposition, i.e. it does not conform to a strict *NP + NP* pattern. Instead, it is introduced by the discourse marker *also*[12] (see Dittmar 2002 and Imo 2012), which marks the following phrase as an explication.

At least for the data of spoken German I searched, then, the claim that there are no true wide appositions where the core element is not a person but a thing or concept can be upheld.

As the discussion of monological data (newscasts and introductory passages in radio interviews and talk programs) has shown, the following types of wide appositions can be set up as possible constructions:
- First, the most common form (seven out of eight instances) would be a wide apposition with a noun phrase denoting a person as the core and a following attributive appositional noun phrase providing specifying, mainly identifying information. Its function is to maximize the informational content of an utterance and to provide for the necessary information for the recipients to understand who the person is that the speaker is referring to. It is restricted to monological passages of talk, which may have to do with the fact that utterances containing wide appositions tend to become unwieldy and difficult to process mentally, so they demand some amount of pre-planning. This first construction could be called *person + information-apposition*.

---

[12] *Also* can be translated into English by a variety of expressions, for example *so, well, anyway, therefore* or *that is*, according to context.

- Second, there is the possibility to present narrow appositions such as *deine Freundin Anna* ('your girlfriend Anna') as wide appositions via prosodic means (supported here by the non-standard combination of definite article and proper name). Again, the main function of this type of apposition is to provide necessary information for the listeners about a person, but there is a gliding scale where this function is no longer plausible and the construction may become a stylistic means for creating a personalized atmosphere in an interaction. It is doubtful whether it is possible to call this pattern a construction of its own. It seems to oscillate between the first type (*person + information-apposition*) and prototypical narrow appositions (*title/status/ function + person*). Using the network metaphor of *Construction Grammar*, both constructs presented in example 5 can be said to be positioned somewhere "in between" more established nodes, i.e. constructions.
- Third, at least in my data, a true wide apposition with a thing/concept as the core does not occur. The only candidate case is one where the discourse marker – *also* ('i.e.') – is added, creating a different syntactic form. This might indeed be a possible construction, but this so far quite speculative hypothesis would have to be tested against a larger corpus as well as a corpus containing more specialized talk (e.g. scientific presentations, instructions).

While appositions in monological passages of talk already show considerable variation, appositions in interactional passages of talk are even more open to variation, as the following examples will show.

5.2 Appositions in interactional passages of talk

So far, data have been presented where the speaker has no (newscasts) or little (introduction periods in interviews or talk programs) fear of being interrupted and, furthermore, where s/he has a lot of (newscasts, interviews) or at least some (introduction of a new caller in a talk program) time to pre-plan his or her utterances. Now, in contrast, I will focus on spontaneous interactions where there is little time for pre-planning one's utterances and where a constant change of turns is expected.

The following transcript is taken from a conversation between a student (K) talking to her grandmother (O). First, both were talking about the grandmother's plans for the evening, but then, in line 51, her grandchild introduces a new topic:

Example 7: private phone call

51	K	→	GEStern wurde doch mariAnne getauft.
			'yesterday Marianne was baptized, wasn't she'
52		→	dein (-) URenkelchen. (–)
			'your little great grandchild'
53	O		GEStern in fÜ[rth,]
			'yesterday in Fürth'
54	K		[ich] mein SCHON;
			'I'm quite certain'
55			GEStern am ersten mAI.
			'yesterday on May the first'
56			Oder,
			'wasn't she'
57	O		im in FÜRTH;
			'in the in Fürth'
58			ja,
			'yes'
59	K		JA:;
			'yes'
60			in FÜRTH.
			'in Fürth'
61			geNAU.
			'right'

The pattern shows considerable similarities with appositions but, on the other hand, there are also striking differences. What this pattern has in common with a wide apposition of the type *NP + NP* is the fact that "dein (-) URenkelchen / your little great grandchild" (line 52) specifies the previous proper name "mariANne" (line 51) in a process of "identification", according to Meyer (1992: 74). The apposition-like structure becomes obvious when one transforms the utterances in lines 51 to 52 into a "proper" wide apposition: *Gestern wurde doch Marianne, dein Urenkelchen, getauft.* ('Yesterday Marianne, your little great grandchild, was baptized, wasn't she?').

The only problem is the position of "dein (-) URenkelchen / your little great grandchild", and this is a problem that makes some difference. The noun phrase that can be called the attributive/appositive part is placed *after* the so-called *right verb brace*, i.e. after the infinite verb "getauft" ('baptized'), which constitutes a very strong signal of syntactic closure in German.[13] According to Auer (2007b: 652), this could be called "a case of straightforward syntactic unit expansion ('incrementing')". Such an expansion "is set off by intonation and constitutes an intonation phrase of its own [...]. Semantically and pragmatically, the expansion specifies the proposition" that was uttered before. Auer (2007b: 652) proposes to call this type of syntactic unit expansion "prototypical expansion".

The problem is that expansions (Auer 2007b: 652–656 continues to list several further types of expansions) are a basic feature of a temporally grounded, progressive and "on-line" (Auer 2000, 2005, 2006a, 2007a, b, 2010) syntax of spoken language and, thus, do not only include phrases that could be described as appositions but also additional adverbs and adverbial phrases or even just co-ordinate clauses and repairs:

> The point is that speakers continually rework and elaborate their own or other speakers' utterances by making use of already existing syntactic structures. They thereby produce 'expansions' of complete syntactic units. These expansions may involve simple continuations but also radical reorganizations. Prosody may camouflage or integrate them. Their information status may be rhematic or thematic, their semantics cohesive or not, and they may constitute new actions or subsidiary ones. (Auer 2007b: 657)

From a *Construction Grammar* point of view, it is difficult to reconcile this piecemeal technique of incrementing in spoken language with a sign-based structure of grammar. Some structures could either be explained as "deplaced" appositions or as mere increments: As Auer (2007b: 657) states, "existing syntactic structures" form the basis for expansions. Therefore, it is indeed possible to view a "stretched" apposition such as the one in example 7 ("GEStern wurde doch mariAnne getauft. dein (-) URenkelchen / yesterday Marianne was baptized, your little great grandchild") as a valid candidate for a wide apposition in spite of the fact that it does not conform to the strict appositional structure of an immediate juxtaposition of two noun phrases.

As has been mentioned before, the function of "dein (-) URenkelchen / your little great grandchild" is that of "identification", which is a typical function of wide appositions. The only thing that is different is that in interactional settings the pursuit of shared understanding is something that develops over time and is oriented to the reactions of the recipients. While in monological settings the speaker can think about possible problems of understandings beforehand and deliver a kind of "preemptive repair" of understanding failures by producing a

---

[13] A common pattern of German main clauses is that of the verb brace, i.e. a finite verb at the so-called second position and the infinite part of the verb at the end of the clause. In example 7, *wurde (was)* constitutes the left and *getauft (baptized)* the right verb brace.

wide apposition, in interactional settings speakers first produce a noun phrase – such as *Marianne* – and then wait and see whether this may not already work. Only when – as is the case in example 7 – no immediate uptake occurs in spite of the fact that the strongly falling pitch signals the end of the turn construction unit, the speaker may conclude that the referent causes problems in terms of understanding and, therefore, he or she provides additional information to support the identification of the referent. The basic difference between monological and interactional settings, therefore, is this: In a monological setting appositions constitute a more or less pre-planned procedure helping recipients understand what is being said while in interactional settings appositions can be described as a context-sensitive, local procedure of reacting to real or potential understanding problems.

The distinction between real and potential problems concerning understanding is important because not always do speakers add an appositive noun phrase after a missing uptake. Sometimes, as in example 8, they seem to realize potential problems while speaking and add a specifying noun phrase immediately without a pause and within a single intonation phrase. This structure then works a bit like a self-repair. Example 8 has already been presented at the beginning of this paper. Two sisters are talking on the telephone; sister 1 (S1) has called her sister (S2) via Skype and not, as she usually does, via her landline telephone. The result is that S2 does not see the number of the caller on her display, which informs her that her sister is not using her landline telephone:

Example 8: private phone call

03	S2		*von wo rufst DU denn an;*
			'where are you calling from'
04			(–)
05	S1	→	*äh von SKYPE weil unser tElefon so rAUscht die Anlage, (-)*
			'erm via skype because our telephone is so noisy the system'
06	S2		*ach SO; (-)*
			'oh all right'
07	S1		*wieso WEIL äh::- (-)*
			'why because erm'
08			*(ma) keine NUMmer angezeigt wurde oder warUm.*
			'(my) no number was shown (on the display) or why'
09	S2		*NE: weil; (.)*
			'no because'
10			*keine NUMmer angezeigt wurde;*
			'no number was shown'

After S2's question where S1 is calling from, S1 replies that she is using her computer and the telephoning software Skype. She explains this change of communicating media by saying that "unser tElefon / our telephone" (line 05) is noisy. After the right verb brace "rAUscht / is noisy" she adds a noun phrase that refers to "unser tElefon / our telephone".[14] In that case, it is not so much the function of "identification" that is important but rather functions that Meyer (1992: 74) groups under the heading of providing "equally specific information". He calls these functions "paraphrase", "reorientation" and "self-correction". Here, a mixture between a "paraphrase" and a "self-correction" can be made out as the functions of the expansion or apposition "die Anlage / the system". It is not a repair, though, because it does not replace "unser tElefon / our telephone". Both expressions are needed to understand what S1 is talking about. With "the system" alone, the recipient would not understand what S1 is talking about, because "system" can refer to anything, not necessarily to the telephone. So both "telephone" and "system" are needed and what S1 does is refocus from the everyday expression "the telephone" to the more technical expression "the system". It is not the physical object "telephone" that is making noise but rather some part of the wider structure of the telephone installation (maybe a faulty speaker in the telephone receiver, a wrong/faulty connection of the telephone to the terminals or even problems with the transmission lines of the phone company). The phrase "the system" therefore refocuses from the single object "telephone" to the complete telephone infrastructure, which helps prevent misunderstandings. S2 can infer that S1 cannot just get a new telephone to solve the problem, as the problem is as yet unspecific and not localized. In a preplanned, monological situation it would very well have been possible to reformulate the utterance by using a canonical apposition: *weil unser Telefon, die Anlage, so rauscht* ('because our telephone, the system, is so noisy').[15]

So far, it would be quite possible merely to expand the definition of the construction *wide apposition* by adding that there are *monological appositions* with direct juxtaposition of both noun phrases and *interactional appositions* where other elements, notably the right verb brace, can intervene.

There is one type of apposition-like structure where one can find the expected pattern of direct *NP + NP* juxtaposition even in interactional language. It is doubt-

---

14 In subordinate clauses, all parts (finite and non-finite) of the verb always have to be produced at the end of the clause. In these cases the subordinating conjunction ("weil / because" in line 05) is taken to constitute the left verb brace while the verb (in this case there is only one verbal part "rAUscht / is noisy") constitutes the right verb brace, which signals the syntactic closure of the clause.
15 The sentence would sound even better if there were a further indication for a shift of semantic focus, such as *unser Telefon, d.h. die Anlage* ('our telephone, that is to say the system').

ful, though, whether one should indeed classify these structures as appositions proper. As mentioned before, Meyer (1992: 74) indeed lists "self-correction" as one possible function of appositions. Strangely enough, he only found about 69 (i.e. less than 3%) self-corrections in a total of the 2941 cases he classified as appositions. The low number seems a bit strange because repair is usually one of the most pervasive features of spoken – and especially spoken interactional – language and I would expect a higher number (in my own data, eight out of 17 instances were repair-like structures, i.e. about half of all examples had to do with repair).

Structures of the type presented in example 9 below are a kind of mixture between appositions proper and nominal self-repairs. Both structures are closely related within the network of constructions and indeed there are some instances of overlap.

Example 9 is taken from a radio talk show; a radio host (H) and a caller (C) are talking about the caller's health problems. The transcript is taken from the middle of the conversation, so both speakers are in a clear interactional mode and both the host and the caller have an equal share of turns and even interrupt each other or produce overlap (see lines 294–295). The caller is talking about the fact that he suffers from the sleep apnea syndrome – he stops breathing, sometimes for several minutes, while sleeping – and that he has been given an automatic respirator by his doctors:

Example 9: radio talk

289	H		*das HEIßT,*
			that means'
290		→	*durch (.) durch diese (.) durch diese Atemgeräusche,*
			by (.) by those (.) by those breathing sounds'
291		→	*die SAUGgeräusche,*
			the sucking sounds'
292			*äh bist du nicht im SCHLAF gestört.*
			ehm do not get disturbed in your sleep'
293			*du KANNST also schlafen.*
			so you can sleep'
294			*[das geht SCHON.]*
			that is o.k.'
295	C		*[.hhhhh] SCHLAfen kann ich,*
			.hhhhh I can sleep'

The caller has just described how his respirator looks and works. He has to put on a breathing mask and the respirator pumps air into his nose and mouth. The caller also complained about the fact that the respirator makes hissing and sucking sounds when pumping air into his lungs, which he had previously said was quite a "killer" for building up a partnership with a woman. The radio host takes up the part about the noise of the respirator and asks whether it does not prevent the caller himself from sleeping. The host first uses the phrase "diese Atemgeräusche / those breathing sounds" (line 290), which he then corrects by the reformulation "die SAUGgeräusche / the sucking sounds" (line 291). The word "breathing" may have been triggered by the fact that both the host and the caller were talking about the breathing problems of the caller all the time. Nevertheless, the problem with the respirator is a special kind of hissing/ sucking noise,[16] not a breathing noise, with which expression the host then repairs his previous utterance. The noun phrase "diese Atemgeräusche / those breathing sounds" can be viewed as "erased" by the following "die SAUGgeräusche / the sucking sounds", which can very well stand alone and does neither specify nor need the previous noun phrase in order to be processed. So while the function of this *NP + NP* pattern is rather one of "self-repair", it nevertheless has strong formal connections with that of an apposition (more about the problems of differentiating between nominal self-repairs and appositions below).

6 Appositions and *Construction Grammar*

So far, only a few types of appositions have been analyzed. I restricted the analysis to wide appositions of the type *NP + NP* and contrasted monological and dialogical passages of spoken interaction. Even then, to get a fuller picture it would be necessary first to extend the analysis to a much larger range of communicative genres (instructions, lectures, counseling sessions, consultations etc.) as well as to include both monologically oriented (books, magazines, legal texts, scientific texts etc.) and interactionally oriented (chat, e-mail, SMS etc.) written language.[17]

---

[16] The caller himself used the expression "FAUCHgeräusch" ('hissing sound') several lines before.
[17] Meyer (1992: 98) discovered a striking inequality in the distribution of appositions across different genres within his corpora: "The genres of fiction and conversation contained the fewest instances of appositions [...], the genres of learned writing and press writing the most [...]. This skewed distribution existed in the corpora because appositions are communicatively more necessary in some genres than in others."

In spite of the meager database of only 23 cases, though, some tentative hypotheses about how a *Construction Grammar* approach to appositions might look like might be ventured:

(i) First, prototypical wide appositions – excluding repair-like cases as presented below in (iii) – are centered round a noun phrase referring to a person (seven out of eight instances). It would be plausible, then, to assume at least one construction called "wide apposition: *person + information about person*". The *formal entry* of this construction would be that there is a core noun phrase which is filled by a proper name or a word/phrase referring to a human being (*his wife, my friend, their boss etc.*) and an appositive noun phrase that follows the core and gives additional information about the status, function or profession of that person. The *functional entry* would be that this type of apposition is used to provide recipients with the necessary pieces of information to identify the person named.

The *sequential entry* – an additional type of information that would be necessary to add from the perspective of *Interactional Linguistics* (see Imo 2007a: 40) – would be that this construction is used preferably in monological situations, where a pre-planning of utterances is possible and where the apposition is a kind of "pre-emptive" attempt to prevent recipients' lack of understanding. On a *prosodic* level, this type of apposition is usually realized within a separate intonation phrase, which reflects the ambiguous status of the apposition. On a syntactic level, it is integrated into an utterance and forms a single constituent together with the core noun phrase it refers to while on a prosodic level the information given in the apposition is marked off as an aside or as background information.

(ii) Second, there might be another type of wide apposition that could be called "wide apposition: *thing/concept + information about thing/concept*". This assumption is rather a speculative one at the moment, though, because only one instance of this type was found in the data I searched and this occurred within a TV newscast for kids. The basic *function* is the same as in the first type of wide apposition. It helps prevent a possible lack of understanding and needs a monological background. An open question would be whether this type of apposition is usually realized with a discourse marker such as *also* (i.e.; 'that is'), *und zwar* ('namely'), *das heißt* ('meaning/that means/that is') etc. or not. Another open question would be whether appositions referring to a core noun phrase denoting a thing/object are more widespread in other communicative genres, such as instructions, lectures etc.

(iii) Third, there is a type of "very wide" or "peripheral"[18] apposition that occurs in interactional settings. It may be called "very wide apposition" because, on a formal level, other words or phrases may occur between the core noun phrase and the appositive noun phrase and, on a functional level, these appositions do not provide background information but rather re-focus, paraphrase or even, at the end of the spectrum, repair the previous utterance (see also Meyer 1992: 74). They occur in interactional settings because they are a result of the ongoing, temporal process of speaking. This temporal process can lead to the choice of wrong or at least less fitting words, which then have to be corrected or "fine-tuned". Another reason is that the absence of recipient reaction (no taking over of a turn) may inform the speaker that further information is needed for the recipient to understand his utterance.

Because of this closeness of appositions and repairs, persons as well as things/concepts can constitute the core noun phrase of "very wide/peripheral" appositions, because anything may be a candidate for repair. At the far end of the spectrum, the *apposition construction* merges with that of repair. How closely "very wide/peripheral" appositions and repairs are related may be illustrated by lines 290/291 of example 9:

290 → durch (.) durch diese (.) durch diese Atemgeräusche,
   by (.) by those (.) by those breathing sounds'
291 → die SAUGgeräusche,
   the sucking sounds'

Preceding the apposition / repair "diese Atemgeräusche / those breathing sounds" and "die SAUGgeräusche / the sucking sounds" are two further self-repairs, namely "durch / by" (line 290), which gets replaced by "durch diese / by those" and then "durch diese / by those", which in turn gets repaired by "durch diese Atemgeräusche / by those breathings sounds".[19] These two self-repairs already hint at an ongoing word search by the host, giving further indications that "those breathing sounds / the sucking sounds" is more of a repair than an apposition proper. Self-repair may be conceptualized as a construction, too, which is defined by a process of breaking off during the production of an utterance and

---

18 Meyer (1992: 132), too, states that the concept of "apposition" becomes fuzzy at the borders. In his data, he had quite a lot of apposition-like candidates that fulfilled only some of the criteria for appositions proper so that he decided to differentiate between more "central" and more "peripheral" appositions, according to how many of the six semantic and syntactic criteria they fulfilled.

19 See Egbert (2009: 101) for a description of the interactional status of such reformulations.

the replacement of an element produced before. Self-repairs are structurally very open. Prepositions can be replaced by prepositions, adverbs by adverbs, adjectives by adjectives, nouns by nouns but also parts of noun, adverb, prepositional or verb phrases by other parts (for a detailed analysis of how self-repairs work in German see Egbert 2009: 53–98). Only when a noun phrase is replaced by another noun phrase do amalgamations between the *self-repair construction* and the *wide apposition construction* occur. If only parts of a noun phrase are realized, the constructs move towards repair proper in the network of related constructions. If the second noun phrase does not plausibly repair the first one (i.e. does not replace it), the given construct moves towards a prototypical *wide appositive construction*.

(iv) Fourth, next to amalgamations of appositions and self-repairs there are also amalgamations of narrow and wide appositions, as in example 5 ("deine FREUNdin, die ANna / your girlfriend, the Anna" in line 165–166 and "deine FREUNdin die Anna / your girlfriend the Anna" in line 175), where stylistic (personalization strategies) and prosodic aspects combine to create a special case of a rather open formal and functional pattern whose constructional status is very unclear.

What this qualitative, empirical study has shown is that, on the one hand, *Interactional Linguistics* can indeed profit by taking up ideas and concepts of *Construction Grammar*. One problem of *Interactional Linguistics* is that analyses within this framework often remain focused on single phenomena which are described very fully but which are not embedded into a larger theory of syntax. *Construction Grammar*, on the other hand, forces one to think in terms of a coherent system of representation, and its concepts of the *symbolic construction* and the *network of constructions* deliver working hypotheses with which to achieve such a representation. The result of almost all previous attempts at combining *Interactional Linguistics* and *Construction Grammar*, though, has been that there is an enormous lack of knowledge about the actual properties of syntactic phenomena. So far, most linguists – and this holds true for *Construction Grammarians*, too – have relied on little or even no empirical data and an overhasty classification of syntactic phenomena, which means that every time a *Construction Grammar* analysis is attempted within the framework of *Interactional Linguistics* the lack of empirically supported knowledge about neighboring phenomena – which is necessary for the establishment of network-based descriptions – is felt severely. What this means is that much more empirically driven work about the *actual use* of syntactic patterns in spoken and written language is needed before a fully satisfying *Construction Grammar* representation of phenomena is really possible.

References

Auer, Peter. 2000. On line-Syntax – oder: was es bedeuten könnte, die Zeitlichkeit der mündlichen Sprache ernst zu nehmen. *Sprache und Literatur* 85: 43–56.

Auer, Peter. 2005. Projection in interaction and projection in grammar. *Text* 25: 7–36.

Auer, Peter. 2006a. Increments and more. Anmerkungen zur augenblicklichen Diskussion über die Erweiterbarkeit von Turnkonstruktionseinheiten. In: Arnulf Deppermann, Reinhard Fiehler and Thomas Spranz-Fogasy (eds.), *Grammatik und Interaktion*, 279–294. Radolfzell: Verlag für Gesprächsforschung.

Auer, Peter. 2006b. Construction Grammar meets Conversation: Einige Überlegungen am Beispiel von 'so'-Konstruktionen. In: Susanne Günthner and Wolfgang Imo (eds.), *Konstruktionen in der Interaktion*, 291–314. Berlin/New York: Mouton de Gruyter.

Auer, Peter. 2007a. Syntax als Prozess. In: Hausendorf, Heiko (ed.), *Gespräch als Prozess: Linguistische Aspekte der Zeitlichkeit verbaler Interaktion*, 95–124. Tübingen: Narr.

Auer, Peter. 2007b. Why are increments such elusive objects? An afterthought. *Pragmatics* 17 (4): 647–658.

Auer, Peter. 2010. Zum Segmentierungsproblem in der Gesprochenen Sprache. *Interaction and Linguistic Structure* 49: 1–19.

Bergen, Benjamin and Nancy Chang. 2005. Embodied Construction Grammar in simulation-based language understanding. In: Jan-Ola Östman and Mirjam Fried (eds.), *Construction Grammars: Cognitive Grounding and Theoretical Extensions*, 147–190. Amsterdam/Philadelphia: John Benjamins.

Boas, Hans C. 2010. The syntax-lexicon continuum in Construction Grammar. *Belgian Journal of Linguistics* 24: 54–82.

Couper-Kuhlen, Elizabeth and Margret Selting. 2001. Forschungsprogramm 'Interaktionale Linguistik'. *Linguistische Berichte* 187: 257–287.

Couper-Kuhlen, Elizabeth and Tsuyoshi Ono (eds.). 2007. Turn continuation in cross-linguistic perspective. *Special Issue Pragmatics* 17 (4).

Couper-Kuhlen, Elizabeth and Dagmar Barth-Weingarten. 2011. A system for transcribing talk-in-interaction: GAT 2. *Gesprächsforschung – online Zeitschrift zur verbalen Interaktion* 12, 1–51 (http://www.gespraechsforschung-ozs.de/heft2011/px-gat2-englisch.pdf).

Croft, William. 2002. *Radical Construction Grammar*. Oxford: Oxford University Press.

Deppermann, Arnulf. 2006. Construction Grammar – Eine Grammatik für die Interaktion? In: Arnulf Deppermann, Reinhard Fiehler and Thomas Spranz-Fogasy (eds.), *Grammatik und Interaktion*, 43–65. Radolfzell: Verlag für Gesprächsforschung.

Dittmar, Norbert. 2002. Lakmustest für funktionale Beschreibungen am Beispiel von *auch* (Fokuspartikel, FP), *eigentlich* (Modalpartikel, MP) und *also* (Diskursmarker, DM). In: Cathrine Fabricius-Hansen, Oddleif Leirbukt and Ole Letnes (eds.), *Modus, Modalverben, Modalpartikel*, 142–177. Trier: Wissenschaftlicher Verlag.

Duden. 2005[7]. *Die Grammatik*. Mannheim: Dudenverlag.

Egbert, Maria. 2009. *Der Reparatur-Mechanismus in deutschen Gesprächen*. Radolfzell: Verlag für Gesprächsforschung (http://www.verlag-gespraechsforschung.de/2009/egbert.htm).

Eisenberg, Peter. 2004. *Grundriß der deutschen Grammatik: Der Satz*. Stuttgart: Metzler.

Fauconnier, Gilles. 2004. Mental spaces, language modalities, and conceptual integration. In: Steven Davis and Gillon, Brendan S. (eds.), *Semantics: A Reader*, 251–279. Oxford: Oxford University Press.

Fillmore, Charles J. 1988. The mechanisms of Construction Grammar. *Proceedings of the annual meeting of Berkeley Linguistics Society* 14: 35–55.
Fischer, Kerstin and Anatol Stefanowitsch. 2006. Konstruktionsgrammatik: Ein Überblick. In: Kerstin Fischer and Anatol Stefanowitsch (eds.), *Konstruktionsgrammatik: Von der Anwendung zur Theorie*, 3–18. Tübingen: Stauffenburg.
Goldberg, Adele E. 1996. Construction Grammar. In: Brown, Keith E. and Jim E. Miller (eds.), *Concise Encyclopedia of Syntactic Theories*, 68–70. New York: Elsevier.
Günthner, Susanne and Wolfgang Imo (eds.). 2006. *Konstruktionen in der Interaktion*. Berlin/New York: Mouton de Gruyter.
Günthner, Susanne. 2006a. Grammatische Analysen der kommunikativen Praxis – 'Dichte Konstruktionen' in der Interaktion. In: Arnulf Deppermann, Reinhard Fiehler and Thomas Spranz-Fogasy (eds.), *Grammatik und Interaktion*, 95–122. Radolfzell: Verlag für Gesprächsforschung.
Günthner, Susanne. 2006b. Von Konstruktionen zu kommunikativen Gattungen: Die Relevanz sedimentierter Muster für die Ausführung kommunikativer Aufgaben. *Deutsche Sprache* 34: 173–190.
Günthner, Susanne. 2006c. 'Was ihn trieb, war vor allem Wanderlust': Pseudocleft-Konstruktionen im Deutschen. In: Susanne Günthner and Wolfgang Imo (eds.), *Konstruktionen in der Interaktion*, 59–90. Berlin/New York: Mouton de Gruyter.
Günthner, Susanne. 2010. Grammatical constructions and communicative genres. In: Heidrun Dorgeloh and Anja Wanner (eds.), *Syntactic Variation and Genre*, 195–218. Berlin/New York: Mouton de Gruyter.
Imo, Wolfgang. 2006. 'Da hat des kleine *glaub* irgendwas angestellt' – ein construct ohne construction? In: Susanne Günthner and Wolfgang Imo (eds.), *Konstruktionen in der Interaktion*, 263–290. Berlin/New York: Mouton de Gruyter.
Imo, Wolfgang. 2007a. *Construction Grammar und Gesprochene-Sprache-Forschung: Konstruktionen mit zehn matrixsatzfähigen Verben im gesprochenen Deutsch*. Tübingen: Niemeyer.
Imo, Wolfgang. 2007b. Der Zwang zur Kategorienbildung: Probleme der Anwendung der Construction Grammar bei der Analyse gesprochener Sprache. *Gesprächsforschung – Online Zeitschrift zur verbalen Interaktion* 8: 22–45.
Imo, Wolfgang. 2008. Individuelle Konstrukte oder Vorboten einer neuen Konstruktion? Stellungsvarianten der Modalpartikel *halt* im Vor- und Nachfeld. In: Kerstin Fischer and Anatol Stefanowitsch (eds.), *Konstruktionsgrammatik II*, 135–156. Tübingen: Stauffenburg.
Imo, Wolfgang. 2009. Konstruktion oder Funktion? Erkenntnisprozessmarker ('change-of-state tokens') im Deutschen. In: Susanne Günthner and Jörg Bücker (eds.), *Grammatik im Gespräch: Konstruktionen der Selbst- und Fremdpositionierung*, 57–86. Berlin/New York: de Gruyter.
Imo, Wolfgang. 2010. 'Mein Problem ist/mein Thema ist' – how syntactic patterns and genres interact. In: Anja Wanner and Heidrun Dorgeloh (eds.), *Syntactic Variation and Genre*, 141–166. Berlin/New York: Mouton de Gruyter.
Imo, Wolfgang. 2011a. Ad hoc-Produktion oder Konstruktion? – Verfestigungstendenzen bei Inkrement-Strukturen im gesprochenen Deutsch. In: Alexander Lasch and Alexander Ziem (eds.), *Konstruktionsgrammatik III*, 141–256. Tübingen: Stauffenburg.
Imo, Wolfgang. 2011b. Die Grenzen von Konstruktionen: Versuch einer granularen Neubestimmung des Konstruktionsbegriffs der *Construction Grammar*. In: Stefan Engelberg, Anke Holler and Kristel Proost (eds.), *Sprachliches Wissen zwischen Lexikon und Grammatik*, 113–148. Berlin/New York: Mouton de Gruyter.

Imo, Wolfgang. 2012. Wortart Diskursmarker? In: Björn Rothstein (ed.), *Nicht-flektierende Wortarten*, 48–88. Berlin/New York: de Gruyter.
Jacobs, Joachim. 2008. Wozu Konstruktionen? *Linguistische Berichte* 213: 3–44.
Langacker, Ronald W. 1987. *Foundations of Cognitive Grammar*. Stanford: Stanford University Press.
Meyer, Charles F. 1992. *Apposition in Contemporary English*. Cambridge: Cambridge University Press.
Molitor, Friedhelm. 1977. Zur Apposition im heutigen Deutsch. Eine Vorstudie. Ph.D. dissertation (Köln).
Östman, Jan Ola. 2005. Construction Discourse: A prolegomenon. In: Jan-Ola Östman and Mirjam Fried (eds.), *Construction Grammars: Cognitive Grounding and Theoretical Extensions*, 121–144. Amsterdam/Philadelphia: John Benjamins.
Östman, Jan Ola and Mirjam Fried (eds.). 2005. *Construction Grammars: Cognitive Grounding and Theoretical Extensions*. Amsterdam/Philadelphia: John Benjamins.
Sag, Ivan A. 2011. Sign-based Construction Grammar: An informal synopsis. In: Ivan A. Sag and Hans C. Boas (eds.), *Sign-based Construction Grammar*, 39–170. Stanford: Center for the Study of Language and Information.
Selting, Margret et al. 2009. Gesprächsanalytisches Transkriptionssystem 2 (GAT 2). *Gesprächsforschung – Online-Zeitschrift zur verbalen Interaktion* 10: 353–402.
Steels, Luc (ed.). 2011. *Design Patterns in Fluid Construction Grammar*. Amsterdam/Philadelphia: John Benjamins.
Taylor, John R. 2002. *Cognitive Grammar*. Oxford: Oxford University Press.
Trijp, Remi van. 2008. Argumentstruktur in der Fluid Construction Grammar. In: Anatol Stefanowitsch and Kerstin Fischer (eds.), *Konstruktionsgrammatik II* [Construction Grammar II], 223–246. Tübingen: Stauffenburg.
Weinrich, Harald. 2005. *Textgrammatik der deutschen Sprache*. Hildesheim: Olms.
Zima, Elisabeth and Geert Brône. 2011. Ad-hoc-Konstruktionen in der Interaktion: eine korpusbasierte Studie dialogischer Resonanzerzeugung. In: Alexander Lasch and Alexander Ziem (eds.), *Konstruktionsgrammatik III*, 155–174. Tübingen: Stauffenburg.
Zifonun, Gisela, Ludger Hoffmann and Bruno Strecker. 1997. *Grammatik der deutschen Sprache*. Berlin/New York: de Gruyter.

Appendix: Transcription conventions (Selting et al. 2009)

Sequential structure
01.	each line represents a single intonation phrase and is marked at the end regarding final pitch movement (see below)
[ ] [ ]	square brackets signal simultaneous talk

Final pitch movements of intonation phrases
?	rising to high
,	rising to mid
–	level
;	falling to mid
.	falling to low

Pauses and lengthening of sounds
(.)	micro pause, estimated, up to 0.2 sec. duration appr.
(-)	short estimated pause of appr. 0.2–0.5 sec. duration
(–)	intermediary estimated pause of appr. 0.5–0.8 sec. duration
(—)	longer estimated pause of appr. 0.8–1.0 sec. duration
(2.5)	measured pause of appr. 2.5 sec. duration
:	lengthening, by about 0.2–0.5 sec.
::	lengthening, by about 0.5–0.8 sec.
:::	lengthening, by about 0.8–1.0 sec.

In- and outbreaths
.hhh	inbreath, increasing number of h indicates longer inbreath
hh.	outbreath, increasing number of h indicates longer outbreath

Accentuation
SYLlable	focus accent
sYllable	secondary accent

Camilla Wide
12 Constructions as resources in interaction: Syntactically unintegrated *att* 'that'-clauses in spoken Swedish

1 Introduction

As shown by Evans (2007) insubordination, that is, conventionalized main clause use of formally subordinate clauses, seems to be a typologically more widespread phenomenon than previously believed. Despite this, the phenomenon remains fairly unexplored both generally and in particular languages (cf. Verstraete, D'Hertefelt and Van Linden 2012: 124–125). According to Evans (2007: 279), insubordinated clauses, which I will call *syntactically unintegrated subordinate clauses*, emerge diachronically via a process of ellipsis and conventionalized ellipsis. In the final stage of the process, when the clauses are re-analyzed as main clauses, constructionalization takes place: the constructions get a meaning or function of their own and the traces of ellipsis may be lost. During this process toward insubordination, the grammatical dependency markers are, as pointed out by Mithun (2008: 3), functionally extended "from sentence-level syntax into larger discourse and pragmatic domains".

The typology of functions of insubordinated clauses presented by Evans (2007) includes a broad selection of functions such as, for example, expressing desire, warnings, requests (indirection and interpersonal control), epistemic and evidential meaning, exclamation (modal insubordination) and contrastive focus and reiteration (signaling presupposed material). In this paper, I will analyze the functions of syntactically unintegrated clauses with the connective *att* 'that' in Swedish from an interactional and Construction Grammar point of view. Syntactically unintegrated 'that'-clauses have been discussed in a number of recent studies (see e.g. Laury and Seppänen 2008; Keevallik 2008; Günthner 2011; Panther and Thornburg 2011; Verstraete, D'Hertefelt and Van Linden 2012; Weinert 2012; Mertzlufft and Wide 2013). The focus in this paper is on the type of 'that'-clauses which according to Verstraete, D'Hertefelt, and Van Linden (2012) express *discourse insubordination*. I will not discuss *att*-clauses with an expressive-evaluative function (Panther and Thornburg 2011; see also Verstraete, D'Hertefelt and Van Linden 2012: 139–142) in clauses like *Att det kunde gå så illa* 'That it had to end that badly' (SAG 4: 759–760, 766). The *att*-clauses I focus on clarify or expand previous utterances similar to the way some of the *dat-* and *dass*-clauses in Dutch and German do (see discussion by Verstraete, D'Hertefelt and Van Linden 2012 for Dutch and Weinert 2012 for German.)

As I will show, *att*-clauses have a rephrasing or a reasoning function. Examples of these two related but yet slightly different functions are shown in (1) and (2) below. In example (1) an informer at a poison control centre explains what she means by *symptom* 'symptoms' when she uses the two *att*-clauses in lines 2–3. In example (2) a teenage boy draws a conclusion about a teacher based on what his sister has just said about the teacher. The conclusion is presented in the form of a syntactically unintegrated *att*-clause. (Both examples are analyzed in more detail in the empirical part of the paper.)

(1) Difficulties breathing? (GRIS: GIC 16519; I = informer C = caller)
    1 I: [...] men du har inga symptom från luftvägarna,
             but you have no symptoms from the respiratory organs
             'but you do not have any symptoms from the respiratory organs'

    →2 **att** du tycker de e jobbit å andas eller **att** de trycker
         ATT you think it is difficult to breathe or ATT it presses
         'that you find it difficult to breath or that it presses'

    ((Overlapping turn by the caller omitted))
    → 3 I: över=bröstet eller nåt sådant?
         over the chest or something like that
         'over the chest or something like that?'

(2) Sculpture class (GRIS: Wallenberg; Anward 2003)
    1 S: Birgitta hon har sådär eh kan ingenting.
         Birgitta she has like knows nothing
         'Birgitta, she has like knows nothing'

    ((5 lines omitted))
    →2 V: jaha **att** då ska ja'nte: välja henne i ↓skulptur.
         PRT ATT then shall I not choose her in sculpture
         'okay, so I'm not choosing her for sculpture class, then'

As shown by Lehti-Eklund (2002) and Anward (2004), the interactional context plays a fundamental role in the use of syntactically unintegrated *att*-clauses in Swedish. The clauses clearly function as resources in certain types of communicative settings (see section 3). Rather than being licensed by the syntactic context they can be seen as licensed by the interactional and pragmatic context. They are typified on the one hand, by the connective *att* 'that', which points both backward and forward in the conversation (see section 3) and, on the other hand, by the paraphrasing or reasoning function of the construction as a whole. The interesting question from an interactionally oriented Construction Grammar point of view is how these two functions should be related to the concept of constructions. Are we dealing with one construction, two constructions or two sub-variants of the same construction? How should the functions be dealt with within a Construction Grammar framework?

The outline of this paper is the following. In the next section, I present my data and the methodological and theoretical background of the study. In section 3, some basic facts on the connective *att* and clauses that use *att* are provided. Findings in previous studies on syntactically unintegrated *att*-clauses and similar clauses in other languages are discussed in the same section. Sections 4–5 form the empirical part of the paper. I start by discussing *att*-clauses with a paraphrasing function in section 4. In section 5 I discuss *att*-clauses with a reasoning function. The results of the analysis are summarized in section 6 where I also discuss the syntactically unintegrated *att*-clauses from a Construction Grammar point of view.

2 Data, method of analysis and theoretical points of departure

My method of analysis is Conversation Analysis (CA). In order to show the function and contextual features of the syntactically independent *att*-clauses I will present and discuss a number of extracts in which the clauses occur. The discussion is based on an analysis of a collection of recurrent occurrences in a number of authentic conversations in Swedish. The Sweden-Swedish examples in the collection are from the corpora of the projects *Grammar in Conversation: A study of Swedish* (GRIS) and *The Language and Music Worlds of High School Students* (GSM). The former corpus includes different types of conversations, such as everyday conversations, various types of institutional conversations, focus group conversations and mediated conversations (in total approximately 11 hours, of which 4 hours have been made available to me for this study). The latter corpus consists of group discussions with high school students on music and music styles (in total approximately 18 hours). All the Finland-Swedish occurrences in the collection are from the corpus of the project *Conversations in Helsinki* (SAM), which includes everyday conversations, meetings and mediated conversations (in total 9 hours of recordings). (For more details on the data, see the list at the end of the paper.)

Combining CA or more generally Interactional Linguistics with Construction Grammar is a feasible but not a completely straightforward task (cf. Östman and Trousdale 2013: 484, 486). As discussed by Wide (2009), an interactional approach to Construction Grammar requires a dynamic and flexible view of constructions. Grammatical patterns must be seen as types that originally emerged out of typified utterances (Langacker 1987: 494; Ono and Thompson 1995; Linell 2009; Anward in prep.). These types, which serve as templates for analogous expressions (Langacker 2008), are based on speakers' and listeners' earlier experiences of situations and contexts (Linell 1998: 113). Constructions are hence affected by cognitive and social constraints arising from the interaction (Ono and Thompson 1995). All the uses in authentic interaction are both influenced by and influence the grammatical patterns themselves (Kemmer and Barlow 2000: ix; Langacker 2000: 1; Croft 2001: 365–366). The patterns can thus be locally managed, negotiated and adapted to new situations (Linell 1998: 113). More stable linguistic units emerge through the process of abstraction but concrete context-dependent uses are always primary to more abstract patterns (Langacker 2000: 35; cf. Fillmore 1989: 33; Croft 2001: 5).

Showing and describing explicitly how participants in a conversation use linguistic resources or patterns in order to do things in the interaction is thus crucial. As the context influences the symbolic linguistic structures, it gives rise to semantic variants (Langacker 2000: 35) which form complex categories that can be described in terms of networks of grammatical patterns (Langacker 2000: 36; see also Croft 2001: 25–26; Croft and Cruse 2004: 262–265). The units in the networks can be of any kind or any size (Langacker 2000: 13). Since more general patterns are abstracted from single uses, the networks include both more specific and more general grammatical patterns. Some patterns can be seen as sub-patterns to other patterns but the patterns at the lowest level (i.e. the most specific patterns) are always the primary ones which specify the distribution of more abstract patterns (Langacker 2000: 28–32).

In this paper I will argue that *att*-clauses with a paraphrasing or reasoning function can be seen as two different but closely related nodes in a network of grammatical patterns or constructions. Before I move on to the empirical analysis of the two types of *att*-clauses, I will present some background information on the connective *att* and *att*-clauses in Swedish as well as 'that'-clauses more generally.

3 The connective *att*, clauses with *att* and previous studies of the phenomenon

The connective *att* is thought to have its origin in the pronoun *þat* (*þät*) 'that' in Old Swedish. In present-day Swedish the form of the pronoun is *det*. As discussed by Lindström and Londen (2008: 112) the development from a pronoun to a connective marker is believed to have taken place as illustrated in example (3). The pronoun originally belonged to the matrix clause (3a) but was then reanalyzed as belonging to the clause following the matrix clause (3b). (See SAOB s.v. *att* konj.; Wessén 1956: 58, 254–259.)

(3) a. *Jag   tror   **det**,   han   kommer.*
       I   think that   he   comes
       'I believe so; he's coming.'

   b. *Jag   tror,   **det** (= att)   han   kommer.*
       I   think that   that he   comes
       'I believe that he's coming.'

In present-day Swedish *att* introduces narrative and consecutive subordinate clauses (example 4, 5) as well as expressive-exclamative main clauses of the type discussed in section 1 above (*Att det kunde gå så illa* 'That it had to end so badly', SAG 4: 766).

(4) *Detta   ledde   till   att   pengarna   snart   tog   slut.*
    this   led   to   that the money soon ran out
    'This led to the situation that the money soon ran out.' (SAG 2: 734)

(5) *Hon   var   så   generös   att   pengarna   snart   tog   slut.*
    She was so generous that the money soon ran out.
    'She was so generous that the money ran out fast.' (SAG 2: 734)

The most prominent function of *att* is to introduce nominal narrative clauses, especially clauses with a mental predicate such as saying, hearing, knowing, believing etc. As pointed out by Lindström and Londen (2008: 113–114), *att* often introduces indirect speech such as is illustrated in example (6).

(6) *I går   sades   det   **att**   fabriken   skulle   slå   igen.*
    Yesterday was said it   that   the factory would close down
    'It was said yesterday that the factory would close down.' (SAG 4: 850)

When *att* introduces adverbial clauses as illustrated in example (5), the connective is usually combined with other connectives, such as *så* 'so' or *för* 'in order to'. The complex connective *så att* can also be used to introduce declarative main clauses expressing conclusions, cf. the two examples in (7) below.

(7) a. Det regnade så (att) sadeln strax blev våt.
      It rained so that the saddle soon became wet
      'It rained so (much) that the saddle became wet fast.'

   b. Det regnade, så (att) sadeln blev strax våt.
      It rained so that saddle became soon wet
      'It rained so the saddle became wet fast.' (SAG 4: 634)

In both the subordinate clause in (7a), where the adverbial *strax* 'soon' precedes the finite verb, and the main declarative clause in example (7b), where *strax* follows the finite verb, *att* can be omitted. The complex connective *så att* is in fact used mainly in spoken language (SAG 4: 943). It sometimes replaces the complex connective *för att* 'in order to' in clauses with purposive meanings, cf. example (8) and (9) with *för att* and *så att* respectively.

(8) – Jag har en hummer i kylskåpet, sa han lågt
      I have a lobster in the refrigerator said he low
      'I have a lobster in the refrigerator, he said in a silent voice'

      för att chauffören inte skulle höra.
      in order to that the driver not would hear
      'so that the driver would not hear it.' (SAG 4: 738)

(9) [...] så gick han alltid undan, så att jag inte skulle se honom.
      so went he always away so that I not would see him
      'then he always went away so that I would not see him.' (SAG 4: 738)

In older Swedish, *att* may be used alone in clauses with a purposive meaning. SAG (4: 546) illustrates this with the example shown in (10). A 19th century example from the Swedish Academy Dictionary (SAOB s.v. *att*, 19, 20) is shown in example (11).

(10) *Lyd din Gud att han icke må vända sitt ansikte från dig.*
      obey your God that he not may turn his face from you
      'Obey your god so that he won't turn his face away from you'

(11) Drick, att kraften   ej   förgår!
    drink that the strength not disappears
    'Drink so that you will not lose your strength' (1844)

As I will discuss in the empirical part of the paper, occurrences of simple *att* can be found also in present-day data in contexts where one would expect complex connectives such as *så att* and *för att* to be used. This is the case especially in syntactically unintegrated *att*-clauses with a reasoning function. The use of *att* alone is particularly frequent in Finland-Swedish varieties (Lehti-Eklund 2002; Lyngfelt 2003), which could be seen as an outcome of contact with Finnish, in which the corresponding connective *että* 'that' is used in similar contexts (see e.g. Laury and Seppänen 2008).

The use of the lexicalized complex connectives *så att* and *för att* (as well as *men att* 'but that') has been studied by Lindström and Londen (2008), who point out that *att* constitutes a formal link from a subsequent unit to a necessary antecedent unit. This is of special import in conversational language "where new utterances regularly build upon prior ones or are constructed *as if* developing from prior utterances in a sequence" (Lindström and Londen 2008: 116). In complex connectives such as *så att* and *för att*, which according to Lindström and Londen (2008: 145) "point back to a preceding discourse source and respond to this and expand from this", *att* has a general linking function whereas *så* and *för* (and *men*) "indicate more clearly the semantic relationship – causal, consecutive, adversative – between the assertions and actions that are joined together" (Lindström and Londen 2008: 146). In this paper I will not include occurrences with complex connectives such as *så att* and *för att* in the analysis. However, since there seems to be a link between at least some clauses with complex connectives and clauses with a simple *att* (cf. example 9 above), it will be necessary to refer to clauses that contain complex connectives in the discussion.

Anward (2004) points out that *att* generally has the function of introducing a known situation into the conversation, which is in line with what, for example, Bolinger (1977: 11) concludes about the corresponding connective *that* in English: "we see that [*that*] is appropriate when the clause in question does not represent a disconnected fact but something tied with a previous matter to which *that* can point back". *Att*-clauses, however, can also bring new information into the situation. The action performed with *att* thus has two sides: it refers to the preceding context but also changes the emerging context by, for example, introducing a new phase in the on-going episode. One of the examples discussed by Anward was shown in (2) above. In this example the syntactically unintegrated clause **att** då ska ja'nte: välja henne i ↓skulptur 'so I'm not choosing her for sculpture class, then' clearly relates to what has been said in the preceding discourse (about a particular teacher). At the same time, it introduces something new, a conclusion regarding what choices the speaker should make when he is planning his school year.

The function of syntactically unintegrated *att*-clauses in Finland-Swedish conversations has been investigated by Lehti-Eklund (2002), who analyzes *att* as a discourse marker in clauses which are not subordinate to any syntactic element in the preceding discourse. In Lehti-Eklund's data *att* occurs in elaborations, conclusions, closings of topics and transitions between communicative acts. As shown by Anward (2004), *att* occurs in elaborations and conclusions in Sweden-Swedish conversations as well (see example 2). Closings of topics and transitions between communicative acts, however, seem to be typical of Finland-Swedish varieties. An example of transitions between acts from Lehti-Eklund (2002) is shown in (12) below. In lines 1–3 and 5, the chair of a board of a political youth organization suggests two possible funding sources that the board should investigate. After the pause in line 6, a transition between acts takes place when the chair reformulates her suggestions as a directive. (I will return to the example in section 4 below.)

(12) It should be checked (SAM: V2; Lehti-Eklund 2002: 102; R = chair person, N = secretary)

1   R: [..] hh så kan man kolla   me   den hä: (.) kult*u*rföreningen (.)
             so   can one check with this   the cultural organization
         'then one can check with this cultural organization'

2   PARTY X' kulturföreningen   om di   vill   ge   pengar? (.)
             the cultural organization   if   they want give money
         'the cultural organization of party X if they want to give us money'

3   di   har   nämligen p*e*ngar
         they have namely   money
         'because they have money'

4   N: j*å*
         PRT
         'yes'

5   R: så kan man kolla   me:d ungdoms- (0.8) centralen
         so can one check with youth-   centre
         'and then one can check with the youth centre'

```
6        (1.5)

→7  R:   att  checka  nu   me    di här för          nu sku    de vara kiva att=
         ATT  check   PRT  with  these  because      PRT would it   be   nice to
         'so check with these because it would be nice to'

8        kunna  ge    någå arvode (.)      [annars    får   vi  bara ge=
         can    give  some remuneration    otherwise  may   we  only gi-
         'be able to give remuneration, otherwise we can only give'

9   (?):                                   [jå
                                           PRT
                                           'yes'

10  R:   =blommor
         flowers
         'flowers'
```

Syntactically unintegrated clauses initiated by *att* alone have been investigated in less detail in Sweden-Swedish data than in Finland-Swedish data. In Sweden-Swedish conversations, clauses with complex connectives such as *så att* and *för att* are more common than clauses with simple *att* (Lyngfelt 2003). Syntactically unintegrated clauses with simple *att* do, however, occur also in Sweden-Swedish varieties. One of the aims of this paper is therefore to explore the use of *att*-clauses in Swedish more generally. Some examples of the functions of *att*-clauses which are typical of Finland-Swedish varieties, will, however, also be discussed in the empirical part of the paper.

As pointed out in the introduction, a number of studies of syntactically unintegrated 'that'-clauses in different languages have been published recently. Some of the papers focus or touch upon the same types of clauses that I am discussing in this paper. Günthner (2011) shows how syntactically unintegrated *dass*-clauses emerge on-line in German conversations. She, however, excludes "Adverbiale *(so) dass*-Konstruktionen (mit finaler, konsekutiver und kausaler Funktion)" (Günthner 2011: 4), that is, 'that'-clauses with a reasoning function, from her study. This is also done by Mertzlufft and Wide (2013), who compare the emergence of 'that'-clauses with a post-modifying function in Swedish and German conversations and argue that there is a continuum between syntactically integrated and syntactically non-integrated *att*- and *dass*-clauses. On the pragmatic level, however, the clauses at both ends of the continuum show similar functions: they modify, explicate or explain something said in the preceding discourse. The function of explaining or explicating something said is also discussed by Verstraete, D'Hertefelt, and Van Linden (2012) in their paper on *dat*-clauses in Dutch and by Weinert (2012) in her paper on *dass/that*-clauses in German and English. Both papers, however, discuss 'that'-clauses in a broader perspective. Verstraete, D'Hertefelt, and Van Linden (2012), who, as pointed out, categorize clauses of the kind discussed in this paper as *discursive insubordination*, only touch upon the phenomenon in Dutch by showing some examples. Weinert (2012) presents a more detailed analysis of unintegrated *dass*-clauses. She concludes the following about unintegrated *dass*-clauses and correlative *dass*-clauses of the type *has du das auch schon mal gehabt (.) dass du träumst du kannst nicht aufwachen*? 'have you ever had the kind of dream from which you aren't able to wake up'?:

> They function as clarifications, elaborations, explications, reiterations, conclusions, subtopics and so on. Since they are anchored in the previous discourse, have a content relation to it and do not function independently, they can therefore still be considered to have a complementing function. Whether the link is achieved through the association of *dass*-clauses with presupposition or through the explicit marking via the complementiser is a moot point. The constraints on unintegrated *dass*-clauses have yet to be defined. (Weinert 2012: 247)

The purpose of this paper is to present a detailed analysis of syntactically unintegrated *att*-clauses in Swedish. As pointed out in the introduction, I will argue that some of the clauses have a rephrasing function whereas others have a reasoning function. Similar to Günthner (2011), who excludes clauses of the adverbial type, I make a distinction between two different types of syntactically unintegrated 'that'-clauses. There are, however, some cases where the difference between the clauses is rather subtle. An example of this will be discussed at the end of section 5. In the next section, I start the empirical analysis by discussing the rephrasing function of *att*-clauses. *Att*-clauses with a reasoning function are discussed in section 5.

4 *Att*-clauses with a paraphrasing function

Let us begin the analysis of syntactically unintegrated *att*-clauses with a paraphrasing function by returning to example (1), which is shown in an extended version in example (13). In the example, the informer at the poison control centre (I) is asking the caller (C) whether she has noticed any symptoms of poisoning in her respiratory organs (line 3).

(13) Difficulties breathing? (GRIS: GIC 16519; I = informer, C = caller)

1   I: [...] se om de här kan ha   nåt   samband,   f[ör   de beror
            see if this   can have some   connection because it depends
            'see if this has any connection, since it depends'

2   C: [ja:,
                                                          yes
                                                          'yes'

3   I: på va   de- (0.6) men du   har inga symptom från luftvägarna,
        on what it-   but you have no   symptoms from the respiratory organs
        'on what i- but you don't have any symptoms from the respiratory organs'

→4   **att** du   tycker de e jobbit   å andas   eller **at[t** de trycker
        ATT you think   it is difficult to breathe or   ATT it presses
        'that you find it difficult to breath or that it presses'

5   C: [nä:
                                                             no
                                                             'no'

→6 I: över= bröstet   eller nåt   sådant?
        over the chest or   something like that
        'over the chest or something like that?'

In lines 4 and 6, I elaborates her question about the symptoms with two co-ordinated *att*-clauses: *att du tycker de e jobbit å andas eller att de trycker över= bröstet eller nåt sådant?* 'that you find it difficult to breathe or that it presses over the chest or something like that'. Pragmatically and interactionally the *att*-clauses make perfect sense: they specify what I has just said, that is, they clarify I's question about C's condition (symptoms = difficult to breathe, pressure over the chest). Syntactically, however, no relationship to an element in the preceding discourse can be found. There is no matrix clause to which the *att*-clauses are subordinate, nor do they syntactically complement a phrasal head. As discussed at the beginning of the paper, informer I at the poison control centre explicates what she means when she asks if the caller has noticed any symptoms in her respiratory organs. The two *att*-clauses which are not syntactically subordinate to any element in the preceding structure give two examples of what the symptoms may be: that it is difficult to breathe and that there is a feeling of pressure over the chest. The informer thus rephrases her question to the patient and makes it more specific. The relation between the *att*-clauses and the preceding discourse could roughly be described as follows:

do you have NOUN X → [that is] do you feel Y or Z...? [EXAMPLES OF X]

In example (13), the element which the *att*-clauses rephrase is a noun (*symptom* 'symptoms'). Example (14) from a focus group discussion on genetically modified food shows a case where the expression which is being rephrased is a verb phrase. In the example, pesticides are being discussed by the farmers participating in the discussion.

(14) Resistance to pesticides (GRIS: L Tema K, GML 4; A, C, F, G, H = farmers).

```
1    G:   ja (0.4)  då     blir     ju    ogräset   resistent  [å    ja=
          PRT       then   becomes  PRT   the weed  resistant  and   PRT
          'well then the grass becomes resistant and well'

2    H:                                                        [ja:¿
                                                                PRT
                                                                'yes'

3    G:   =(0.2) så    måste  [man ( )
                 then  has     one
                 'then one has to'

4    H:                       [>å    sen    får  vi  hitta på  e<
                               and   then   get  we  invent    a
                               'and then we have to invent a'

5                             nytt  s[prutmedel  [å    [sen¿
                              new    pesticide    and then
                              'new pesticide and then'

6    G:                             [ja:¿              [.ja
                                     PRT                PRT
                                     'yes'              'yes'

7    C?:                                               [°(mm)°

8    C?:  °(mm)°

9    H:   blir   de resistent emot   de   å   sen   får  m- (0.4)
          becomes it resistant against that and then  gets o-
          'it becomes resistant against that and then one has to'

10        så    [går   de så¿
          then   goes  it so
          'then it goes like that'

11        ((4 lines omitted))
```

12	C:		[a	just	ogräsmedel	blir		ju	↓kanske'nte
			PRT	precisely	pesticide	becomes		PRT	perhaps not

'well, pesticides do not perhaps become'

13			resistent↓	[m[en	de	e	ju	däremot		svampar=
			resistant	but	that	is	PRT	on the other hand		fungi

'resistant, it is rather the fungi that are that'

14 A: [n [ä:,
                 PRT
                 'no'

15 F: [nä,
                 PRT
                 'no'

→16 C: =å [bakterien **att** dom (0.2) ↓förändras ju=
         and bacteria ATT they   change   PRT
         'and bacteria, they change'

17 F: [a:o (.) a:o.
                 PRT   PRT
                 'yes'   'yes'

18 C: =å [virusarna dom ä[ndras [ju↓.
         and the viruses they change PRT
         'and the viruses, they change'

19 F: [mm::.   [mm:.

20 H: [>a j-<
                                        PRT I-
                                        'yes I'

At the beginning of the example, G says that grass becomes resistant to pesticides (line 1). H responds to this by concluding that new pesticides then have to be invented (lines 4–5). In lines 5 and 9–10, when H says that *it* (Swe. *de(t)*) in turn becomes resistant to *that* (*å sen blir de resistent emot de* 'it becomes resistant against that'), the reference is ambiguous. C's contribution in lines 12–13 and 16–18 could be seen as a reaction to this. He points out that it is not the pesticides that become resistant but rather the fungi, viruses and bacteria. During this contribution he uses a syntactically unintegrated *att*-clause: *att dom förändras ju* 'that they change' (line 16).

As in example (13), the *att*-clause in example (14) refers to something specific in the preceding discourse which is rephrased in some way. In lines 13–16, C says that fungi and viruses are resistant: *a just ogräsmedel blir ju kanske'nte resistent men de e ju däremot svampar å bakterier* 'well, pesticides do not perhaps become resistant, it is rather the fungi and bacteria that are that'. When he continues by saying that *att dom förändras ju* 'that they change' he rephrases the characterization expressed by the verb in the previous clause: fungi and bacteria are resistant → fungi and bacteria change. The function of this *att*-clause seems to be to strengthen the point C is making about the contrast between pesticides, on the one hand, and bacteria and fungi, on the other hand. As in example (13), the *att*-clause occurs within the same turn and directly after the clause with the word which is rephrased. The relationship between the *att*-clause and the preceding discourse could be summarized as follows:

they VERB X are Y → [that is] they VERB Z [EMPHASIZING A POINT MADE]

In some cases syntactically independent *att*-clauses are also used when speakers rephrase specific acts in the preceding discourse. This is the case in example (15), which is from a different call to the poison control centre than the call in example (13). The caller has just told the informer that he has been stung by a bee in his tongue. When the informer hears this she suggests that the caller should go to the hospital (line 1).

(15) Stung by a bee (GRIS:GIC 16784; I = informer C = caller)
```
→1   I:  [ja  tycker att  du    ska   åka in ti sjukhus.
          I   think that  you   shall go  in to hospital
         'I think you should go to the hospital'

 2       ((four lines left out))

 3   I:  [...] om man får   de i  munnen    eller i  ansiktet¿
               if  one gets it in the mouth or    in the face
              'if you get it in your mouth or face'

 4   C:  jaha.
         PRT
         'oh'

 5   I:  eller speciellt  inne  i  munnen,
         or    especially inside in the mouth
         'or especially inside your mouth'
```

6   C: *jaa¿*
        PRT
        'okay'

7   I: *så kan de eh (0.2) kan de svullna, så att man ehm (0.2) får*
        so can it   can it swell   so that one   gets
        'it can it can swell so that one gets'

8   *svåriheter, (.) som du säjer svårihet me andning å så*
        difficulties   as you say difficulty with breathing and so
        'difficulties as you say difficulty with breathing and so'

9   *vidare,*
        further
        'on'

10 C: *jaa¿*
        PRT
        'uhu'

11   (0.5)

12 I: *e:h=*

13 C: *=ha?=*
        'so:: eh?'

→14 I: =**att** *eh (0.6) de e därför   tycker ja de e bra   om du:, (0.2)*
        ATT   it is therefore think I it is good if you
        'that is why I think it is good if you'

→15   *åtminstone e på sjukhus å (0.2) så att dom kan, eh*
        at least   are in hospital and   so that they can
        'at least were in the hospital and, so that they can'
        (0.8)

16 C: *bedöma då [(om),*
        assess then if
        'assess then whether'

→17 I: [*a bedöma de, å ha dej kanske under*
                 PRT assess that and have you perhaps under
                'yes assess that and have you perhaps under'

→18   *observation en stund,*
        observation a while
        'observation for a while'

In the four lines omitted from example (15), the informer says that people in her profession are normally quite cautious with bee stings of the kind the caller has told her about. The caller reacts to this with a minimal response. When the informer continues by explaining why one should be cautious when you get stung by a bee in your mouth or face (you can get a swelling which makes it difficult to breathe), the caller still reacts only with minimal responses (*jaha* 'oh' in line 4, *jaa* 'okay/uhu' in lines 6 and 10). In line 12, the informer, after a 0.5 second-long pause, makes a hesitation sound (*eh* 'uh'). The caller responds to this by saying *ha?* 'so:: eh?', which indicates that he needs more information in order to draw a conclusion. Following this, in lines 14–17, the informer rephrases her suggestion that the caller should go to the hospital by producing a syntactically independent *att*-clause. The clause starts with a reference to what the informer herself has just said about swelling: *att eh (0.6) de e därför* 'that is why'. By using *därför* 'because' as a pivot, the informer can then continue by saying that she thinks it would be good if the patient were in the hospital. She is then on her way to explicate her suggestion further when she interrupts herself: *så att dom ka̲n, eh* 'so that they can' (line 15). After a 0.8 long pause, the caller begins to complete the informer's unfinished clause by saying *bedö̲ma då om* 'assess then whether' (line 16). He is overlapped by the informer who repeats what the caller has said and adds that the caller can also be under observation for a while at the hospital (lines 17–18). In the context following the example, the caller grasps the seriousness of the situation.

The context of the *att*-clause in example (15) is more complex than the contexts of the clauses in examples (13) and (14). In this case, it is not only a specific word or expression which is paraphrased but rather a suggestion which has been expressed with a main clause some turns earlier: you should go to the hospital → you should at least be in the hospital so that they can... As in examples (13) and (14), the speaker returns to something previously said in order to clarify what she means. The function seems to be to strengthen a point made, more specifically to restate a suggestion (cf. example 14). The informer is trying to persuade the caller to go to the hospital, but the caller does not seem to respond to this before the informer rephrases her suggestion in lines 14–16 and 17–18. The relationship to the preceding discourse could be described as follows:

you should VERB X to Y→ [I really think] you should at least VERB Z in Y so that...
[RESTATING A SUGGESTION]

Example (15) is similar to the example shown in (12) in section 3, which also exhibits a rephrasal. In (12), the chair person of a political youth organization (R) makes some suggestions as to how the organization could get funding for an event they are planning to organize (lines 1–3, 5). The other members of the board do not seem to pick up these suggestions. Following a 1.5 second-long pause at the end of the example, the chair in line 7 uses a syntactically independent *att*-clause (*att checka nu me di här* 'so check with these') to rephrase her suggestions as a directive. Instead of pointing out what *one* could do, R uses an imperative form of the verb *checka* 'check', which is semantically equivalent to *kolla* 'check' in lines 1 and 5. She thus makes her request explicit and directs it to the other members of the board, perhaps the secretary N in particular. Directly after the request she provides a reason for why her request should be met: *nu sku de vara kiva att kunna ge någå arvode (.) annars får vi bara ge blommor* 'it would be nice to be able to give [them] remuneration, otherwise we can only give [them] flowers' (lines 7–8, 10).

As pointed out by Lehti-Eklund (2002: 2) in her analysis of the same example, the *att*-clause in example (12) occurs at the transition between acts. When R rephrases her statements that certain organizations should be contacted as a directive, she moves from discussion to decision-making. Nonetheless, the contents of the *att*-clause rephrase something that has been said in the preceding discourse. The function of the clause seems to make the request explicit and thus "add it to the records" in the sense discussed by Anward (2004). The relationship to the preceding discourse could be described as follows:

one could contact x → [I really want you to] contact x [MAKING A REQUEST EXPLICIT]

To summarize, the syntactically unintegrated *att*-clauses in all the examples discussed in this section paraphrase something said in the preceding discourse. In examples (13) and (14) a specific wording in the preceding discourse is specified, clarified or modified. The wordings concern a concept expressed by a noun (symptoms) and an outcome expressed by a verb phrase (being resistant) respectively. In example (15), a specific clause with a suggestion (you should go to the hospital) is repeated and specified and in example (12), which was shown in section 3, previously presented suggestions are rephrased as a directive. The contents of all the *att*-clauses in question have already been expressed in some way in the preceding discourse. By using the syntactically independent *att*-clauses, the speakers present the contents again by adding more specific information or specifying an act such as a suggestion or request. All the examples occur in situations in which the speakers either react to something that has been said or not said and/or want to a get a certain reaction from the other speaker(s). The syntactically unintegrated *att*-clauses thus clearly function as communicative resources of a particular kind in the conversations and could be seen as constructs of a construction with a certain function (rephrasing for example questions or suggestions in order to make them more explicit). In the next section, I will discuss *att*-clauses with a reasoning function, which occur in slightly different contexts than *att*-clauses with a paraphrasing function.

5 *att*-clauses with a reasoning function

Example (16) shows an extended version of example (2) which was discussed in the introduction. In the example, S and V are talking to their mother (U) about their schedule at school. S, who is V's older sister, is describing a particular teacher (Birgitta), of whom she does not seem to be very fond.

(16) Sculpture class (GRIS: Wallenberg; Anward 2003; U = mother, S = daughter, V = son)

```
1    S: Birgitta hon har sådär eh kan      ingenting.
        Birgitta she  has  like       knows nothing
        'Birgitta, she has like knows nothing'

2       (0.8)

3    S: [hon har skulptur: å    så   [sen så säjer hon=
        she has  sculpture and then  then so  says  she
        'she teaches sculpture class and then she says'

4    U: [nähä.                          [jaha.
        PRT                              PRT
        'oh'                             'oh'

5    S: .hhh ↑prata↑ me    min O- .hh min eh bror    O::scar¿
             talk    with my               my        brother Oscar
        'talk to my to my brother Oscar' ((artificial voice))

6    U: ↑jaså de e hon: jaha.
        PRT  it is she  PRT
        'oh it's her I see'
        (0.6)

→7   V: jaha att då    ska  ja'nte: välja   henne i  ↓skulptur.
        PRT  ATT then shall I not  choose  her    in sculpture
        'okay, so I'm not choosing her for sculpture class, then'
```

In line 1, S says that Birgitta, the teacher, knows nothing. She then goes on to say that Birgitta teaches sculpture and says "talk to my brother" (lines 3, 5).

Her mother (U) reacts to this by concluding *jaså de e hon: jaha* 'oh it's her I see' in line 6. After a 0.6 long pause S' brother V takes the floor and draws the conclusion *jaha att då ska ja'nte: välja henne i skulptur* 'okay, so I'm not choosing her for sculpture class, then'. This conclusion is presented in the form of a syntactically independent *att*-clause which is preceded by the response particle *jaha* 'okay'.

In a similar way as the examples discussed in section 4 above, the syntactically independent *att*-clause in example (16) clearly relates to something said in the preceding discourse. However, in contrast to the *att*-clauses discussed in section 4, the *att*-clause in example (16), does not rephrase something that has been said. Instead, it expresses a consequence of what another speaker has said. In the example, *att* has the same meaning as the complex connective *så att* 'so (that)' (cf. example 7b in section 3; Lindström and Londen 2008). The relationship of the *att*-clause here to the preceding discourse is thus clearly different from the examples discussed in section 4. It could be described as follows:

person x is y → [so] I should not choose x [DRAWING A CONCLUSION]

Example (17) shows a case in which a speaker draws a conclusion based on what she has just said herself. In the example, which is from the same meeting within a youth organization as example (12), speaker H uses a syntactically independent *att*-clause to expand her description of the so-called Cable Factory, that is, the cultural centre where the youth organization is considering organizing a party.

(17) Party at The cable factory (SAM:M2; Lehti-Eklund 2002: 6; R = chair person, H = participant at annual meeting)

```
1    H:  men   den e   den e  nog enorm (.)   de  e    [liksom fem meter   ti
         but   it  is  it  is PRT huge        it  is like    five meters to
         'but it's huge, it's like five meters to'

2    R:                                                  [jå
                                                         PRT
                                                         'yes'

→03  H:  take       °eller någå       sånt°    att de sku      liksom va:
         the ceiling or     something like that ATT it should like     be
         'the ceiling or something like that so it would have to be'

→04      smockfullt me    människor för       att de ska   bli   (någå)=.
         packed     with  people    in order to that it    would become something
         'packed with people in order for it to work'
```

In line 1, speaker H says that the space in the Cable Factory is huge. She then elaborates on this by saying that it is five meters to the ceiling "or something like that". Having said this, she continues with a syntactically unintegrated *att*-clause and says *att de sku liksom va: smockfullt me människor för att de ska bli någå* 'so it would have to be packed with people in order for it to work'. The *att*-clause here expresses a consequence of the fact that the Cable Factory is huge: in order for the party to be a success, the place would have to be packed with people.

The fact that the *att*-clause in example (17) is used to elaborate something said makes it partly similar to the *att*-clauses discussed in section 4, which also clarify, specify or emphasize something said. However, just like the *att*-clause in example (16), the *att*-clause in example (17) does not paraphrase something already said; rather it presents a consequence of what has just been said. Instead of specifying or modifying a word or clause, the *att*-clause expands the line of reasoning. H points out that there has to be a lot of people at the party if it is to be organized at the Cable Factory (since the space there is so huge). The relationship between the *att*-clause and the context in which it occurs could be presented as follows:

place x is y → [so] there must be z in x in order to… [PRESENTING A PREREQUISITE]

Example (18) from a group discussion about music and music styles shows a slightly different use of an *att*-clause with a reasoning function. In the example, the high school students participating in the discussion are answering the moderator's questions about whether they listen to music on CDs or on tapes.

(18) CDs are better (GSM: 5; K3, K4, K5, K6 = female high school students)
```
    1   K5: men de e  ändå tråkigt (0.7) me   band också
            but it is still tedious        with tapes also
            'but it is also tedious with tapes as well'
((four lines omitted))

    2   K4: nä- när   man har band så e de en   låt  så  vet   man inte
            whe- when one has tapes so is it  one song then knows one not
            'wh- when one has a tape it's one song, then one doesn't'

    3       på vicken låt   man e  så ska man sp- [ja de- nej de e-]
            on what   song one is so has one pl- yes it-  no  it is-
            'know what song one is on, then one has to pl-, yes i- no it is'
```

4	K3:		[a: de e otymp]ligt e de (.)
			PRT it is unconvinient is it
			'yes it is unconvienient it is'

5		då e [de bättre] me CD [men ändå ( )]
		then is it better with CD but still
		'so it's better with CDs but still'

6	K5:	[a:]
		PRT
		'yes'

→7 K6:   [att man liksom kan] (.) hoppa (lit-) till
                          ATT one PRT   can   jump litt- to
                          'that one like can skip a litt-(le) to'

8   liksom (.) den lå[ten som   e sist] när   man e på första typ
         PRT   that song which is last when one is on first PRT
         'like the song which is last when one is like on the first one'

9   K3:   [mm-m   ]

10 ?:   mm-m
         (0.2)

11 K5: men de e ju mest   såna som har   en speciell musiksmak då
         but it is PRT mostly those who have a   special music taste PRT
         'but it's those who have a special music taste'

12   som köper skiver
         who buy   records
         'who buy records'

At the beginning of the extract shown in the example, K5 says that tapes are tedious. K4 elaborates on this in lines 2–3 when she points out that you do not know where you are on tapes. K3 agrees with K4 (line 4) and states that it is better with CDs (line 5). This line of thought is then picked up by K6 who presents an argument for why it is better with CDs: you can skip, for example, from the first song to the last. When she presents this argument in lines 7–8, she uses a syntactically non-integrated *att*-clause. The *att*-clause expresses the benefit of choosing CDs. Just like all the *att*-clauses discussed in sections 4 and 5, this *att*-clause elaborates on something just said in the discourse. However, rather than rephrasing something in the way that the *att*-clauses analyzed in section 4 do, the *att*-clause in example (18) extends the line of thought. This is similar to the way the other *att*-clauses discussed in this section function: K6 presents a reason for why it is better to use CDs.

it is better with y than x → [because] you can do z [Presenting an argument]

It could, however, be argued that the *att*-clause in example (18) also explicates something in the preceding discourse (why CDs are better) in a way that is similar to, for example, the *att*-clause in example (13) (see above). The difference between the two types of *att*-clauses, *att*-clauses with a paraphrasing function and *att*-clauses with a reasoning function, can thus be rather subtle. Is there then a large enough difference between the two types that they need to be analyzed as two different types of constructions? Or are we dealing with two different types of uses of the same construction? This question will be discussed in the next section.

To summarize, the syntactically independent *att*-clauses discussed in this section show similarities to the examples discussed in section 4 in the sense that they elaborate a topic under discussion. The *att*-clauses in this section, however, introduce a new perspective rather than specify information that has already been presented. Furthermore, all the *att*-clauses in this section draw conclusions based on something said whereas the *att*-clauses in section 4 rephrase a specific word, phrase or clause. As the last example shows, the difference between *att*-clauses with a rephrasing and reasoning function respectively, is, however, sometimes rather subtle.

6 Discussion

In sections 4 and 5 I have presented a number of examples of syntactically unintegrated *att*-clauses in two different types of interactional contexts in Swedish. In both cases the clauses are clearly linked to the preceding discourse even if they are syntactically not subordinate to any specific element in it. The relationship to the preceding discourse is of a different nature in the two types of clauses. In the first type, the *att*-clauses rephrase something specific that has been said in the preceding discourse. In examples (13) and (14), a specific wording was explained or explicated, and, in examples (12) and (15), suggestions were either restated or reformulated as directives. The way in which the *att*-clauses brought a new perspective into the emerging context (Anward 2004) varies. In (13), examples of a phenomenon were given in order for the other participant of the conversation to be able to answer a question of importance for the on-going activity (clarifying the symptoms of poisoning). In (14), some facts presented in the preceding context were corrected, and, in (12) and (15), suggestions or directives were put forth in order to persuade the other participants in the conversations to do certain things (check the possibility to get funding from certain organizations; go to the hospital).

The examples show clear resemblances with some of the examples of discourse insubordination and unintegrated *dass*-clauses respectively discussed by Verstraete, D'Hertefelt and Van Linden (2012) and Weinert (2012). Verstraete, D'Hertefelt and Van Linden (2012: 48) discuss the possibility to insert a predicate like *ik bedoel dat* 'what I mean to say is that' into the syntactically unintegrated *dat*-clauses expressing discourse insubordination. As they conclude, "even that may be reading too much into the data". Nonetheless, their formulation quite nicely captures the relationship between the context and the rephrasing type of 'that'-clauses which I have been analyzing in this article. In the schematic presentations of the *att*-clauses discussed in section 4, I used expressions such as "that is", "I really think" or "I really want to" to describe the semantic/pragmatic link between the clauses and the preceding context.

In the other type of *att*-clauses discussed in this paper, syntactically un integrated clauses with a reasoning function, the relationship to the preceding context was of a different kind. Rather than rephrasing something said, the *att*-clauses in examples (16)–(18) explicated consequences of something that had been said in the preceding discourse. The consequences were of slightly different types. In example (16), a conclusion was drawn based on something said in the preceding discourse. In example (17), a prerequisite for an event (a party at a particular place) was presented based on the information given (by the same speaker) in the immediately preceding context. In example (18), an argument for an evaluation just presented was put forth. In all cases, the line of argumentation was expanded when the syntactically unintegrated *att*-clauses were used. Instead of rephrasing something already presented in the conversation, the *att*-clauses brought new information into the conversation. The relationship to the preceding context could in most cases be described with "so" (cf. Lindström & Londen 2008: 128–145).

Even though both *att*-clauses with a reasoning function and *att*-clauses with a rephrasing function elaborate on something said in the preceding discourse, the elaboration is of two different kinds. The two types of clauses are – at the most specific level of language – used as communicative resources in different types of interactional settings. As pointed out above, a distinction between the two types of syntactically unintegrated 'that'-clauses has also been drawn e.g. by Günthner (2011) and Mertzlufft and Wide (2013), who focus on interaction in a similar way as I have done in this paper. When investigating syntactically unintegrated *att*-clauses from an interactional point of view, the difference between the two types of clauses becomes salient: speakers use the two types of clauses for different purposes in interaction. But does this make it possible to see the two types of *att*-clauses as two different constructions?

If this question is approached from a mainstream Construction Grammar point of view, where the role of context has been considered only to a limited extent (Bergs and Diewald 2009: 2), the answer could be no. The motivation would then, for example, be that differences in meaning or function have to be reflected in differences in form (cf. Boogaart 2009). Such an approach, however, implies that form is given priority over function even though most versions of Construction Grammar stress that constructions are holistic form-function/meaning constellations. If, on the other hand, form and function are given equal weight in the form-function constellations, one could argue that the same form can develop into two different constructions with different functions. If constructions are seen as nodes in networks of grammatical patterns, it is also possible to treat the two different types of *att*-clauses as different constructions. As discussed in section 2, the influence of context can give rise to different semantic variants (cf. Langacker 2000: 35–36). However, in the case of the two types of syntactically unintegrated *att*-clauses, it remains unexplored whether they have even developed from the same source. As shown in examples (10)–(11), clauses with simple *att* (with a reasoning function) seem to have been more widely used in older Swedish in contexts where complex connectives such as *så att* and *för att* are used today. As discussed for instance in connection to example (16), simple *att* with a reasoning function still today sometimes occurs in similar contexts as the complex connective *så att*. *Att*-clauses with a rephrasing function, on the other hand, do not occur in contexts where *att* can as easily be replaced with a complex connective. What we could thus be dealing with are actually two syntactically different types of *att*-clauses (narrative vs. adverbial) to begin with. Whether this is really the case, however, needs to be explored in future research.

Another possibility is to treat the relationship to the prior context as a form-related feature. If this is done the two types of syntactically unintegrated *att*-clauses discussed in this paper can indeed be seen as reflecting a difference in form since they occur in different types of interactional settings and perform different types of acts (rephrasing something said vs. extending the line of reasoning). As Östman and Trousdale (2013: 488) point out, context features are seen as part of constructions within discourse approaches to constructions. In line with Linell (2009) it could be argued that the two types of *att*-clauses have a different external syntax (the discourse context) even though their internal syntax (on the clause level) is the same.

7 Conclusion

When one investigates the use of syntactically unintegrated *att*-clauses in actual use in authentic conversations in Swedish, it becomes quite clear that we are dealing with two different constructions or patterns: one which rephrases something said and one which expands the line of reasoning by relating to something said. Through the process of abstraction the two types of clauses can be seen as forming a more general construction: syntactically unintegrated *att*-clauses which relate to the preceding discourse and elaborate upon it. As argued by Langacker (2000: 35; cf. also Fillmore 1989: 33; Croft 2001: 5), the more specific constructions at the lowest levels of language, in this case *att*-clauses with a rephrasing function and *att*-clauses with a reasoning function, must, however, be seen as primary to such an abstract and more general construction.

Data

GRIS = The kernel corpus of Swedish conversations made available within the project *Samtalsspråkets grammatik* (Grammar in conversation: a study of Swedish), see http://www.tema.liu.se/tema-k/gris/.

GSM = The corpus of group discussions with teenagers made available within the project *Gymnasisters språk- och musikvärldar* (The Language and Music Worlds of High School Students). Department of music sciences and Department of Swedish, University of Gothenburg.

SAM = The corpus of Helsinki Swedish conversations made available in the project *Svenska samtal i Helsingfors* (Swedish conversations in Helsinki). Department of Finnish, Finno-Ugrian and Scandinavian Studies, University of Helsinki.

References

Anward, Jan. 2004. 'att' ['that']. *Språk och stil* 13: 65–85.
Anward, Jan. In prep. Interaction and Constructions. In: Benjamin Lyngfelt and Camilla Wide (eds.), *Constructions*, Special issue on Swedish constructions.
Bergs, Alexander and Gabriele Diewald. 2009. Contexts and constructions. In: Alexander Bergs and Gabriele Diewald (eds.), *Context and Constructions*, 1–14. (Constructional Approaches to Language 9.) Amsterdam/Philadelphia: John Benjamins.
Bolinger, Dwight. 1977. *Meaning and Form*. London/New York: Longman.
Boogaart, Ronny. 2009. Semantics and pragmatics in construction grammar. The case of modal verbs. In: Alexander Bergs and Gabriele Diewald (eds.), *Context and Constructions*, 213–241. (Constructional Approaches to Language 9.) Amsterdam/Philadelphia: John Benjamins.

Croft, William. 2001. *Radical Construction Grammar. Syntactic Theory in Typological Perspective*. Oxford: Oxford University Press.

Croft, William and D. Alan Cruse. 2004. *Cognitive Linguistics*. Cambridge: Cambridge University Press.

Evans, Nicholas. 2007. Insubordination and its uses. In: Irina Nikolaeva (ed.), *Finiteness. Theoretical and Empirical Foundations*, 366–431. Berlin/New York: Mouton de Gruyter.

Fillmore, Charles J. 1989. Grammatical Construction Theory and the Familiar Dichotomies. In: Rainer Dietrich and Carl F. Graumann (eds.), *Language Processing in Social Context*. Amsterdam: North-Holland/Elsevier.

Günthner, Susanne. 2011. *Dass*-Konstruktionen im alltäglichen Sprachgebrauch – Facetten ihrer "interaktionalen Realität". *Gidi Arbeitspapiere* 35. [http://noam.uni-muenster.de/gidi/arbeitspapiere/arbeitspapier35.pdf]

Keevallik, Luule. 2008. Conjunction and sequenced action: The Estonian complementizer and evidential particle *et*. In: Ritva Laury (ed.), *Crosslinguistic Studies of Clause Combining. The Multifunctionality of Conjunctions*, 125–152. (Typological Studies in Language 80.). Amsterdam/Philadelphia: John Benjamins.

Kemmer, Suzanne and Michael Barlow. 2000. Introduction: A Usage-Based Conception of Language. In: Michael Barlow and Suzanne Kemmer (eds.), *Usage-Based Models of Language*, vii-xxviii. Stanford: CSLI Publications.

Langacker, Ronald W. 1987. *Foundations of Cognitive Grammar*. Volume 1. Theoretical Prerequisites. Stanford: Stanford University Press.

Langacker, Ronald W. 2000. A Dynamic Usage-Based Model. In: Michael Barlow and Suzanne Kemmer (eds.), *Usage-Based Models of Language*, 1–63. Stanford: CSLI Publications.

Langacker, Ronald W. 2008. *Cognitive Grammar. A Basic Introduction*. New York: Oxford University Press.

Laury, Ritva and Eeva-Leena Seppänen. 2008. Clause combining, interaction, evidentiality, participation structure, and the conjunction-particle continuum: The Finnish *että*. In: Ritva Laury (ed.), *Crosslinguistic Studies of Clause Combining. The Multifunctionality of Conjunctions*, 153–178. (Typological Studies in Language 80.) Amsterdam/Philadelphia: John Benjamins.

Lehti-Eklund, Hanna. 2002. Om *att* som diskursmarkör [About *that* as a discourse marker]. *Språk och stil* 11: 81–118.

Linell, Per. 1998. *Approaching Dialogue: Talk, interaction and contexts in dialogical perspectives*. (IMPACT: Studies in Language and Society 3.) Amsterdam/Philadelphia: John Benjamins.

Linell, Per. 2009. Grammatical constructions in dialogue. In: Alexander Bergs and Gabriele Diewald (eds.), *Context and Constructions*, 97–110. (Constructional Approaches to Language 9.) Amsterdam/Philadelphia: John Benjamins.

Lindström, Jan and Anne-Marie Londen. 2008. Constructing reasoning. In: Jaakko Leino (ed.), *Constructional Reorganization*, 105–150. (Constructional Approaches to language 5.) Amsterdam/Philadelphia: John Benjamins.

Lyngfelt, Benjamin. 2003. Samordnande *att* – en talspråklig sambandsmarkör sedd från ett syntaktiskt perspektiv [Co-ordinating *that* – a spoken language connective marker seen from a syntactic perspective]. In: *Texten framför allt. Festskrift till Aina Lundqvist på 65-årsdagen den 11 september 2003*, 139–149. University of Gothenburg: Department of Swedish Language.

Mertzlufft, Christine and Camilla Wide. 2013. The on-line emergence of postmodifying *att*- and *dass*-clauses in spoken Swedish and German. In: Eva Havu and Irma Hyvärinen (eds.),

Comparing and Contrasting Syntactic Structures. From Dependency to Quasi-subordination, 199–229. (Mémoires de la Société Néophilologique de Helsinki 86.)

Mithun, Marianne. 2008. The extension of dependency beyond sentence. *Language* 83: 69–119.

Norén, Kerstin and Per Linell. 2007. Meaning potentials and the interaction between lexis and contexts: An empirical substantiation. *Pragmatics* 17: 387–416.

Östman, Jan-Ola and Graeme Trousdale. 2013. Dialects, discourse and Construction Grammar. In: Thomas Hoffman and Graeme Trousdale (eds.), *The Oxford Handbook of Construction Grammar*, 476–490. Oxford: Oxford University Press.

Ono, Tsuyoshi and Sandra A. Thompson. 1995. What can conversation tell us about syntax? In: Philip W. Davis (ed.), *Alternative Linguistics. Descriptive and Theoretical Modes*, 213–271. (Amsterdam Studies in the Theory and History of Linguistic Science. Series IV – Current Studies in Linguistic Theory.) Amsterdam/Philadelphia: John Benjamins.

Panther, Klaus-Uwe and Linda L. Thornburg, Linda. 2011. Emotion and desire in independent complement clauses: A case study from German. In: Mario Brdar, Stefan Th. Gries and Milena Žic Fuchs (eds.), *Cognitive Linguistics. Convergence and Expansion*, 87–114. (Human Cognitive Processing 32.) Amsterdam/Philadelphia: John Benjamins.

SAG. 1999. Teleman, Ulf, Staffan Hellberg and Erik Andersson. Svenska Akademiens grammatik [The Swedish Academy Grammar]. Stockholm: Svenska Akademien (distr. Norstedts ordbok).

SAOB. 1898–. Ordbok över svenska språket [Dictionary of Swedish]. Utg. av Svenska Akademien [Published by the Swedish Academy]. Lund.

Verstraete, Jean-Christophe, D'Hertefelt, Sarah and Van Linden, An. 2012. A typology of complement insubordination in Dutch. *Studies in Language* 36 (1): 123–153.

Weinert, Regina. 2012. Complement clauses in spoken German and English: Syntax, deixis and discourse-pragmatics. *Folia Linguistica* 46 (1): 233–265.

Wessén, Elias. 1956. *Svensk språkhistoria III. Grundlinjer till en historisk syntax*. [The history of Swedish III. Main lines of a historical syntax.] Stockholm: Almqvist and Wiksell.

Wide, Camilla. 2009. Interactional Construction Grammar: Contextual features of determination in dialectal Swedish. In: Alexander Bergs and Gabriele Diewald (eds.), *Context and Constructions*, 111–142. (Constructional Approaches to Language 9.) Amsterdam/Philadelphia: John Benjamins.

Transcription and glossing symbols

[	utterances starting simultaneously
]	point when overlapping talk stops
=	a single continuous utterance or two "latching" utterances
.	a falling intonation contour
,	a continuing intonation contour
?	a rising intonation contour
¿	a somewhat rising intonation contour
↑	prosodic up-step
↓	prosodic down-step
wo<u>r</u>d	emphasis
wo:rd	lengthening of the sound
>word<	compressed or rushed talk
<word>	slower talk or drawl
º wordº	quiet or soft voice
(word)	uncertain transcription
( )	talk not discernible
wo-	an audible cut-off
.word	a word pronounced with a audible inhalation
hh	audible exhalation
.hh	audible inhalation
(.)	silence shorter than 0.2 seconds
(0.5)	silences measured in tenths of a second
((laughs))	transcriber's comments
(?):	uncertain speaker identification
PRT	discourse particle

Index

adaptive system (language as a complex –) 141–143, 167, 172
affixoids 77–105
agentivity 150–155, 159–167, 174
analogy 120, 49, 55–59, 85, 86, 235, 236, 256, 258, 277
apposition 321–350
auxiliary fronting 58

Berkeley Construction Grammar 3
borrowing 83, 91–93

case 107–137
causative constructions 17–46
change from above 181, 186, 191
chunking 115, 118, 119, 121, 125–128
clause integration 155–158, 170–172, 174
Cognitive Construction Grammar 3, 28
Cognitive Sociolinguistics 6–7
computational modeling 47–72
conserving effect 115, 118, 120
constructional diffusion 181, 191–202
constructional idioms 77–105
constructional networks 1–2, 4, 6, 141–175, 239–246, 265–266, 325, 338, 347, 356
constructionalization 239–243, 353
contrastive 8–9, 259–267, 275–276, 278
conventionality 193, 252–281

Data-Oriented Parsing 47–72
debonding 82, 87
deflection 110, 118, 159, 166
degeneracy 141–143, 159, 163, 167, 170, 172–175
degrammaticalization 82, 227
degree modifiers: *see intensifiers*
degree of clause integration: *see clause integration*
dialogue 322, 338–350
– dialogical construction 312–313
distributional hypothesis 22
ditransitive 144–148, 240, 264–267, 271–275

elative compounds 93
Embodied Construction Grammar 4, 49, 143, 323
emphatic coordination 83, 93
epistolary formulae 181, 191–195, 197, 198, 200
expansion 332, 340–342
experiencer (verbs) 151–155, 159–167, 174–175
external syntax 376

fake direct object 145, 273
Fluid Construction Grammar 4, 49, 143, 323

gender 110, 111, 113, 116–123, 125, 128
genitive 107, 108, 110–113, 115–118, 120–122, 124–128, 131–135
grammaticalization 6, 161, 169, 210–211, 238–239, 325

hierarchical lexicon 80, 81, 83, 99, 102, 103
hyperbole 207–216, 225–226, 244, 263, 270–274

increment 322, 326, 340
insubordination 353
– discourse insubordination 375
intensifier 207–246 83–87, 94–97, 268, 271, 301
Interactional Construction Grammar 323–326, 347, 355–356

language acquisition 47–49, 55–59
learning mechanisms 49, 59, 72

monological 329–338

network: *see constructional networks*

pattern of coining 254–256
prefixoids 78, 84, 85, 87, 91, 93–95, 97
productivity 49, 54, 80, 83, 85–87, 95, 108, 119, 132, 133, 251–281

quantifiers 207–213, 216–219, 221, 228–230, 234–245

Radical Construction Grammar 3, 28, 143, 323
reinterpretation 82, 83, 87, 88, 90, 235
relative clauses 182–205
relativization 181, 182, 186, 190, 191, 197, 200, 201
repair (self repair) 285, 307, 340–347
replication 83, 91, 93, 210
resultative 145–148, 251–281

semantic (verb) classes 17–21, 23, 25, 27, 28, 32–36, 39, 42
semantic polygenesis 220–221

Semantic Vector Spaces 19, 22–29, 31, 33
Sign-Based Construction Grammar 3, 143, 323
social diffusion 181, 186, 189–191, 201
social rank 181, 186, 187, 188, 190, 191, 202
subordination 155–158, 167–172
suffixoids 78

topic 192, 285–318, 338, 360, 374
– hanging topic 290
topical keyword 290
topical antecedent 290
typified utterances 356

verb-second (V2) 144, 149–150, 155, 156, 158–159, 172, 174

www.ingramcontent.com/pod-product-compliance
Lightning Source LLC
Chambersburg PA
CBHW071810230426
43670CB00013B/2415